The Turks and Islam in Reformation Germany

Although their role is often neglected in standard historical narratives of the Reformation, the Ottoman Turks were an important concern of many leading thinkers in early modern Germany, including Martin Luther. In the minds of many, the Turks formed a fearsome, crescent-shaped horizon that threatened to break through and overwhelm. Based on an analysis of more than 300 pamphlets and other publications across all genres and including both popular and scholarly writings, this book is the most extensive treatment in English on views of the Turks and Islam in German-speaking lands during this period. In addition to providing a summary of what was believed about Islam and the Turks in early modern Germany, this book argues that new factors, including increased contact with the Ottomans as well as the specific theological ideas developed during the Protestant Reformation, destabilized traditional paradigms without completely displacing inherited medieval understandings. This book makes important contributions to understanding the role of the Turks in the confessional conflicts of the Reformation and to the broader history of Western views of Islam.

Gregory J. Miller is Professor of History at Malone University.

Routledge Research in Early Modern History

For a full list of titles in this series, please visit www.routledge.com

The Turks and Islam in Reformation Germany

Gregory J. Miller

Routledge
Taylor & Francis Group

NEW YORK AND LONDON

First published 2018
by Routledge
711 Third Avenue, New York, NY 10017

and by Routledge
2 Park Square, Milton Park, Abingdon, Oxon OX14 4RN

Routledge is an imprint of the Taylor & Francis Group, an informa business

© 2018 Taylor & Francis

British Library Cataloguing-in-Publication Data
A catalogue record for this book is available from the British Library

Library of Congress Cataloging-in-Publication Data
A catalog record for this book has been requested

ISBN: 978-1-138-30023-1 (hbk)
ISBN: 978-1-315-13607-3 (ebk)

Typeset in Sabon
by Apex CoVantage, LLC

For Carter, *endlich*

Contents

Figures

1   Sixteenth-Century Bestsellers

Once only on the edges of early modern European scholarship and on the margins of maps, the Ottoman Turks have begun to be recognized as an important part of the mental world of sixteenth-century Europeans. As is the case with many kinds of otherness, when one becomes aware of them, the Turks seem to be everywhere in the period. In the first half of the sixteenth century alone, for example, over 600 books, pamphlets, ballads, and broadsheets with the Turks and/or Islam as the main subject were published in Western Europe. Throughout Europe, pamphlets reported one Ottoman victory after another. As far away as England, the 'Turk' was a catchword for unexpected attack and invasion. The confluence of this perceived danger with the Renaissance interest in the exotic produced a knowledge hunger that was fueled by the development of new print technology. Although it is tenuous to argue that the quantity of publication on a topic alone demonstrates the level of contemporary importance, it seems clear that sixteenth-century Europeans were fascinated with the Ottomans.[1]

One particularly important subgenre of this *Turcica* was captivity narratives. For much of Western Europe in the Late Middle Ages and Renaissance, these narratives were among the few available sources concerning life in the Ottoman Empire behind what might be termed the 'crescent curtain.' Apart from Venetian news reports, until the mid-sixteenth century reports from former captives provided the most extensive information.[2] The wide distribution and multiple editions of these writings reflect a perennial human interest in stories about adventure, danger, and the exotic. There seems to have been something particularly intriguing about those that had been subjected to slavery and lived to tell the tale. The insider information they brought back both intrigued and scandalized their readers.[3]

Captivity narratives played a much greater role than simply entertainment, however. They had an enormous impact on the shaping of Western views of Islam. These ex-slaves wrote with authority. They could speak the languages of the Ottoman Empire. They had spent long years inside Turkey, seeing society in a way that, for example, a reporting itinerant traveler could not.[4] Of course, the former captives did not and could not perfectly translate Turkish culture into written Latin. (Although there is much that is of interest in these writings even to historians of the Ottoman Empire.) The primary value of these writings is what they say about developing attitudes within Europe, and in particular, Western understandings of the Turks and Islam (See Figure 1.1).

In Reformation Germany two publications by former slaves of the Turks were particularly important. The *Tractatus de moribus Turcarum*, (c.1480) [Pamphlet on the Customs of the Turks] attributed to George of Hungary, and Bartholomew Georgijevic' two-part publication *De Turcarum ritu et caeremoniis* [On the Rituals and Ceremonies of the Turks] and *De afflictione tam captivorum quam etiam sub Turcae tributo viventium Christianorum* [On the Afflictions of the Captive Christians Living under the Tribute of the Turks] (both 1544).[5] Both of these publications were reprinted numerous times and in whole or in part were translated into several vernaculars. These two authors are especially important for three reasons. Taken together, they give significant insight into the type of information about Islam that was widely circulated in Europe during the period. In comparison with material on Islam from earlier in the medieval period, considerably more information, and more accurate information, is known. In addition, because both authors claim to have written out of the experience of Ottoman slavery and escape, these documents can add to our understanding of religious boundaries between Islam and Christianity as imagined and constructed by early modern Europeans. These texts draw boundaries in a myriad of ways, from religious practices to bathroom etiquette and food culture. Finally, although the supposed regional origins and life stories of both former captives are remarkably similar, because they were penned almost seventy years apart, a comparative reading demonstrates considerable diversity in European responses to Islam and points to important developments in Western responses to the Muslim Ottomans from the Late Middle Ages to the early modern period that highlight the important transitional nature of the period. One central focus of this study is the analysis and comparison of these two publications (See Figure 1.2).

Of course, escaped slave reports make up only a fraction of the body of Western literature about Islam and the Turks in early modern Europe. The historical confluence of Ottoman expansion and the development of widespread moveable type printing created an explosion of small booklets and broadsheets about the 'exotic' Turks. This production was directly tied to the military conflict with the Ottoman Empire. Some pamphlets on the Turks were published each year, but production soared during periods of more intense military confrontation, especially the 1529 siege of Vienna, the 1532 Ottoman campaign, and the 1542 annexation of Hungary. When the threat increased, general interest in the Turks increased as well.

Although nearly every land with a printing industry published "little booklets on the Turks" (in German: *Türkenbüchlein*) the majority were published in Italy, France, the Low Countries, and especially in Germany. During the first half of the sixteenth century alone, more than 350 pieces

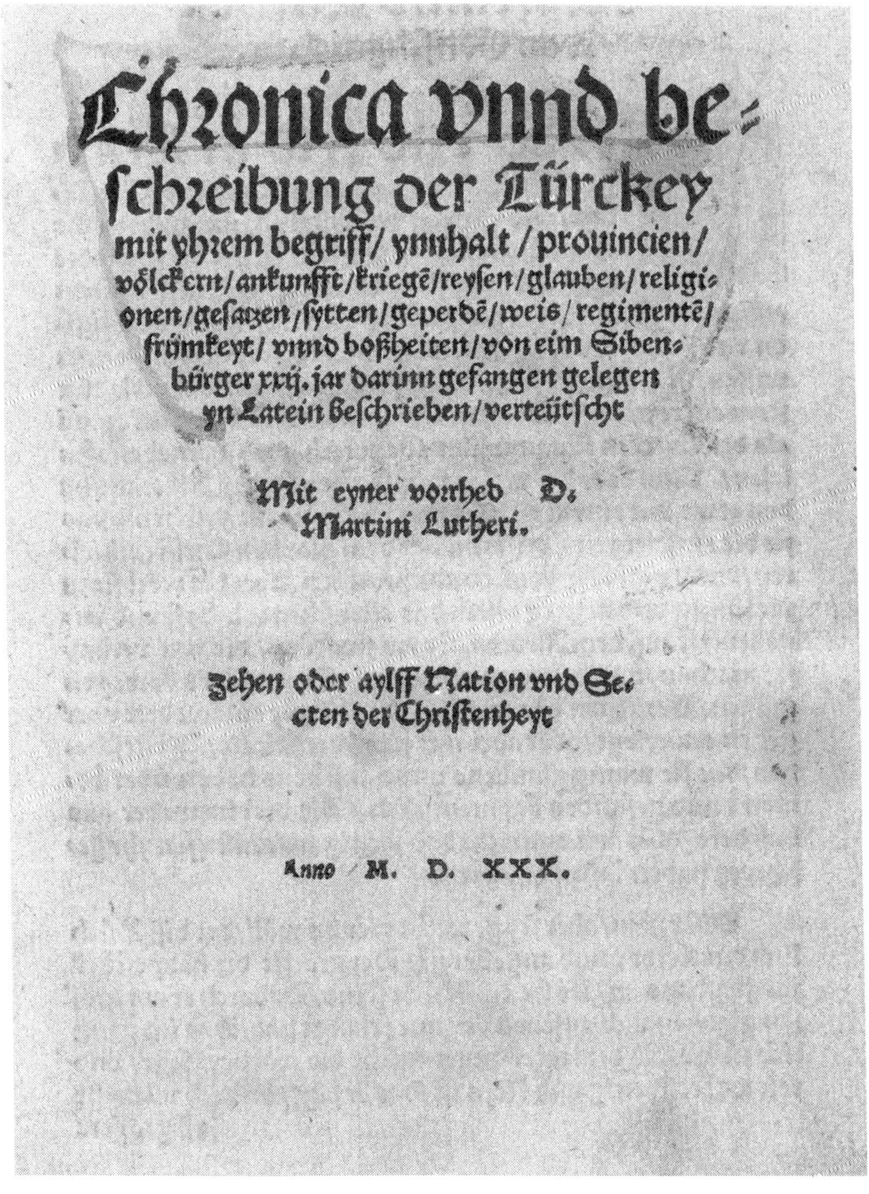

Chronica vnnd be-
schreibung der Türckey
mit yhrem begriff/ ynnhalt / prouincien/
völckern/ ankunfft/ kriegē/ reysen/ glauben/ religi-
onen/ gesatzen/ sytten/ geperdē/ weis/ regimentē/
frümkeyt/ vnnd boßheiten/ von eim Siben-
bürger xxij. jar darinn gefangen gelegen
yn Latein beschrieben/ verteütscht

Mit eyner vorred D.
Martini Lutheri.

Zehen oder aylff Nation vnd Secten der Christenheyt

Anno M. D. XXX.

Figure 1.1 Martin Luther's edition of George of Hungary, 1530

Courtesy of Houghton Library, Harvard University. *GC5 L9774 En530t, Houghton Library, Harvard University

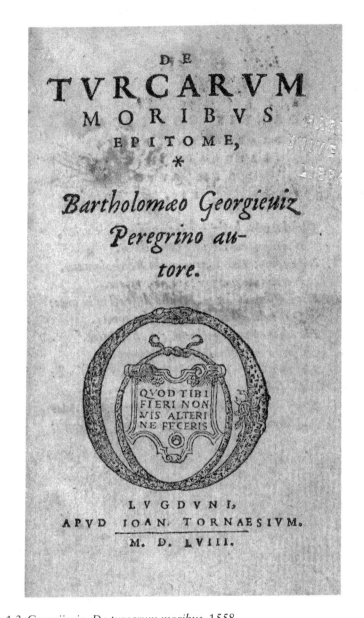

DE
TVRCARVM
MORIBVS
EPITOME,
*

Bartholomæo Georgieuiz
Peregrino au-
tore.

QVOD TIBI
FIERI NON
VIS ALTERI
NE FECERIS

LVGDVNI,
APVD IOAN. TORNAESIVM.
M. D. LVIII.

Figure 1.2 Georgijevic, *De turcarum moribus*, 1558

of literature specifically on the Turks were published in German-speaking lands. Very little of the significant body of sixteenth-century *Turcica* has been translated into English,[6] despite the importance of this genre of literature in early modern Europe. This specific period is not only interesting because of the large number of publications on the Turks. It represents a high point of the Ottoman Empire's push into Central Europe and, at the same time, a significant event in the intellectual history of Western Europe due to the development of the Protestant Reformation. From the beginning of Protestantism, understandings of the Turks and evaluations of appropriate responses to them became embroiled in confessional debates.

Interest in the Turks was not limited to any genre. All printed genre contain works on the Turks. As has been expertly analyzed by Charlotte Colding Smith, visual images, some proclaiming their basis in eyewitness accounts, were broadcast by means of single-leaf woodcuts and illustrated publications small and large.[7] Secular ballads and spiritual hymns concerning the Turks were printed. Sermons and prayers against the Ottomans were published along with political speeches and *Reichstag* decisions. Early newspapers (in German: *Neue Zeitungen*) kept interested people up to date on the latest events.[8] In fact, according to Andrew Pettegree, "by far the greatest stimulus to the growth of the European news industry was the relentless encroachment of the Ottoman Empire."[9]

Organization of the Study

This study summarizes the views of Islam and the Turks presented in the great outpouring of literature on the Ottomans produced in German-speaking lands during the first half of the sixteenth century, that is, during the first generation of Protestant Reformers. While some of this literature originated outside of German-speaking lands, vernacular translations brought them into the German milieu and blended with the already significant number of native publications. Germans seemed to have been particularly interested in the Turks, in part due to the Hapsburg-Ottoman rivalry but also because the first generation of German Reformers (especially Martin Luther) were themselves interested in the Turks and Islam.[10] In order to understand these publications, two layers of context need to be established. I begin with a short summary of the intellectual context through a survey of the development of Western attitudes toward Islam and the Turks prior to 1520. The political context is established through a summary of the engagement between the Ottomans and Europe in Reformation-era Germany.

A central contribution of this study is the content analysis of more than 300 publications from German-speaking lands that discuss the Turks and/ or Islam and were printed between 1520 and 1550, that is, between the accession of Sulaiman the Magnificent and publication of the final edition of Theodor Bibliander's Qur'an. Most of the authors of these publications make no distinction between the 'Turks' and Islam and often use the terms as synonyms. However, for reasons of topical analysis, I devote one chapter to descriptions of social, cultural, and military aspects of the Turks in particular. A second chapter surveys understandings of religious aspects of Islam that sometimes were applied to the Muslim world more generally.

There are two questions at the heart of most of these publications: why are the infidel Turks seemingly invincible against Christendom? What is the appropriate Christian response? The chapter 'Holy Terror' surveys the answers to the first question found in these pamphlets and the chapter 'Holy War' discusses answers to the second. Here, too, the Protestant Reformation, as seen for example both in Martin Luther's absolute denunciation of the Crusade as a blasphemous confusion of spiritual and temporal, and in various Anabaptist disavowals of all warfare, was a catalyst for new developments that influenced the history of Christian-Islamic relations. I conclude with a more detailed comparison and contrast of the two main escaped slave narratives in the broader context of the Reformation in Germany. In appendices are found lengthy selections both of George of Hungary and Bartholomew Georgijevic. No modern English translation of either of these influential publications has previously been available. The translations have been made from their printings accompanying the first published Latin Qur'an, Theodor Bibliander's *Machumetis saracenorum principis* (1543, second edition 1550). This three-volume equivalent of an 'encyclopedia of Islam' is the form in which these pamphlets would have been read by scholars throughout Europe during the sixteenth and seventeenth centuries.[11] Because of their attempt to provide Europeans not only with theological and political guidance concerning the Turks but also because they attempted to portray all aspects of life and culture concerning the Ottoman, George of Hungary and Bartholomew Georgijevic provide the best short summary of the general understandings of Islam and the Turks available to Western Europeans (See Figure 1.3).

Paradigm Shifts

Over the last twenty-five years, several studies of the perceptions of the Muslim world in Western Europe have challenged the dominant metanarrative that early modern Europeans had a binary understanding of their relationship with the Islamic world. The most interesting work recently has been done in the area of early modern English dramatic literature.[12] These studies have demonstrated that 'Islam and the West' in the early modern period is more complicated than it has been portrayed. Matthew Dimmock and Jonathan Burton demonstrate, for example, how Marlowe's *Tamburlaine* continuously violates stereotypes and common lines of division, highlighting the "period's conditional suspension and activation of anti-Islamic prejudice."[13] Gerald MacLean describes an "ambiguous representation of the Ottoman Empire" as both a "realm of tyrannous slavery and a space where Britons might do rather well for themselves."[14] Thus, "attitudes

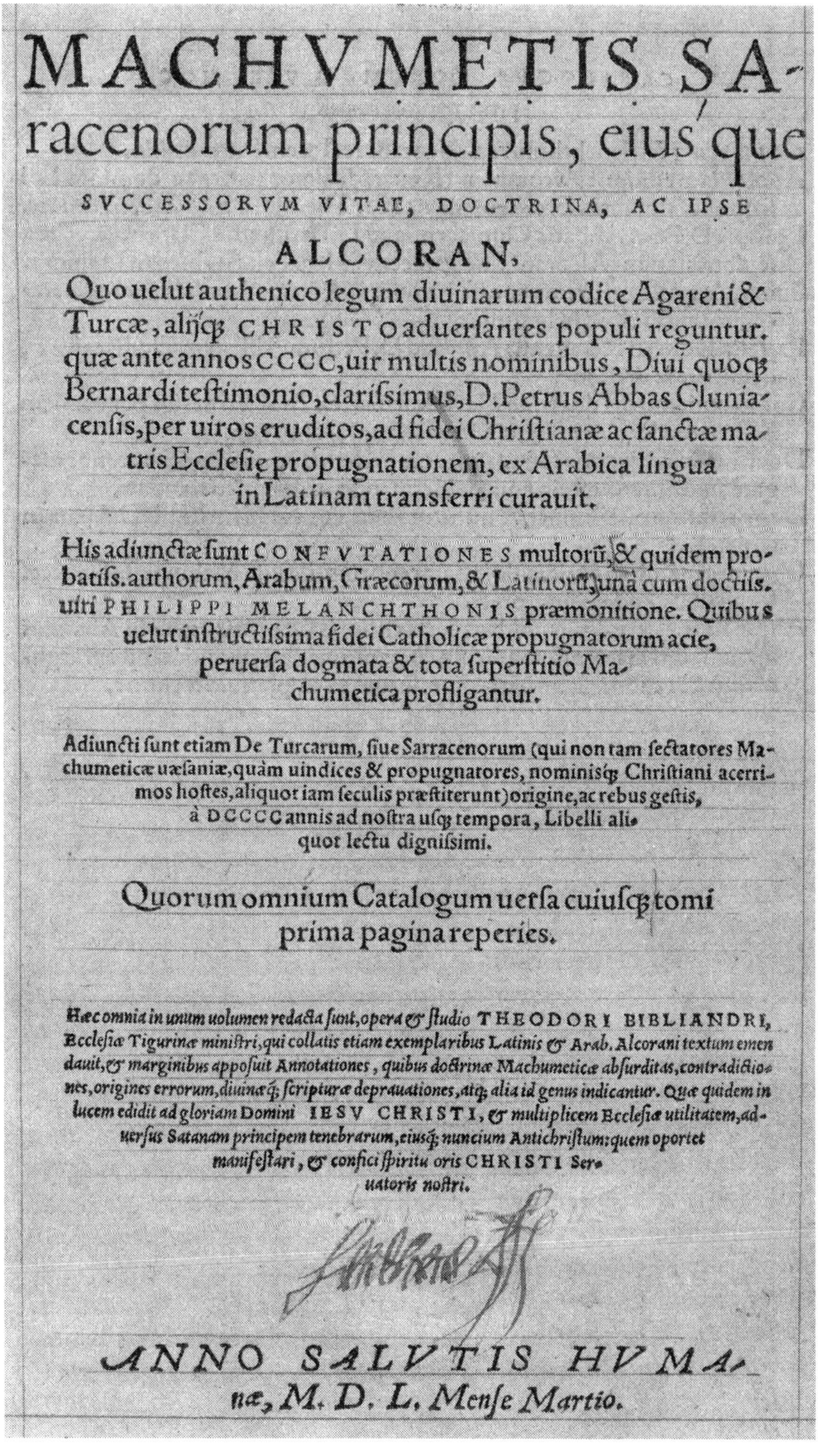

MACHVMETIS SA-
racenorum principis, eiusque
SVCCESSORVM VITAE, DOCTRINA, AC IPSE
ALCORAN,
Quo uelut authenico legum diuinarum codice Agareni &
Turcæ, aliiq; CHRISTO aduersantes populi reguntur.
quæ ante annos CCCC, uir multis nominibus, Diui quoq;
Bernardi testimonio, clarissimus, D. Petrus Abbas Clunia-
censis, per uiros eruditos, ad fidei Christianæ ac sanctæ ma-
tris Ecclesię propugnationem, ex Arabica lingua
in Latinam transferri curauit.

His adiunctæ sunt CONFVTATIONES multorũ, & quidem pro-
batiss. authorum, Arabum, Græcorum, & Latinorũ, unà cum doctiss.
uiri PHILIPPI MELANCHTHONIS præmonitione. Quibus
uelut instructissima fidei Catholicæ propugnatorum acie,
peruersa dogmata & tota superstitio Ma-
chumetica profligantur.

Adiuncti sunt etiam De Turcarum, siue Sarracenorum (qui non tam sectatores Machumeticæ uæsaniæ, quàm uindices & propugnatores, nominisq; Christiani acerri-
mos hostes, aliquot iam seculis præstiterunt) origine, ac rebus gestis,
à DCCCC annis ad nostra usq; tempora, Libelli ali-
quot lectu dignissimi.

Quorum omnium Catalogum uersa cuiusq; tomi
prima pagina reperies.

Hæc omnia in unum uolumen redacta sunt, opera & studio THEODORI BIBLIANDRI,
*Ecclesiæ Tigurinæ ministri, qui collatis etiam exemplaribus Latinis & Arab. Alcorani textum emen
dauit, & marginibus apposuit Annotationes, quibus doctrinæ Machumeticæ absurditas, contradictiones, origines errorum, diuinæq; scripturæ deprauationes, atq; alia id genus indicantur. Quæ quidem in
lucem edidit ad gloriam Domini* IESV CHRISTI, *& multiplicem Ecclesiæ utilitatem, ad-
uersus Satanam principem tenebrarum, eiusq; nuncium Antichristum: quem oportet
manifestari, & confici spiritu oris* CHRISTI *Ser-
uatoris nostri.*

*ANNO SALVTIS HVMA-
næ, M. D. L. Mense Martio.*

Figure 1.3 Title page of Bibliander's Qur'an compilation, 1550

Courtesy of Houghton Library, Harvard University. GC5 B4716 543md, Houghton Library, Harvard University.

towards peoples and cultures of Muslim North Africa . . . were certainly more complicated, varied, and indeed more self-reflexive than some twentieth century historians would have us believe."[15] Similar ambiguity is demonstrated by the work of Thomas Burman on the study of the Qur'an in the late medieval and early modern periods. Burman's research contradicts the common presumption that polemics always trumped philology in Western study of the Qur'an. In fact, he demonstrates that scholars used a variety of reading strategies from derogatory polemic to pure linguistic interest—and sometimes within the work of the same translator.[16] Charlotte Colding Smith's conclusions on the way that the Turks were represented visually in Germany during the sixteenth century also supports this position.[17] Of course, it is possible to find enough material from the received tradition in early modern European accounts to argue that the understanding of Islam which developed in the medieval west persisted long after the end of the Middle Ages (or indeed even down to the present day). But this obscures the interesting fluidity of early modern Western approaches to Islam and can lead to an inaccurate essentializing—this time not of 'Islam' but of western views of Islam.

With due respect to the enormous influence of Edward Said's *Orientalism*, I argue for what might be termed a 'post-Said' understanding of the West's views of Islam in the early modern period. Said argued that a certain discourse about the Muslim world in the West created a binary of 'occident' and 'orient' for the express purpose of domination and control, and located the origin of that discourse in the early modern period.[18] In contrast, I argue that despite many shared images and themes, early modern European understandings of Islam did not originate in an attempt to dominate or to justify domination—nor could they in light of Ottoman political and military power. In addition, I argue that there was much more diversity and ambiguity in Western views of Islam than Edward Said recognizes. My study, then, can be seen in part as a continuation of the one made by Margaret Meserve in *Empires of Islam* concerning how fifteenth-century humanists understood the origins of the Turks. She argues that "there was no one Oriental other" in the fifteenth century, either in geopolitical reality or in the conceptions of Europeans.[19] Likewise, the writings on Islam that form the center of this study do not speak with a single voice or perspective. They reveal to us how knowledge about Islam gets translated, modified, re-used, altered in its purposes, and adjusted to an audience and the demands of authority structures. These publications are often at odds with themselves and self-contradictory. Although most of these authors would not have desired a new view of Islam to develop, the ambivalence of these texts helped to destabilize and create space for new information and new perspectives to break through. This is a complexity of which cursory readings are oblivious. Residual, emergent, traditional, and innovative perspectives all can occur at the same time in a culture, some of which may be more dominant than others. It is important to identify trends, emergences, changes, and especially underlying shifts in the framework of understanding. There is much more going on in early modern understandings of Islam than simple 'medieval' disparagement or the seeds of a later orientalism. And the Reformation was a critical factor in these developments.

Notes

1. For the broader context of medieval and early modern Western understandings of Islam, see especially: Nancy Bisaha, *Creating East and West: Renaissance humanists and the Ottoman Turks*; John Victor Tolan, *Saracens: Islam in the Medieval European Imagination*; Margaret Meserve, *Empires of Islam in Renaissance Historical Thought*; David R. Blanks and Michael Frassetto, *Western Views of Islam in Medieval and Early Modern Europe: Perception of Other*; Samuel Chew, *The Crescent and the Rose*; Norman Daniel, *Islam and the West: The Making of an Image*, 2nd ed.; Clarence Rouillard, *The Turk in French History, Thought and Literature*; and Richard Southern, *Western Views of Islam in the Middle Ages*.

2. For European captivity narratives in general, see Linda Colley, *Captives*; Ellen G. Friedman, *Spanish Captives in North Africa in the Early Modern Age*; Nabil Matar, *Turks, Moors and Englishmen in the Age of Discovery*; and Daniel J. Vitkus, ed., *Piracy, Slavery, and Redemption: Barbary Captivity Narratives from Early Modern England*.

3. "Bis zur Mitte des 16. Jahrhunderts waren es—abgesehen von der venezianischen Nachrichtenerhebung—vor allem ehemalige Gefangene gewesen, die dem von der *Türkengefahr* erschütterten Europa ausführlichere Einblicke auf das Leben am Bosphorus ermöglichten." Almut Höfert, *Den Feind beschreiben: "Türkengefahr" und europäisches Wissen über das Osmanische Reich 1450–1600*, 226. Until the mid-sixteenth century almost exclusively reporters who described the Ottoman Empire from extended experience were captives; after 1550 it was diplomats. It might even be possible to detect a hint of this transition even within the writings of the Hapsburg diplomat Busbecq. His first letter depends at least in part on earlier publications, the remaining letters seem not to be dependent on any previous sources and express his own understandings. See *The Turkish Letters of Ogier Ghiselin de Busbecq: Imperial Ambassador at Constantinople 1554–1562*.

4. Traveler's reports and captivity narratives should be considered distinct genres of Western European/Christian writings on the Muslim world. On traveler's reports in general, see: Gerald MacLean, *The Rise of Oriental Travel: English Visitors to the Ottoman Empire, 1580–1720*; Ivo Kamps and Jyotsna G. Singh, eds., *Travel Knowledge: European "Discoveries" in the Early Modern Period*; Kenneth Parker, ed., *Early Modern Tales of Orient: A Critical Anthology*; and Gerald MacLean, ed., *Re-orienting the Renaissance: Cultural Exchanges with the East*.

5. Especially in light of the significance of these two writings, not a great deal of research has been done on them. The most important work has been done by Reinhard Klockow who has published a scholarly edition of George of Hungary with introduction: *Georgius de Hungaria. Tractatus de moribus, condictionibus et nequicia Turcorum. Traktat über die Sitten, die Lebensverhältnisse und die Arglist der Türken. Nach der Erstausgabe von 1481 herausgegeben, übersetzt und eingeleitet von Reinhard Klockow*. He has also edited (with Monika Ebertowski) a limited edition, hand typeset museum printing of a different Georgijevic writing, *De captivitate sua apud Turcas*. In 1920 a short biographical

and bibliographical pamphlet concerning Georgijevic's life was written for the Vienna Nationalbibliothek by Franz Kidric, *Bartholomaeus Gjorgjevic: Biographische und Bibliographische Zusammenfassung*. In English the only writings I am aware of on these two authors are: Michael Heath "Bartholomaeus Georgiewitz: Exile, Slave, and Propagandist" and J.A.B. Palmer, "Fr. Georgius de Hungaria, O.P. and the Tractatus de Moribus Condicionibus et Nequicia Turcorum." There are numerous scholarly works on early modern pamphlet literature, travel writing, etc. which mention these two authors and provide brief descriptions, most importantly, Carl Göllner, *Turcica: Die europäischen Türkendrücke des XVI. Jahrhunderts*.

6. Two of Luther's main three writings on the Turks can be found in the American Edition. (*On War Against the Turks* (v. 46, pp. 155–205) and *Admonition to Prayer Against the Turks* (v. 43, pp. 213–241). Otherwise, I am aware of only Johann Brenz' *Booklet on the Turk: How Preachers and Laymen Should Conduct Themselves if the Turk were to Invade Germany* (1537) and Veit Dietrich's *How Preachers Should Exhort the People to Repentance and Earnest Prayer Against the Turk* (1542) have been translated, both by John Bohnstedt in "The Infidel Scourge of God: the Turkish Menace as Seen by German Pamphleteers of the Reformation Era."

7. See Charlotte Colding Smith, *Images of Islam, 1453–1600: Turks in Germany and Central Europe*.

8. Although each year brought some publications on the Turks, the quantity peaked during the more intense times of Ottoman-Hapsburg conflict and especially during the years surrounding the 1529 siege of Vienna. There was considerable variety in these publications, from single-sheet woodcuts emphasizing Turkish atrocities to Theodor Bibliander's 1543 several hundred-page collection of more learned polemics and descriptions of Islam. In terms of numbers alone, the largest single type of pamphlet concerning the Turks were the sixteenth century equivalent of the newspaper, the *Avisso* or *Neue Zeitung*. No scrap of news seemed to be too small for these short publications. One *Neue Zeitung* featured a dialogue with a captured Turk despite the fact that most of the answers the Turk gave were simply "Ich weiss nicht."

9. Andrew Pettegree, *The Book in the Renaissance*, 141.

10. The most extensive treatment of Martin Luther's engagement with Islam is *Martin Luther and Islam: A Study in Sixteenth-Century Polemics and Apologetics* by Adam Francisco.

11. Together, they make up almost one-third of the final volume of Bibliander's Qur'an. In fact, it appears that the new availability of the Geogijevic pamphlets was the primary motivation for the production of the second edition of Bibliander's work. See Gregory J. Miller, "Theodor Bibliander's *Machumetis saracenorum principis eiusque successorum vitae, doctrina ac ipse alcoran* (1543) as the Sixteenth Century 'Encyclopedia' of Islam."

12. For example, see Richmond Barbour, *Before Orientalism: London's Theatre of the East, 1576–1626*; Matthew Dimmock, *New Turkes: Dramatizing Islam and the Ottomans in Early Modern England*; Jonathan Burton, *Traffic and Turning: Islam and English Drama 1579–1624*; and Daniel Vitkus, *Turning Turk: English Theater and the Multicultural Mediterranean, 1570–1630*. In terms of sixteenth- and seventeenth-century English history writing, the same ambiguity is described by Anders Ingram in *Writing the Ottomans: Turkish History in Early Modern England*, 140.

13. Dimmock, 135–161. The quote is from Burton, 54.

14. Gerald MacLean, *Looking East: English Writing and the Ottoman Empire before 1800*, 87.

15. MacLean, *Looking East*, 68.
16. See Thomas Burman, *Reading the Qur'an in Latin Christendom, 1140–1560*.
17. Smith, 177–179.
18. Part of the opposition to Said is due to misunderstanding and oversimplifying his arguments. However, there is increasing criticism even among those who have accurately read him. For example, Ivan Kalmer has chided Said's failure to engage theology in any significant way. For example, see Ivan Kalmar, *Early Orientalism*.
19. Meserve, 11.

References

Barbour, Richmond. *Before Orientalism: London's Theatre of the East, 1576–1626*. Cambridge: Harvard University Press, 2003.

Bisaha, Nancy. *Creating East and West: Renaissance Humanists and the Ottoman Turks*. Philadelphia: University of Pennsylvania Press, 2004.

Blanks, David R. and Michael Frassetto. *Western Views of Islam in Medieval and Early Modern Europe: Perception of Other*. New York: St. Martin's, 1999.

Bohnstedt, John. "The Infidel Scourge of God: The Turkish Menace as Seen by German Pamphleteers of the Reformation Era." *Transactions of the American Philosophical Society* NS 58:9 (1968).

Burman, Thomas. *Reading the Qur'an in Latin Christendom, 1140–1560*. Philadelphia: University of Pennsylvania Press, 2007.

Burton, Jonathan. *Traffic and Turning: Islam and English Drama 1579–1624*. Newark: University of Delaware Press, 2005.

Chew, Samuel. *The Crescent and the Rose*. New York: Octagon Books, 1937.

Colley, Linda. *Captives*. New York, NY: Pantheon Books, 2002.

Dimmock, Matthew. *New Turkes: Dramatizing Islam and the Ottomans in Early Modern England*. New York: Routledge, 2005.

Forster, Edward, trans. *The Turkish Letters of Ogier Ghiselin de Busbecq: Imperial Ambassador at Constantinople 1554–1562*. Baton Rouge: Louisiana State University Press, 2005.

Francisco, Adam. *Martin Luther and Islam: A Study in Sixteenth-Century Polemics and Apologetics*. London: Brill, 2007.

Friedman, Ellen. *Spanish Captives in North Africa in the Early Modern Age*. Madison: University of Wisconsin Press, 1983.

Göllner, Carl. *Turcica: Die europäischen Türkendrücke des XVI. Jahrhunderts*. 3 vols. Bucharest: Editura Academiei, 1961–78.

Heath, Michael. "Bartholomaeus Georgiewitz: Exile, Slave, and Propagandist." *Journal of the Institute of Romance Studies* 2 (1993): 151–163.

Höfert, Almut. *Den Feind beschreiben: "Türkengefahr" und europäisches Wissen über das Osmanische Reich 1450–1600*. Frankfurt: Campus Verlag, 2003.

Ingram, Anders. *Writing the Ottomans: Turkish History in Early Modern England*. New York: Palgrave, 2015.

Kalmar, Ivan. *Early Orientalism*. New York: Routledge, 2012.

Kamps, Ivo, and Jyotsna G. Singh, eds. *Travel Knowledge: European "Discoveries" in the Early Modern Period*. New York: Palgrave, 2001.

Kidric, Franz. *Bartholomaeus Gjorgjevic: Biographische und Bibliographische Zusammenfassung*. Vienna: Verlag Ed. Strache, 1920.

Klockow, Reinhard, ed. *Georgius de Hungaria. Tractatus de moribus, condictionibus et nequicia Turcorum. Traktat über die Sitten, die Lebensverhältnisse und die Arglist der Türken. Nach der Erstausgabe von 1481 herausgegeben, übersetzt und eingeleitet.* Cologne: Böhlau, 1993.

Klockow, Reinhard, and Monika Ebertowski, eds. *De captivitate sua apud Turcas.* Berlin: Druckwerkstatt im Kreuzberg-Museum, 2000.

MacLean, Gerald. *Looking East: English Writing and the Ottoman Empire before 1800.* New York: Palgrave, 2007.

MacLean, Gerald, ed. *Re-Orienting the Renaissance: Cultural Exchanges with the East.* New York: Palgrave, 2005.

MacLean, Gerald. *The Rise of Oriental Travel: English Visitors to the Ottoman Empire, 1580–1720.* New York: Palgrave, 2004.

Matar, Nabil. *Turks, Moors and Englishmen in the Age of Discovery.* New York: Columbia University Press, 1999.

Meserve, Margaret. *Empires of Islam in Renaissance Historical Thought.* Cambridge: Harvard University Press, 2008.

Miller, Gregory J. "Theodor Bibliander's *Machumetis saracenorum principis eiusque successorum vitae, doctrina ac ipse alcoran* (1543) as the Sixteenth Century 'Encyclopedia' of Islam." *Islam and Christian-Islamic Relations* 24:2 (April 2013), 241–254.

Norman, Daniel. *Islam and the West: The Making of an Image.* 2nd ed. Oxford: Oneworld, 1993.

Palmer, J. A. B. "Fr. Georgius de Hungaria, O.P. and the Tractatus de Moribus Condicionibus et Nequicia Turcorum." *Bulletin of the John Rylands Library* 34 (1951/52): 44–68.

Parker, Kenneth, ed. *Early Modern Tales of Orient: A Critical Anthology.* New York: Routledge, 1999.

Pettegree, Andrew. *The Book in the Renaissance.* New Haven: Yale University Press, 2010.

Rouillard, Clarence. *The Turk in French History, Thought and Literature.* Paris: Boivin, 1941.

Said, Edward. *Orientalism.* New York: Vintage Books, 1978.

Smith, Charlotte Colding. *Images of Islam, 1453–1600: Turks in Germany and Central Europe.* London: Pickering and Chatto, 2014.

Southern, Richard. *Western Views of Islam in the Middle Ages.* Cambridge: Harvard University Press, 1962.

Tolan, John Victor. *Saracens: Islam in the Medieval European Imagination.* New York: Columbia University Press, 2002.

Vitkus, Daniel, ed. *Piracy, Slavery, and Redemption: Barbary Captivity Narratives from Early Modern England.* New York: Columbia University Press, 2001.

Vitkus, Daniel. *Turning Turk: English Theater and the Multicultural Mediterranean, 1570–1630.* New York: Palgrave, 2003.

2 The Intellectual Context

Western Views of Islam in the Late Middle Ages

I stood and stared; he saw me and stared back; then with his hands wrenched open his own breast, crying "See how I rend myself! What rack mangles Mahomet! Weeping without rest, Ali before me goes, his whole face slit by one great stroke upward from chin to crest. All those whom thou beholdest in the pit were sowers of scandal, sowers of schism abroad while they yet lived; therefore they now go split.

Dante, *Inferno*, Canto XXVIII

By the end of the crusading period in the Levant, the long-term foundation of Christian Europe's understanding of Islam had been established. Drawing on a wide variety of sources, medieval scholars collected a body of knowledge concerning Islam and detailed permissible responses to the Islamic threat.[1] With few exceptions this corpus was simply reinforced and repeated through the remainder of the period and, in part, persisted long into European history. With little variance from author to author, late medieval depictions of Islam were so similar because they used each other in a chain of sources, simply repeating the information on Islam which had been passed down to them.

Accurate information concerning the essentials of Islamic belief was available to medieval scholars and, to a lesser degree, even to the general population. However, Christian writers developed a picture of Islam which was intentionally distorted. They interpreted data specifically in a manner favorable to Christianity and unacceptable to Islam. There was little attempt to understand what was known or to communicate with Muslims.

Among other assertions, Muhammad was portrayed as dishonest and insincere as a prophet, as a promoter of violence in order to establish his religion, self-indulgent concerning sexuality, and a Christian heretic and schismatic. In aggregate form these inaccuracies created what Norman Daniel described as a "frontier of mental attitudes", that was "emphatically defined and crossed only with the greatest difficulty."[2]

One of the reasons these inaccuracies proved to be so intractable was because they served a specific purpose in the foundation of the concept of

Europe. When Europe began to recover from the turmoil and invasions of the Early Middle Ages, because of a strong religious element, it began to identify itself more and more with Christianity. Europe needed a negative image against which it could fight; this was provided by a distorted image of Islam, a psychological 'shadow side' of European identity.[3] As Suzanne Akbari has described in her excellent study *Idols in the East*, the wide range of European writings on Islam, from the fanciful to the scholarly, were united in projecting an idolatrous orient in direct opposition to the true faith of Christendom.[4] A proper understanding of this foundational medieval view of Islam provides the necessary background from which sixteenth-century developments can be analyzed.

Late Medieval Scholars of Islam and Their Sources

Western scholars in the late medieval period who desired information concerning Islam had access potentially to a variety of sources. Polemic writings from the East and travelers' accounts made accessible firsthand knowledge of the Muslim world. The Qur'an was available, both in Arabic and in translation. Authentic Muslim sources were less frequently used, however. Christian scholars invariably preferred Christian sources. When Muslim sources were used, such as in the Iberian corpus (see below), deliberate editing in the service of polemics frequently took place.[5] If there were discrepancies among accounts, for example, the Christian account was always accepted over the Muslim. Thomas Burman's research on Latin translators of the Qur'an, however, has demonstrated how complex this process could be and how pure linguistic interest often superseded polemic.[6]

Available Eastern Christian anti-Muslim polemical writings include the "Syrian Apology" and the works of John of Damascus.[7] The struggle for survival of minority Christian groups in Muslim lands helps to explain the violent, imaginative language used in this literature. These lurid stories were an important source of the West's misconceptions.[8] Although his work did not circulate widely in the Middle Ages,[9] an example of an important medieval source on Islam from a traveler to the Levant is Ricoldo de Monte Croce. As was the case with many Eastern sources, although Ricoldo spent a number of years in direct contact with Islam, his anti-Muslim writings remained extreme and are filled with errors and calumnies.[10]

Iberian sources were particularly influential and represented the single largest group of writings available to medieval scholars.[11] The popularity of these few works was probably due to their combination of amusement, instruction, and controversy in an easy-reading format.[12] The most important of the Iberian manuscripts is the so-called Cluniac corpus.[13] This collection of writings on Islam was begun under the initiative of Abbot Peter the Venerable who in 1141–43 visited Benedictine Abbeys in Spain and became interested in Islamic polemics.

The centerpiece of the Cluniac corpus was the *Liber legis Saracenorum quem Alcoran vocant*, a Latin paraphrase of the Qur'an with many marginal and interlinear notations. This work was completed in 1143 by the Cluniac monk Robert of Ketton with the help of a native translator.[14] Mark of Toledo later authored a more literal translation of the Qur'an, but it was Ketton's work (a paraphrase intended to explain or illumine the original text) rather than Mark of Toledo's literal translation that was widespread during the Middle Ages.[15]

Of the medieval scholars who worked on Islam, Nicholas Cusa, deserves special comment.[16] Because of direct involvement in the East-West negotiations leading to the Council of Florence, Cusa developed an intense interest in Islam and produced two works that had a significant influence on later views: *De Pace Fidei* and the *Cribatio Alchoran*.[17]

In *De Pace Fidei* Cusa suggested an international colloquium as the best approach for peace and the conversion of Muslims. The *Cribatio*, the more important of the two writings, was a complex polemic that 'sifted' the Qur'an and found elements of (Christian) truth. Both works were characterized by careful scholarship and attempted accuracy, even though he had only Ketton's Qur'an and Ricoldo for sources.[18] In an age dominated by Crusade ideology and scholastic theology, Cusa's scholarship is unique in both its relatively irenic tone and in the use of a methodological reductionism to reconcile Christian and Muslim beliefs (of course, in the end always convincing Muslims of the truth of Christianity).

Late Medieval Knowledge and Depictions of Islam

The audience for Western writings concerning Islam was Christian, despite the popularity of the Muslim-Christian dialogue format. The writings "were admirably formulated to uphold faith. They would suitably horrify those who were at a distance from actual Muslims, but they would also fortify those who could not be guarded physically from Islamic realities. All alike would be confirmed in their suspicion and contempt."[19] Since it was certainly easier to win an argument against a paper opponent, and since the Christians always won, these writings tended to give Christendom a certain self-respect in dealing with a civilization in many ways its superior.

Because of the polemic context of their writings, medieval authors concerned themselves with Islamic subjects not to describe Islam accurately, but to compare it with Christianity. One point is clear: the paradigmatic understanding of Islam in the Middle Ages was that it was a Christian heresy. This underlying argument of the superiority of Christianity not only dictated which Islamic subjects would be discussed (and which would not), but also the order in which Islamic subjects would be treated.

The traditional first and dominating argument was that Muhammad could have been no true prophet and certainly no Messiah. Arguments concerning the inferiority and inconsistency of the Qur'an and of Muslim theology and spirituality followed. Only toward the end of the Middle Ages did scholars demonstrate any sustained interest in the institutions and history of Islam and the Ottoman Turks.

Christian polemicists depicted Muhammad as the central figure and originator of Islam, and used his life as the starting point of their arguments. His claim to be the divine mouthpiece (prophet) was known and transmitted through the Latin translation of the *shahadah*: "Non est deus nisi Deus, Mahamad est nuncius Dei." [There is no God except God; Muhammad is God's representative.][20] For the Christian scholastics, a prophet demonstrated his divine call by purity of life, presentation of true miracles, and the fulfillment and truthfulness of all his sayings. Every Latin writer presented Muhammad's life in such a way as to prove his incompatibility with the three aspects of this definition.[21] If they disproved his prophetic calling, they considered themselves to have disproved Islam itself.

Several themes were consistently used to demonstrate the depravity of Muhammad's life. Many sources emphasize his 'low birth,' pagan, or idolatrous background. Even the medieval etymology of the designation 'Saracen' was wrongly seen as a claim to descent from 'Sara' to cover up Agarene (that is, from Hagar), barbarian blood.

Muhammad also was shown to have schemed himself into authority through deception. Some portrayed him as a renegade Christian, a cardinal who had been denied the papacy and in return maliciously initiated a heretical schism, as seen in Dante's *Inferno*. With the help of instructors in heresy or black magic, such as the Nestorian monk Sergius, he was able to deceive the ignorant Arabs into believing he was a divine messenger. Medieval scholars attempted to disprove the validity of Muhammad's miracles, and instead credited demonic power, trained animals, or magic devices.[22] Muhammad's deceptive revelatory utterances were seen as demonically inspired, or at best, self-generated. The claim that he suffered from epileptic (or self-induced) fits was common. Frequently, demonic possession was added as the source of his inspiration.

After gaining power by means of deception, Muhammad was said to have maintained his power by violence and by allowing lascivious sexuality. Muslim violence and the extension of Islam by the sword was consistently stressed, especially in contrast to humble, peripatetic Christian missionaries. Usually writers attributed Muhammad's violence to a base desire for plunder and possessions, but emphasized Muslim hatred and destruction of things Christian.

Even without invention or exaggeration, no Christian would have believed Muhammad's sexual life to be proper. Polygamy proved that he was lascivious; in fact, some argued that he made up 'revelations' on the spot to justify his lecherous actions.[23] The ability to have multiple wives and concubines was widely believed to be one of the chief enticements of Islam.

Because a good death is the proof of a saintly life, Muhammad was given a horrible death by Latin writers. Some writers could not determine the most horrible of the different traditions and so simply listed them all. Frequently used themes included: death and devouring by swine, poisoning by a Jewess, death in Aishah's arms (with sexual innuendo), and the problems of a rotting corpse faced by disappointed followers who had expected an angelic ascension.[24]

After painting such an evil portrait of Muhammad, scholars were left to answer how he could have been accepted at all. The solution was found in the cunning of the Prophet, the ignorance of the pagan Arabs, and the maliciousness of Arabian Jews and heretics. Clearly, however, Muhammad was no true prophet.

Medieval scholars knew the Muslim belief that the Qur'an is the infallible, direct revelation of God and therefore superior to the Christian Bible. In addition, there was some knowledge of the *tahrif*, the Muslim claim that the biblical text is corrupt (especially concerning the prophecy of the coming of Muhammad). These points were vigorously denied by a comparison of the two writings. The task was simplified considerably by the fact that the scholastics used arguments based primarily on their own scripture and made no significant attempt to examine Muslim claims.

The primary arguments against the Qur'an centered on style and content. The style was characterized as redundant and vain. (Of course, the Qur'an was generally known only through poor Latin translations.) There is no evidence that the Muslim proof of inspiration by the beauty of language was seriously considered. Furthermore, the content was not meaningful enough for divine revelation, contained inherent absurdities and contradictions, and was generally irrational. Dissonance with scripture (Old Testament discrepancies were blamed on the Talmud, New Testament discrepancies on heretics) further illustrated the Qur'an's weakness.[25]

Sometimes side-by-side with these arguments, many scholars also claimed that the Qur'an did contain some divine revelation—just enough to prove the validity of Christianity and the Christian Bible. Those scholars who had access to a copy of the Qur'an took great pains to show that the Qur'an actually establishes the Trinity, the divinity of Jesus, and other key Christian doctrines. Since the Qur'an proved scripture, it also invalidated Islamic belief.

Christian scholars did not thoroughly investigate Muslim theology, but concentrated on a few key doctrines. An extensive analysis was not necessary since Islam was seen as a Christian heresy. How could it be otherwise? It was born from a malignant combination of Christian heresy and Samaritan/Talmudic Judaism, claimed John of Damascus and others.[26] Although the term also was used colloquially, scholars made serious attempts to demonstrate Islam's heretical nature by the measure of agreement they found with some classic heresies, especially Nestorianism. The Saracens were placed (along with Judaism) in contemporary lists of heresies and confronted in manuscripts *contra haereticos*.[27] In addition to the charge of heresy, Islam sometimes also was viewed as a schism, with the concomitant additional penalties (as by Dante).

Concerning Muslim theology, medieval scholars knew the intensity of the Muslim doctrine of the unity of God, and that this proclamation was the purpose of the Prophet's mission. Claims of Muslim idolatry were very rare among the educated, although mentioned in some literary sources. Rather than a fault, the unity of God was seen as a point of contact. According to the thirteenth-century Spanish mystic and missionary, Raymond Llull, the Islamic doctrine of God was 'incomplete' rather than false.

The primary problem in the relationship between the two theological systems, however, was Muslim Christology and soteriology. From evidence in the Qur'an itself, Latin scholars knew the Muslim teaching that Jesus was born of a virgin and sinless. They could not understand how the same book that proclaimed his sinlessness could also deny that he died and that he was divine.[28] Moreover, Islamic determinism seemed to deny the free exercise of human will (cooperation with God) that was necessary for salvation. This fatalism was most repugnant when God was seen as the author of evil. To its discredit, in the eyes of medieval writers Islam offered a salvation by 'faith alone,' that is, by the mere repetition of the *shahadah* or by Muhammad's intercession on the Day of Judgment.[29] Without stress on the use of works, Islam was seen as giving license to sin. It was a 'wide path' as opposed to the true Christian 'narrow path.' According to medieval scholars, writes Norman Daniel, "Islam not only permitted sin, it reconciled religion with illicit fun; it encouraged people to think that they could be saved some easy way."[30] Since salvation was so easy, it was no surprise that paradise was also indulgent. The historical details of Muhammad's personal life, the looseness of Islamic sexual ethics, and the sensual paradise of the Qur'an "were linked together to constitute one single theme. Islam was essentially built upon a foundation of sexual license which was plainly contrary to the natural and the divine law."[31]

There was much ignorance, little interest, and practically no systematic comparison of the interior life of the two religions. Some authors who had direct contact with Islamic lands noted and appreciated Muslim piety, but only as a means to shame Christians and not to commend Muslims.[32] At times a grudging admission of the popular strength of Muslim devotion was made (e.g., medieval scholars knew Muslim respect for the name of God, the prophets, saints, and holy places, and had some appreciation of the details of Islamic rituals), but Islamic spirituality made little impression on the medieval West. Scholars frequently made comparisons between rituals and institutions important to Christianity and their supposed Muslim counterparts. However, since it was assumed that Islam was fundamentally Christian (albeit corrupted), the communal rather than clerical/sacramental tendencies of Islam were unknown.

Since Friday was the day of Venus, Friday prayers commonly were seen as a false parallel to Christianity with sexual overtones. The *qiblah* was believed to be south (as opposed to the Christian east). The five-time daily prayer was known, but there was no knowledge of the Muslim strict avoidance of the appearance of sun worship. Some thought the *salat* was the worship of Muhammad. Latin scholars assumed that Islam had clergy (*fuqaha* were not understood as teachers/lawyers) and had a little knowledge of traveling ascetic monks who did bizarre acts. The Caliph was equated with the Pope, the *qadi* with cardinals and bishops. Islamic washings were understood as 'baptisms' for the remission of sin, to which the Christian writers responded by sermonizing about the need for interior rather than exterior cleanliness. In another tie to sexuality, the washing of private parts was emphasized. The prohibition of wine and swine and the requirement of circumcision was emphasized.

The Islamic counterpart to the Christian sacrament of marriage attracted considerable attention. Typical was Pedro de Alfonso's claim that a man may have four wives (who could be divorced and replaced for any reason) and sexual relations with any number of slaves (including the freedom to buy or sell them as long as there was no pregnancy). Christians had particular problems with the permissive Muslim divorce laws. The woman should be the partner (*socia*) rather than the servant (*serva*), they declared.[33] Muslim desecration of the sacrament of marriage was another evidence of Islamic sexual license deriving from the example of the Prophet himself. Although not known as such, the Latin West was familiar with the Five Pillars of Islam. The medieval Christian interpretation of the Confession of Faith *(shahadah)* and five-times daily prayer is given above. The *hajj*, the fast of Ramadan, and *zakat* were also interpreted in relation to Christian rituals. The *hajj* most frequently was seen as a pilgrimage to Muhammad's grave. Scant knowledge existed of the circumlocution, stoning, and sacrifice. Both the *Kaaba* and Muhammad's tomb (understood to be the same thing) were a source of controversy. While some scholars affirmed the medieval tradition of the myth of Muhammad's tomb suspended in air, others denied it. Some understood the *Kaaba* as the *Domus Dei* founded by Adam and used by Abraham and Ishmael in worship, although others saw it as a center of pagan idol worship that Muhammad had been unable to cleanse from the Arabs and therefore simply incorporated.[34] The fast of Ramadan was compared to Christian fasts, to the detriment of the former (evening sexual license and feasting were mentioned). There was little knowledge of the reason for the fast. Muslim almsgiving *(zakat)* was known, but mentioned infrequently (only as 'something Christians should do'); some scholars mentioned the mandatory nature of the almsgiving. Concerning the so-called 'Sixth Pillar,' the *jihad* (holy war), scholars believed that the Qur'an commanded the use of violence against Christians and therefore that violence was central to Islam. Muslim expansion was credited primarily to the material and spiritual benefits promised in the *jihad*. Muslims fought so fearlessly, it was said, because death in battle meant that one would go immediately to Paradise.

Finally, Islamic sects and divisions were largely unknown. The Shi'a were essentially seen as a schism;[35] Shi'a forms of religious expression were quite unknown.[36] The Assassins were known as a separate group from crusader contacts, but their 'religious' aspects were not understood.

Late Medieval Depictions of the Ottoman Turks

Many late medieval writers (outside of Spain) used the term 'Turk' as a synonym with 'Islam.'[37] What was true of one was assumed to be true of the other. However, until the last half of the fifteenth century few Europeans had direct contact with the Ottoman culture. The combined result of these factors was an almost complete lack of knowledge of the unique character of Ottoman Turkish history, institutions, or culture.[38]

One characteristic was frequently mentioned, however, especially in the military accounts: the Turks were unusually cruel. Many argued that the Turks were descendants of the war-like Trojans. Others connected them with the ancient Scythians who were noted for their barbarity and cruelty.[39] Although the details differed, the themes were constant: brutality (especially to women and children), wanton shedding of blood, violent sexuality, pollution of the holy places, seizure and destruction of wealth and property, and barbaric slavery. With their intricately detailed descriptions of Turkish atrocities, Western chroniclers established the image of the Turks as savage and bloodthirsty barbarians who swooped down on innocent Christians and massacred them indiscriminately. The Turks were seen as eager for world domination. Frequently the rhetoric reached fever pitch, as when Pope Nicholas V (30 September 1453) addressed a Crusade bull to all Christendom and declared Mehmed to be the "cruelest persecutor of the Church of Christ, the son of Satan, the son of death who thirsted for the blood of Christians."[40] Similar descriptions appeared regularly.

If Turks were barbarians, however, they were also militarily inferior. Pius II expressed a familiar idea when he described the Turks as courageous, aggressive, and ready to die for their faith, but yet militarily untested. The Greeks were considered by many in the West to be cowardly, unarmed weaklings.[41] As was commonly suggested, all that was needed was for Christians to take up the defense of the faith. Christendom would then soon triumph.

Medieval Understandings of the Ottoman Threat and Its Causes

Historians are divided over how intense the Ottoman threat was perceived by late medieval Europeans. Islamic expert Hans Joachim Kissling argued that the beginning of a strong fear of the Turks *(Türkenfurcht)* can be seen in the fallout of the battle of Nikopolis (1396) and political weakness after the death of King Sigismund of Hungary (1437).[42] Ottoman historian Aziz Atiya claimed that the fall of Constantinople was the key event, and that it was received throughout Western Europe with utter bewilderment and great bitterness.[43] Most scholars, however, claim that the West (specifically the Germans) was unperturbed by Ottoman advances, even after the fall of Constantinople.[44] According to Steven Runciman, the West thought it was in no immediate danger from the Ottomans and "they were unwilling to fight for their faith unless their immediate interests were involved."[45] "Only the papacy and a few scholars and romanticists scattered about the West had been genuinely shocked at the thought of the great historic Christian city passing into the hands of the infidel . . . the conscience of Western Europe had been touched but not roused."[46]

One primary reason why the Ottoman advance was not taken too seriously was because of Latin hatred of the Greeks. Why shed blood to save those recalcitrants? Would not the angry ghost of Virgil (honorary Christian and prophet) say that the Turks, the descendants of the Trojans, were getting revenge for the horrors of the sack of Troy? The occupation of the Byzantine territories was seen as inevitable and only signified the end of the Greek age.

Still, two hundred years of continual Ottoman victories had to be explained. The answer was found in Christian weakness rather than in Ottoman strength. Military losses often were blamed by contemporaries on numerical inferiority, although modern scholars argue that Ottoman victories were won not by greater numbers, but by better tactics, stricter discipline, better leadership, and greater loyalty and devotion.[47] Late medieval Christians would not have agreed. Pius II declared

> The courage of Christians had always been the terror of the Turks and they [the Christians] had never been worsted unless betrayed or overpowered by too great odds, when they were weary of conquest, or because our Lord God was angry at our sins.[48]

According to the contemporary De Mezieres, the reason for the failure at Nicopolis was a lack of the four virtues of good governance: order, discipline, obedience, and justice and instead the dominance of vanity, covetousness, and luxury.[49] A similar interpretation for the fall of Constantinople was also given: the Greeks were guilty because of their deceitfulness, indolence, and failure to work to end the schism and therefore God justly punished them. If only Christians would unite, a small force (50–60,000 men) was sufficient to halt the Turkish advance and perhaps push them out of Europe.[50] Less frequently, the Turkish threat was declared to represent God's punishment for the sins of Christendom. Calls to repentance were made, especially by Franciscan friars who delivered *ex tempore* sermons (mostly running commentaries on a Crusade bull or indulgence) to plaza crowds and sold expiation from Crusade pledges for monetary contributions. Even if one did not need forgiveness from sins, it was argued, in his providence God did allow the Turks to continue to exist as an *exercitio bonum* (an opportunity for good work) and a *salutis facilitas* (an easier salvation) for those who would never perform long penances.[51]

Late Medieval Responses to Islam

The 'good work' mentioned in popular preaching was, of course, the Crusade.[52] Even though the last of the Crusader strongholds in the East fell in 1291, Crusade ideology continued to dominate late medieval thinking concerning Islam.[53] The output of Crusade literature and propaganda during the fourteenth and fifteenth centuries was immense. According to Andrew Pettegree, one of the most significant types of publication in pre-Reformation Germany was an indulgence for the purpose of raising money to fight against the Turks.[54] The crusading ideal was still strong enough in 1396 to draw 100,000 knights from all over Europe for the Nicopolis campaign. The failure at Nicopolis, however, marked a turning point in Crusade history. The Crusades ceased to be an organized movement of Christendom against Islam for the deliverance of the Holy Land, and instead took on defensive characteristics in the much closer area of the Balkans. Otherwise, however, Crusade ideology survived intact. The same motivations, leadership, and justifications were offered in the fifteenth century as in the twelfth. After Nicopolis, Hungary became the chief focus of defense and the bulwark of Christendom for the West. The so-called Hungarian Crusade is illustrative of Christian responses to the Ottoman Turks in the Late Middle Ages. In the years preceding the fall of Constantinople, John Hunyadi of Hungary (in conjunction with King Ladislas of Poland, George Brankovitch despot of Serbia, and John Castriota (Scanderberg) of Albania) engaged in a series of campaigns (1442–43) that inflicted heavy losses upon Ottoman Sultan Murad II and forced a ten-year truce and his abdication into central Anatolia.

However, Cardinal Caesarini persuaded Hunyadi to break the truce (since it was made with an infidel and was thus null) and attack Ottoman Bulgaria, in return for which he would receive the Bulgarian throne. The first attack was at Varna on the Black Sea in 1444. Victory appeared to be in sight when the Sultan reappeared at the head of a picked army of 40,000 that had been transported by the Genoese for profit and trade rights. Caesarini was killed and Hunyadi forced to retreat. While Hunyadi recovered, the rebellion continued under Scanderberg in Albania, but at the second Battle of Kossovo (1448) the rebels were routed and the Hungarian Crusade effectively at an end.

Although some Western European adventurers and mercenaries participated, campaigns like this were primarily fought by Balkan armies for Balkan leaders in the Balkans. They were, however, 'Europeanized' by the continual papal calls for action, pleas for financial aid, and Crusade bulls of indulgence. Furthermore, both churchmen and representatives of Balkan leaders would often universalize the conflict using traditional Crusade rhetoric and by making ties to the crusading tradition. For example, during the relief of the siege of Belgrade (1456) John Capistrano begged for more troops from the West by promising that "the day of the salvation of Christendom has dawned" and that Europe, the Greek empire, the Holy Land, and Jerusalem could be recovered.[55] Such calls for assistance and papal declarations of Crusade were made in response to every seeming Christian advantage or crisis in the last half of the fifteenth century and the early sixteenth century.[56] Some local rebellions succeeded momentarily, some battles were won, but all efforts at stopping the Ottoman advance eventually failed, frequently because of in-fighting and treachery among the Christian leaders.

A key point of discussion in the late medieval crusading movement was therefore unity among Christian princes. Both as an excuse for non-participation and as a legitimate desire, European peace was seen as a necessary precursor to any successful Crusade. Repentance for disunity and prayers for brotherhood frequently were urged by the Church hierarchy and scholars. Robert Schwoebel in *The Shadow of the Crescent* goes so far as to argue that the Turkish threat worked to revive the idea of the *Respublica Christiana* and gave new life to the idea of a unified Christianity to oppose Islamic advances.[57] As the instrument of Almighty God, a united Christendom could not fail to overcome his enemies, Cardinal Bessarion proclaimed.[58] With God's help and Christian unity, they believed they could destroy Islam.

Although the Crusade continued to be the paradigmatic response to Islam, other approaches were suggested.[59] Atiya credits Raymond Llull with the novel approach that it might be more appropriate if he tried to win the Muslims over to Christ. By saving their souls from sin, he would eventually bring the Holy Land and the whole world of Islam into the fold of the faithful without violence or the spilling of blood.[60] Llull also attempted to find a means of communication by learning Arabic and Islamic theology.[61] R. W. Southern's *Western Views of Islam in the Middle Ages* also highlights efforts at evangelization and rapprochement. Southern saw a 'Moment of Vision' in the 1450–60 work of John of Segovia[62] and Nicholas Cusa. By the late fifteenth century, it was inevitable that negotiations would have to be made with the growing Ottoman power.[63] By necessity the Turks became part of the European political system.[64] Negotiations were not new, but the frequency of diplomatic correspondence and temporary alliances increased dramatically. Through this direct, peaceful contact and increased relations a body of descriptive and historical literature was produced that was more sober and more accurate. It was this new material delivered into a new religious context that gave sixteenth century scholars an opportunity to reevaluate medieval views of Islam.

Notes

1. The most important source for the medieval view of Islam is Norman Daniel, *Islam and the West: The Making of an Image*. A new edition was released in 1993. Although it is not without its detractors (it has been criticized for its completely synchronic, topical presentation of information), it remains the standard work on the subject. By far the two most important recent studies have been Thomas Burman's *Reading the Qur'an in Latin Christendom, 1140–1560* and Suzanne Akbari's *Idols in the East: European Representations of Islam and the Orient, 1100–1450*. Also important for medieval views of Islam, R. W. Southern, *Western Views of Islam in the Middle Ages*; C. F. Beckingham, *Between Islam and Christendom: Travelers. Facts and Legends in the Middle Ages and the Renaissance*; James E. Biechler, "Christian Humanism Confronts Islam: Sifting the Qur'an with Nicholas of Cusa"; John Ferguson, "Northern Europe and

Islam in the Middle Ages"; Nicholas Rescher, "Nicholas of Cusa on the Qur'an: A Fifteenth Century Encounter with Islam"; Maxime Rodinson, *Europe and the Mystique of Islam*; Robert Schwoebel, *The Shadow of the Crescent: The Renaissance Image of the Turk (1453–1517);* and Jean-Jacques Waardenburg, "Two Lights Perceived: Medieval Islam and Christianity." (Oxford: Clarendon, 1985) 1957).

2. Daniel, 45.
3. W. Montgomery Watt, "Muhammad in the Eyes of the West," 62–63.
4. See Akbari, especially 1–20.
5. Daniel, 270.
6. Burman's study is a masterpiece of historical-religious-linguistic research and has become the primary shaper of my own understanding of Western views of the Qur'an in the Late Middle Ages.
7. Concerning the literature on Byzantine anti-Muslim polemic, see Waardenburg, 273–277, and John Meyerdorff, "Byzantine Views of Islam."
8. Waardenberg, 268.
9. The *Confutatio Alcorani* owes its fame to the Renaissance retranslation of a fifteenth-century Greek version by Demetrius Cydones, Daniel, 234. In 1542 Martin Luther translated and published a German version under the title, *Verlegung des Alcoran Bruder Richardi* (WA 53, 261–396). Since the *Confutatio Alcorani* included selections supposedly from the Qur'an, Luther sometimes is identified erroneously as a translator of the Qur'an. The *Confutatio* is responsible for many mistaken understandings of the Qur'an even through the seventeenth century.
10. "From all the polemic that he inherited, both the books and the living tradition, he constructed an encyclopedic refutation of Islam, from which nothing he ever learned was omitted. . . . So much of what he wrote did nothing to illumine Islam for his contemporaries." Daniel, 66–67.
11. Many different individuals and groups were involved in this research, including Peter the Venerable, the abbot of Cluny, Mark the bishop of Toledo, the Franciscan Raymond Llull, and the Dominicans St. Raymond de Penyaforte (General of the Order in 1238) and Raymond Marti. The most important manuscripts included: Pedro de Alfonso's *Dialogue*, the *Corozan* (fables), Peter of Toledo's translation of the *Risalah* (this was perhaps the greatest Cluniac contribution to the biography of Muhammad and the history of early Islam), and the Cluniac corpus. See Burman, 60–87.
12. Daniel, 234.
13. In addition to Ketton's Qur'an, the Cluniac corpus contained the *Epistola Saraceni cum rescripto Christiani* translated by Peter of Toledo (a Christian Arab polemic purporting to be the correspondence of two friends at the court of al-Ma'mun, AD 813–833), *De generatione Machumet* by Hermannus Dalmata (a discussion of the transference of the prophetic light through the generations from Adam to Muhammad including biographical comments on Muhammad's birth and early life), *De doctrina Machumet* by Hermannus Dalmata (the conversion legend of the Median Jews by Muhammad's answer to their questions), and the *Chronica Mendosa et ridiculosa Saracenorium* by Ketton (a legendary chronicle of the creation of the world and a summary of Islamic history concerning Muhammad and the first seven caliphs).
14. This was a paraphrase rather than a translation; the text was reworked so that logical conclusions and connections which were unexpressed were made clear. It was a strongly interpreted and 'Christianized' text (for instance, Ketton did not use the word 'Muslim' and its related forms). For information on the Cluniac Qur'an, see Burman's *Reading the Qur'an*, M. T. D'Alvery, "Deux traductions

latines du Coran au Moyen Age," and James Kritzeck, *Peter the Venerable and Islam.*

15. Ketton was also the foundation for Bibliander's Latin Qur'an. On Mark of Toledo's Qur'an and its impact, see Burman, 122–148.

16. Concerning Cusa's work with Islam, see Southern, Biechler, and Rescher. The *Cribatio Alchoran* and *De Pace Fidei* are found in Nikolaus von Kues *Werke.*

17. Cusa and Ricoldo were the only two scholarly sources on Islam available to Martin Luther until late in his life.

18. Rescher, 197.

19. Daniel, 263.

20. Daniel, 207.

21. Daniel, 73.

22. Daniel, 74.

23. Daniel, 102.

24. Daniel, 107.

25. Daniel, 57–67. See also Burman, 36–59.

26. For John of Damascus, see Chapter 101 of his book on heresies, *Pege tes gnoseos.* For the influence of the Damascene's view on Latin scholars, see especially Waardenburg, 270.

27. For example, in Alan of Lille's *De fide catholica contra haereticos sui temporis,* he wrote 76 chapters against Albigensians, 25 against Waldensians, 21 against Jews, and 14 against Muslims.

28. Daniel, 175.

29. Daniel, 159–160.

30. Daniel, 156.

31. Daniel, 152.

32. For example, Ricoldo recorded from his personal contact with Muslims in Baghdad, "Who will not be astounded, if he carefully considers how great is the concern of these vile Muslims for study, their devotion in prayer, their pity for the poor, their reverence for the name of God and the prophets and the Holy Places, their sobriety in manners, their hospitality to strangers, their harmony and love for one another." Daniel, 190.

33. Daniel, 146.

34. According to Pedro de Alfonso, the Kaaba was the center of pagan idolatry. Two holy stones (named Chamos and Mercurius by Ammon and Moab, the sons of Lot) were worshipped by Arabs at separate solar festivals. Muhammad, unable to destroy the worship, had the Saturn stone set backwards in the wall of the Kaaba and the Mars stone buried in the ground. Daniel, 217.

35. [Dante] "Ali was its anti-prophet."

36. Daniel, 319.

37. See among others, Rodinson, 36 and Schwoebel, 226.

38. One exception to this was the Burgundian court of Philip the Good (r.1419–1467) where a revival of courtly chivalry produced a great deal of effort (including the use of spies) to gain knowledge about the Turks. The Ottoman peril was linked with courtly chivalry and holy war in the language and romantic literature of his court.

39. Schwoebel, 148. Pilgrim accounts usually mentioned the Trojans version, see Schwoebel, 189.

40. Schwoebel, 31.

41. At times, in an effort to strengthen Western resolve, the military ability of the Turks would be downplayed, as in an oration before the Roman Curia in 1452, when Aeneas Sylvius declared that the "Turks are unwarlike, weak, effeminate, neither martial in spirit, nor in counsel; their spoils were taken without sweat or blood."

42. Hans Joachim Kissling, "Türkenfurcht und Türkenhoffnung im 15/16. Jahrhunderts: zur Geschichte eines 'Komplexes'," 6.
43. Aziz Atiya, *Crusade, Commerce, and Culture*, 117.
44. For example, Stephen Fischer-Galati, *Ottoman Imperialism and German Protestantism, 1521–1555*, 9–10.
45. Steven Runciman, *The Fall of Constantinople, 1453*, 13–14.
46. Runciman, *Fall*, 179–181. This argument has been challenged. Robert Schwoebel specifically took issue with Runciman's claim that only a few scholars, intellectuals, and the papacy were shocked by the fall of Constantinople and found any real significance in the event. This may be true in the source material of the elites, Schwoebel stated, but significant collections of popular ballads, lamentations, and apocryphal accounts display alarm, the need for military action, guilt and insecurity. Religious reform sentiment and resentment toward Rome for allowing this to happen are also evident. Schwoebel does admit, however, that this literature was primarily aimed at strengthening imperial or papal loyalty. Schwoebel, 19–22, 23.
47. Atiya, 160.
48. Quoted in Schwoebel, 74.
49. Atiya, 111.
50. A spy of the Burgundian prince Philip the Good stated that a well-ordered army only one-half the size of the Turkish army could defeat them. Schwoebel, 105.
51. Daniel, 129.
52. The literature on the medieval crusades is enormous. Classic studies include Steven Runciman, *A History of the Crusades* and Kenneth Setton, ed., *A History of the Crusades*.
53. As different as the Crusade literature was in details (some emphasizing the bravery of the Germans, others prayer and repentance), "in dem einen sind sie sich gleich, sie erwarten alle das Heil von den beiden Haupten der Christenheit," *WA 30II*, 89.
54. Pettegree, 93.
55. Schwoebel, 49.
56. For example, the fall of Constantinople produced another series of calls for Crusade from around Europe. Nicholas V addressed a Crusade bull to all Christendom and guaranteed a plenary indulgence for all who would take part or furnish a combatant for six months. When Innocent VIII (1484–92) gained custody of Sultan Bayezid II's brother Djem, he renewed a call to crusade in hopes of inciting rebellion in Turkey.
57. Although his claim that "it may be said that the fall of Constantinople contributed to postponing the Protestant revolt" is certainly overstated. Schwoebel, 23. A similar argument was made by Denys Hay in *Europe*.
58. Quoted in Schwoebel, 160.
59. Pacifistic objections to the crusade did exist, but were very rare in the Middle Ages. According to Elizabeth Siberry in *Criticism of Crusading 1095–1274*, information concerning them only survived because they were recorded by crusading apologists. Modern ecumenical scholarship has tended to exaggerate the extent of these objections. From the beginning there was criticism of Crusade abuses (that is, especially criticisms of Crusader morality), but fundamental criticism of the concept is rare.
60. On his third trip to North Africa in 1314, Llull ended his life as a martyr, Atiya, 96. On Llull see also, Daniel, 120–121, 258–259.
61. Others who suggested missionary work include Thomas Aquinas and St. Francis. On medieval missionary motivations, see Daniel, 117–120.
62. John of Segovia (d. 1458) was a Spanish bishop who argued for a conference in which the leaders of Christianity and Islam would discuss their religious

beliefs. War was not the answer. Although preaching was not allowed in areas dominated by Islam, a conference would be good for peace even if it was not successful in converting the Muslims. He even wrote to Cusa in an attempt to generate enthusiasm for the project.

63. In *The Shadow of the Crescent*, Schwoebel argued that as early as the mid-fifteenth-century negotiation became the primary response to Islam (the Turks) and emphasized secular power-politics as dominating the relationship. In my opinion, this optimistic modern appraisal cannot explain the emotional intensity or amount of Crusade propaganda produced beyond the fifteenth and well into the sixteenth century.

64. Especially during the Italian Wars, whenever a European state found itself in desperate straits it asked for help from the Ottomans. Milan, Ferrara, Mantua, and Florence all applied to the Turks for financial aid against France and Venice.

References

Akbari, Suzanne. *Idols in the East: European Representations of Islam and the Orient, 1100–1450*. Ithaca: Cornell University Press, 2009.

Atiya, Aziz. *Crusade, Commerce, and Culture*. New York: John Wiley, 1962.

Beckingham, C. F. *Between Islam and Christendom: Travelers. Facts and Legends in the Middle Ages and the Renaissance*. London: Variorum Reprints, 1983.

Biechler, James E. "Christian Humanism Confronts Islam: Sifting the Qur'an with Nicholas of Cusa." *Journal of Ecumenical Studies* 13 (1976): 1–14.

Burman, Thomas. *Reading the Qur'an in Latin Christendom, 1140–1560*. Philadelphia: University of Pennsylvania Press, 2007.

D'Alvery, M. T. "Deux traductions latines du Coran au Moyen Age." *Archives d'histoire doctrinale et litteraire du Moyen Age* 16 (1948): 69–131.

Daniel, Norman. *Islam and the West: The Making of an Image*. Edinburgh: Edinburgh University Press, 1962.

Ferguson, John. "Northern Europe and Islam in the Middle Ages." *Theological Review* 5:2 (1982): 69–78.

Fischer-Galati, Stephen. *Ottoman Imperialism and German Protestantism, 1521–1555*. Cambridge: Harvard University Press, 1972.

Hay, Denis. *Europe: The Emergence of an Idea*. Edinburgh: Edinburgh University Press, 1957.

John of Damascus. *Pege tes gnoseos* in *Patrologia Grecae*, Vol. 94, cols.764–773.

Kissling, Hans Joachim. "Türkenfurcht und Türkenhoffnung im 15/16. Jahrhunderts: zur Geschichte eines 'Komplexes'." *Südost-Forschungen* 23 (1964): 1–18.

Kritzeck, James. *Peter the Venerable and Islam*. Princeton: Princeton University Press, 1964.

Luther, Martin. *Verlegung des Alcoran Bruder Richardi*. WA 53, 261–396.

Meyerdorff, John. "Byzantine Views of Islam." *Dumbarton Oaks Papers* 18 (1964): 115–132.

Pettegree, Andrew. *The Book in the Renaissance*. New Haven: Yale University Press, 2010.

Rescher, Nicholas. "Nicholas of Cusa on the Qur'an: A Fifteenth Century Encounter with Islam." *Muslim World* 55:3 (July 1965): 195–202.

Rodinson, Maxime. *Europe and the Mystique of Islam*. Roger Veinus, trans. Seattle: University of Washington Press, 1987.

Runciman, Steven. *The Fall of Constantinople, 1453.* Cambridge: Cambridge University Press, 1965.

Runciman, Steven. *A History of the Crusades.* 3 vols. Cambridge: Cambridge University Press, 1951–54.

Schwoebel, Robert. *The Shadow of the Crescent: The Renaissance Image of the Turk (1453–1517).* New York: St Martin's Press, 1967.

Setton, Kenneth, ed. *A History of the Crusades.* 6 vols. Madison: University of Wisconsin Press, 1969ff.

Siberry, Elizabeth. *Criticism of Crusading 1095–1274.* Oxford: Clarendon, 1985.

Southern, R. W. *Western Views of Islam in the Middle Ages.* Cambridge: Harvard University Press, 1962.

Waardenburg, Jean-Jacques. "Two Lights Perceived: Medieval Islam and Christianity." *Nederlands Theologisch Tijdschrift* 31:4 (1977): 267–289.

Watt, W. Montgomery. "Muhammad in the Eyes of the West." *Boston University Journal* 22:3 (Fall 1974): 62–63.

Wilpert, Paul, ed. *Nikolaus von Kues Werke.* 2 vols. Berlin: Walter de Gruyter, 1966–67.

3 The Political Context
Hapsburg-Ottoman Relations in the Sixteenth Century

In order to understand the historical context in which early modern views of Islam were developed in Germany, it is necessary to survey the European advance of the Ottoman Turks. Fourteenth- and fifteenth-century sultans established the stage for Ottoman Imperialism, but it was during the leadership of Sulaiman the Magnificent (r. 1520–1566) that the Ottoman Empire reached its height. When Sulaiman began his reign, Germans were generally complacent about Ottoman expansion. A series of European campaigns, however, including the siege of Vienna (1529) and the direct annexation of most of Hungary (1541), brought the Muslims to the very door of Central Europe. A Hapsburg-Ottoman peace treaty was signed in 1545 that temporarily stabilized the region and decreased attention on Ottoman expansion, but during the preceding twenty-five years the Turks had become one of the most prominent subjects in Germany.[1]

When Sulaiman ascended the Ottoman throne in 1520, he inherited an empire that had been growing steadily since the fourteenth century. Founded by the Seljuk vassal chieftain Osman in the early 1300s, the Ottoman Empire was built piece by piece through *ghazi* attacks on the remains of Byzantine territories in Asia Minor. Expanding from its first victory at Bursa in 1326, by the reign of Osman's second successor Murad I (1359–1389), the Ottomans had captured Western Asia Minor, crossed the Hellespont, and taken most of the central Balkans.

Despite defeats by the armies of Timur the Lame (in Asia Minor c. 1395–1430) and desultory attacks by Balkan princes, by 1453 the chief Ottoman goal, the capture of Constantinople, had been attained by Muhammad II the Conqueror (1451–1481).[2] Muhammad II, one of the most brilliant of the Ottoman Sultans, further solidified Ottoman power by re-capturing all of Asia Minor, conquering all of the Balkans south of the Danube except for a few isolated strongholds and some islands, and building a significant navy. His expansion was limited only by a defeat at Belgrade (1456), an abortive attack on Italy (Otranto 1480), and the failure to capture the eastern fortress of the Knights of St. John on Rhodes (1481).

Selim I (r. 1512–1520), the ninth Ottoman Sultan and grandson of Muhammad II, turned his attention to the East. After first winning Syria from a reconstituted Persian Empire under the leadership of Shah Ismail I, Selim added both Egypt and the guardianship of the Holy Cities Mecca and Medina to his realm through the capture of Cairo in 1517. At Selim's death in 1520 the Ottoman Empire was both the leader of the Muslim world and a significant threat to Christian Europe.

Western European leaders of the early sixteenth century were not completely blind to the danger represented by the might of Selim's Empire. The two powers most interested in Ottoman activities were Venice and the Holy Roman Empire under the leadership of Maximilian I (r.1493–1519). In the early sixteenth century, Venice had the reputation of being the most dangerous enemy in the West for the Turks and the only power who could really damage them.[3] Venice used this reputation not to fight the Turks, however, but to gain mercantile privileges. The Republic of St. Mark became the Ottoman Empire's most intimate conversation partner as well as being considered by the Turks as the only reliable source of information in the West.[4] While occasionally forced into military action against the Ottomans (to protect trading stations or under the guise of a united Christendom), Venice preferred a more profitable economic partnership and avoided as much antagonism as possible. When forced to fight, Venice chose to focus their strategy on the scientific fortification of important strongholds and brief but decisive naval campaigns.[5]

In contrast, Maximilian formulated his aggressive policy concerning the Turks in connection with his designs on Hungary and the Balkans. By the Treaty of Vienna (1515) he was able to secure the betrothal of his granddaughter Mary to King Ladislav of Hungary's infant son Louis, thereby securing the succession. As future ruler of 'the bulwark of Christendom' facing Ottoman incursions into Hungary, Styria, Carinthia, and Carniola, and with dreams of a Hapsburg-Byzantine empire in the East, Maximilian became an energetic advocate of the Crusade.[6] Because he did not have the personal resources to fulfill his Imperial ambitions, Maximilian turned to the German *Reichstag* for assistance. This type of request was not new. From 1466, *Reichstäge* had dealt with the Turkish situation. Contributions had always been modest (considered a joint donation from both *Kaiser* and *Reich*) but were renewed with some regularity.[7]

In an effort to increase funding, Maximilian encouraged the production of a significant body of pro-Crusade propaganda.[8] In the hope that the Diets might grant him subsidies, he purposely exaggerated the Ottoman threat. The lack of response, however, indicated that the members of the Reichstag did not agree with Maximilian and his supporters that a strong Turkish policy was essential for the welfare of the Empire and the Hapsburgs.

In 1515 Maximilian attempted to convince Pope Leo X to consider the renewal of hostilities against the Turks in conjunction with King Francis I of France, but their plan remained only discussion. Finally, in 1517 the general peace that was considered a prerequisite for military action against the Turks was finally arranged. On 13 March 1518, Leo X formally proclaimed a Crusade and a five-year peace.[9] There were great expectations of a dramatic Christian victory. Court poets even sang of the re-conquest of the Holy Land.[10] This Crusade never materialized, however, as the participants became deadlocked in the early stages of planning over the division of the to-be-conquered lands. Although diminished in importance, Turkish affairs continued to play a role in the Holy Roman Empire, even in the Imperial election of 1519 when Charles V ascended to the Hapsburg throne.[11]

When the news of the death of Selim I reached Europe, it was greeted with great joy and relief. Western leaders thought that the Turkish danger could be set aside, perhaps forever, and that the Ottomans could at last be forced out of Europe. The contemporary historian Paolo Giovo reported that Selim's son Sulaiman

> has neither the talent nor the will to continue down the road of the conquerors as his father; he is a child without experience and high ability, a soft, peace-loving personality that thinks little about war and the glory of arms, a lamb that follows the lion.[12]

It quickly would be seen how wrong this initial appraisal was.[13]

Sulaiman's first action as head of state was to arrange a settlement with Venice. In 1520 he extended an existing agreement of commerce protection and aid against pirates, which was heartily welcomed by Venetians.[14] Turning to the East, by a show of strength he secured the existing Ottoman holdings against Persian aggression. This quick settlement of the Venice and Safavid situations was the primary factor in allowing Sulaiman a free hand to deal with his two main concerns: Hungary and Rhodes.

Sulaiman's first target was Belgrade. He considered the Hungarian town to be an absolutely essential key to the control of southeast Europe. Its position on the Danube made it both an important defensive position as well as a forward base for future operations.[15] It was the Hungarians' primary defensive southern fortress.

By early 1521, as it became clear that preparations were being made by Sulaiman for an attack, Hungarians sent representatives throughout Europe asking for assistance. Hungary's representative at the Worms *Reichstag*, Hieronymus Balbus, gave a fiery speech: Germany must give military support now so as not later to see the enemy in their own land.[16] A Croatian official also asked for help as the first defense of the German nation. Both pleas were in vain; the Diet refused to do anything at present, although they promised future help.

Meanwhile, Sulaiman and his army had left Constantinople. By early August the Ottoman forces were in position to attack the Danubian fortress. Due to the success of heavy artillery bombardments and successive waves of Janissary attacks, the siege lasted only one month. As would become his standard procedure, after looting the city, massacring the defenders, and enslaving large numbers of inhabitants, Sulaiman converted the major church into a mosque, installed a Muslim administration, and left behind a significant Janissary garrison. Within a year of his accession, Sulaiman had accomplished a military victory that had eluded the Ottomans for four generations. The last significant barrier had been removed from the route to central Europe.

Sulaiman's second target, the primary obstacle to Ottoman expansion in the Mediterranean, was the island of Rhodes. This difficult military obstacle held by the Knights of St. John had been unsuccessfully attacked in 1480 by Muhammad II. Despite huge losses during a bitter five-month siege, Sulaiman's forces captured the island in 1522. Although the Knights survived (they were offered exceptionally easy terms to encourage their surrender), Sulaiman could rightly claim to be the greatest *ghazi* warrior since the Conqueror himself. Europeans began to take the Ottoman threat more seriously.[17]

After the fall of Belgrade and Rhodes, the Turkish threat continued to be presented at the *Reichstäge* by representatives of King Louis of Hungary, now joined in his appeal by Ferdinand, brother of Emperor Charles V and Hapsburg ruler of Austria. Ferdinand took particular interest in the Turkish advance, due both to the Turkish raids on his own territory and because of his own desire for the Hungarian crown.

At the Nürnberg *Reichstäge* of 1522 and 1524, however, little aid was granted, despite emotional appeals concerning the Turkish menace to Christianity made by Hungarians and representatives of the Austrian territories of Styria, Carniola, and Carinthia.[18] One reason that aid for Hungary was so difficult to get from the *Reichstäge* was because of German-Hungarian antagonism. Many Germans believed that the Hungarians were bluffing about the seriousness of the threat. There was considerable bitterness about the papal annates and taxes for anti-Turkish campaigns that never materialized.[19] Furthermore, Charles V was primarily interested in the West; he did not push the *Reichstäge* to grant aid for Eastern Europe against the Turks.

Faced with a lack of German support, Ferdinand turned to the papacy for taxes on his Hapsburg possessions, borrowed heavily from banking houses, and supported a propaganda campaign aimed at convincing the German people of the severity of the Muslim threat.[20] At no time, however, were his resources significant enough to relieve him of the need to negotiate with the *Reichstag*.[21]

For the German *Reichstag*, internal problems always took precedence over Ferdinand's appeals for aid. At the Diet of Speyer in 1526, Ferdinand's opening speech (as usual) was an appeal for immediate aid to Hungary. But this time the need was urgent; information had been received concerning a new Turkish offensive in Europe. The Diet, however, declined to consider the question of aid before dealing with the German religious situation. As a result, Ferdinand (after gaining the consent of Charles V) agreed to a demand for a church council. But Charles's statement of his decision to negotiate with Pope Clement VII with a view to summoning a council (27 July 1526) was perceived by both sides as too vague. Although Ferdinand had no authority to make a more specific commitment, because of the severity of the situation he made a significant promise: a council would be convened within eighteen months and the party in support of Luther was to be given guarantees of safety until the council was convened. With the primary religious issue temporarily settled, the Diet examined the request for aid against the Ottoman Turks. They agreed to send a large contingent of 24,000 men. The army was never sent, however; the Diet adjourned 27 August 1526 and the battle of Mohács took place just four days later.[22]

After his conquest of Rhodes, Sulaiman had remained in Constantinople for three years enjoying the pleasures of the Ottoman court. But the Turkish soldiery grew restless. A rebellion of the Janisseries in 1525 had convinced Sulaiman that a new campaign was necessary. The target was partially determined by European power politics, as the French king Francis I began to work with the Turks in an attempt to distract the Hapsburgs. After the defeat of the French forces at Pavia (1525), Francis used a letter concealed in the sole of a boot to smuggle out a plea from his Madrid prison for the sultan to help him.[23] In response to Francis, and knowing the internal division of the kingdom, Sulaiman made preparations to attack Hungary.

Sulaiman left his capital in April 1526 with a force of some 45,000 infantry and cavalry, as well as a well-trained artillery contingent. They marched north toward the capital Buda along the west bank of the Danube, building bridges across the undefended Sava and Drava Rivers. Meanwhile, the Hungarian nobility gathered in Buda to discuss the defense of the kingdom. King Louis, twenty years old and pleasure-minded, was considered unable to coordinate the defense, so the military leadership of the c.20,000 strong Hungarian army was given to the martial Archbishop of Kalocsa, Tömöri.[24] Rather than wait for reinforcements which were in route, or retreat to more defensible terrain, Tömöri decided to remain and fight on the plain near Mohács.

The two armies met late in the afternoon on 1 September 1526. In less than two hours the entire Hungarian force was destroyed. Superior numbers and tactics, as well as an ill-advised frontal charge against the Ottoman center, gave the battle to the Turks. King Louis was drowned as he attempted to flee; Tömöri, many Hungarian nobles, and all of the higher clergy except six of the Roman Catholic bishops of Hungary lost their lives.[25] Hungary's ability to defend herself from the Turks was effectively destroyed. On 10 September Sulaiman entered Buda unopposed. Because of the approaching winter and the distance of the Hungarian capital from Constantinople, however, Sulaiman did not permanently occupy the city. After four days of looting and burning in Buda and Pest, the Ottoman force headed for home. Sulaiman had again proved the superiority of the Ottoman military and the vulnerability of Central Europe.

The battle of Mohács had left Hungary in a leaderless chaos. Two rival factions battled for the crown, one led by Ferdinand, whose claim to the throne rested on earlier agreements made by Maximilian, and the second led by the *voivode* (governor) of Transylvania, John Zapolya. Zapolya quickly gained the support of the 'national' faction and was crowned King of Hungary by a group of nobles who disregarded the Hapsburg treaties, claiming that no foreigner should wear the crown of St. Stephen. Zapolya was made king even though some blamed him for the loss at Mohács because he did not aggressively attack the Turks with his large contingent of Transylvanian reinforcements.[26] Ferdinand was crowned by a rival diet (the 'German' faction) a few days later. Many considered him the only hope to preserve Hungary from Turkish domination.[27] Although supported by different nobles, both Zapolya and Ferdinand were crowned with the same crown of St. Stephen, by the same archbishop. It appears that the Hungarians were willing to risk civil war to see who could effectively accomplish their goals: the re-creation of the integrity of the kingdom and defense against the Turks.

Zapolya entered Buda first, but was pushed out by an aggressively led Hapsburg army. Although Ferdinand commanded a much smaller force, the professional German mercenaries quickly captured the territory held by the national faction and drove Zapolya into Poland. Defeated, John Zapolya took a decisive step and appealed to Sulaiman for help. The sultan considered Hungary his to bestow through conquest and saw the advantage of using a weak vassal to frustrate Hapsburg Imperialism. In 1528 Sulaiman concluded a treaty with Zapolya which made him an Ottoman vassal and promised support for him to regain the crown. When Ferdinand received the report concerning Zapolya's Turkish alliance, he withdrew the bulk of his army from Hungary, leaving only small garrisons in Buda and some northwestern fortresses. In 1529 Sulaiman moved to fulfill his promise of support for Zapolya against the Hapsburgs in a campaign that ended in the famous siege of Vienna. A large force, including between 120,000 and 200,000 men, 20,000 camels, 400 pieces of artillery, and a fleet of 400 Danubian river boats, left Constantinople on 10 May.[28]

Due to a large feudal cavalry component, the Ottoman military was limited to summer campaigns from mid-April to late October. Since Hungary was 90–100 days' march from Constantinople, the late start in mid-May effectively limited the Ottoman attack in northern Hungary to a period of less than one month. Heavy rains further slowed the 1529 advance, and forced Sulaiman to abandon much of his heavy artillery. The aggregate delays cost the Ottomans nearly a month and made the success of the attack highly improbable.

It was not until August that Sulaiman reached Mohács, where he received homage from Zapolya. The Ottoman force then advanced to Buda, defeated the Hapsburg garrison, and installed Zapolya as king of Hungary. Although the end of the campaigning season was near, Sulaiman proceeded to Austria, not to annex the land, as was commonly thought, but to warn and intimidate Ferdinand.[29] The Austrian capital was besieged on 23 September.

With advance warning of the Ottoman approach, Vienna was prepared for defense; the walls had been fortified and there were plentiful supplies in the city.[30] Also, the delay in the Ottoman advance had allowed some 10,000 last-minute reinforcements to enter the city, which raised the total number of defenders to c.20,000 with an artillery force of 72 canon. Overall command was in the hands of an able general, Nicholas Salm, who had previous experience fighting the Turks. In addition, both Charles V and the German princes (now convinced of the severity of the threat) had promised still more aid; an army of relief was forming upriver at Krems. The Germans clearly had the advantage.

The siege lasted from 23 September to 15 October 1529. Because most of the Ottoman heavy artillery had been left behind, Sulaiman relied on mining operations to breach the walls. The primary attacks and mining attempts were made at the southern gate known as the *Kärnthnertor*. Although the wall was damaged, the defenders repeatedly beat off the furious Ottoman attacks. After four large-scale assaults, the Turks had exhausted their supplies. The area surrounding Vienna had been denuded both by the Turks and by the Austrians themselves who had used a scorched-earth defense.[31] Discouraged and faced with the coming of winter, on 14 October Sulaiman gave the command to withdraw.[32] A cry of relief was heard throughout Christendom. Pamphlets reported that it had been the intention of Sulaiman to winter in Hungary or Vienna and then proceed to conquer more of Germany. Thanks to God's help through the defense of Vienna, Christian Europe had been saved.[33]

In reality there was little chance of Ottoman success at Vienna and no real chance of a deeper penetration of Europe. Like the battle of Tours some 800 years earlier, the Muslim army had overextended its supply lines. Although the Ottoman feudal troops did on occasion winter on the Mesopotamian frontier, they would not have subjected their horses to an Austrian winter. The Ottoman loss at Vienna was almost guaranteed due to the quality of the Imperial troops and artillery, Sulaiman's lack of heavy artillery, food shortages, and disease in the Ottoman camp, the approaching cold, and the nearby presence of a German relieving army.[34]

The German victory at Vienna was not without its costs, however. Many Austrian homes had been destroyed by both sides. The Turks had been particularly vicious in their raids on the communities surrounding Vienna. Some 30,000 persons were enslaved or killed; as many as 2000 people were reported to have been massacred in one single incident. The nearness of the Muslims, as well as their gruesomeness, left a deep and lasting impression on the psyche of the German population.[35] They were convinced that the Turkish army would return to avenge their loss.

After 1529, Charles V increasingly came to believe that it was his personal responsibility to lead all Europe against the 'archenemy of Christendom,' the Turk. He saw himself as the *princeps pacis* and the *advocatus ecclesiae*.[36]

In order to combat Islam, however, Hapsburg resources would need to be increased.

A nominal peace was therefore necessary to successfully challenge the Turks. From 1529 to 1532 (specifically at Speyer and Regensburg) Charles negotiated with the German Diets in an effort to satisfy their immediate internal concerns so that attention could be paid to the Ottoman threat. In essence, this required postponing a religious settlement until after Sulaiman had been defeated. The emperor believed that a military triumph against the Turks would give him the leverage he needed to convince Clement VII to convene a council.[37] The papacy gave the Hapsburg effort whole-hearted support; Ferdinand's claim to the Hungarian crown was made official by the excommunication of Zapolya on 22 Dec 1529.[38]

Charles and Ferdinand worked together to gather the military strength necessary to face the anticipated return of Sulaiman's army. In 1529 Ferdinand occasioned a papal appeal to the Reichstag at Speyer to take part in the war and also convinced Clement VII to authorize his legates to sell some possessions of the northern German churches and cloisters to help speed an army against the Turks.[39] The next year the Pope agreed to a six year tithe-grant worth the significant sum of three million gulden. In 1531 a regular tax for defense was established and refugees from the South-Slavic and Albanian lands were funded to move north to serve as a defensive military buffer.[40] In 1532, the largest army ever put together by the empire (in the judgment of contemporaries), some 222,000 on foot and 74,000 on horse, was put on alert. Although they emphasized that it was for defensive purposes only, the significant force of 44,000 on foot and 38,000 on horse (the largest German commitment to date) was pledged from the Regensburg *Reichstag*.[41]

As anticipated, Sulaiman did attack Austria for the second time, leaving Constantinople at the head of his army in the spring of 1532. This time, rather than moving north along the Danube as he did in 1529, the Sultan led his army northwest, as if to drive deeper into central Europe. However, the Hapsburg military preparations proved to be more than adequate. An effective use was made of the combination of native resources in Croatia and Slavonia and a sparse supply of professional Spanish, Italian, and Walloon infantry in a deep defense of crude earthen forts along the Austrian-Hungarian border. At one small fortress on the Austrian border, Günns (modern Koszeg, c.100 km south-east of Vienna), the entire Turkish army, some 100,000 regular troops, was held up by a garrison of less than 800 men.[42] Although the garrison did surrender after three weeks (the long holdout produced very favorable surrender terms by the Turks in order to save face), by this time it was too late to attack Vienna.

Sulaiman had probably hoped that the Imperial army would attempt to meet the Ottoman forces and therefore give him an opportunity for a large-scale battle. But he was disappointed; Charles remained at Ratisbon (300km upriver on the Danube) and the bulk of the army never left Vienna. As in 1529, Sulaiman proclaimed victory on the basis that the Emperor was too afraid to face him in the field, but in reality the campaign was another failure.[43]

Three weeks of plunder followed as the Turks retreated through Austrian Styria. The Ottoman raiders looted and burned several hundred villages and more than a dozen cities, killing over 1000 persons and enslaving many more.[44] Again, central Europe had been successfully defended, but the enemy was believed to be too strong for Germans to go on the offensive. In addition, the *Reichstag* had agreed to the use of troops only on defense. When the Turkish threat was gone, the large Imperial army was dispersed.[45]

Since the German estates would not support Ferdinand's attempt to take Hungary by force, after the 1532 campaign he was left with the single option of negotiation. Frustrated with his failure in Austria and needing to turn his attention to pressing problems in the East, Sulaiman was willing in 1533 for the first time to exchange representatives with the Hapsburgs and negotiate a truce. Ferdinand's desire for eastward expansion was finally fulfilled when a perpetual truce was signed in July 1533 that supported an Ottoman-supervised division of Hungary between Zapolya and Ferdinand.

For the next few years relations were generally peaceful, but with Ferdinand, Zapolya, and Sulaiman all claiming control, Hungary and the northern Balkans remained highly unstable. The peace was first broken when continued raids into Croatia and Slavonia by the Ottoman Pasha of Bosnia resulted in an unsuccessful punitive expedition sent by Ferdinand in 1537. In 1538, the region became more threatened by Ottoman attack as Zapolya, having lost the favor of the Sultan, made a secret peace with Ferdinand (the Treaty of Grosswardein) which divided Hungary between them and declared that Ferdinand was to become sole king after Zapolya's death. However, two weeks before Zapolya's death in 1540, a son, John Sigismund, was born to him, which reversed his plans of allowing Ferdinand to succeed according to the arrangement of 1537.[46] Instead of relinquishing the crown to Ferdinand after her husband's death, Zapolya's widow Isabella proclaimed their infant son John Sigismund to be king. Ferdinand immediately attacked but was unable to take Buda. In response, Isabella appealed to Sulaiman for help. Hungary was again faced with civil war.[47]

In 1541 rumors spread that Sulaiman was preparing a force to reconquer Hungary. To forestall a military confrontation, Ferdinand attempted to negotiate with the Sultan for the purchase of Hungary by a huge annual *Ehrengeschenk* of 50,000–100,000 *Goldgulden;* this was rudely rejected.[48] Ferdinand put his last hope on assistance from the German *Reichstag*. Little help was given, with the result that Ferdinand's army and the small contingent of troops from the German estates were quickly driven out of Hungary.

By September Sulaiman was once again in Buda. The infant John Sigismund was proclaimed king with the Sultan as regent, but in reality south and central Hungary (the majority of the kingdom) was directly annexed by the Ottomans with a governor and permanent garrison in the capital. Sulaiman converted the principal church into a mosque and established a continuing presence and stronghold in the city which lasted until 1699.[49] People in nearby Austria and Germany shuddered at the thought of a major Muslim stronghold so near the border.

The Speyer *Reichstag* in April 1542 finally did respond to this renewed urgent threat. A large force of 25,000 foot soldiers and 5000 cavalry was placed under the leadership of Joachim II, Margrave of Brandenburg, to march against the Ottoman forces. The troops were gathered in Vienna by May, but because of the threat of a shortage of money, the entire force went into open mutiny on the march to Buda and Joachim was forced to make a rapid retreat.[50] Because there was widespread fear that Hungary would become a base of Ottoman action against Europe, in 1544 the *Reichstag* was willing to contribute to an offensive war (even Francis I promised to send troops). However, by that time the military situation had significantly worsened. Many fortifications in Hungary and Croatia had been taken by the Turks. Under the circumstances Charles V and Ferdinand began to consider a lasting peace with the Turks based on the status quo. Francis, eager to preserve his good relations with the Sultan, eagerly accepted the idea and offered to serve as intermediary. The news of the emperor's plans worked like a bomb in Hungary. Ferdinand's support was largely based on the fact of promised help; this seemed gone and both brothers appeared to the Hungarians as liars and betrayers.[51] In 1545 negotiations were begun that led to the signing of the Truce of Adrianople with Sulaiman. This treaty officially recognized the tripartite division of Hungary which had actually existed since 1541. For a price of 30,000 ducats per annum,[52] Ferdinand received a thin slice of Hungarian territory on the Austrian border. A small vassal kingdom was also created in Transylvania, but the Ottomans directly controlled the vast majority of the center and south of the former 'bulwark' of Christendom.

After the Truce of Adrianople, the Christian-Islamic confrontation shifted its focus from the Balkans to naval encounters on the Mediterranean Sea. Intermittent attacks continued (both small-scale raids and two inconsequential campaigns, 1552 and 1566), but the danger from a massive invasion from the East declined. By the early 1550s central Europe displayed a growing lack of concern and absence of fear of the Turks. For the next few decades a general feeling of confidence returned; the Muslim menace became not only geographically but also more emotionally remote.[53]

The period from the accession of Sulaiman to the Truce of Adrianople had a lasting influence, however, on both the ideological and the political history of Eastern Europe. The Ottoman occupation of Hungary and the northern Balkans had significant effects. Heavy financial demand because of the Turkish defense greatly affected Imperial tax and administrative systems.[54] In addition, the Turkish threat was one of the most important elements in Austria becoming an independent and important European power.[55]

Through their connection with Ferdinand and the Hapsburg claims on Hungary, from 1520 to 1545 Germans throughout the Empire also were brought face to face with the Islamic Turks in a more significant way than ever before. Twenty-five years of intense interest and involvement with Turkish themes produced new views of the nature of Islam and re-examined permissible responses to the Ottoman advance, in part because this period also corresponds almost perfectly with the first generation of Protestant Reformers. With the decline of the threat in the mid-1540s, however, understandings of Islam and the Turks solidified into new, but standardized conceptions. Petitions continued to be made to the *Reichstäge* for aid against the Turks, pamphlets on Islam continued to be published in Germany, but little that was original was added to the knowledge and ideas which had been put forward in the first half of the sixteenth century. Not until the late 1600s with the re-acquisition of Hungary and the gradual retreat from the Balkans of the declining Ottomans did a changing political situation cause Germans to reevaluate and alter their views of Islam.

Notes

1. The overall survey that has most shaped my understanding of Ottoman-Hapsburg relations in the sixteenth century is *The Ottoman Empire and Early Modern Europe* by Daniel Goffman.
2. See Steven Runciman's classic work, *The Fall of Constantinople.*
3. For extensive information on the complicated relations between Venice and the Ottoman Empire, see Kenneth Setton, *A History of the Crusades* vol. 6, and Kenneth Setton, *The Papacy and the Levant*, vol. 3, 1–197.
4. Phillipe Braunstein, "Venedig und der Türk, 1450–1570," 60–61, 70.
5. Paul Coles, *The Ottoman Impact on Europe*, 133.
6. Maximilian was "motivated by traditional crusading ideal with a strong admixture of personal and dynastic ambition." John W. Bohnstedt, "The Infidel Scourge of God: The Turkish Menace as Seen by German Pamphleteers of the Reformation Era," 9.
7. Given at the 1477, 1474, 1500, and 1512 *Reichstäge*. Horst Glassl, "Das Heilige Romische Reich und die Osmanen im Zeitalter der Reformation," 61–62.
8. For example: *Hilfanschlag in Folge des Reichstages zu Coblenz zum Kriege gegen Türken und Franzosen* and Riccardo Bartolini, *Richardi Bartolini Perusini Oratio ad Imp. Caes. Maximilianum Aug. ac potentis. Germania Principes de expeditione contra Turcas suscipienda.*
9. Setton, *Papacy*, 172–197.
10. In connection with this promised campaign, court poet Jorg Graff reworked a fifteenth-century song to show Maximilian guiding the ship of the church against the strong wind of the Turks. Quoting from a prophecy of Methodius he added: "ain newer cristen könig würt (sein nam Maximilian si redten) der würt das hailig land ersetten und fullen mit cristen galuben." R. V. Liliencron, *Die historischen Volkslieder der Deutschen vom 13 bis 16. Jahrhundert*, 212–215.
11. Part of the pledge of Francis I was the promise to organize more effective help against the Turks. Glassl, 63.
12. "[H]abe weder das Talent, noch den Willen, auf der Bahn der Eroberung fortzuschreiten, die ihm sein Vater vorgezeichnet; er sei ein Jungling ohne Erfahrung und ohne Begabung, ein sanfter, friedliebender Charakter, der wenig am Krieg und Waffenruhm denke, ein Lamm, das dem Lowen gefolgt." Quoted in Johann Wilhelm Zinkeisen, *Geschichte des osmanischen Reiches in Europa*, vol. 1, 611.

13. For general information on Sulaiman see: Antony Bridge, *Suleiman the Magnificent: Scourge of Heaven* and Roger B. Merriman, *Suleiman the Magnificent: 1520–1566.*
14. Zinkeisen, vol. 1, 614–615.
15. Hans Joachim Kissling, "Die Türkenfrage als europaisches Problem," 53, 55.
16. Adolf Wrede, ed., *Deutsche Reichstagsakten unter Kaiser Karl V*, vol. 2, 758–759.
17. The capture of Rhodes was proclaimed in a number of different German pamphlets. At least four different pamphlets were published on the siege in 1522 and seven descriptions of the capture were published in 1523.
18. Johann Loserth, *Innerösterreich und die militärischen Massnahmen gegen die Türken im 16. Jahrhundert*, 24–25. See also Stephen Fischer-Galati, "Ottoman Imperialism and the Lutheran Struggle for Recognition in Germany, 1520–1529," 52–53.
19. Some Hungarians had allegedly asserted that they would prefer the Sultan as ruler rather than to put up with the consequences of Imperial aid. Many Germans thought that the Hungarians were as bad as the Turks. Setton, *Papacy,* 219.
20. "Inzwischen hatte Erherzog Ferdinand eingesehen, dass eine wirksame Reichshilfe nur durch eine gezielte Propaganda auf den Reichstagen erreicht werden konnte." Glassl, 64.
21. Franz Thaller, *Glaubensstreit und Türkennot 1519–1648: Geschichte Österreichs in Einzeldarstellungen, no. 6,* 20.
22. Concerning the Speyer negotiations, see: Fischer-Galati, "Lutheran Struggle," 56–58; Fischer-Galati, *Ottoman Imperialism,* 25–26. According to Merriman, an embassy was sent to Buda to inquire about the severity of the situation and that the aid proclamation was made the day before the battle. Merriman, 83–84.
23. Recounted by Merriman, 129.
24. This is the reason that Luther characterized it as a *Pfaffenheer. WA 30II,* 114.
25. Hugo Hantsch, "Zum ungarisch-türkischen Problem in der allgemeinen Politik Karls V," 58. See also Merriman, 76–96.
26. Zapolya reached the east bank of the Danube opposite Mohács on the day after the battle with a force as large as 20,000 soldiers. When he saw that the main Hungarian force had been routed, he quickly retreated back to Transylvania. Accusations of betrayal were made in many *Türkenbüchlein.* Carl Göllner, "Betrachtungen Betrachtungen zur öffentlichen Meinung über die Schlacht von Mohács (1526)," 73.
27. Sturmberger emphasized the battle of Mohács as the foundation of the Hapsburg Empire in modem times. It was believed, and not just by the Hapsburgs, that Ferdinand was the only prince who could defend central Europe against the Turks. He was elected King of Croatia 1 Jan 1526. Hans Sturmberger, "Türkengefähr und österreichische Staatlichkeit," 134–136.
28. Merriman, 104.
29. Bohnstedt, 7.
30. The 1529 siege of Vienna produced a considerable amount of contemporary literature. For example: *Ein new Lied, wie der Türk Wien belegert, Ein newes Lied der gantz handel der turckischen belegerung der Stat Wienn,* Hans Lutz, *Grundige und warhafftige bericht der geschichten unnd kriegshandlung so sich, neben und usser der Stat Wien belegerung heruss,* Hans Sachs, *Die Türkisch belagerung der Stat Wien, mit sampt seiner Tyrannischen Handlung,* Peter Stern, *Belegerung der Start Wienn, jm jar, als man zallt nach Cristi geburt, tausent fünffhundert unnd im newn und zwaintzigisten beschehn kürtzlich angezaigt,* etc. For a complete bibliography of contemporary and modern literature concerning the siege see, Kabdebo and Sturminger.

31. The Austrians themselves burned some 834 houses to prevent Ottoman resupply. Thaller, 20.
32. For a description of the end of the siege, see Setton, *Papacy*, 326–327.
33. "Alle Christen menschen un zuvorderst Teutsche land gott lob un danck sagen sollen." Vienna would have been "ein porten un schlussel zu teutschen landen." Peter Stern, *Warhafftige handlung Wie und welcher massen der Turck die stat Ofen und Wien belegert*, a2b, c4a.
34. Contemporary accounts primarily credited the cold weather and concern over German reinforcements for Sulaiman's decision to retire. For example, Stern, *Warhafftige handlung*, d2a.
35. *Die Belagerung der Statt Wien in Österreich, von dem allergrawsamesten Tyrannen*, b2b. The emphasis in most 1529 tracts on the Vienna siege was on the gruesomeness of the Turks, thanks for God's help in saving the city, and deep fear of the return of the Turks next year.
36. Hantsch, 62–63.
37. Ascan Westermann, *Die Türkenhilfe und die politisch-kirchlichen Parteien auf dem Reichstag zu Regensburg* 1512, 20.
38. On papal activity during this period, Setton, *Papacy*, 335–354.
39. Wrede, ed., *Deutsche Reichstagakten*, vol. 7, 689.
40. Thaller, 20.
41. Almost all of Europe participated, including Spain, Belgium, Burgundy, and Italy (half the Italian troops had to be sent home because there was no room for them), but the force consisted mainly of Germans and Austrians. The army was well organized and provisioned. Glassl, 65ff; Hantsch, 65–66.
42. The siege is described by a contemporary observer in: *Sendbrief un warhafte urkundt Türckischer belägerung*. See also Coles, 120–122.
43. Merriman, 118–119.
44. Thaller, 21. Despite the pillaging on the retreat, the raiders also suffered defeats by Austrian and German forces. Setton, *Papacy*, 366.
45. Hantsch and others have argued that this was a missed opportunity for a significant Imperial victory. Why was the Imperial force not used? When it appeared that Sulaiman would not attack Vienna, Charles V considered the Hungarian problem to be Ferdinand's and thus departed with a large part of the army, signalling the breakup of the force. "In der Geringschätzung der innerungarischen Verhältnisse, in der Verkennung ihres engen Zusammenhanges mit den Tiirkenproblem eine weltgeschichtliche Stunde versäumt hat." Hantsch, 65–66.
46. Thaller, 22–23.
47. Setton, *Papacy*, 455.
48. Franz Babinger, "Die Osman auf dem Balkan," 9–10.
49. Babinger, 8.
50. Joachim was accused by German Catholics of being a traitor who purposely let the army be destroyed because he feared the military power of the emperor. Concerning the 1542 campaign: Setton, *Papacy*, 478ff., Babinger, 9ff., and Richard Ebermann, "Die Türkenfurcht: Ein Beitrag zur Geschichte der öffentlichen Meinung in Deutschland während der Reformationszeit," 41ff.
51. The Protestant opposition in Germany was frequently blamed for this abandonment. Hantsch, 67–68.
52. Thaller stated that the tribute amounted to 30,000 ducats per year. Thaller, 22–23. Glassl listed the amount at only 10,000 ducats. Glassl, 71–72.
53. See for example, Stephen Fischer-Galati, "The Turkish Question and the Religious Peace of Augsburg," 295–296.
54. This is claimed by Ranke. Quoted in Sturmberger, 132–133.
55. Concerning the effect of the Turkish threat on the development of Imperial government and taxation, see especially: Karl Otto Bull, "Die Türkensteuerlisten

als Geschichtsquelle: Aufschlüsse über die wirtschaftliche und sozialen Struktur des Herzogtums Württemberg im 16. Jahrhundert," 5–11, Vesselka Garkova, "Sachsen und Südosteuropa 15–17. Jahrhundert: Politik, Wirtschaft und Kultur im Zeichen der Auseinandersetzungen mit dem osmanischen Reich," Josef V. Polisensky, "Bohemia, the Turk, and the Christian Commonwealth (1462–1620)," 82–108, and Winfried Schulze, *Reich und Türkengefahr im späten 16. Jahrhundert: Studien zu der politische und gesellschaftliche Auswirkungen einer äusseren Bedrohung.*

References

Babinger, Franz. *Zwei baierische Türkenbüchlein (1542) und ihr Verfasser.* Munich: Verlag der Bayerischen Akademie der Wissenschaften.

Bartolini, Riccardo. *Richardi Bartolini Perusini Oratio ad Imp. Caes. Maximilianum Aug. ac potentis. Germania Principes de expeditione contra Turcas suscipienda.* Augsburg: Wirsung, 1518.

Bohnstedt, John W. "The Infidel Scourge of God: The Turkish Menance as Seen by German Pamphleteers of the Reformation Era." *Transactions of the American Philosophical Society* NS 58:9 (1968).

Braunstein, Phillipe. "Venedig und der Türk, 1450–1570." In *Die wirtschaftliche Auswirkungen der Türkenkriege: die Vorträge des I. Internationalen Grazer Symposions zur Wirtschafts-und Sozialgeschichte Südosteuropas*, Othmar Pickl, ed. Graz: Selbstverlag der Lehrkanzel für Wirtschafts-und Sozialgeschichte der Universität Gräz, 1971, 59–70.

Bridge, Anthony. *Suleiman the Magnificent: Scourge of Heaven.* New York: Franklin Watts, 1983.

Bull, Karl Otto. "Die Türkensteuerlisten als Geschichtsquelle: Aufschlüsse über die wirtschaftliche und sozialen Struktur des Herzogtums Württemberg im 16. Jahrhundert." *Beilage zur Staatsanzeiger für Badenwürttemberg* 2 (1974): 5–11.

Coles, Paul. *The Ottoman Impact on Europe.* London: Thames and Hudson, 1968.

Die Belagerung der Statt Wien in Österreich, von dem allergrawsamesten Tyrannen und verderber der Christenheit, genant der Türgkisch Keyser. n.p., 1529.

Ebermann, Richard. "Die Türkenfurcht: Ein Beitrag zur Geschichte der öffentlichen Meinung in Deutschland während der Reformationszeit." Ph.D. diss., Halle University, 1904.

Ein newes Lied der gantz handel der turckischen belegerung der Stat Wienn. n.p.: Gutknecht, 1529.

Ein new Lied, wie der Türk Wien belegert. n.p., 1529.

Fischer-Galati, Stephen A. *Ottoman Imperialism and German Protestantism, 1521–1555.* Cambridge, MA: Harvard University Press, 1972.

Fischer-Galati, Stephen. "Ottoman Imperialism and the Lutheran Struggle for Recognition in Germany, 1520–1529." *Church History* 23 (1954): 46–67.

Fischer-Galati, Stephen. "The Turkish Question and the Religious Peace of Augsburg." *Südostforschung* 15 (1956): 290–311.

Garkova, Vesselka. "Sachsen und Südosteuropa 15–17. Jahrhundert: Politik, Wirtschaft und Kultur im Zeichen der Auseinandersetzungen mit dem osmanischen Reich." Ph.D. diss., Leipzig University, 1987.

Glassl, Horst. "Das Heilige Romische Reich und die Osmanen im Zeitalter der Reformation." In *Südosteuropa unter dem Halbmond: Untersuchungen über Geschichte und Kultur der Südosteuropaischen Völker während der Türkenzeit.* Peter Bartl and Horst Glassl, eds. Munich: Trefenik, 1975, 61–72.

Goffman, Daniel. *The Ottoman Empire and Early Modern Europe.* Cambridge: Cambridge University Press, 2002.

Göllner, Carl. "Betrachtungen zur öffentlichen Meinung über die Schlacht von Mohács (1526)." *Revue roumaine d'histoire* 6:1 (1967): 67–76.

Hantsch, Hugo. "Zum ungarisch-türkischen Problem in der allgemeinen Politik Karls V." In *Festschrift Karl Eder zum Siebzigsten Geburtstag*, Helmut J. Mezler-Andelberg, ed. Innsbruck: Universitätsverlag Wagner, 1959, 57–69.

Hilfanschlag in Folge des Reichstages zu Coblenz zum Kriege gegen Türken und Franzosen. n.p., 1505.

Kabdebo, Heinrich. *Bibliographie zur Geschichte der beiden Türkenbelagerungen Wiens, 1529 und 1683.* Vienna: Verlag Von Faesy and Frick, 1876.

Kissling, Hans Joachim. "Die Türkenfrage als europaisches Problem." *Südostdeutsches Archiv* 7 (1964): 39–57.

Liliencron, R. V. *Die historischen Volkslieder der Deutschen vom 13 bis 16. Jahrhundert.* Vol. 3. Leipzig: F. C. W. Vogel, 1869.

Loserth, Johann. *Innerösterreich und die militärischen Massnahmen gegen die Türken im 16. Jahrhundert.* Graz: Verlag Styria, 1934.

Lutz, Hans. *Grundige und warhafftige bericht der geschichten unnd kriegshandlung so sich, neben und usser der Stat Wien belegerung heruss.* Regensburg: Khol, 1530.

Merriman, Roger B. *Suleiman the Magnificent: 1520–1566.* New York: Cooper Square Publishers, 1966.

Polisensky, Josef V. "Bohemia, the Turk, and the Christian Commonwealth (1462–1620)." *Byzantinoslavica* 14 (1953): 82–108.

Runciman, Steven. *The Fall of Constantinople.* Cambridge: Cambridge University Press, 1965.

Sachs, Hans. *Die Türkisch belagerung der Stat Wien, mit sampt seiner Tyrannischen Handlung.* n.p., 1529.

Schulze, Winfried. *Reich und Türkengefahr im späten 16. Jahrhundert: Studien zu der politische und gesellschaftliche Auswirkungen einer äusseren Bedrohung.* Munich: Beck, 1978.

Sendbrief un warhafte urkundt Türckischer belägerung, sturmung und handlung des Schloss und der Stat Güns. n.p., 1532.

Setton, Kenneth. *A History of the Crusades.* Vol. 6. Madison: University of Wisconsin Press, 1989.

Setton, Kenneth. *The Papacy and the Levant.* Vol. 3. Philadelphia: American Philosophical Society, 1984.

Stern, Peter. *Belegerung der Stadt Wienn, jm jar, als man zallt nach Cristi geburt, tausent fünffhundert unnd im newn und zwaintzigisten beschehn kürtzlich angetzaigt.* Vienna: Vietor, 1529.

Stern, Peter. *Warhafftige handlung Wie und welcher massen der Turck die stat Ofen und Wien belegert.* n.p., 1530.

Sturmberger, Hans. "Türkengefähr und österreichische Staatlichkeit." *Südostdeutsche Archiv* 10 (1967): 132–145.

Sturminger, Walter. *Bibliographie, Ikonographie, und der Türkenbelagerungen Wiens 1529 und 1683.* Graz: Verlag Hermann Böhlaus, 1955.

Thaller, Franz. *Glaubensstreit und Türkennot 1519–1648: Geschichte Österreichs in Einzeldarstellungen, no. 6.* Graz: Styria, 1946.

Westermann, Ascan. *Die Türkenhilfe und die politisch-kirchlichen Parteien auf dem Reichstag zu Regensburg 1512.* Heidelberg: Carl Winter Universitätsbuchhandlung, 1910.

Wrede, Adolf, ed. *Deutsche Reichstagsakten unter Kaiser Karl V.* Vol. 2. Gotha: Perthes, 1896.

Zinkeisen, Johann Wilhelm. *Geschichte des osmanischen Reiches in Europa.* Vol. 1. Gotha: Perthes, 1840.

4 Knowledge and Depictions of Islam and the Religious Life of the Ottoman Turks in Reformation Germany

> How could there be a more gruesome, dangerous, frightening imprisonment than to live under such a system?
> Lies destroy the secular estate, murder destroys the spiritual estate, illegitimacy destroys the married estate.[1]
>
> Martin Luther

Sixteenth-century interest in the Turks manifested itself through published descriptions of an amazing range of facets of Ottoman society. More than any other area, however, references to the religious aspects of Turkish culture abound. Several important writers even gave a more or less systematic description of what they considered to be the essential nature of Islam. As in the Middle Ages, these descriptions did not thoroughly analyze Islam or use Islamic categories of understanding. Publications on the Turks in German-speaking lands primarily compared Islam with Christianity, concentrating on differences or areas that were considered to be particularly important to Christians. It is important to note that for sixteenth-century Germans almost all knowledge about Islam was filtered through their understanding of the Ottoman Turks. Although most writers on the Turks knew of the ethnic and historical differences between Arabs and other 'followers of Machomet,' little emphasis was placed on these distinctions. Whatever was believed or done by the Turks was considered to be normative for Muslim life as a whole.[2]

One key to understanding sixteenth-century views of the essential nature of Islam is by an analysis of the specific terms used to describe Muslims and their religion. This process of classification not only illustrates German knowledge of Islam, but also is important for the development of Western understandings of 'religion' in general.

The primary designation used for Muslims in the early sixteenth century was derived from the name 'Muhammad,' either in noun (e.g., *Mahometisten*) or adjectival (e.g., *Mahmetischen*) form. Spellings were not standardized, even within the works of individual writers.[3] Surprisingly, 'Saracen' was less frequently used as a designation for all Muslims;[4] when so used its primary usage was in polemic arguments disputing Muhammad's supposed claim of descent from Abraham's wife Sarah.[5]

The terms *Ungläubigen* (German) and *infideles* (Latin) were commonly used, most often in pamphlets by anonymous authors relating to military campaigns against the Turks.[6] Some reference is made to the Turks as *Heiden* (especially in relation to Psalm 79). Most often, however, 'heathen' was a distinct category referring to the 'barbarian' or 'uncivilized' and not to the Turks.[7] Two other less frequent designations, *Seckt* and *Kirchen*, point to the continuation of the medieval understanding of Islam as a Christian heresy.[8]

Only one author used a derivative of the accurate term "Muslim" in the literature published from 1520–1545. Although fundamentally misunderstood to be a cognate of the Turkish word for 'circumcised' (German: *Beschnitter*), former Ottoman captive Bartholomew Georgijevic in 1544 identified Muslims or Muslim converts as *musluman*.[9] Georgijevic understood this term to be a designation based on the use of circumcision as a ceremony of admission into the Islamic faith, similar to Christian baptism. He was more accurate in reference to women, who became *musluman* not through circumcision, but through a confession of faith.[10] This is perhaps the first published reference to followers of Muhammad as "Muslims" in Western literature, and demonstrates the subtle but important gains made in knowledge of Islam through the sixteenth-century contact with the Turks. This will be discussed in more detail in Chapter 8.

Not including designations such as *Grewel* or *Lügen* (abomination, lies, etc.),[11] when sixteenth-century Germans needed a term to refer specifically to the religious aspects of Turkish culture, they almost universally used *Glaube* in German or *fides* in Latin (faith) preceded by an adjectival identifier.[12] This term has had a broad spectrum of meanings. It was used both to refer to the totality of religious life, as well as to an inward, personal attitude toward God (piety).[13] Indications of the developing specialization of the term can be found in its use as a member of a series, e.g. "Von der Türken glaube, gesatz, gebet"[14] and "Glaub und gesatz der Türken."[15] Other words used to describe Turkish religious life include *Leer*[16] (modern German: *Lehre*, teaching), and two terms used especially in literature written by Protestants, *Gestaz* (modern German: *Gesetz*, law) and *Gottesdienst*.[17] The word *religion* was also employed in both German and Latin.

The use of *religion* is particularly important in this context because of its later Enlightenment use as *the* term for a reified, abstract system of belief and practice. During the sixteenth century one can observe increasing use of the designation 'religion' in literature written about the Turks.[18] Some of the first widely circulated pamphlets which utilized the word *religion* were the German editions of George of Hungary (Captivus Septemcastrensis). The title pages of various editions are inconsistent and therefore provide an opportunity to observe sixteenth-century uses of the term.

1530– Nürnberg, Franck, translator

Chronica unnd beschreibung der Türckey mit yhrem begriff, ynnhalt, provincien, völckern, ankunfft, kriege, reysen, *glauben, religionnen, gestazen,* sytten, geperde, weis, regimente, frümkeyt, unnd bossheiten.

1530– Augsburg, Franck, translator

Cronica, Abconterfayung und entwerffung der Türckey mit yrem begirff, Inhalt, Provincien, Völckern, ankunfft, Kryeegen, Sigen, niderlagen, *glaube, Religio, Gestazen,* sitte, Regiment, Pollicey, reüterey, fromkeit, und bossheit.

1530– Strassburg, translator unknown

Türckei. Chronica, *Glaube*, Sittenn, Herkomen, Weiss, und alle Geberden, der Türcken.

1530– Zwickau, translator unknown

Turckey. chronica, *Glaube, Gesatz*, Siten, Herkomen, Weis unalle geberden der Türcken.

1530– Strassburg, translator unknown

Saracenisch, Türckisch, un Mahometisch Glaub, Gesatz, Chronic, Gotsdienst, Ceremonien, Alle Gebräuch, Ordnungen, Disiplinen, in Kriegs unnd Fridenszeitten.

1530– place unknown, translator unknown

Ausz Ratschlage Herren Erasmi . . . *Türckisch un Machometisch Glaub, Gesatz,* Chronic, *Gotsdienst, Ceremonie,* alle gebraüch, Ordnungen, Disciplinen, in Kriegs unnd Friedenszeiten.

1531– Augsburg, Franch, translator

Cronica Abconterfayung und entwerffung der Tükey mit jrem begriff, Inhalt, Provincien, Völckern, ankunnft, Kriegen, Sigen, nyderlagen, *glawben, Religon, Gesatzen,* siten, Regiment, Policey, reutterey frommkeit und bossheit

As one can see from the use or omission of the term, in the 1530s Germans were familiar with the term 'religion,' but its usage was not universal. The term most frequently used as an alternative was *Gottesdienst* and in the descriptions this refers to the external aspects of religious practice (ceremonies, etc.). This is further demonstrated in Justus Jonas's translation of

Luther's introduction to *Libellus de ritu et moribus Turcorum* from Latin into German (1538).[19] When Luther used the term *religion*, Jonas once retained the usage, a second time retained the Latin word but added the term *Gottesdienst* to clarify is meaning to his German readers,[20] and then a third time substituted the term *religion* in German as a synonym for *fides* (and *Glaube*).

Luther

Nunc enim video, quid causae fuerit, quod a Papisti sic occuleretur *religio Turcica* . . . si ad disputandum *de religion* veniatur, totus Papatus cum omnibus suis caderet nec possent *fidem suam tueri et fidem Mahometi* confutare, cum ea confutare porteret, quae ipsimet maxime probant et quibus maxime nituntur, et ea tueri, quae illi maxime probant et quibus maxime nituntur.

Jonas' Translation

Und nu mercke ich erst warumb die Papisten und Curtisan zu Rom von der *Türcken Religion un Gottesdienst* . . . wen sie mit den Türcken oder andern *von der Religion* zu redden kemen, so müste das gantze Bapsthumb fallen und könten die Papisten *jren glaube nicht verteidige noch den Mahome-tischen* verdamen, den sie musten das verdammen das sie selbs thun, nemblich solche gleisnerei darauff das gantze Bapsthumb stehet oder *musten des Türcken Religion schüzen und verteidigen dan sie hat jhe so viel möncherey und gleisnerey als das Baptsthumb*.

In his classic study *The Meaning and End of Religion*, Wilfred Cantwell Smith argued that the use of the term 'religion' as a description of a foreign, separate system of religious beliefs is anachronistic if used before the late seventeenth/early eighteenth century. It was only in the time of the Enlightenment that the Reformation concept 'religion' as equivalent to 'piety' was superseded by a concept of systematic externalization.[21] Smith bases this argument on the fact that he found no use of the plural 'religions' or connections with external religious practices by Protestants until the middle of the seventeenth century.[22] More recently, Peter Harrison in *'Religion' and the Religions in the English Enlightenment* has refined but not substantially altered Smith's thesis. Harrison included a short section on the Reformation in the chapter 'Antecedants,' emphasizing Luther's use of the Turks in inter-confessional conflict. He stated that this lead eventually to the comparison of 'religions' and finally to the discipline of comparative religion. But for Harrison as well as for Smith, the real change happened during the Enlightenment.[23] Some sixteenth-century continuities with the medieval paradigmatic understanding of Islam as a Christian heresy would seem to support this view. However, as in the previous examples, an analysis of the sixteenth-century terminology used for the Ottoman Turks substantiates the claim that an important stage in the development of the reification of the concept of religion occurred in the matrix of the confessional conflicts of the sixteenth century combined with general interest in the Turks and the attention demanded by the Ottoman advance. The sixteenth-century contribution to this reification can easily be missed if the range of popular pamphlets are not examined and only the major figures and their central works of theology are investigated. The process began as much with the way material was organized and presented as with the content itself, as Almut Höfert has argued and my research supports.[24]

Islamic Views of Christ

One of the primary differences between sixteenth century and medieval depictions of Islam lies in the splintering that occurred as a result of the confessional divisions during the Reformation. Roman Catholic depictions of Islam in the sixteenth century followed medieval sources and continued to concentrate on Muhammad and his prophetic vocation; not surprisingly, Catholic discussion of Muslim Christology primarily reiterated earlier arguments.[25] A significant shift in emphasis, however, occurred with the Lutherans. Luther and those who followed him focused their entire discussion of Islamic theology on the difference between the Christian and Muslim understanding of Christ.

The most extensive treatment of the connection between Martin Luther and Islam on Christology and other topics is *Martin Luther and Islam: A Study in Sixteenth-Century Polemics and Apologetics* by Adam Francisco. Relying on a close reading of Luther's primary publications dealing with the Turks, Francisco's primary argument is that Luther engaged Islamic theology much more intentionally than generally believed and that his approach should be considered to be more apologetic than polemic. Luther never met a Muslim and never had real Muslims in mind when he wrote about Islam. His primary concern was to defend Christianity against Islam for the sake of Christians.[26]

Francisco is certainly correct, and his overall reading of Luther on Islam is quite similar to mine. However, as helpful as Francisco's account of Luther's engagement with Islam is, it could create a misleading impression. Luther's significant engagement with Islam certainly included apologetic elements. It seems to me, however, that this should not be singled out as Luther's primary mode of engagement with Islam. Almost always when Luther writes about the Turks he is simultaneously writing about other things, such as the wickedness of the Papists, depravity of his Germans, or to encourage early Protestants to spiritually and militarily defend the fatherland against the Ottomans. While it is incorrect to go so far as to argue that Luther simply uses the Turks rhetorically to combat enemies closer to home, an emphasis on this broader rhetorical context is essential in understanding Luther's writings on Islam. In addition, pastoral concerns are central to Luther's writings on the Turks. One does not want to draw too fine a distinction here, but it seems to me that Luther is less interested in apologetically defending 'Christianity' against 'Islam' than he is helping individual Christians to endure the troubles of the Last Days or perhaps even spiritually survive Turkish captivity. This should be kept in mind whenever I describe any aspect of Luther's understanding of the Turks and Islam.

For Martin Luther, the foundation of all orthodoxy and the difference between theological truth or falsehood was a correct understanding of the person and the work of Jesus.[27] Because of their denial of the divinity of Christ, all of Islamic theology was categorically false. In conjunction with the denial of Christ's divinity, Luther thought two other Muslim doctrines were particularly blasphemous: the Muslim denial of the death of Christ on the cross (the centerpoint of Luther's *theologia crucis*) and the Muslim exaltation of Muhammad over Christ.[28]

Due to this christological emphasis, the Lutheran critique of Islam was significantly harsher than that of the Middle Ages. Luther had read Cusa's *Cribatio* ('sifting') of the Qur'an but chose not to republish it as he did with another medieval source on Islam, Ricoldo de Monte Croce. For Luther, there was nothing valuable to sift out of the Qur'anic *Teufelslehre* (devil's doctrine).

Other Lutherans also focused their discussions of Islam on Christology.[29] Melanchthon's treatment of Islam was concerned almost exclusively with the Islamic denial of the divinity of Jesus.[30] Melanchthon saw the Muslim view of God as limited to creator and judge, and therefore placed it in a series stemming from Platonic (philosophic) ideas of God.[31] Without a divine Jesus, the God of Muhammad was really no God at all, but an idol. He even took the recognized Islamic monotheism and turned it into polytheism: "Wer Gott nicht zum Herr hat, hat viele Herrn." [Whoever does not have God as Lord has many Lords.][32]

A typical exposition of the Lutheran understanding of Islam which demonstrates this Christological focus is found in sermons on the Turks by Tübingen professor Jacob Andreä.[33] Andreä lists the three primary blasphemies of the Qur'an as 1) the denial that Jesus was God's son, 2) the forbidding of prayer to Jesus, and 3) the denial of Christ's death on the cross. His exposition of the faith of the Turks (*Türkenglaube*) consists of the tripartite explanation of how Muhammad attempts to deny the divine sonship of Christ by stating that if God has a son he must also have a wife, he must be divided in his sovereignty, and the son would have been more glorious than the despised Jesus. Andreä then refutes these points from the Qur'an itself by arguing that the Qur'an speaks of God in the plural, that the Qur'an demonstrates the divine sonship of Jesus (using his German translation of Bibliander's Qur'an: "Wir haben dem Sohn Mariae unser Seel zu eigen gegeben"), and that in the Qur'an Jesus speaks of his own death.

Except for the change in emphasis to an almost exclusive focus on Christology and the addition of the criticism that Muslims do not allow prayers directed to Jesus, the entire argument can be found in medieval polemic.

The Lutheran conclusion, however, goes much further than most medieval arguments: if Jesus is not the Son, God is not the Father. Therefore, Muslims believe in a different God than Christians.[34] Islam is no longer a Christian heresy, rather it worships a different God, which is the devil, according to Luther.[35] The Lutheran shift to a Christological focus was so strong that its influence can be seen even in later popularly written Catholic pamphlets and subtly changed the nature of Christian polemic against Islam.[36]

Islamic Soteriology

A similar confessional division is found in the interpretation of Islamic soteriology. The Muslim doctrine of Divine Decree was mentioned by both Roman Catholics and Lutherans. Catholic writers followed the medieval argument that this doctrine destroys free will and eliminates the human role in salvation. Lutherans, however, did not critique what they called 'Turkish predestination,' but simply showed their hope is in vain.[37] Catholic and Lutheran interpretations are even more diametrically opposed concerning the Islamic means of salvation. While Roman Catholic sources criticized Islam for believing that a person is saved by confession of faith alone (the *shahadah*), Lutherans viewed Islam as fundamentally a religion of works-righteousness.[38] For Luther, Islam is so strongly stamped by *Werkerei* that every works-righteousness within or without Christianity could be characterized as *Turcae*.[39]

This Lutheran understanding of Islamic soteriology led to some interesting interpretations of other aspects of Muslim life. Lutherans relegated the *shahadah* to a minor status within Islamic life. It was grammatically "meaningless," Luther wrote.[40] Many rituals were understood to have been established specifically as a means of salvation. Ritual washings and almsgiving are frequently mentioned in this context.[41] Also, since Muslims were saved by their works and since no one could completely please God, Muslims themselves must admit how insecure their salvation is.[42]

Some scholars, including Erasmus, Zwingli, and to a lesser extent, Melanchthon, articulated a further, important understanding of Islamic soteriology during this period. These scholars saw Islam as a branch of the law-religions built upon the Decalogue, an expression of the *religio naturalis,* which has been given to all of mankind.[43] Although still understanding Islam to be a religion of works, this more positive interpretation held out the real possibility of salvations for some of the followers of Muhammad.

Knowledge and Depictions of Muhammad

Nowhere is the difference between medieval and early modern depictions of Islam more clearly evident than in the lack of attention paid to the life of Muhammad in the Lutheran literature published in the early sixteenth century. Few pamphlets on the religion of the Turks dealt extensively with

Muhammad's life.[44] In part, this is due to the dominance of the immediate military threat. However, even in those writers who are most concerned with a spiritual defense against Islam, polemic biographic plays little or no role. It is not the content of the biographical information that represents a change (for it largely repeats medieval calumnies), but the relative de-emphasis on the topic.

The Christological focus of Luther's arguments against Islam appears to be an important factor in this shift from the traditional medieval polemic. Luther stated specifically that he is not concerned with Muhammad's biography or personality, but only with his teaching.[45] He was not in the least interested in the medieval legends about Muhammad. "Personalia, quae dicunt de Mahomet, me non movent, aber die Lehr der Türken müssen wir angreifen."[46]

Despite this biographical de-emphasis, there were numerous brief references made to Muhammad and his life scattered throughout the *Türkenbüchlein* of the sixteenth century.[47] Because it is a typical summary, the biography by Heinrich Knaust, *Von geringem herkommen schentlichern leben schmehlichem ende des Türckischen abgots Machomets* (1542), deserves to be summarized. *Von geringem* is a collection of the most vicious medieval legends of Muhammad, pieced together with no attempt at harmonization or analysis. This particularly sharp rhetoric was specifically written for a popular audience, explicitly with the intention to dissuade Christians who might be tempted to become Muslims.

Knaust found several aspects of Muhammad's life particularly important. First, Knaust was determined to prove false Muhammad's claim to be the vehicle of divine revelation. Muhammad suffered without doubt from epilepsy. It was during these fits that he claimed to speak with the angel Gabriel and receive his revelation.[48] Muhammad used false signs to give credence to the law as he gave it to the people, such as a trained dove which would fly to him, sit on his shoulder, and eat grain out of his ear—to deceive the people into thinking that the Holy Spirit was speaking to him.[49] Instead of a divine source for his teaching, Muhammad received his blasphemous doctrines from Judaism (his mother was Jewess[50]) and from heretical Nestorian and Arian monks.[51]

Knaust portrays the character of Muhammad as power-hungry, prideful, presumptuous, lying, and lecherous—just like his father Lucifer.[52] On one of his merchant trips to Cana, his drive for power led him to deceive the princess and ruler of Cana, Tagida, along with many Jews and Saracens, into believing that he was the Jewish messiah. This was done through many false miracles by the devil's power.[53] The princess married him and thus he came to power. After a failed preaching attempt in Cordoba, Spain, where he was driven out by the archbishop, Muhammad escaped to Africa and won over many people. According to Knaust, Heraclius sent a force to Africa to bring Muhammad's revolt under subjection, but it was defeated by the false prophet and his followers. Muhammad then went to Damascus, was crowned king, and ruled for ten years.[54]

As in the medieval biographies, Knaust also emphasized Muhammad's death. According to Knaust's biography, Muhammad had often stated that after his tenth year of ruling, he would die, and after three days, ascend to heaven. To test his truthfulness, a disciple poisoned him to see if this would be so, but he did not rise again. In fact, after a few days his body was eaten by dogs. Only the bones remained which were then buried, after which many of his followers fell away.[55]

Knaust ended his biography with a selection of fables supposedly drawn from the Qur'an[56] including the only published account of the period of the *miraj* (the nighttime journey to heaven).[57] Knaust accepted the tradition as both authentic and essential to Islamic theology. Frequently interjecting very sharp polemical commentary, this became the pinnacle of Knaust's anti-Islamic argument. In summary, Muhammad was an imposter inspired by Satan to found a cult capable of challenging and eventually destroying Christianity. Already the Muslims have been appallingly successful in decimating the ranks of the Christians by massacre and conversion. Any Germans captured by the Turks and tempted to apostatize (soldiers are specifically mentioned), should strengthen their faith by recalling the diabolical origin of Islam and the devilish history of Muhammad. Although he was not typical in his focus on polemic biography, Knaust demonstrates both the inaccuracy of Western knowledge of Muhammad as well as the use of medieval depictions to encourage the Christian defense against the Ottoman Turks in the context of the Reformation.

Knowledge and Depictions of the Qur'an

In their effort to defend Christianity against Islam, Protestants demonstrated considerable interest in the Qur'an. Surprisingly, I could find no extensive examination of the Qur'an in the Roman Catholic literature published in German-speaking lands during the first half of the sixteenth century. One reason for this may be that the Catholics were content with their medieval sources, while the Protestants sought independent, non-Catholic sources. Luther, for instance, personally displayed considerable hesitation in using Catholic sources on Islam, accused them of intentionally falsifying their material, and made numerous calls for accurate information on both the Qur'an and Islam in general.[58] In addition, the theological focus of Protestantism on Christian scripture in its original languages encouraged a correspondingly fresh engagement with Islamic scripture.

As early as 1529, Luther lamented that he had no accurate Latin translation of the Qur'an. About this time, Theodor Bibliander also appears to have initiated his study of the Arabic Qur'an, with the intention of publishing an accurate Latin edition.[59] By 1542, Bibliander had completed an edition based on Ketton's medieval translation, supposedly with corrections made from two Arabic copies, one from the University of Basel, another purchased through an Italian merchant from Algeria. Bibliander's Qur'an was widely considered to be a scholarly edition, but was not, despite the claim on the title page that the text was improved through comparison with Latin and Arabic texts. Due to his weak Arabic, Bibliander was only able to add a few marginal comments and did not improve the quality of the translation. The majority of changes concerned the removal of scholastic terminology and the de-Catholicizing of Ketton's translation and its marginal comments. The controversy surrounding the printing of the book demonstrates that the first published Qur'an was a direct result of widespread Protestant interest in Islam.

German Protestants were in agreement on the necessity of an accurate edition of the Qur'an, but displayed some interesting differences in their interpretation of Muhammad's "*Gesatzbuch.*" Luther's interpretation of the Qur'an is illustrative of much of early sixteenth-century Protestant thought. As in the other areas, Luther displays both his interest in 'accuracy' and also in the development of knowledge over the period. In 1530, for instance, he translated the word Qur'an to be "*predigt oder lerebuch*" but by 1542 had changed his interpretation to "*Summa oder versamlung, Nemlich der Go(e)ttlichen Gebot.*" This translation to closer to the actual meaning and highlights Luther's understanding of the Qur'an to be fundamentally a collection of laws, a book not on a par with the Bible, but rather with the Papal Decretals.

Furthermore, these laws were not morally good, or even neutral; the Qur'an is a "*faul schendlich buch*" [foul, shameful book].[60] For Luther, the Qur'an contained only human wisdom without God's word and spirit, it was the evil human eyes on the horn in the prophecy of Daniel Chapter 7.[61] "For his law teaches nothing other than what human reason can easily bear. What he found in the Gospel that was too difficult or lofty to believe he left out, particularly that Christ is God and that he has saved us through his death."[62]

Luther supported the publication of the Qur'an in Latin because he considered public knowledge of its hideousness to be the greatest weapon against Islam. This would help preachers to better preach the gruesomeness of the Turks and help people to have courage to fight.[63] Both Papists and Muslims themselves had tried to hide the truth of this shameful book.[64] Luther even claimed that most Muslims don't believe the majority of the Qur'an,[65] or believe in it only because of the Muslim success of arms and not for any inherent value.[66] The claim of the miraculous nature of the Arabic Qur'an was completely lost on Luther who believed that Muhammad simply composed it in the common language of the people he sought to seduce.[67]

Melanchthon's critique of the Qur'an is similar to Luther's, especially in the fundamental designation of the Qur'an as a book of human wisdom. The reason that the Qur'an uses only human reason was to accommodate the uneducated, mercenary Arabs who were Muhammad's followers and thus to unify the scattered Arab tribes.[68] Melanchthon also analyzed the style of

Figure 4.1 Alcoran and Decretals, Matthias Gerung, 1530

the Qur'an and argued that it cannot be a divine revelation because of the structure of its composition.[69] Melanchthon makes a great deal out of the argument that the Qur'an is 500 years younger than the Bible and claims to use the apostles and prophets as a source, but does not follow them accurately.[70]

Finally, an alternative view is found in the Zürich reformer Theodor Bibliander. In contrast to Luther and Melanchthon, Bibliander argued that the Qur'an had some positive value, included some genuine scripture, and that it contained nothing more false than many heathen philosophies.[71] Like Raymond Llull before him, Bibliander placed the highest hope and stress on the study of the Arabic language. If there were a common linguistic understanding between Christians and Muslims, many would be soon converted.

Knowledge and Depictions of Islamic Rituals and Spirituality

The area in which the most dramatic development in Western knowledge concerning Islam took place was in new descriptions of Islamic rituals and spirituality. Sixteenth-century writers were particularly interested in descriptions of the exotic Turkish culture, especially in their religious practices. These new descriptions were a result of particularly close cultural contact: in Hungary and Austria, on military and diplomatic assignments, but especially through the published narratives of escaped Turkish captives like George of Hungary and Bartholomew Georgijevic. The new forms of mass media, both textual and visual, spread these descriptions and perhaps increased the market for information concerning the cultural 'other.'

Sixteenth-century descriptions of Turkish religious life continued the medieval methodology of interpreting Islamic practices to be 'versions' of their nearest Christian counterparts. However, the emphasis of the *Türkenbüchlein* on descriptions of the exotic rather than polemic gives the early modern literature a considerably different character than its medieval counterpart. A general guide to the topics that sixteenth-century Germans found particularly interesting can be found through an analysis of the contents of George of Hungary and Georgijevic as will be seen in Chapter 8. Considerable attention was paid to the practices of the 'monks' of the Turks, as well as anything to do with sexuality. Other topics that received significant treatment include Muslim corporate prayer, almsgiving, and for the first time, extended discussions of Islamic mysticism and the division within Islam.

Confession of Faith, Ramadan, Pilgrimage

There is no designation of the 'Five Pillars of Islam' or even any consistent mention of required Islamic practices in the early sixteenth-century literature. A reader of this literature might even conclude that marriage was the most strongly emphasized religious requirement.[72] The Islamic confession of faith (the *shahadah*: "There is no God but God and Muhammad is his prophet") was mentioned but not emphasized. The Ramadan fast was accurately described, but Bartholomew Georgijevic, for example, was more interested in recounting the Muslim 'Easter' feast that followed it.[73] The medieval perspective on the pilgrimage, which incorrectly saw the *hajj* as an annual requirement of the followers of Muhammad to visit his tomb in Mecca, remained prominent. In the sixteenth century, however, alternate explanations began to circulate. Georgijevic, for example, simply listed Mecca as the foremost among many pilgrimage holy places. Mecca was venerated as the Christians venerated Jerusalem, he claimed, but the Mecca pilgrimage was more for trade than veneration. Georgijevic did not mention any pilgrimage requirement.

Almsgiving

Muslim almsgiving and charity was often mentioned, but again there seems to have been no understanding of the required nature of this activity. Several topics of institutional charity were emphasized, including endowed hospitals, schools, and inns.[74] Personal charity was also frequently mentioned. In *Das siebend Capital* Justus Jones described Turks carrying well water through the streets of the large seaport cities so that the inhabitants would have something to drink and also providing hospitality for poor strangers in an effort to demonstrate their own holiness and gain favor with God. Georgijevic mentioned that it was considered an act of great charity to free a slave (or even a captive animal) and that some Turks set aside a portion of their estate for this kind of activity. According to Georgijevic, the Turks also considered the feeding of wild animals and the distribution of food to the poor to be acts which earned them special favor with God and perhaps the answer to prayers for their own or a loved-one's crisis.[75]

Prayer and Worship

The requirement of five-times daily prayer was known, but generally the corporate rather than the individual aspects of prayer was emphasized.[76] This is especially true for Georgijevic, whose extended description had a wide circulation and influence and will be examined in greater detail in Chapter 8. According to Georgijevic, the call to prayer as initiated by a *pfaff* in a high tower who put his fingers in his ears so that he could yell, and said three times: "Ein warer Got allein." [There is one true God.] People gathered in response to this call, with the largest gathering on Friday, the Muslim holy day.[77] Before prayer, the people must wash their feet and private parts and put water on their heads three times, saying: "Honored and praised be my God."[78] Ritual purity and discipline is important. No one may enter the temple wearing shoes. Christians are not allowed to enter and are considered to pollute the temple. Women are not allowed with the men but have a special place where they cannot be seen or heard.[79]

Georgievic described the Turkish temples (called by him *meschit*) as large and expensive, decorated not by pictures or statues, but only by letters (including the *shahadah* and other statements such as "There is no one stronger than God"). The interior is lit by oil lamps and rugs cover the floor.

The corporate prayer consists of the men putting their hands to their head as if they were removing their linen hat, and then falling to their knees and kissing the ground several times. When the *pfaff* comes to the pulpit, the priest with all the people turn their bodies from side to side and mumble, "There is no more than one God."[80] On Friday a sermon is said, of which we have two apparently authentic Turkish examples translated by George of Hungary. If his two examples were also typical in content, they were primarily ethical admonitions with an emphasis on death and on the judgment according to deeds. Protestants would emphasize that this confirmed their understanding of Islam as a religion of works, not faith.[81]

Georgijevic made clear that in contrast to Christianity, among the Turks there is almost no distinction between clergy and laity. Turkish clergy need no special training, only to be able to read and translate Arabic. The common people choose them, but they are paid by the king. Sixteenth-century authors expressed surprise that the Turkish clergy had wives, dressed like the laity, and even worked.[82]

Rituals "from the Jews"

The Muslim prohibition of wine and pork are often mentioned, but generally only under the rubric of "rituals derived from Judaism."[83] This was also true of circumcision, which was believed to be directly copied from Judaism in an effort to prove Muslim affinity with Abraham and the Abrahamic covenant.[84] For Luther, these rituals were simply another indication of the external works-righteousness of Islam. Georgijevic, however, stressed the importance of circumcisions in Turkish spirituality. He described it as *the* initiation ceremony of Islam and even the meaning of the term *musluman* (Muslim). He dedicated a considerable portion of his description of Turkish ritual to circumcisions, especially in the context of Christian conversion to Islam.[85]

Islamic Mysticism

The first extensive descriptions of Sufism[86] and Islamic mysticism published in the West are found in the German *Türkenbüchlein* of the early sixteenth century. These descriptions are remarkable for the intense interest they reflect in this aspect of Turkish life. Although they often display a naïve credulity and contain obvious inaccuracies and exaggerations, the German descriptions show an awe of the religiosity of the 'Turkish monks' that was based in part on actual contact.

The reputation of the holiness of Islamic mystics was so widespread that Martin Luther, for example, could use it as a rhetorical device against his papal opponents. "Their 'spirituals' live such a strict life that they put our monks to shame; they are more like angels than men," Luther wrote. "They are often in ecstasies in which they do miracles, but because they do not hold to the second article [of the creed], these are false miracles and ecstasies done through the devil's power."[87]

Ecstasy was one of the most frequently mentioned characteristics of the Turkish Sufis. This ecstasy could be gained through self-deprivations, dance (the Dervish whirling dance was specifically mentioned), or drugs.[88] Publications in German also emphasized severe asceticism, specifically fasting, begging, nakedness, bodily mutilation, and homelessness.[89] Grave sites were mentioned both as pilgrimage centers and as the locations of the miraculous healings. Female mysticism was also mentioned; descriptions were given of the loss of consciousness during prayer and of mystical pregnancy.[90]

Several different Sufi orders were distinguished by their maintenance of the specific Muslim saints' graves or by differences in ascetic practice. It is clear that George of Hungary, for example, considered the mystic orders to be genuinely religious (although deceived, Luther would add) as opposed to the hypocritical 'secular' clergy. There are even indications that some considered the Sufis and the regular religious leaders to be mutually antagonistic.[91]

Shi'a Islam

It was only after Shah Ismail (d. 1524) had re-established Persian power that the West became significantly interested in Shi'a Islam.[92] The first published literature in the West on the Shi'ites was in the *Türkenbüchlein* of the early sixteenth century. The antagonism between Shi'a Persia and the Sunni Ottoman Empire was both a comfort to a divided Europe and a political boon to the Hapsburgs. Understanding the advantages of a two-front war against the Turks, the Hapsburgs sent repeated negotiators to work out an alliance with Persia. Germans hoped for the defeat of the Ottomans by the Persians and celebrated any rumor of Persian military victory.[93] In fact, reports of the military conflicts between the Persians and Ottomans serve as the primary vehicle for Western descriptions of the party of Ali.

Little was actually known about Shi'a theology or spirituality. However, such a strong connection was made between Shi'a Islam and Sufism ("a Persian order like our monks, among which are priests which one calls *sophi*"[94]) that the leader of Persia was simply referred to as the 'Sophi' in the early sixteenth century. Germans also believed that the Shi'a represented a separate religious tradition based on a different (new) exposition of Muhammad's law and that they were considered to be heretical by the Ottomans.[95] The primary demarcation between Sunni and Shi'a Islam, the acceptance of the leadership of Ali's descendants, was at least partially understood. The description given in the 1536 *Warhaffte beschreibung* was typical. Islam is divided into two parts: the *Gesider* who followed Machomet, Hebubachir, Homer, and Isinan; and the *Refasier* who followed Hali.[96] At times, however, this division became exaggerated into the rumor that the Shi'a were opposed even to Muhammad.[97]

From what is known of Muslim life in the sixteenth century, these descriptions of Islamic ritual and spirituality are often exaggerated and only partly accurate, but they do seem to reflect a Christian interpretation based on contact with genuine Islamic spirituality. Even though comparisons continue to be made with Christian practices, in contrast to medieval depictions the overall tone of the *Türkenbüchlein* is investigative. The most derogatory comments came from the ecclesiastical literature of the Lutherans. Luther always used the same argument: no matter how spiritual it looks, without Christ they are damned. Miracles are no evidence of authenticity, for satanic power is great and can appear as an 'angel of light.'[98] The Lutheran attack on the genuineness of Muslim spirituality was not only to protect people from converting to Islam (this was believed to be a very real danger) but most importantly to prove the vanity of any works-righteousness, be it the rigorous discipline of the Turks or the comparatively shameful hypocrisy of the Papists.

The Relationship of Islam with Judaism and Christianity

German pamphleteers of the early sixteenth century knew the exclusiveness of the claims of Islam, but it is not clear if they understood the assertion that Islam was the successor to corrupted forms of religion found in Judaism and Christianity. Instead, two different views were held concerning the relation of Islam to Christianity and Judaism. First, the medieval idea that Islam was a type of Christian heresy remained influential. Second, Islam was viewed by some as putting aspects of Judaism and Christianity together to create a new religion, a 'devil's brew' of false belief. Sebastian Franck was an important but isolated exception to these two views. In his writings the earliest beginning of an understanding that Islam was a separate religious system can be found.

Since the primary understanding of Islam in the Middle Ages was as a Christian heresy, it is not surprising that this view remained strong in the early sixteenth century, especially with those most influenced by the medieval sources on Islam. This view remained the dominant one among Catholics, who used it in their Augustinian justification of war against the Turks. Protestants, however, often used similar language.[99] Bibliander, for instance, called Islam the "enemy of the people of God" and a "dangerous heresy." Muhammad was a false prophet who must be rejected in order for Turks to become the sons of God.[100] Melanchthon clearly identified Muhammad's teaching with Christian heresy, particularly Arianism.[101] According to Melanchthon, Muhammad taught nothing original and added only a few ceremonies to distinguish his teaching from others.[102] In literature written for popular consumption the tendency to identify Islam with Christian heresy could reach absurd levels. In Knaust's *Von geringem*, for example, he accused Turks of Sabellianism, Arianism, Manichaeism, Doceticism, Macedonianism, Origenism, Anthropomorphism, Anabaptism, and even gave them credit for some heretical doctrines that no one had ever thought of before![103]

Luther, however, avoided designating the faith of the Turks as heresy. For him, it was worse; the Turks worshipped a different God, the devil himself. Islam was something essentially different from Christianity, "a faith created from Jewish, Christian, and Heathen faiths".[104] If anything, Luther considered Islam to be closer to Judaism than to Christianity.[105] The similarity, or at least the compatibility of Judaism and Islam, was frequently mentioned in popular publications.[106]

Sebastian Franck was an important exception to these two views because his interest in Islam resembled that of a world chronicler, almost a 'student of world religions.' In the preface to his "Corigieret und gebeesert" *Chronica*, Franck announced that his work was a "beschreibung aller land inn Affrica, Europa, und Asia gelegen mit yrem glawben, religionen, Regimenten, Policeyen, siten, gestalten, Vo(e)lkern."[107] In a description of religious divisions, he also seemed to make a much stronger distinction between Christianity and Islam as separate systems:

> Here we see that the Christian faith is divided into at least sixteen or seventeen divisions . . . it goes with us just like the Turks in Turkey— actually worse because they are divided into only four sects, we, on the other hand, in more than a thousand.[108]

Most of the time, however, when pamphleteers related the *Glaube* of the Turks to Christianity it was in the service of confessional polemic rather than as an investigation into the nature of Islam itself. Both Catholics and Lutherans used the image of the Turks as a weapon against their ecclesiastical opponents.

There are numerous references in Catholic literature to the equation of 'Turks and Lutherans.'[109] For example, Johannes Cochlaeus specifically declared that Luther's teaching conformed to the Qur'an.[110] *Ein Sendbrieff* stated that Lutheran morality was no better than the Turks:

> The Turk tears down churches and destroys monasteries—so does Luther, the Turk turns convents into horse stables and makes cannon out of church bells—so does Luther. The Turk abuses and treats lasciviously all female persons, both secular and spiritual. Luther is just as bad for he entices monks and nuns out of their monasteries into false marriages.[111]

In the eyes of the papacy and its representatives, Lutherans were actually worse than the Turks.[112] The correspondence of Cardinal Legate Alessandro Farnese was typical:

> The Turks are better than the Protestants, for when they allow Christians to live, they allow them to live as Catholics. The Protestants, on

the other hand, when they allow men to live they destroy their souls under the pretense of reforming them.[113]

The Catholic equation of Lutheran and Turk was not intended to describe Islam. Rather, whenever a Catholic representative wanted to malign an opponent no epitaph was more derogatory than calling them a 'Turk.'

I have already mentioned the importance of the Turks in the anti-Catholic polemic of the Lutherans.[114] In demonstrating the religious 'superiority' of the Turks over the Papists, Luther wanted to highlight not only the meaninglessness of works-righteousness, but also the fact that Roman Catholics did not do very well even at what they claimed to honor.[115] The discipline of the Turks would shame any Catholic so much that Luther thought no one would remain in his faith if he were to spend just three days with the Turks.[116]

The concept of the 'Turk' became a Lutheran metaphor for any 'anti-Christian' activity within the church. Not only Catholics but also Anabaptists and stubborn, unbelieving Germans were called 'Christian Turks.'[117] Like the Catholic propagandists, Lutherans also argued that their Christian opponents were much worse than the Turks.[118] According to Luther, the Turks do not force anyone to deny Christ, but simply "tempt and entice" them [versuchen und locken]. The Turk kills the body, but fills heaven with saints; the Pope kills both body and soul and fills hell with supposed Christians.[119]

Many Protestant writers drew parallels between Catholic and Turkish doctrine and morality and used pamphlets to attack not only Turks but also their Catholic opponents.[120] This was especially true of the Lutheran pamphlets written to support the 1542 campaign of Joachim of Brandenburg against the Ottomans.[121] Luther, Dietrich, and Jonas seem to be genuinely concerned about the Turkish threat and bring in their opponents only tangentially. Osiander, however, primarily used the Turkish theme as a vehicle for this anti-Catholic rhetoric.[122]

One of the strongest propagandistic uses of the image of the Turks in the confessional conflict was done through broadsheets and woodcuts. As Charlotte Colding Smith has demonstrated, the art of Matthias Gerung is particularly dramatic in this regard.[123] In a series of woodcuts Gerung makes the equation Turks and Pope = devil (directly equated with two devils crowned as sultan and pope, see Figure 4.2), while the true believers (the Protestants) were protected by Jesus (sometimes preaching, sometimes bearing a sword) or by the four evangelists (representing the true gospel). In most of the broadsheets, the Turks and the Papists are linked in their activity in attacking the true believers and/or being dragged into hell. In one important example, a direct visual link was made between the Alcoran and the Papal Decretals (importantly, not the Qur'an and the Bible), thus demonstrating that both are sets of false laws. (See Figure 4.1.) Both satanic connections and atrocities are shown (no real distinction is made between the physical destruction

Figure 4.2 Two Devils Crowned as Sultan and Pope, Matthias Gerung, 1530

Used by permission of the Universität- und Forschungsbibliothek Erfurt. UB Erfurt, Dep. Erf. 03-Na 4° 00287 (58).

Figure 4.3 Pope and Sultan, Matthias Gerung, 1530

Used by permission of the Universität- und Forschungsbibliothek Erfurt. UB Erfurt, Dep. Erf.
03-Na 4° 00287 (44).

wrought by pope or Turk)—yet Christ is also shown to be triumphant— physically defending the church, slaughtering its enemies and forcing them into hell. The Turkish/papal attacks are shown to be ultimately ineffective, as ineffective as a wagon pulled in opposite directions. (See Figure 4.3.)

Notes

1. Luther, *Vom Kriege*, 127.
2. For example, Luther stated that all Islamic powers form one Reich, be they Turkish or Egyptian, because they are all of the same faith. *Heerpredigt*, 167. For a large portion of Europe (except Spain), the image of the Turk and the image of Islam was one and the same. Rouillard, 8, Rodinson, 36, Schwoebel, 226. Therefore, unless otherwise specified, I will use the terms 'Muslim' and 'Turk' (with their cognates) synonymously.
3. For instance, Melanchthon used Mahometus, Mahumetus, Mahmetus in his Latin writings, Mahometh, Mahmet, and Machmet in his German works. See *Opera, Corpus Reformatorum* 25, 499ff., also, Manfred Köhler, *Melanchthon und der Islam: Ein Beitrag zur Klärung des Verhältnisses zwischen Christentum und Fremdreligionen in der Reformationszeit*, 29ff.
4. It was frequently used as an ethnic designation for Arabs, as in the series: Turks, Jews, Saracens. Josef Grünpeck, *Ein Dyalogus Doctor Joseph Grünpeck von Burckhausen*, a3a. Saracen was actually a word borrowed from the Greek *sarakegoi*, a corruption of the Arabic *sharquiin*, meaning easterners.
5. According to Justus Jonas, *Das siebend Capitel Danielis von des Türken Gottes lesterung und schrecklicher moderey mit unterrich*, d2d. For a similar argument attributed to Luther, *WA TR* 3, 418–419 (#3571).
6. For example, *Bäbstlicher heilikeit*, a2a and *Römischer Keyserlicher Maiestat*.
7. Giovo, gla. Concerning Muhammad the conqueror: "das er jhe so viel der Christlichen Religion, oder auch Haidnischem glauben, allls des Mahomets glauben angehangen." Luther's Large Catechism: "For whatever stands outside of Christianity, be it heathens, Turks, Jews, or pseudo-Christians and hypocrites." *WA 301*, 192.
8. Only rarely used by Protestants, most often by those greatly influenced by the medieval literature on Islam, e.g., Knaust. For an example of Roman Catholic use: "Machumetischen Seckt nachvolger", "Machometischen kirchen" are frequent in Grünpeck, especially a3a-a4a.
9. See appendix 3, "Of Their Circumcision." In pamphlet form in German translation, see Bartholomew Georgijevic, *Von der Türken gebreuchen, gewonheyten und Ceremonien*, b4a.
10. Since it was not customary to circumcise wives, they were not considered *musluman* until they "die vorgeshrybene wort geschworen haben." Georgijevic, b4a.
11. Also included in this category is the use of the terms *Abgötterei* (idolatry) and *Aberglauben* (superstition). These designations were used by both Protestants and Catholics, most often in highly charged rhetorical passages. It is clear that the German usage of these terms was rhetorical rather than descriptive due to the fact that they can be found in passages which demonstrated knowledge that Islam clearly *was not* idolatrous or pagan.
12. Such as *machometische Glaube, Saracenische Glaube, Türckische Glaube*, etc. Used separately or in conjuction with other terms, *Glaube* or *fides* is found in almost every writing on the Turks I examined.
13. For example, Luther uses the term in his writings on the Turks in both abroad sense (in reference to the totality of religion): "Also ist ein glaube, zu samen geflickt aus der Juden, Christen, und heiden galuben." (in context of the Islamic

praise of Christ, use of circumcision, etc, *Vom Kriege,* 122) and narrow sense (in reference to inward belief and piety): "Und durch diesen artickel wird unser glaube gesondert von allen anderen glauben auff erden: (in context of the discussion of the second article of the creed against Catholics and Turks, *Heerpredigt,* 186)

14. George of Hungary, Chapter 19.
15. *Aus Ratschlage,* Chapter XVIII.
16. For example, Heinrich Knaust, *Von geringem herkommen schentlichern leben schmehlichem ende des Türckischen abgots Machomets und seiner verdamlichen und Gotsslesterischen Ler,* ala: "Mahomet" and his "verdammlichen und Gottlesterlichen Leer."
17. Luther often uses the word in reference to Christianity. "The Turks think that they have the correct (true) Gottesdienst and the true Religion and mock our Christliche Religon", *WA TR 1,* 452 (#904).
18. Wilfred Cantwell Smith argues that exteriorization is the first step toward the reification of the concept of "religion." According to Smith, Roman Catholics introduced the plural "religions" because the term had a concrete reference for them (the outward pattern of religious life). "Protestants, with their concern with inner piety and personal faith, were not ready to take this step until they had exteriorized and reified their concept, which as we have just seen was only in the seventeenth century." Wilfred Cantwell Smith, *The Meaning and End of Religion,* 42. However, my research demonstrates that both Protestants and Catholics used an exteriorized concept of "religion" much earlier than Smith believed.
19. This is found in Giovo, *Ursprung des Turkischen Reichs bis auff den itzigen Solyman druch D. Paulum Jouium Bischoff Nucerin an keiserliche Maiestate Carolum V. inn welcher sprach geschrieben er nach aus dem Latin F. Bassainatis verdeutschet durch Justum Jonan,* xlaff.
20. This was done in other locations in the translation as well. For example, when Luther states, "Scilicet *Christianam religionem* longe aliud esse quam bonos mores seu bona opera" Jonas translates, "*Die Christliche Religione un rechter Christlicher Gottesdienst* viel ein höhere sache ist den menschliche gute wreck oder eusserliche scheinende tugend."
21. According to Wilfred Cantwell Smith, in the sixteenth century "religion" was "the sense of piety that prompts men to worship. It is innate in every man and is the one characteristic that lifts man above the brutes. It is an inner personal attitude." Smith, *Meaning,* 36. For his treatment of the Reformers, see also 320–337. However, "in the seventeenth and early eighteenth century this was largely superseded by a concept of systematic externalization that reflected, and served, the clash of conflicting religious parties, the emergence of a triumphant intellectualism, and the emerging new information from beyond the seas about the patterns of other men's religious life. These provided the foundations of the concept of the modern word." Smith, *Meaning,* 44. However, from the examples given above, it appears that this transition was beginning as early as the first half of the sixteenth century.
22. "Protestants, on the other hand, had to wait more than a century until they had exchanged their use of *religio* as inner piety for an externalized systematic one, before they had a plural available that they could apply to the observables of other men's religious life." Smith, *Meaning,* 237.
23. Peter Harrison, *'Religion' and the Religions in the English Enlightenment,* 7–10.
24. Höfert, 303–309.
25. This is reflected even in the more popularly written literature which, in contrast to pamphlets influenced by Luther, began their critique of Islam with a discussion of Muhammad. For example, Benedict Kuripecic, *Ein Disputation*

oder Gesprech zwayer Stalbuben So mit künigklicher Maye. Botschafft bey dem Türckischen Keyser zu Constantinopel gewesen Dieweil sy allda in jhrer beherbergung vo dem Türcken verspert beschehen, c2a-b.

26. See Francisco, especially 211–231.

27. Concerning the second article of the creed: "Und durch diesen artickel wird unser glaube gesondert von allen andern glauben auff erden." Luther, *Heerpredigt*, 186. According to the second article of the *Confessio Augustana*, the correct understanding of the person and work of Christ was the chief differentiator between truth and false religion. See also Ludwig Hagemann, *Martin Luther und der Islam*, 20–26, Nicolaus Heutger, "Luther und der Islam: Scharfe Äusserungen blieben glücklicherweise ohne Nachwirkung," 498, and Harmut Bobzin, "Martin Luthers Beitrag zu Kenntnis und Kritik des Islam," 280–283.

28. Luther believed Muslim Christology to consist of the following (chiefly negative) doctrines: 1) Jesus was without sin, 2) but nothing more than a prophet, 3) Jesus is not God's son or true God, 4) Jesus is not the world's savior, 5) Jesus did not die on the cross, and 6) Muhammad is higher than Jesus because his office is still in force. Luther responded with a categorical rejection of Islam: "Denn wer die stu(e)cke an Christo verleugket, das er Gottes son ist und fur uns gestorben sey und noch izt lebe und regire zur rechten Gottes: Was hat der mehr an Christo? Das ist Vater, Son, heiliger giest, Tauffe, Sacrament, Euangelion, glaube und alle Christliche lere und wesen dahin, Und ist an stat Christi nichts mehr, den Mahometh mit seiner lere von eigen wercken und sonderlich vom schwerd: das ist das heubtstu(e)cke des Tu(e)rckisschen glaubens, darynn auff einem hauffen alle grewel, alle yrthum, alle Teuffel auf einem hauffen ligen." Luther, *Vom Kriege*, 122ff.

29. This was true even of Knaust, the Protestant who demonstrates the most influence by the medieval literature. His first four critiques of Islam equate Islam with the Christological heresies of Sabellianism, Arianism, and "Manichaeism" (a denial of Christ's death on the cross). Knaust, d3a.

30. "Qui non honorat filium, non honorat patrem." *CR 12*, col. 1077. Also, Köhler, 48.

31. Köhler, 48

32. *CR 13*, 966; Köhler, 55–57.

33. Siegfried Raeder, "Die Türkenpredigten des Jakob Andreä," 103–106. See also Susan Boettcher, "German Orientalism in the Age of Confessional Consolidation: Jacob Andreae's *Thirteen Sermons on the Turk*, 1568."

34. Raeder, 106.

35. The "Tu(e)rcken Gott (das is der Teu(e)ffel)." Luther, *Vom Kriege*, 116.

36. For instance, in Kuripecic, c2b-3a, he stated that all Muslim works are in vain because they do not believe in God's son.

37. Giovo, t3a; Luther, *Vermanhnung*, 615.

38. According to Andreä, despite man's inability to live a sinless life before God, it was an unbreakable rule with Turks and Jews "was ein Mensch für Sünden getan habe . . . die muss er auch selbst büssen." Raeder, 106–116. Also, see Luther's preface to George of Hungary, *Libellus de ritu et moribus Turcorum*, 205ff. and Jonas, *Das siebend*, passim.

39. Walter Holsten, *Christentum und nichtchristliche Religion nach der Auffassung Luthers*, 131.

40. Holsten, *Christentum*, 131.

41. Turks must "frequently wash with water for the forgiveness of sins—almost like the Anabaptists." Knaust, d3a. According to Melanchthon, *CR 12*, 1076, Turks obtain remissions of sins on the basis of good deeds (almsgiving is specifically mentioned).

42. Melanchthon, *Opera, CR 14*, 381; Köhler, 95.

43. For Melanchthon there was no real difference between the Turks and heathens such as Plato, Xenophon. Melanchthon, *Opera, CR* 7, 584; Köhler, 95–97.
44. The most widely circulated were medieval reprints found in Theodor Bibliander, *Machumetis Saracenorum Principis, Eiusque Successorum Vitae, Ac Doctrina, Ipseque Alcoran, Quo uelut authentico legum diuinarum codice Agareni & Turcae.*
45. Bobzin, 285; Göllner, *Turcica*, vol. 3, 207; Helmut Lamparter, *Luthers Stellung zum Türkenkrieg*, 34.
46. Luther, *WA TR 5*, 221.
47. For example, *Beschreibung aller Türcischen Khayser*, a2a; Melanchthon, *Opera, CR 25*, 499.
48. Knaust, c4a-b.
49. Knaust also mentioned that Muhammad deceived the people by use of trained oxen that would come to him with the Qur'an tied to their horns. Knaust, d2a-b.
50. Knaust, b2a.
51. Knaust emphasized Muhammad's training by 1) a Jewish prophet, 2) an Egyptian heretic monk ("Vonn dem selbigenn hatt er vil hinder listige stuck/betriegerey und verfelschung der schrift gelernet"), and 3) an Egyptian Arian who also trained him in the teaching of Nestorius. "Unnd haben also samptlich auss der Judenn unnd Christen leer einen ku(e)chen gebachenn/unnd ein sonderlich Gesetz darauss gemacht." "Daher man nun wol spüren unnd merckenn kan den ursprung unnd das herkommen der Gottlesterlichen unnd schentlichen Secten des Mahomets. Wo kompt die her? eben auss der schu(e)l der Juden un Müncke unnd ihres Maysters des Teüffels." Knaust, b3b-4a.
52. "Erstlich hat diser bo(e)sswicht ein unrein uneerlich unzüchtig leben vor der welt gefu(e)rt in allerlay hu(e)rerey und ehebruch." Knaust, b4b. For the connection with Lucifer and homosexuality, see Knaust, c1a-b.
53. Knaust, c1b-2b.
54. Knaust, c2b.
55. Knaust, d1a-b.
56. This collection of fables supposedly in the Qur'an was intended to show its lies and foolishness. Included are: Solomon's miracles, talking to animals, Muhammad dividing the moon with his fingers, the origin of the prohibition of drinking wine by the incident of two angels which came to earth and became drunk, a woman who became the Morning Star, the origination of the pig from the refuse of the elephant, the origination myths of the rat and mouse, and the myth that God will kill all creatures at the end of the world to be alone and will then raise them up again. That Knaust believed these miracle stories to be in the Qur'an and accepted by Muslims demonstrates that Knaust had no firsthand knowledge of the Qur'an or of genuine Turkish spirituality. His influences were entirely medieval. Knaust, d4a-e2a.
57. Knaust, e2c-4b
58. See Luther's introduction to *Libellus*, 205; *Vom kriege*, 107–110.
59. Rudolf Pfister, "Reformation, Türken und Islam," 353. Although Thomas Burman's *Reading the Qur'an* is extraordinary in dealing with late medieval Latin Qur'an editions, he unfortunately neglects Bibliander's work beyond a few brief mentions.
60. Luther, *Vom Kriege*, 121–122.
61. Luther called the Turkish faith "Epicurean" (meaning purely rational). Luther, *Vermahnung*, 614. A similar view was presented by Justus Jonas: "The Qur'an contains nothing but unadulterated, shameless lies and horrible blasphemy; for therein Muhammad boasts of being a prophet sent by God to alter the teachings of the gospel. He denies and negates the divinity of Christ and rejects the

true Christian teachings of grace, forgiveness of sins, and faith—which constitute the true and genuine service of God. But in order to give a semblance of truth to these diabolical lies, he accommodates his doctrine to human reason." Jonas, *Das siebend Capital*, e3a. (Bohnstedt translation)

62. "Denn sein gesetz leret nichts anders, den was menschliche witze und vernunfft wol leiden kan. Und was er ym Euangelio funden hat, das zu schweer und hoch zu gleuben gewest, das hat er ausgethan, sonderlich aber das Christus Got sey und uns erlo(e)set hat mit seinem tode." Luther, *Heerpredigt*, 165–167.

63. Luther's introduction to Bibliander's Qur'an, 565.

64. Luther interpreted the Islamic teaching on the un-translatableness of the Qur'an to be a secret concession of its falsehood on the part of the Muslims. Bobzin, 276.

65. Luther's source for this was a corrupt edition of Ricoldo de Monte Croce. Karl-Heinz Bernhardt, "Luther und der Islam," 88–89.

66. "Die grosse Massenden Muslime habe sich aus deshalb an den Koran gehalten, weil der Islam in seiner Geschichte so erfolgreich gewesen ist." Bobzin, 280; Luther, *Vom Kriege*, 141.

67. *WA TR* 1, 454 (#904).

68. The Qur'an is therefore "lex accomodata ad militare genus hominum." Melanchthon, *Opera*, CR 25, 499. "Because he knew that divisions rise through articles difficult [to understand] that cannot be discerned by reason, he removed the doctrine of the thre persons of the trinity and held solely that God was a single person." Melanchthon, *Opera*, CR 12, 1074. See also, Köhler, 31–32.

69. In "bound not free speech." Melanchthon, *Opera*, CR 11, 865; Göllner, *Turcica*, vol. 3, 213.

70. It is also interesting that Melanchthon prefers to quote the Qur'an in Greek. Since I cannot find any evidence of a Greek Qur'an that would have been available in sixteenth-century Wittenberg, Melanchthon likely adapted them from the inaccurate Greek translation of Ricoldo de Monte Croce's *Confutatio Alcoran*. Köhler, 46; Melanchthon, *Opera*, CR 12, 1075–1077.

71. Holsten, "Reformation und Missions," 24, 28.

72. See Appendix 2, Chapter 13.

73. "After the fast is their Easter (Bairam) three day feast, when they paint their fingernails and toenails red, (also horses' tails and hooves). The women do not paint only nails, but their entire hands and feet." See Appendix 3, "Of Their Pilgrims." Also the German translation, Georgijevic, b3a.

74. See Appendix 2, Chapter 13, Appendix 3, "Of Their Almsgiving." *Ausz Ratschlag Erasmi*, 17b. Georgijevic, c2b, c3a.

75. They made offerings of food at graves, freed captive birds, gave bread to fish, thinking that they would receive some reward from God for these activities. Georgijevic, see Appendix 3, "Of Their Tombs," *Von den Türcken gebreuchen*, c3b.

76. In fact, it appears that sixteenth-century writers misunderstood every call to prayer to be a call for corporate gathering at the mosque.

77. According to Georgijevic, Friday was honored because that was the day that Muhammad was born. See Appendix 3, "Of Their Temples." See also Köhler, 55.

78. Concerning washings, see also Appendix 2 Chapter 13. Luther saw in the washings an imitation of the Nazarites. Luther, *Vom Kriege*, 122.

79. According to Georgijevic, women rarely go to church, sometimes on Easter (for Georgijevic this was the Muslim celebration following Ramadan), sometimes on Fridays. They do, however, pray in the churches at night from nine to midnight. See Appendix 3, "Of Their Temples." Luther knew that the women were veiled and went to a separate place to pray "with great quietness, reverence, and discipline." Luther, *Heerpredigt*, 187.

80. See Appendix 3, "Of Their Temples." In the original pamphlet *Von den Türcken gebreuchen*, b2b.
81. For example, Kuripecic, c2a-b.
82. See Appendix 3, "Of Their Priests." *Von den Türcken gebreuchen*, b4b.
83. Köhler, 55.
84. Luther, *WA TR 5*, 532, 740 (6195). Melanchthon, *Opera, CR 12*, 1076.
85. See Appendix 3, "Of Their Circumcision." In the German translation, the most important section is Georgijevic, b3b-4a.
86. The designation 'Sufi' (Sophi) is found in the sixteenth-century literature, but as the name of the leaders of Shi'a Persia and not for the Turkish mystics. However, the use of terms such as 'Dervish' make it clear that the descriptions of 'Turkish monks' did indeed refer to Sufi brotherhoods.
87. Luther, *Heerpredigt*, 187. The external, "false" religion of these Turks became an important ingredient in Luther's anti-papal polemic.
88. See Appendix 3, "Of Their Monks."
89. In addition to the material from Georgijevic, see also Jonas, *Das siebend Capitel*, e2b.
90. Georgijevic stated that mystical pregnancies ("children of the holy spirit") were a regular occurrence. See Appendix 3, "Of Their Temples."
91. See Appendix 2, Chapter 20. This chapter listed four antithetical religious groups in Turkey: 1) Priests hold the main offices and positions; 2) Dermscher who believe that not the law but mercy saves, their following is from the most pious and spiritual of the people; 3) Czofilar who believe that they are saved by service, not mercy or law, with emphasis on special prayers; and 4) Horife (or heretics) a secret group (because they are persecuted) who believe that each people is a law unto themselves and that religious beliefs must not be imposed on anyone.
92. Almost nothing was known about the Shi'a in the Middle Ages. See Daniel, 318–319.
93. For example: *Neüwe Zeitung vom Türcken. Warhafftige anzeyge: kommende vo Constantinopel, von dem mercklichen schaden un niderlag, die der Türckisch Keyser vom Sophi dem grossen König in Persia* (Worms: Wagner, 1535), *Newe Zeyttung des rathschlags und reisse der kriegssrüstung, so der Türck, newlich wider Carolum den Romischen Kaiser und die Christen fürgenohmen, mit anzeigung der niderlag, so er von dem Sophi erlitten hat. Auch mit warhafftigen beschreiben der Religion, und weise zu kriegen, so die Perser gebrauchend erlitten hat* (Dresden: Stöckel, 1536), *Newe Zeyttung von Kayserlicher Maiestat, vo dem Türcken, un von dem grossen Sophi etc.* (Augsburg: n.p., 1535).
94. *Warhaffte beschreibung wie der Sophi auss Persia*, a1b.
95. Hismael Sophi "gros vnd namhafftig worden, den er hette des Mahomets gesetz mit newen auslegungen vercleret, vnd ein newe Religion eingefu(e)ret." Later the Shi'a are called a "sect" that greatly alarmed the Ottoman Turks. Giovo, r1a.
96. *Warhaffte beschreibung wie der Sophi auss Persia*, a1b.
97. Chew, 53.
98. Luther, *Heerpredigt*, 188.
99. Even though they often did not use the term *Ketzerei* (heresy) or its equivalent, the stronger Protestant anti-Turkish rhetoric grew, the closer it sounded like medieval denunciations of Islam as heresy. See, for example, Andreas Osiander, *Unterricht und vermanung*, a2b. "verzweyffelten [verdammten] Machmeds verfu(e)ische, gottsslesterliche, teuffliche gruel und le(e)gen."
100. Rudolf Pfister, "Das Türkenbüchlein Theodor Biblianders," 449–450.
101. In his introduction to Giovo's *Ursprung*, Melanchthon stated that Arabia was the birthplace of all kinds of heresy. Giovo, b3a-b. In the first article of the

Confessio Augustana, the *Mahometisten* are listed together with the Arians as deniers of the divinity of Christ. Bernhardt, 265. See also, Göllner, *Turcica*, vol. 3, 213; Köhler, 88.

102. "Diende ut distinctionen suae multitudinis a caeteris gentibus faceret, et aliqua religionis species esset, ceremonias addidit, sed paucas, quia turba militaris non patitur multa talia vincula." Melanchthon, *Opera, CR 12*, 1076.

103. Knaust, d3a.

104. From Christians they took praise of Mary, Christ, the Apostles, and other saints; from the Jews they took the prohibition of wine, fasting during certain times of the year, washings like the Naserei, and eating off of the ground. Luther, *Vom Kriege*, 122–123.

105. "The Jew and the Turk argue against the truth of God; neither believes the trinity or baptism. Both agree on circumcision and in other external ceremonies." *WA TR 5*, 532 (#6195).

106. For example, *Vier warhafftige Missiue*, especially c3a.

107. Franck's German edition of George of Hungary, *Chronica*, a2b. Notice the separation of *Glaube* and *Religion*, as well as the plural 'Religions.'

108. The identification of the four divisions of Islam comes directly from George of Hungary. "Hie sehen wir das allain der Christlich glawb in sechtzehen oder sibenzehen Sect und hauptglawben zerthailt ist wyll nit sagen yn wie vil ketzerey ein yeder glawb in im selbs zerthailt und gehet gerad mit uns zu als mit den Türcken inn der Türckey, ya vil erger weil sy allain in vier sect wir aber mehr dann in tausent zerthailt seyndt." *Chronica*, Franck trans., a2a. See also Bernhard Capesius, "Sebastian Francks Verdeutschung des 'Tractatus de ritu et moribus Turcorum'," 116–124.

109. For example, Matthias Kretz, *Ein sermon von dem Turckenzug durch Doctor Mathiam Krecz zu Mosspurg in sant Castelsstifft gepredigt* (n.p., 1532); Johann Faber, *Oratio De origine, Potentia, ac tyrannide Thurcorum, Ad Serenissimum & potentissimum Henricum Angliae & Franciae Regem* (Vienna: n.p., 1528). Similarities with Islamic predestination were also used against Calvinism by Catholics, in fact the two greatest Catholic Orientalists (Postel and Widmanstetter) brought their Islamic study expressly into fight against French Protestantism. Bobzin, 286–87. Göllner, *Turcica*, vol. 3, 197.

110. Göllner, *Turcica*, vol. 3, 214.

111. *Eyn sendbrieff wie eyner in der Türkei wont seinem freundt in Deutsche landt* (n.p., 1527). Quoted in Bohnstedt, 24.

112. Papal nuncio Francesco Chieregato stated that "We [the papal court] are occupied with the negotiations for the general war against the Turk, and for that particular war against that nefarious Martin Luther, who is a greater evil to Christendom than the Turk." Quoted in Kenneth M. Setton, "Lutheranism and the Turkish Peril," 147.

113. "Die Türken sind besser als die Protestanten, den wenn sie die Christen leben lassen, so erlauben sie ihren als Katoliken zu leben. Die Protestanten dagegen, wenn sie das Menschen leben lassen, vernichten die Seelen unter dem Vorwand, sie zu reformieren." Quoted in Hans Pfeffermann, *Die Zusammenarbeit der Renaissancepäpste mit den Türken*, 156.

114. Luther stated that the Roman Catholic church never seriously dealt with Islam, because if they did, they would be attacking their own religion. "Turca et papa in formis religionis nihil differunt neque variant nisi vocabulis et ceremoniis." Lamparter, 44–45.

115. Luther, *Heerpredigt*, 187; Rudolf Mau, "Luthers Stellung zu den Türken," 656.

116. Luther stated that the Turks outdo even our strictest monks, in fact their works are so enticing, that no Pope, monk, or cleric would remain in his faith if he spent just three days with the Turks. "Ego plane credo nullam Papistam,

monachum, clerum aut eorum fidei socium, si inter Turcos triduo agerent, in sua fide mansurum." Luther's forward to *Libellus*, 206.

117. "Christlischen Türken" in Luther, *Vermahnung*, 391; Bobzin 269. The Turks combine fanaticism with popular teaching "sicut fit ab Anabaptistis." Melanchthon, *Opera, CR 12*, 1075–1076.

118. The Pope is the true antichrist; although the Turks are a danger, they are not as bad as the Pope. *WA BR 1*, 270 (#121).

119. Luther, *Heerpredigt*, 195.

120. For example the Kinderlied also puts "gotlosen Lehren und Tyrannen, falschen Christen und den Türken" in parallel. See Martin Luther, *Ein Kinderlied and* Spangenberg, *Der LXXIX Psalm*.

121. See Luther, *Vermahnung*, Dietrich, *Wie man das Volck zur Busz*, Jonas, *Christlicher und kurtzer unterricht*.

122. Osiander, *Unterricht und vermahnung*, a1a-a2b.

123. Smith, *Images*, 77–83.

References

Ausz Ratschlage Herren Erasmi von Roterdam die Türcken zubekriegen Der ursprung unnd alle geschichten der selbigen gegen Römische Keyser unnd gemeyne Christenheit vo anbegin des türckischen namenn nach der kürtze new verteutscht. n.p., 1530.

Bäbstlicher heilikeit sampt Römscher Keiserlicher Maiestat auch anderer kristlichen Künig un Fürste botschaffte anschlag wider die Türken. n.p., 1518.

Bernhardt, Karl-Heinz. "Luther und der Islam." *Standpunkt* 11 (1983): 263–265, 328–330; 12 (1984): 87–91.

Beschreibung aller Türcischen Khayser. Von jrem ursprung un anfang her wie vil derselben biss auff dise unser zeit und jar geregiert was auch derselben jeder von Landt und Leut Bestritten uberkhomen und in seinen gwalt unnd herschung gebracht. n.p., 1531.

Bibliander, Theodor. *Machumetis Saracenorum Principis, Eiusque Successorum Vitae, Ac Doctrina, Ipseque Alcoran, Quo uelut authentico legum diuinarum codice Agareni & Turcae.* Basel: Oporin, 1543 and 1550.

Bobzin, Harmut. "Martin Luthers Beitrag zu Kenntnis und Kritik des Islam." *Neue Zeitschrift für Systematische Theologie* 27:3 (1985): 262–289.

Boettcher, Susan. "German Orientalism in the Age of Confessional Consolidation: Jacob Andreae's *Thirteen Sermons on the Turk*, 1568." *Comparative Studies of South Asia, Africa and the Middle East* 24:2 (2004): 101–115.

Bohnstedt, John W. "The Infidel Scourge of God: The Turkish Menace as Seen by German Pamphleteers of the Reformation Era." *Transactions of the American Philosophical Society* NS 58:9 (1968).

Burman, Thomas. *Reading the Qur'an in Latin Christendom, 1140–1560.* Philadelphia: University of Pennsylvania Press, 2007.

Capesius, Bernhard. "Sebastian Francks Verdeutschung des 'Tractatus de ritu et moribus Turcorum'." *Deutsche Forschung in Südosten* 3:1 (March 1944): 103–128.

Chew, Samuel C. *The Crescent and the Rose.* New York: Octagon Books, 1974.

Dietrich, Veit. *Wie man das Volck zur Busz und ernstlichem gebet wider den Türcken auff der Cantzel vermanen sol.* Nürnberg: Berg, 1542.

Eyn sendbrieff wie eyner in der Türkei wont seinem freundt in Deutsche landt. n.p., 1527.

Faber, Johann. *Oratio De origine, Potentia, ac tyrannide Thurcorum, Ad Serenissimum & potentissimum Henricum Angliae & Franciae Regem.* Vienna: n.p., 1528.

Francisco, Adam. *Martin Luther and Islam: A Study in Sixteenth-Century Polemics and Apologetics.* London: Brill, 2007.

George of Hungary. *Chronica unnd beschreibung der Türckey mit yhrem begriff, ynnhalt, provincien, völckern, ankunfft, kriege, reysen, glauben, religionen, gesatzen, sytten, geperde, weis, regimente, frükeyt, unnd bossheiten.* Sebastian Franck, trans. Nürnberg: Peypus, 1530.

Georgijevic, Bartholomew. *Von der Türken gebreuchen, gewonheyten und Ceremonien.* Nürnberg: Guldenmunde, 1544.

Giovo, Paolo. *Ursprung des Turkischen Reichs bis auff den itzigen Solyman druch D. Paulum Jouium Bischoff Nucerin an keiserliche Maiestate Carolum V. inn welcher sprach geschrieben er nach aus dem Latin F. Bassainatis verdeutschet durch Justum Jonan.* Augsburg: Steiner, 1538.

Göllner, Carl. *Turcica: Die europäischen Türkendrucke des XVI. Jahrhunderts. Vol. 3. Die Türkenfrage in der öffentlichen Meinung Europas im 16. Jahrhundert.* Bucharest: Editura Academiei, 1968.

Grünpeck, Josef. *Ein Dyalogus Doctor Joseph Grünpeck von Burckhausen.* Landshut: Weissenburger, 1522.

Hagemann, Ludwig. *Martin Luther und der Islam.* Altenberge: Verlag für christliche-islamische Schriften, 1983.

Harrison, Peter. *'Religion' and the Religions in the English Enlightenment.* Cambridge: Cambridge University Press, 1990.

Heutger, Nicolaus. "Luther und der Islam: Scharfe Äusserungen blieben glücklicherweise ohne Nachwirkung." *Luther Monatsblatt* 22 (1983): 497–498.

Höfert, Almut. *Den Feind beschreiben: "Türkengefahr" und europäisches Wissen über das Osmanische Reich 1450–1600.* Frankfurt: Campus Verlag, 2003.

Holsten, Walter. "Reformation und Missions." *Archiv für Reformationsgeschichte* 44 (1953): 1–32.

Holsten, Walter. *Christentum und nichtchristliche Religion nach der Auffassung Luthers.* Gütersloh: Bertelsmann, 1932.

Jonas, Jonas. *Christlicher und kurtzer unterricht von vergebung der Sünder, und Seligkeit Item, Ein Gebet D. Martini Luther, wider den Türcken, und alle Feinde der Christlichen Kirchen.* Wittenberg: n.p., 1542.

Jonas, Justus. *Das siebend Capitel Danielis von des Türken Gottes lesterung und schrecklicher moderey mit unterrich.* Wittenberg: Lufft, 1529.

Knaust, Heinrich. *Von geringem herkommen schentlichern leben schmehlichem ende des Türckischen abgots Machomets und seiner verdamlichen und Gotsslesterischen Ler.* Berlin: Weisen, 1542.

Köhler, Manfred. *Melanchthon und der Islam: Ein Beitrag zur Klärung des Verhältnisses zwischen Christentum und Fremdreligionen in der Reformationszeit.* Leipzig: Klotz, 1938.

Kretz, Matthias. *Ein sermon von dem Turckenzug durch Doctor Mathiam Krecz zu Mosspurg in sant Castelsstifft gepredigt.* n.p., 1532.

Kuripecic, Benedict. *Ein Disputation oder Gesprech zwayer Stalbuben So mit künigklicher Maye. Botschafft bey dem Türckischen Keyser zu Constantinopel gewesen Dieweil sy allda in jhrer beherbergung vo dem Türcken verspert beschehen.* Augsburg: Steiner, 1531.

Lamparter, Helmut. *Luthers Stellung zum Türkenkrieg.* Munich: Lempp, 1940.

Luther, Martin. *Ein Kinderlied, zu singen, wider die zween Ertzfeinde Christi und seiner heiligen Kirchen, den Bapst un Türcke, etc.* Wittenberg: Klug, 1543.

Luther, Martin. *Heerpredigt wider den Türken* (1530). *WA 30II,* 160–197.

Luther, Martin. *Large Catechism* (1530). *WA 30I,* 125–238.

Luther, Martin. *Verlegung des Alcoran Bruder Richardi, Prediger Ordens. Verdeutscht und herausgegeben von Martin Luther* (1542). *WA 53,* 261–396.

Luther, Martin. *Vermahnung zum Gebet wider den Türken* (1541). *WA 51,* 585–625.

Luther, Martin. *Vier tröstliche Psalmen An die Königynn zu Hungern aussgelegt durch Martinum Luther.* n.p., 1527.

Luther, Martin. *Vom Kriege wider den Türcken* (1529). *WA 30II,* 107–148.

Luther, Martin. *Vorrede zu Theodor Biblianders Koranausgabe* (1543) *WA 53,* 569–572.

Luther, Martin. *WA Briefwechsel (BR)* 1, 270–272 (#121).

Luther, Martin. *WA Tischrede (TR)* 1, 448–456 (#904).

Luther, Martin. *WA Tischrede (TR)* 3, 418–419 (#3571).

Luther, Martin. *WA Tischrede (TR)* 5, 532 (#6195).

Luther, Martin and Philip Melanchthon. *Zwen trostbriefe geschriben an der Durchleuchtigen und hochgebornen Fürsten und Herrn Herrn Joachim Churfürste und Marckgraven zu Brandenburger vom Türcken zuge.* Nürnberg: Berg, 1532.

Mau, Rudolf. "Luthers Stellung zu den Türken." In *Leben und Werk Martin Luthers von 1526 bis 1546.* Helmar Junghans, ed. Göttingen: Vandenhoeck and Ruprecht, 1983, 647–662.

Melanchthon, Philip. *Opera: Corpus Reformatorum.* Vols. 7, 11, 12, 25. Halle: Schwetschke, 1843ff.

Neüwe Zeitung vom Türcken. Warhafftige anzeyge: kommende vo Constantinopel, von dem mercklichen schaden un niderlag, die der Türckisch Keyser vom Sophi dem grossen König in Persia. Worms: Wagner, 1535.

Newe Zeyttung des rathschlags und reisse der kriegssrüstung, so der Türck, newlich wider Carolum den Romischen Kaiser und die Christen fürgenohmen, mit anzeigung der niderlag, so er von dem Sophi erlitten hat. Auch mit warhafftigen beschreiben der Religion, und weise zu kriegen, so die Perser gebrauchend erlitten hat. Dresden: Stöckel, 1536.

Newe Zeyttung von Kayserlicher Maiestat, vo dem Türcken, un von dem grossen Sophi etc. Augsburg: n.p., 1535.

Norman, Daniel. *Islam and the West: The Making of an Image.* Edinburgh: Edinburgh University Press, 1962.

Osiander, Andreas. *Unterricht und vermanung wie man wider den Türcken beten und streyten soll. Auff ansuchung etlicher gutter Herrn und Freunde. An die jhenigen gestalt bey denen der Türck schon angriffen und schaden gethon und sie desselben noch alle tag gewertig sein müssen.* n.p., 1542.

Pfeffermann, Hans. *Die Zusammenarbeit der Renaissancepäpste mit den Türken.* Wintherthur: Mondial Verlag, 1946.

Pfister, Rudolf. "Das Türkenbüchlein Theodor Biblianders." *Theologische Zeitung 9* (1953): 438–468.

Pfister, Rudolf. "Reformation, Türken und Islam." *Zwingliana* 10:6 (1956): 345–375.

Raeder, Siegfried. "Die Türkenpredigten des Jakob Andreä." In *Theologen und Theolgie an der Universität Tübignen* Martin Brecht, ed. Tübingen: J. C. B. Mohr, 1977, 96–122.

Rodinson, Maxime. *Europe and the Mystique of Islam*. Roger Veinus, trans. Seattle: University of Washingon Press, 1987.

Römischer Keyserlicher Maiestat Christenlichste Kriegs Rüstung wider die unglaubigen, anzug in Hispanien un Sardinien, Ankunfft in African, und eroberung des Ports zu Thunisi im monat Junio Anno 1535. n.p. 1535.

Rouillard, Clarence Dana. *The Turk in French History, Thought, and Literature, 1520–1660*. Paris: Boivin, 1940.

Schwoebel, Robert. *The Shadow of the Crescent: The Renaissance Image of the Turk, 1453–1517*. New York: St. Martin's Press, 1967.

Setton, Kenneth M. "Lutheranism and the Turkish Peril." *Balkan Studies* 3 (1962): 133–168.

Smith, Charlotte Colding. *Images of Islam, 1453–1600: Turks in Germany and Central Europe*. London: Pickering and Chatto, 2014.

Smith, Wilfred Cantwell. *The Meaning and End of Religion*. New York: Harper and Row, 1978.

Spangenberg, Johann. *Der LXXIX Psalm auff die weise, Aus tieffer not*. n.p., 1545.

Vier warhafftige Missiue, eyne der Frawen Isabella, Künigin un nachgelassne Wittib in Ungern, wie untreulich der Türck und die jhren mit jhr umbgangen. n.p., 1542.

Warhaffte beschreibung wie der Sophi auss Persia den Türcken erlegt, die Statt Babilonia eingenommen, auch was Glauben, Sitten, und Kiegsrüstung er im brauch habe. n.p., 1536.

5 Knowledge and Depictions of the Turks

> When I consider history, I find that there has been no nation that has prac-
> ticed more blasphemy of God, brutality, shameful fornication, and every
> kind of wild and chaotic living than the Turks.[1]
>
> Philip Melanchthon

In addition to interest in Islam, Germans during the Reformation were also
interested in the Turks as a cultural/ethnic unit. Although they were most
often conflated, separating Islam from the Turks in analysis enabled them to
do two things. First, they could respect, admire, and even grudgingly praise
Turkish cultural and political institutions without having to deal with the
baggage of a blasphemous religion. Second, and this is in the opposite direction, they could link the Turks with other ethnic barbarian groups noted
for their cruelty without having to explain the 'glittering righteousness' of
their religious practices. Yet there was no clear-cut sacred-secular dichot-
omy. The religious life of the Turks was often placed in a separate category
of description, but because Islam of course pervaded all aspects of society
religious justifications for social and political things appear throughout the
descriptions.

There was some understanding that the Turks were ethnically different from Arabs, but little attention to Arabs was paid. It is interesting that
Reformation-era Germans generally were not concerned with general Muslim or Arabic history. Outside of limited biographical interest in Muhammad, only the relation between the Roman Empire and the rapid expansion
of Islam was frequently discussed. The standard explanation for the rise of
Islam was that Rome was to blame.[2] Islamic power was launched when
Heraclius did not deal fairly with Arabic mercenaries used in the Persian
wars, who then turned against their former masters and defeated them.[3]
Using false signs and wonders, with promises of plunder and sexual freedom, Muhammad then enticed many of the Christians of the Eastern Roman
Empire to convert. Other than this brief summary, there is almost a complete lacuna of information on early Islam. The primary areas concerning
the Turks that interested sixteenth-century Germans were the history of the

Ottoman Sultans, questions concerning the ethnic origin of the Turks, the brutality and sexual perversity of the Turks, and aspects of Turkish society, government, military, and slavery.

One aspect of Turkish society that received considerable attention was history. (See Figure 5.1) Sustained historical interest in the early sixteenth century began with the rise of the Turks. In fact, some authors seem to believe that Islamic history *is* the history of the Turks. This is reflected in the fact that many pamphlets claimed Turkish rule began in AD 755 or even as late as AD 900.[4] There were mixed motivations behind the numerous publications of the history of the Turks. The use of history in the service of war propaganda should not be underestimated. Reminders of the increasing power of the Turks, the past greatness of Christian kings and kingdoms, and the occasional vulnerability of the followers of Muhammad could serve as a powerful encouragement for a war or Crusade.[5]

However, there were other reasons than propaganda for historical writing in sixteenth-century Germany. Melanchthon's introduction to *Ursprung*

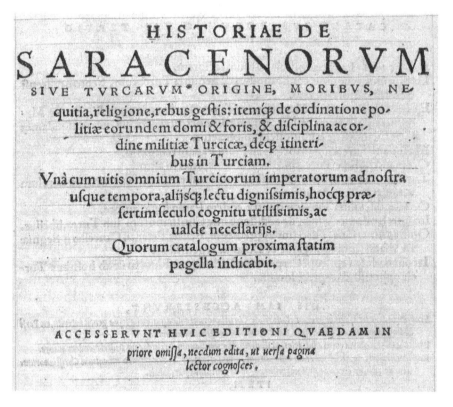

Figure 5.1 Contents page of volume 3 of Bibliander's Qur'an, 1550

des Türckischen Reichs was an extended apology for the value of princes facing contemporary problems of the study of the 'rise and fall of kingdoms.'[6] The German translation of Paolo Giovo's *History* and Sebastian Franck's *Chronicle* are good representatives of a more journalistic reporting of events. Several other pamphlets and broadsheets offer non-derogatory summaries of the reigns of Turkish sultans for apparently no other reason than public interest in the unknown or foreign.[7]

As has been examined at length by Margaret Meserve in the context of fifteenth-century Italian humanist writers, the ethnic origin of the Turks also was considered especially important in Reformation-era publications. For sixteenth-century Germans, the confrontation between Islam and the West stood in a close connection with the question of the ancestry of the Turks.[8] In pamphlets, the medieval view that the Turks were descended from the Trojans was known, but generally discounted.[9] To equate the Turks with Aenaeus' kin would have been to relate barbarity too close to civilization. Instead, sixteenth-century scholars traced the Turks' descent from the biblical Esau[10] and/or from statements originating in Pliny and Herodotus that they are a type of Tartar or Scythian from the vicinity of *Iura* or *Turcae* in or beyond the *Tyssagetis* (Caucasus), as did the fifteenth-century Italian humanists Meserve has analyzed.[11] Luther gave an important alternate explanation based upon his eschatological exposition of Ezekiel Chapters 38 and 39.[12] According to his *büchlein* translation of these two chapters, the Turks were the biblical Magog (shortened to Gog in several scriptural texts by the Holy Spirit out of fury and rage).[13] Luther traced the etymology of Gog from Hebrew for *Dach* [roof], meaning *Dachman* or one who lives under a roof. This is a perfect description of the Turks, Luther wrote, for their huts are open on all sides, "so that they can carry on their perversity like animals."

According to the early sixteenth-century documents, the Turks first became involved in the course of history when they were invited as mercenaries by (the sources disagree) the King of Armenia, the Persians, or the Saracens themselves. After their conversion to Islam, the Turks gained power over the remainder of the followers of Muhammad due to internecine rivalry and divisions.[14] About 1200 the Turkish leader Soldan captured the East and appointed seven governors: Othman, Ermem, Germem, Garchan, Andin, Menthess, and Caroman. Rivalry brought a war in which Othman became king of Turkey and Caroman conquered the remaining Islamic territories.[15]

The history of the Turks after Othman (also called Ottoman) was written in a series of plain, brief descriptions of the reigns of the twelve (generally, but also eleven) Turkish sultans through Sulaiman.[16] The conquests of each ruler is emphasized; a short side note was added occasionally concerning the fratricide that accompanied the Sultans' ascension. Almost no other information is given. These lists sometimes consider party leaders to be official Sultans during interregnums, but are otherwise accurate. Through the frequent publication of *Neue Zeitungen*, there was much more information available on Sulaiman than on any of the preceding sultans.

Depictions of the Character of the Turks

"When I consider history", Melanchthon wrote, "I find that there has been no nation that has practiced more blasphemy of God, brutality, shameful fornication, and every kind of wild and chaotic living than the Turks."[17] This was quite a judgment for a humanist scholar well acquainted with the conventional representations of evil in the Western tradition. In most of the literature of the early sixteenth century, the Turks were not simply considered evil, cruel, barbarous—but the very epitome of these characteristics. This was due in part to rhetoric in the service of the Hapsburg-Ottoman military conflict. Crusade propaganda alone does not fully explain the extreme nature of these judgments, however, especially since they are found in those who emphasized a spiritual rather than a military response. Rather, in the Ottoman advance Germans faced a cultural and religious 'other' that struck holy terror deep within the social consciousness of the people. In Luther's language, the Turks were the devil incarnate: inhumanly violent, treacherous, and demonically lascivious.[18] They were indeed an enemy of cosmic proportions.

The primary characteristic of the Ottoman Turks depicted in the *Türkenbüchlein*, broadsheets, and *Lieder* was excessive violence and cruelty. This violence was especially frightening because it was directed specifically at Christians. In fact, the *raison d'etre* for the Turks was to extirpate Christianity. They were portrayed as enjoying nothing more than the indiscriminate killing of all who call themselves Christians, "For he [the Turk] is the enemy of the Christian name."[19]

What is worse, several authors declared, the Turks consider this violence to be a righteous deed, pleasing to God. Muhammad had commanded his followers to commit perpetual aggression, to conquer lands and peoples and to spread his teaching by means of the sword. The Qur'an itself was designed to appeal to the violent nature of unredeemed man. It not only allowed war, murder, looting, but actually commanded them and promised a sensual paradise to those that died in the service of this aggression.[20]

Additional evidence of Turkish cruelty was found in the treatment of their enemies. *Neue Zeitungen* covering the European campaigns of the Turks reported wholesale massacres of Christians and the enslavement of hundreds of thousands, most of them innocent non-combatants.[21] Furthermore, rather than displaying chivalric honor, the Turks shamefully abused their captives-mutilating, raping, and murdering them.

German pamphleteers employed images of attacks on innocent and helpless victims to prove the inhuman barbarity of the Ottomans. First, the Turks murdered the elderly. One broadsheet graphically displayed this

Figure 5.2 Turkish Cruelty, Matthias Gerung, 1530

Used by permission of the Universität- und Forschungsbibliothek Erfurt. UB Erfurt, Dep. Erf. 03-Na 4° 00287 (50).

violence and added the text: "We beat the elderly to death to make fun of the Christian faith."[22] The rape, murder, and mutilation (especially slicing off breasts) of women was frequently mentioned. (See Figure 5.2) When the Turks conquered a city they would pass around the women like gifts and then behead them when they were finished.[23] The Turks were also displayed as grotesque slaughterers of children, beasts who even ripped unborn babies from their mother's wombs.[24] (See Figure 5.3) The image of a Turk impaling a Christian child became so common as to achieve almost iconic status in the publications of the period.[25]

German pamphlets also declared the Turks to be perfidious liars. They claimed that the Qur'an states a Muslim does not need to keep promises made with those of another religion.[26] Historical examples were given to prove this; surrender terms and offers of tolerance given by the Turks were blatant deceptions.[27] Nothing the Turks said could be trusted, so Christian soldiers should fight to the bitter end.

Lasciviousness was another chief characteristic of the Turks. The critique of the Turkish character was based primarily on views of polygamy, the treatment of women, rapine practiced in the Turkish raids on Christian territory, and charges of sexual perversity. "Mars and Venus, say the poets, want to be near one another."[28] It was common knowledge that Muhammad permitted multiple wives, a sure sign of sexual perversity. Concerning this highly sensitive issue, no German author demonstrated accurate knowledge of Muslim polygyny. The best educated stated that Muslims may have twelve wives and as many concubines as they desire;[29] popular pamphlets stated that the number of wives was limited only by the amount of their lust.[30]

Permissive divorce particularly bothered the German pamphleteers. It was reported that women were bought and sold like cattle, mistreated and despised.[31] The Turks set aside their wives for any reason any time they want.[32] The ability of the man to break the marital bond whenever he chose was considered a blasphemy to the marital estate. "That is no true marriage if the man may abandon the wife as it pleases him and may take as many other women as he wants; true marriage is an eternal contract."[33] Turkish marriage is nothing but *whorerei* [whoredom], thus all Turkish children are children of whores.[34]

It was widely believed that Muhammad permitted (or at least did not discourage) various kinds of sexual perversity. Homosexuality was most frequently mentioned in this context, both in ecclesiastical and popular literature.[35] According to some *Türkenbüchlein*, the Turks did not consider it a sin. A whole host of additional charges of sexual perversity were made, including sodomy, bestiality, and child molestation.[36] The majority of pamphlets from every confession agreed with Cochlaeus: Turkish morality has nothing in common with humanity, "the life of the Turks consists of the worst of everything."[37]

Despite the universality of the preceding condemnations, there were many indications of a grudging admiration of the Turks, and even a few voices

Figure 5.3 Turks as Wild Bear, Matthias Gerung, 1530

that actually praised Turkish morality. The most positive statements came from fictitious captured Turks or Turkish representatives in dialogue pamphlets. They declared that the reports of the Turkish atrocities were only false rumors; Sulaiman was no murdering tyrant.[38]

Pamphlets that reported the experiences of formerly captured Christians or travelers to Turkey also presented positives of Turkish society. Turks do not drink wine, gorge themselves as Germans, wear flashy clothes, build pretentious buildings, or swear very much. Rather, they are humble, disciplined, modest, unpretentious, hospitable, and obedient to authority—in short, everything that the German Christians should be, but are not.[39] Much of this admiration must be seen in the context of Protestant attempts to reform Christian living or to discredit Roman Catholicism.[40] A German congregation being told that the Turks were more moral than they were was hardly a tribute to Islamic ethics. "Es ist kein mensch so arg, dass er hat kein guts an sich." There may be some good in Turkish society, but even the best was only Satan masquerading as an angel of light.

Knowledge and Depictions of Turkish Society and Government

The rigorous organization and disciplined life of the Ottoman Empire held an attraction to many in Christendom.[41] When German pamphleteers examined Turkish society and government, they examined it mirror in hand, and consciously related Christian weakness to supposed Turkish strengths.[42] In the final verdict, however, the Turks were 'barbarians' compared with the Christians. Justus Jonas, for example, noted that several books praised the morality and discipline of the Turks, but argued that the entire social structure is nevertheless completely contrary to both divine and human law because it is based upon war and violence.[43] This paradoxical combination of grudging admiration alongside sharp denunciation is found throughout the early sixteenth-century *Türkenbüchlein*.

The ringing denunciations did not stop German pamphleteers from being interested in every conceivable aspect of Turkish society from personal toiletry to military organization. Most of this information was gained through contemporary reports from the Balkans or from the escaped slaves George of Hungary and Georgijevic. The frequency with which the following descriptions are repeated demonstrates the importance that contemporary sources had for the formation of Western images of Islam in the sixteenth century.

Descriptions of everyday life in Turkey are especially interesting. The silence, modesty, and obedience of Turkish wives were noted with approval.[44] Furthermore, descriptions stated that anything pretentious, superfluous, unclean, or vain was forbidden.[45] There is no gambling, no seals for letters, no bells, and no chairs.[46] They take off their shoes to show respect in homes. Bathroom habits emphasize modesty and cleanliness. They urinate and defecate privately, wash two or three times a day (changing the water each time), and remove all bodily hair except male beards.[47] The Turks criticize Christian clothing because it is too sensual and demonstrates pride and vanity. "Heissen sie es assen." [They call it asinine.][48] Allowing animals in the house while eating pollutes a meal. They avoid unclean foods, especially pork and wine. They eat simple foods such as bread, rice, fruit, and mutton with no ostentation, using their fingers.[49] Each pamphlet carried the same theme: the Turks far surpass the Christians in modesty and cleanliness. "Sie verachten allen urberfluss und hoffart in allen dingen."[50] [They despise all superfluity and pride in all things.]

Similar conclusions were made concerning the arts in Turkey. They have no particular enjoyment of architecture and build few houses of stone, outside of the great lords, mosques, and baths.[51] Part of their holiness is not allowing any illustrations, so they put only letters on their buildings and coins.[52] Although they have no music, they do study poetry, astronomy, philosophy, grammar, logic, metaphysics, metaphor, geometry, syntax, philology, astrology, and rhetoric in schools for both women and men (taught separately). Georgijevic even included examples of translated Turkish school-poetry.[53]

The Sultan Sulaiman and his government was another frequent theme in the descriptive literature. German travelers depicted the sultanate court as spectacular and majestic.[54] Contemporary illustrations of Sulaiman and his officials (supposedly based on eyewitness accounts of features, clothing, and appearance at Vienna in 1529) emphasized wealth and nobility, at times with no hint of gruesomeness.[55]

Some German publications appreciated the fact that the sultan did not allow any non-approved inter-generational inheritance, so no independent noble families could be established.[56] Descriptions of the Turks mention some major officers such as the Grand Vizier of Pascha and regional governors (*sanjakbeys*), but the exact organization and the nature of the Turkish government was not understood in the early sixteenth century.[57] It was believed that everyone was directly subject to the Sultan. The absolute nature of the Sultan's rule and the reverent obedience which he received was admired.[58] Crime and disobedience were infrequent because the Turkish government ruthlessly punished lawbreakers.[59] The closest political analogy for the sixteenth-century scholars was classical Sparta.[60]

It is not surprising that the Turkish military both interested and intimidated the Germans. Individual Turkish military units and their uniforms and duties were depicted in both text and illustrations.[61] In woodcuts from Schoen and Stoer, Persian archers, Turkish horseback musicians, camels, dromedaries, cannon, army trains, horsemen, horse archers, Stradioth (light cavalry that attacks from the rear), and Turkish noblemen were all brilliantly illustrated.[62]

Praise for the Turkish military, however, was limited primarily to areas in which the Germans considered their own military to be weak. These popular broadsides and pamphlets, therefore, served as a type of critique of the military policies of the Holy Roman Empire. It was noted, for example, that the Turks have no problem raising troops; they come eagerly in great numbers, without concern about pay. They are hardy warriors and supberb horsemen, able to suffer weather, hunger, etc., without complaint and still be able to make long, fast journeys. They do not take anything with them into battle that would hinder them, such as superfluous baggage trains.[63] They serve at least once every three years against the Christians and understand this to be their sacred duty.[64]

It was extremely frustrating to the German pamphleteers that the Turkish military included former Christians and children of Christians. In *Ein Disputation*, the author was convinced that almost all of the Turkish military manpower came from these captured Christians—even the population of Constantinople was believed to be only one-third Turkish.[65] "The best [Turkish] soldiers are mere former Christians that were stolen from their parents."[66] These soldiers were known as *janis*, that is, from Christian lands.[67] They used muskets and throwing axes and formed an elite force completely dependent on and obedient to the sultan.[68] The potential use of captured and/or former Christians against the West was such a grave ideological problem that Luther considered refusal to fight against Christians to be the *only* justifiable cause for disobedience against Turkish governmental authority.[69]

The Turkish policy of religious toleration was well known.[70] However, due to the very real danger that some would 'turn Turk' or (worse yet) support the Turkish advance into central Europe, this was the subject of long polemical discourses. Some argued that Turkish tolerance was not genuine because it was limited. Others declared it an outright sham designed to lure Christians into perpetual slavery.

"Sometimes the Turks are praised because they allow one to believe what they will," Luther stated, "but this is false." In Turkey no one can publicly confess Christ, evangelize, or preach against Muhammad. "What kind of freedom of faith is this since one cannot preach Christ? Yet one must confess him, for our salvation is based in that same confession." Without preaching, a person lacks the bread of the soul and will easily fall prey to the enticements and temptations of the Turks.[71] Justus Jonas' argument is similar:

> Some uneducated persons say that the Turkish emperor allows freedom of faith to everyone. But this is far from the truth. Consider what the Turk does to all those [Christians] who come under his control. He forcibly takes from parents one of every three children; then the parents must look on helplessly while their own beloved children are indoctrinated in the Mohamedan errors and taught to become accustomed to Turkish ways.[72]

Since they are not allowed to preach or have schools, Christians become so weak that when they see how much better Turks live than the despised *arme hunde* [poor dogs] under their feet they easily convert to Islam. Catholic pronouncements echoed these concerns.[73]

Several writers offered evidence that Turkish religious tolerance was pure deception. Georgijevic wrote that if a Muslim was wounded by a Christian or if Muhammad was blasphemed then that Christian was forced to convert to Islam.[74] In the *Turcken peuchlein*, when a Turk claimed that his *Kaiser* has a better government than the Christians since he permitted each to believe as he chose, a rebuttal story is told of one who went to the Turks for protection but was immediately taken as a slave. According to *Zweyen Turk newlich gefangen*, Christians who went to Turkey were not only suspected of being spies, but were put in the army to be used as cannon fodder, given only bread and water, forced to sleep on the ground, and abandoned when injured. When not enough Christian men for the front lines were available, women with shorn hair were dressed in men's clothing and forced to fight.[75]

Oppressive Ottoman taxation added to the burden of Christians in Turkey. Not only had the Turks built their empire on the backs of the Christian soldiers but also through the money of Christians. Taxation was depicted to be as high as one-third or one-half of all income. Non-payment brought slavery and hard labor.[76] In fact, any Christian property could be confiscated at any time.[77]

Of all the aspects of Turkish life and society discussed in the early sixteenth century, German writers were most concerned with the slavery of Christians. It is clear from the tone of the writings that the possibility of becoming a Turkish slave was believed to be very real. Entire pamphlets were written instructing people what to do if they should be captured. In addition, the theme of 'our Christian brothers and sisters in cruel bondage' was a powerful motivator for military action.

Slavery was permitted in Islam if an individual was not already Muslim and not under treaty to pay a poll-tax. In its golden age, the Ottoman Empire took advantage of this allowance and built their entire society around a slave system. There were two principal ways that one could become a Turkish slave: by the *devshirme* or through capture.

The *devshirme* was a human tribute or tax of Christian boys age 6–20 from the conquered lands. The boys (some girls were taken for the harem, but this was rare) were trained for positions in the government, military (Janissary corps), household staffs, or the general labor force, based on each individual's ability. At any given time in the sixteenth century, around 80,000 slaves were in the Ottoman system, of which about 3,000 per year came from the *devshirme*. Although these children were not forced to convert to Islam, peer pressure to do so was strong and conversions were rewarded with promotions and celebrations. Conversion was the norm, not only for rewards, but also because slaves had no security or legal protection whatsoever if they did not convert to Islam.[78]

Understandably, sixteenth-century German reports concerning *devshirme* were highly critical.[79] The number of children taken was exaggerated;[80] positive aspects were completely ignored. Only a 'devil-inspired enemy of Christendom' would take children away from their parents, entice them into denying Christ, and then send them back to kill Christians. The young Christian captives, trained from childhood for war, became the most bloodthirsty enemies of Christendom. "It is a great shame that the Turks use Christian blood to shed Christian blood."[81]

The most frightening aspect of Turkish slavery for early sixteenth-century Germans, however, was the possibility that they themselves might be captured on a Turkish raid or military campaign. Soldiers were very much at risk, but even civilians in Austria, Bohemia, and Bavaria took extra precautions upon every rumor of a Turkish advance. All of Germany was concerned to some extent. Popular prophesies claimed that the Turks would get as far as Cologne; others predicted they would overrun all of Germany.

According to sharia, the Turks first had to ask a besieged city or occupied area to convert. If the people converted they were respectfully treated, if not, the Turks had the legal right to kill or enslave as many as they chose.[82] Slavery was, therefore, very common and became the usual way the Ottoman Turks subdued an area.[83]

The German pamphleteers' depictions of the fate of those captured by the Turks (called a 'Babylonian captivity'[84]) were as brutal as possible. Slave traders[85] travel with the army, carrying long chains that can hold up to 50–60 people. The old are most often simply killed, for they do not sell well. The captives are chained together at the hands (so that they will not stone their captors), since there are but ten merchants for each 500 Christians. Families are separated. Captives suffer hunger, thirst, and exposure to the elements. (See Figure 5.4) At night "the merchants satisfy themselves with them. One hears a pitiful cry in the darkness as both boys and girls, even six- or seven-year-old children are abused, even against nature."[86]

Things are even worse after they get to Turkish territory. Firsthand descriptions of a Turkish slave market, such as the broadsheet *Wie die Türcken mit den gefangenen Christen handeln so sie die kauffen oder verkauffen* [How the Turks treat captured Christians when they buy or sell them], are typical.[87] Each town has a separate place for a slave market. The sultan gets a percentage of all slaves and the young boys 10–15 years old. Young children are sent to a special place where they are taught and much effort is placed into their conversion. Some children are made eunuchs and forced to perform homosexual acts.[88] Both men and women are displayed naked at the market; they are forced to run and spin around to display their health. Many writers emphasized that Christian slaves are bought and sold in Turkey like livestock (twenty or thirty times), with no concern for father, mother, child, or wife.[89]

> The son is sold in the view of his mother. The man has his wife, his own flesh taken away and given to another, sold and ridiculed like a whore. They take the child from the breasts or arms of their mother. Rank is not considered, a priest goes for as much as a layman, a knight or nobleman is valued no more than a peasant.[90]

omnibus liberum eſt vel Chri-
ſtianã fidem reſeruare, aut ſpem
libertatis,quàm diu viuit, conci-
pere.

*Quomodo reliqui Turcæ cum man-
cipijs agant.*

H Actenus quid Imperator
Turcarum agat, diximus:
nunc quid priuati iſti, cùm pri-
mũ nouitios adepti ſunt, omnibus minis, promiſsis, blanditiis
agunt,

Figure 5.4 Illustration of slavery from Georgijevic, 1558

Both hard labor and deprivation follow their purchase. They are faced with "an eternal slavery with no hope of freedom or release as long as one lives. All evil labor is hung around their neck, neither day or night are given any rest, comfort, or concern. In their anguish many call out for death but it does not come."[91] Slaves are often put in chains, branded on the back or forehead, or have their nose or ears cut off to make escape difficult. Escape techniques and the violent and magical means Turkish masters used to recapture their slaves were described in detail.[92] There was great concern about the souls of those who are taken in such captivity. It was feared that they would give up all hope and abandon God. Clearly, Turkish slavery represented a severe threat to both body and soul.

Notes

1. Martin Luther and Philip Melanchthon, *Zwen trostbrieve geschriben an der Durchleuchtigen und hochgebornen Fürsten und Herrn Herrn Joachim Chürfurste und Marckgraven zu Brandenburger vom Türcken zuge*, 4b.
2. This was also the case for the fifteenth-century Milanese humanist Andrea Biglia, for example. See Meserve, 173–178. Raeder, 116–118.
3. The reason that Muhammad so quickly came to power was the *status corruptissimus populi Christiani*. Much blame was laid on Heraclius for indecent living, weakness in dealing with corruption in the East, and a propensity for monothelitism. See among others, Melanchthon, *Opera, CR 12*, 1074.
4. The dates range widely. 800AD: George of Hungary, 755AD: Bibliander, 900AD: Piscatorius.
5. Ehrenfried Herrmann, "Türke und Osmanreich in der Vorstellung der Zeitgenossen Luthers: Ein Beitrag zur Untersuchung des deutsche Türkenscriftens," 110–111.
6. In Giovo, a2a-b1b.
7. For example, Michael Ostendorfer and broadsheets by Beham, Stoer, and Schoen.
8. Göllner, *Turcica*, vol. 3, 229.
9. For example, Johannes Piscatorius, *Herkommen Ursprung unnd Auffgang des Türckischen unnd Ottomannischen kayserthums unnd was die selben für künigreich Länder und Stett so in kurzen Jaren den Christen abgetrungen sollen haben*, a3a. For the heavily influential fifteenth-century background, see Meserve, 22–64.
10. For example, Martin Bucer, *Opera, Corpus Reformatorum, CR 13*, 823–1003. George H. Williams, "Erasmus and the Reformers on Non-Christian Religions and Salus Extra Ecclesiam," 351, 354.
11. Piscatorius, a3a, Melanchthon, *Opera, CR 12*, 1075, Giovo, d2a, George of Hungary, *Chronica unnd beschreibung der Türckey mit yhrem begriff, ynnhalt, provincien, völckern, ankunfft, kriege, reysen, glauben, religionen, gesatzen, sytten, geperde, weis, regimente, frükeyt, unnd bossheiten*, b2a. For the fifteenth-century background on the supposed 'Scythian' origin of the Turks, see Meserve, 65–116.
12. See my introduction to Luther's pamphlet publication: Gregory J. Miller, "Preface to the Thirty-Eighth and Thirty-Ninth Chapters of Ezekiel on Gog" in *Luther's Works* (American Edition) Vol. 59.
13. This interpretation was not without critics. Bibliander, for example, did not find the connection with Gog and Magog to be either historical or biblical. Pfister, 445–449.

14. The Persians, hardpressed by the Arabs, asked for foreign help. The Turks (from the Tartars in the Caucasus) were so successful that they themselves captured a large portion of Asia and in the meantime had converted to Islam, "das aus Tur(e)ken und Sauaceren jnn Asia ein volckund ein leib ward." Jonas, d2b.

15. *Ausz Ratschlag Erasmi*, 10a.

16. *Beschreibung aller Turckischen Khayser* gives the following list with some dates when each Sultan began his reign: 1) 1300 Ottoman, 2) Orchanis, 3) Marat, 4) Paiazei, 5) Calepin, 6) 1400 Moyses, 7) Machomet, 8) Murat, 9) 1451 Machomet the Great, 10) 1481 Paiazer, 11) Zelim, 12) 1519 Soleyman; Johannes Piscatorius, *Herkommen* lists: 1) Ottomannus, 2) Orcannes, 3) Amurhates, 4) Baiazetes, 5) Ciriscilebes or Caeepinus, 6) Mahometes, 7) Amurhates, 8) Mahometes II, 9) Maiazetes II, 10) Selimus, 11) Solymannus; Ostendorfer, *Der Türgkyschen Keyser herkomen* lists: 1) Ottomanus 1300, 2) Orchanes 1335, 3) Amurates 1363, 4) Pazaites 1386, 5) Calepinus 1394, 6) Moyses 1400, 7) Mahumetes 1408, 8) Amurates 1422, 9) Mahumetes 1451, 10) Paiazetus 1481, 11) Zelimus 1512, 12) Soleymannus 1519. Other than the addition of two Sultans during the 1403–1413 interregnum (Moyses and Calepinus) and slight differences in the dates of ascension, the sixteenth-century lists are largely accurate.

17. "[S]o finde ich das nie Keyn Nation gewesen ist die mer Gottes lesterung wuterey schendlicher unzucht unnd allerley wustes unnd wildes leben geubet hat den die Türcken." They not only destroy the true teaching and Gottesdienst but also all good morals and discipline. They do whatever they desire with the people and subject them to cruel slavery. Luther and Melanchthon, *Zwen trostbrieve geschriben*, 4b.

18. One sees "wie grewlich er die leut, kind, weiber, iung und allt erwu(e)rget, spiesset, zu hacket . . . und sohandelt, als sey er der zornige teuffel selbs leibhafftig, Denn nie kein ko(e)nigreich also getobet hat mit morden und wu(e)ten, als er thut." Luther, *Heerpredigt*, 162.

19. "Denn er ist dem Christlichen namen feind." This was a common designation for the Turks. Luther, *Heerpredigt*, 170. Concerning the single-mindedness of Turkish attacks, "Aber des Mahomets schwerd und reich an yhm selber ist stracks wider Christum gericht, als hette er sonst nichts zu thun und ku(e)nne sein schwerd nicht besser brauchen, den das er wider Christum lestert und streitet, wie den auch sein Alkoran und die that dazu beweisen." Luther, *Heerpredigt*, 172.

20. There are no greater robbers and murderers, because Muhammad commanded them to prevail with the sword, and his followers believe that they do a service to God thereby. The devil is a liar and murderer; therefore, since Muhammad possessed a lying spirit and the devil kills the soul through the Qur'an, it was natural that he must also take the sword and kill the body. Luther, *Vom Kriege*, 123–125. On Melanchthon's understanding of the role of violence in the rise of Islam, see especially Köhler, 99–100.

21. Georg Schreiber, "Das Türkenmotiv und das deutsche Volkstum," 43. For example: *Die Belagerung der Statt Wien*, d2a-d3a, *Hernach volgt des Bludhundts* (includes gruesome drawings, with the theme of the hacking to death of children), *Des Türckische Kaysers heerzug*, a3a.

22. "Die alten schlagen wir zu todt, Dem Christen glawben zu eym spot." Schoen woodcut "Turkish Atrocities."

23. *Ein newes Lied der ganz handl*, with women captives "sie habent schendlich gethon die nacht, darnach die armen frawen hat die thirannisch schar all lebendig zhuawen, der doch ob tausent war." Christoph Zell, *Ein neues Lied in welchem* includes cutting off the breasts of girls, etc., printed in a *Flugblatt* with an accompanying illustration of the cruelties). Dappach, "Die kindlein steckens an die spies, den weibern schnytens ab die bryst." *Hernach volgt des Bluthundts*, "Auch was sye der Junger weiber und meydlin erwischen, treiben sye jren

muttwillen mit, scheckts einer dem andern. Wann sy sych dann dero genuten, so schlahen sy inen die kopf ab."

24. Zell, "erwudigt die leut, beid man und weib, die kinder auch im muterleib kunten for im nit bleiben." *Ein neues Lied, in welchem fursten,* a3b: "sie kinder auch zeryssen."

25. This was a very common theme, but the most typical example is *Der armen Leut klag,* a frequently reproduced broadsheet representing a supposedly historical massacre outside Vienna in 1529. Bible illustrations and paintings of the child massacre of Bethlehem also anachronistically used Turkish figures. See Smith, 41–47 and Schreiber, 44–45.

26. Bernhardin Türck, *Das der Türck ein Erbfeind aller Christen,* bla.

27. One example was the promise not to harm the surrendering guards of Ferdinand at Buda, which were subsequently massacred. "Auss de mist nun eynem yeden Christen menschen ab zunehmen in zu gedencken was auff des Türcken zusagen trawen und glauben zu halten ist." Stern, *Warhafftige handlung,* a3b.

28. "Mars and Venus, sagen die Poeten, wollen bei einander sein." Luther, *Vom Kriege,* 126–127.

29. The following sources state that Turks are allowed twelve wives: Jonas, f3b-4b; Luther, *Heerpredigt,* 190. The information likely came from George of Hungary, see Appendix 2, "Of the Honorableness of Their Women."

30. Kuripecic, *Ein Disputation,* c2a, Knaust, d3a.

31. In "disen landen die weyber die jämsten und verochtesten creature die auff erden leben/heypt ewere weyber in ewren landen got vor dem Türckischen gebrauch Behu(e)tten." *Auszug eines Briefes,* a3a. Georgijevic also emphasized that Turkish women are completely in the control of their husbands. In the German translation, Georgijevic, *Von der Türcken,* c2a.

32. Knaust, d3a; Luther, *Vom Kriege,* 126–127.

33. "Das ist kein rechter ehestand wann der man das weib mag verlassen seins gefallens und mag Ander weiber nemen so viel er wil Dann ein rechter ehestand ist ewig verbundnis." Jonas, f3b-4b.

34. Easy divorce demonstrates that this is really no true marriage at all. Luther, *Heerpredigt,* 190. Ebermann, 28–29.

35. This was frequently stated, for example: "Gebrauchen sich der lesterlichen sünd mit den büben wider natur un habe vil unmentschlich wesen." Kuripecic, *Ein Disputation,* d3a. Knaust stated specifically that it was not considered a sin. Knaust, d3a.

36. The Turks permit the "laster der sodomia oder stumend su(e)nd mit knaben weybern un unvernu(e)rffftigen thieren ganz gemeyn." *Auszug eines Brieffs,* a3a. Muhammad the conquerer is said to have used small children who had been captured. Giovo, f4b.

37. "Ut omnium turpissima sit vita Turcica." Herrmann, 55.

38. For example, there is a considerable difference in vocabulary (no gruesomeness) in *Ain gründtlicher und warhaffter bericht.* A captured Turk reports: "des er unnd seins gleichen gut Kriegssvolck seyen, prennen nicht, schlagen auch die leüt nicht zu tod." *Ain gundtlicher,* c3b.

39. Giovo reported that there was great discipline and no hate among the Turks. Giovo, t2b. Their cleanliness, frequent worship, and hospitality to strangers was often noted by sixteenth-century travelers. Chew, 53.

40. Holsten, 133–134, Pfister, 453–454.

41. Herrmann, 92–99.

42. The motive for the admiration of the Turkish administration is shown by frequently stated hope that the Germans could participate in the advantages of this form of government and administration. Vogler, Luthers Geschichtsauffassung im Spiegel seines Türkenbildes," 120.

43. Jonas, e1b-f2b.
44. See George of Hungary, Appendix 2, "Of the Honorableness of Their Women." In German translation, *Chronica*, e4a. *Ausz Ratschlag Erasmi*, 16b: "Der zu(e) chtig wandel jrer frawen."
45. In German translation, "Summa alle dise ding und der gleichen darin ein über-fluss und missbrauch mag gespürt warden und nit von no(e)ten ist warden bei jhen für eitel und grewel gehalten." *Ausz Ratschlag Erasmi*, 15a. See Appendix 2, "Concerning Specific Experiential Reasons."
46. See George of Hungary, Appendix 2, "Concerning Specific Experiential Reasons." In the German translation, *Ausz Ratschlag Erasmi*, 15a.
47. See George of Hungary, Appendix 2, "Concerning Specific Experiential Reasons." Georgijevic emphasized the frequent washings (changing the water each time seems to have been especially surprising) and hair removal (in fact he described at some length Turkish methods for removing pubic and body hair). See Appendix 3, "Of Craftsmen and Agriculturalists." In German translation, Georgijevic, *Von den Turcken*, d4a.
48. See Appendix 2, "Of the Various Types of Reasons Why People are Persuaded by this Sect and Prefer it to the Christian Faith." The German translation is from *Ausz Ratschlag Erasmi*, 13b.
49. See Appendix 3, "Of Their Meals." See also Merriman, 200–201.
50. See Appendix 2, "Of the Various Types of Reasons Why People are Persuaded by the Sect and Prefer it to the Christian Faith." In German translation, *Ausz Ratschlag Erasmi*, 14b.
51. See Appendix 2, "Concerning Specific Experiential Reasons." In German translation, *Ausz Ratschlag Erasmi*, 14b; Luther, *Vom Kriege*, 126; Merriman, 200–201.
52. Luther, *Vom Kriege, WA 30II*, 128.
53. See Appendix 3, "Of their Schools." In German translation, Georgijevic, *Von den Türken*, c1a, d1a; Merriman, 198–199.
54. Kuripecic, *Itinerarium* and *Beschreibung der Kaiserlichen Statt Constantinopel*. See also Göllner, *Turcica*, vol. 3, 212–213.
55. For example, Erhard Schoen woodcuts of Sulaiman and his wife, as well as Michael Ostendorfer, (although Ostendorfer's date appears to be 1548, this wood-cut probably circulated earlier). The Schoen prints (dated 1530) were surely based on Ostendorfer, although the wife's appearance is pure imagination-unveiled and covered with jewelry. Charlotte Colding Smith's extensive treat-ment of Ottoman dress in German-printed costume books of the sixteenth century is particularly demonstrative of this point. See Smith, 123–150.
56. See Appendix 3, "Of the Estate of the Nobility." In German translation, Georgi-jevic, *Von den Türken*, c4b.
57. Georgijevic mentioned two princes called *sanjak beys*, the timar (feudal) cav-alry, and various military orders, but was not aware of most of the governmen-tal offices or of the use of slaves in governmental positions. See Appendix 3, "Of the Military." In German translation, Georgijevic, *Von den Türcken*, c4a.
58. The Sultan "is alone lord over all in his land." Luther, *Vom Kriege*, 128. See also Kuripecic, *Itinerium*.
59. It is "in Tu(e)rckischen landen vor raubery sicher"; there "ist eyn solch gehorsam im volck." *Auszug eines Brieffs* related a story of how the Sultan had six men kill themselves in front of him to prove the obedience of his subjects. *Auszug eines Brieffs*, a2a-b. Georgijevic also emphasized the quick, stern justice. Geor-gijevic, *Von den Türcken*, d4b. This positive(?) appraisal was not universal in the early sixteenth century. Both Luther and Brenz when rhetorically to their advantage stated that there was no true justice in Turkey, only exploitation of the weak by the strong. Ebermann, 28–29; Bohnstedt, 48.

60. Melanchthon, *Opera*, CR 12, 1077.
61. Georgijevic, *Von den Turcken*, d3b.
62. See the Schoen and Stoer woodcut series. Special attention was paid to camels and dromedaries captured from the Turks at Vienna (although Stoer identified the camel/dromedary pair as male/female!). See Smith, 49–55.
63. *Ausz Ratschlag Erasmi*, 11a-b, 15b. George of Hungary, *Saracenisch*, d4b. Giovo, t3a.
64. Georgijevic, *Von den Türcken*, d3b.
65. Kuripecic, *Ein Disputation*, b2b.
66. Dietrich, c2b.
67. Giovo, d1b. According to Giovo, the Janisseries were created by Sultan Murat from the children of a captured daughter of a Serbian despot. Giovo, f1b.
68. *Ausz Ratschlag Erasmi*, 13a.
69. He understood that such disobedience would result in death, but did not consider this to be suicide. In contrast, he counsels absolute sexual submission to Turkish masters. Luther, *Vermahnung*, 621.
70. For example: "Die Türcke zwingen niemans in jrem land seinen glaube zuverleugnen oder den jfren anzunemen." *Ausz Ratschlag Erasmi*, 16a. "[U]nd yeder bey seynem glauben bleiben lassen," the Turk said concerning the leniency of Turkish rule over Christians in *Turcken peuchlein*.
71. "Was ist aber das fur eine freiheit des glaubens, da man Christum nicht predigen noch bekennen mus, so doch unser heyl ynn dem selbigen bekentnis stehet." Luther, *Vom Kriege*, 120–121. Concerning the Turkish "*versuchen und locken*" of Christians, see Luther, *Heerpredigt*, 195, Holsten, *Christentum*, 132, Göllner, *Turcica*, vol. 3, 223, Lamparter, 26.
72. "Ob auch wol etlich unerfaren leuth sagen/er las jederman gleuben/was er will/ so helt sichs doch nicht also/das allen den ihenigen/so er unter sein gewalt bringt/ da nimst er den eltern mit gewalt das dritte kind/das mussen sie sehen und ho(e) ren/das jhr eizen liebesten kinder jhn dem schendlichen Mahometischen irrtumb ausser sagen/und zu allen Tu(e)rckischen sitten gewest und unterweiset warden." Jonas, e4a-b.
73. *Auszug eines Brieffs*, a2a and Sadoleto. See Carl Göllner, "Die Auflagen des *Tractatus de ritu et moribus Turcorum*," 608.
74. See Appendix 3, ""The Situation of Those Attacked." In German translation, Georgijevic, *Von den Türcken*, b4b.
75. Ebermann, 33.
76. *Auszug eines Brieffs*, a2b-a3a, Georgijevic, *Von den Türcken*, e1a, Kuripecic, *Itinerarium*, c3b, Kuripecic, *Ein Disputation*, a4b.
77. "Ich oder keyn man in der Tu(e)rckey darff sich Berhu(e)me das seyne gu(e)tter seyn sonder sie seyen unser herrs der keyser." *Auszug eines Briefs*, a1b.
78. Concerning devshirme and the Turkish slave system, see especially Krstic and Goffman, 67–68. On women and the harem, see Peirce and Albert Hourani, 119–121.
79. For contemporary depictions of devshirme, see: *Ain Sendbrief*, a1b, c3a-b; Kuripecic, *Ein Disputation*, c2b-3a; Giovo, s1b-s2a.
80. It was claimed that the devshirme took one of every three sons. *Auszug eines Brieffs*, a2b-a3a.
81. *Ein kleglich ansuchen*, c1a.
82. Kissling, 18.
83. Concerning the ravages of Ottoman resettlement, *Auszug eines Brieffs*, a4a.
84. "Ach der ellerden Babylonische gefengknis." Kuripecic, *Itinerarium*, c1b.
85. Actually a significant amount of the slave trade in the Balkans as carried on by non-Muslims. Babinger, 203.

86. "Die fu(e)rka(e)uffer gond jre mutwillen nach mit jne um da ho(e)rt einer ein
    ellend geschrey in der finsternuss do wirt so knab so meydlin gescha(e)ndt ja
    sechs oder siben ia(e)rige kind die weden also missgebraucht so gar wider die
    Natur." Georgijevic, *Türckey oder von yetziger Türcken gepräng*, g2a.
87. See Eisenkorn.
88. Georgijevic, *Türckey*, g2a.
89. They sell Christians twenty or thirty times. Kuripecic, *Ein Disputation*, c3a. In
    Ein Disputation, the remarkable suggestion was made that if Turks fight so well
    for human booty, perhaps Christians should buy and sell Turks!
90. George of Hungary, c1a.
91. "[V]il ruffen in diser angst dem tode und er will nitt komen." George of Hun-
    gary, c1b.
92. See Appendix 3, "Concerning Turkish Incantations Against Fugitives." *Ausz
    Ratschlag Erasmi*, 12bff. George of Hungary, c2a-c3b. Georgijevic, *Türkey*, g4b.

References

*Ain gründtlicher und warhaffter bericht Was sich under der belegerung der Statt Wyen
Newlich im MDxxix Jar zwyschen denen inn Wyen und Turgken verlauffen Beges-
sen und zugetragen hatt von tag zu tag klerlich angezaigt und verfasst.* n.p., 1529.

*Ain Sendbrief Wie sych der Turckisch kaysser So grausamlich für die stat Rodis
belegert, und gewonnen hat.* n.p., 1523.

*Ausz Ratschlage Herren Erasmi von Roterdam die Türcken zubekriegen Der
ursprung unnd alle geschichten der selbigen gegen Römische Keyser unnd gemeyne Christenheit vo anbegin des türckischen namenn nach der kürtze new verteutscht.* n.p., 1530.

*Auszug eines Briefes wie einer so in der türkey wonhafft seinem freünd in dise landt
geschriben un wessen sey und wie Türcken Regiment un wessen sey und wie er es
mit den landen so er erobert zu halten pflegt kürtzlich in Teütsche sprach gebracht
nützlich diser zeyt zu wissen.* Wittenberg: Schirlentz, 1526.

Babinger, Franz. "Die Osman auf dem Balkan." In *Völker und Kulturen Südosteuropas: Kulturhistorische Beiträge.* Balwin Saria, ed., 211–217. Munich: Südosteuropa Verlaggesellschaft, 1959.

*Beschreibung aller Türcischen Khayser. Von jrem ursprung un anfang her wie vil
derselben biss auff dise unser zeit und jar geregiert was auch derselben jeder von
Landt und Leut Bestritten uberkhomen und in seinen gwalt unnd herschung
gebracht.* n.p., 1531.

*Beschreibung der Kaiserlichen Statt Constantinopel derselben gegendt gelegenhait
Erbawung und bewonung* Augsburg: Kriesstein, 1543.

Bibliander, Theodor. *Ad nominis christiani socios consultatio, Qua nam ratione Turcarum dira potenia repelli possit ac debeat a populo christiano.* Basel: Brylinger,
1542.

Bucer, Martin. *Opera, Corpus Reformatorum.* Vol. 13. Halle: Schwetschke, 1843ff.

Chew, Samuel C. *The Crescent and the Rose.* New York: Octagon Books, 1974.

Dappach, Jörg. *Ein lied, gemacht wie es im Osterlandt ergangen ist als man schreybt
1529 jar.* n.p., 1529.

*Des Türckische Kaysers heerzug wie er von Constantinopel Mit aller rüsting zu Ross
und Fuss zu wasser und land gegen kriechische Weyssenburg kummen und fürter
für die königlichen stat Ofen yn Ungern unnd Wien yn Osterreich gezoge die*

belegert un gestürmt und mit angehenckter ermanung der grausamen tyranny des Türken wyder christliche Nation. Nurnberg: Zell, 1530.

Dietrich, Veit. *Wie man das Volck zur Busz und ernstlichem gebet wider den Türcken auff der Cantzel vermanen sol.* Nürnberg: Berg, 1542.

Ebermann, Richard. "Die Türkenfurcht: Ein Beitrag zur Geschichte der öffentlichen Meinung in Deutschland während der Reformationszeit." Ph.D. diss., Halle University, 1904.

Ein Kleglich ansuchen des ausschus der V. nider osterreichischen lande belangend die grosse jtzige fahr des Türcken halben. Wittenberg: Klug, 1540.

Ein neues Lied, in welchem fursten und herren und andere stend des reichs mit sampt allen frummen lanzknechten zu fryd und einickeit, auch got, den allergrossmechtigsten Keiser und herren mit hochstem fleiss anzurufen und in seinem namen auch umb seiner eer willen ritterlichen zu straiten wyder den Turcken treulich vermant weden. Nürnberg: n.p., 1529.

Eisenkorn, Max. *Wie die Turcken mit den Gefangen Christen handeln, So sie die kauffen oder verkauffen.* Nürnberg: Meldemann, 1532.

George of Hungary. *Chronica unnd beschreibung der Türckey mit yhrem begriff, ynnhalt, provincien, völckern, ankunfft, kriege, reysen, glauben, religionen, gesatzen, sytten, geperde, weis, regimente, frükeyt, unnd bossheiten.* Sebastian Franck, trans. Nürnberg: Peypus, 1530.

Georgijevic, Bartholomew. *Türckey oder von yetziger Türcken kirchen gepräng, Sytem unnd leben, auch was grausamen jochs, was unsäglichen jamers die gefangnen Christen under den selben gedulden müssen, sampt Namenbüchlein Persischer in der Türckey gängen sprachen.* Basel: Cratander, 1545.

Georgijevic, Bartholomew. *Von der Türken gebreuchen, gewonheyten und Ceremonien.* Nürnberg: Guldenmunde, 1544.

Giovo, Paolo. *Ursprung des Turkischen Reichs bis auff den itzigen Solyman druch D. Paulum Jouium Bischoff Nucerin an keiserliche Maiestate Carolum V. inn welcher sprach geschrieben er nach aus dem Latin F. Bassainatis verdeutschet durch Justum Jonan.* Augsburg: Steiner, 1538.

Goffman, Daniel. *The Ottoman Empire and Early Modern Europe.* Cambridge: Cambridge University Press, 2002.

Göllner, Carl. "Die Auflagen des *Tractatus de ritu et moribus Turcorum.*" *Deutsche Forschung im Südosten* 3:1 (March 1944): 129–151.

Göllner, Carl. *Turcica: Die europäischen Türkendrucke des XVI. Jahrhunderts. Vol. 3. Die Türkenfrage in der öffentlichen Meinung Europas im 16. Jahrhundert.* Bucharest: Editura Academiei, 1968.

Hernach volgt des Bludhundts der sych nennedt ein Türckischen Keiser gethaten so er und die seinen nach eroberug der Schlacht auff den xxviij. tag Augusti nech stuer gange geschehe an unsern mitbrudern der Ungrische lant schaffen gatz unmeschlich tribe hat un noch teglichs tut. n.p., 1526.

Herrmann, Ehrenfried. "Türke und Osmanreich in der Vorstellung der Zeitgenossen Luthers: Ein Beitrag zur Untersuchung des deutsche Türkenscriftens." Ph.D. diss., University of Freiburg, 1961.

Holsten, Walter. *Christentum und nichtchristliche Religion nach der Auffassung Luthers.* Gütersloh: Bertelsmann, 1932.

Hourani, Albert. *Western Attitudes Towards Islam.* Southampton: Southampton University Press, 1974.

Jonas, Justus. *Das siebend Capitel Danielis von des Türken Gottes lesterung und schrecklicher moderey mit unterrich.* Wittenberg: Lufft, 1529.

Kissling, Hans Joachim. *Rechtsproblematiken in den christlich-muslimischen Beziehungen, vorab im Zeitalter der Türkenkriege.* Graz: Universitäts Buchdruckerei Styria, 1974.

Knaust, Heinrich. *Von geringem herkommen schentlichern leben schmehlichem ende des Türckischen abgots Machomets und seiner verdamlichen und Gotsslesterischen Ler.* Berlin: Weisen, 1542.

Köhler, Manfred. *Melanchthon und der Islam: Ein Beitrag zur Klärung des Verhältnisses zwischen Christentum und Fremdreligionen in der Reformationszeit.* Leipzig: Klotz, 1938.

Krstic, Tijana. *Contested Conversions to Islam: Narratives of Religious Change in the Early Modern Ottoman Empire.* Stanford: Stanford University Press, 2011.

Kuripecic, Benedict. *Ein Disputation oder Gesprech zwayer Stalbuben So mit künigklicher Maye. Botschafft bey dem Türckischen Keyser zu Constantinopel gewesen Dieweil sy allda in jhrer beherbergung vo dem Türcken verspert beschehen.* Augsburg: Steiner, 1531.

Kuripecic, Benedict. *Itinerarium Wegrayss K. May. Potschafft gen Constantinopel zu dem Türckischen Kayser Soleyman Anno xxx.* n.p , 1531.

Lamparter, Helmut. *Luthers Stellung zum Türkenkrieg.* Munich: Lempp, 1940.

Luther, Martin. *Heerpredigt wider den Türken* (1530). WA 30II, 160–197.

Luther, Martin. *Vermahnung zum Gebet wider den Türken* (1541). WA 51, 585–625.

Luther, Martin. *Vom Kriege wider den Türcken* (1529). WA 30II, 107–148.

Luther, Martin and Phillip Melanchthon. *Zwen trostbrieve geschriben an der Durchleuchtigen und hochgebornen Fürsten und Herrn Herrn Joachim Chürfurste und Marckgraven zu Brandenburger vom Türcken zuge.* Nürnberg: Berg, 1532.

Melanchthon, Philip. *Opera. Corpus Reformatorum.* Vol. 12. Halle: Schwetschke, 1843ff.

Merriman, Roger B. *Suleiman the Magnificent: 1520–1566.* New York: Cooper Square Publishers, 1966.

Meserve, Margaret. *Empires of Islam in Renaissance Historical Thought.* Cambridge: Harvard University Press, 2008.

Miller, Gregory J. "Preface to the Thirty-Eighth and Thirty-Ninth Chapters of Ezekiel on Gog." In *Luther's Works* (American Edition). Vol. 59, 277–286. St. Louis: Concordia Press, 2012.

Ostendorfer, Michael. *Der Türgkyschen Keyser herkomen unnd geschlecht bis auff den grossen Soleymannum welcher den rechst vergangen summer den Künig vonn Hungern im Feldt erschlagen hatt.* n.p., 1527.

Peirce, Leslie Penn. *The Imperial Harem: Women and Sovereignty in the Ottoman Empire.* New York: Oxford, 1993.

Pfister, Rudolf. "Das Türkenbuchlein Theodor Biblianders." *Theologische Zeitung 9* (1953): 438–468.

Piscatorius, Johannes. *Herkommen Ursprung unnd Auffgang des Türckischen unnd Ottomannischen kayserthums unnd was die selben für künigreich Länder und Stett so in kurzen Jaren den Christen abgetrungen sollen haben.* Augsburg: Steiner, 1542.

Raeder, Siegfried. "Die Türkenpredigten des Jakob Andreä." In *Theologen und Theolgie an der Universität Tübingen.* Martin Brecht, ed. Tübingen: J. C. B. Mohr, 1977, 96–122.

Sachs, Hans. *Die Türkisch belagerung der Stat Wien, mit sampt seiner Tyrannischen Handlung.* n.p., 1529.

Sadoleto, Jacobo. *Iacobi sadoleti Episcopi Carpentoracensis, uiri doctissimi, de bello Turcis inferendo.* Basel: Plater, 1538.

Schoen, Erhard. *Der armen Leut klag.* (broadsheet) Nürnberg: Guldemunde, 1530.

Schoen, Erhard. *Turkish Atrocities.* (broadsheet) Nürnberg: Guldemunde, 1530.

Schreiber, Georg. "Das Türkenmotiv und das deutsche Volkstum." *Volk und Volkstum* 3 (1938): 9–54.

Smith, Charlotte Colding. *Images of Islam, 1453–1600: Turks in Germany and Central Europe.* London: Pickering and Chatto, 2014.

Stern, Peter. *Warhafftige handlung Wie und welcher massen der Turck die stat Ofen und Wien belegert.* n.p., 1530.

Türck, Bernhardin. *Das der Türck ein Erbfeind aller Christen.* n.p., 1542.

Turcken peuchlein. Ein Nutzlich Gesprech, oder underride etlicher personen, zu besserug christlicher ordnung un lebens. n.p., 1522.

Vogler, Günther. "Luthers Geschichtsauffassung im Spiegel seines Türkenbildes." In *450 Jahre Reformation.* Leo Stern and Max Steinmetz, eds. Berlin VEB Deutscher Verlag der Wissenschaften, 1967, 118–127.

Williams, George H. "Erasmus and the Reformers on Non-Christian Religions and Salus Extra Ecclesiam." In *Action and Conviction in Early Modern Europe.* Theodore K. Robb and Jerrold E. Seigel, eds. Princeton: Princeton University Press, 1969, 319–370.

Zell, Christoph. *Ein neues Lied in welchem aufz angebung deren so von anfang mit und darbey gewesen Die gantz handlung des Turcken in Ungern und Osterreych nemlich der belegerung der Stat Wien begryffen ist.* Nurnberg: Peypus, 1529.

6 Holy Terror

Depictions of the Islamic Threat and Its Causes

The majority of Church leaders dream of nothing else except war against the Turks, but that means not war against their own sins, but war against God's rod, even against God himself.[1]

Martin Luther

From a modern perspective, the Germans should not have been overly concerned about the Ottoman Turks. The sixteenth-century Turkish military realistically could not have attacked beyond Vienna; the long march, the limited campaign season, and the difficulty of supply hampered even attacks into Austria. Yet, Germans all over the Empire felt threatened by the Ottoman advance. This social fear transcended political propaganda. Even those who did not support Hapsburg Imperialism believed the danger to be very real.

The perceived seriousness of the threat is clearly reflected in German publications on the Turks during the Reformation. Both hearth and soul were in danger. The Turks did not pose a simple military threat, like any other European power. Rather, their vicious attacks would destroy the land and enslave the people. Worse yet, the very survival of Christendom was at stake. The chief desire of the Turks was to destroy the Church and to convert individual souls to Muhammad's blasphemous teaching. The Turks were perceived to be a fearful enemy that could destroy not only the body but also the soul.

As in all times of social stress, German pamphleteers sought a cause, a reason why Christendom was so severely threatened. Almost never did the Turks receive credit for their successes. Some of these perceived causes were also heard in medieval laments over failed Crusades. Due to the Protestant Reformation, however, new understandings of the reason for Islam and its successes emerged. Different Christian failings were blamed, and most importantly, an eschatological paradigm for understanding Islam was developed that was influential for centuries.

The Seriousness of the Threat

There is significant evidence in early sixteenth-century pamphlets, broadsheets, and songs that the Turkish threat was perceived to be very serious.

Both Roman Catholic and Lutheran writers emphasized the danger posed to the material and spiritual life of Christendom. Everyone did not perceive the danger to be serious, however, nor did it plague the minds of Germans continually.[2] Especially in the period before Mohács (1526), some intellectuals completely discounted the threat. Ancient authors were cited on the weakness of Asiatics.[3] Others followed Ulrich Hutten and claimed that the Turk was only a papal pretext designed to wring money out of Germany.[4] This humanist, nationalist influence can be seen also in Luther's 1518 remark about the Turkish war, "to fight against the Turks is to fight against God himself who is punishing our sins."[5]

The lack of German military action against the Ottomans is cited by modern historians as further evidence that the *Türkenfurcht* (fear of the Turks) was only an element of political propaganda and never deeply penetrated German culture.[6] While the large number of pamphlets, broadsheets, and *Lieder* against the Turks written with urgent language by a wide range of people demonstrate this conclusion to be incorrect, throughout the period (especially before 1526), the majority of Germans did stress that the settlement of internal religious was a higher priority and should be undertaken before campaigning against the Turks. Despite the urgent problems at home, however, whenever the Ottoman Turks campaigned against the West, the level of fear intensified; even the suspicious, divided German *Reichstag* gave military support and funding in response to each Ottoman campaign.

The fear of the Turks was also reflected in the actions of common people. There is no doubt that not only the residents of the borderlands but also Bavaria, Saxony, and Brandenburg had a pressing fear of the Turks. For example, after Mohács even in Breslau people were arming themselves against the appearance of the Turk. During the siege of Vienna, the city of Regensburg expected the arrival of Turks at any moment and ordered repairs to the city's fortifications. It was reported that the number of people in the Regensburg churches was so great (especially women) that some had to stand in the street.[7]

Further evidence that the threat was taken very seriously is found in the Lutheran response to the Ottoman advance. Although they were a group that would have benefited a great deal from Turkish success in Austria, Luther and those who followed him were actually some of the strongest voices concerning the seriousness of the threat and the need for a response. In a letter to Amsdorf (19 October 1529), Luther reported that the news of the Turkish siege of Vienna actually made him physically ill.[8] Luther was deeply concerned with the Turkish problem and not a shrewd negotiator of Turkish aids in exchange for Protestant liberties, as some modern scholars have argued.

Since Luther's early statements concerning the Turks had been misinterpreted in such a way to discount the Ottoman threat, he wrote *Vom Kriege wider den Türken* and *Heerpredigt* as a clarion call to earnest action. Do not underestimate the Turks as we Germans are inclined to do, Luther stated. Fighting the Turk is not like fighting against the King of France, Venice or the Pope. "This Gog and Magog is a different kind of power than our kings and princes."[9] The Turk has both money and human resources—he can continually mobilize 300–400,000 men, has a territory greater than Europe, and can fight two, three, or four large battles one after another. Perhaps the princes do not know the Turkish power, or don't believe it, or are not in earnest—or are following the Pope's example and simply raking German money, Luther argued.[10] Even after the withdrawal of the Turks from Vienna, Luther admonished the Germans not to go back to sleep. Action is needed, not complacency. The entire purpose for the *Heerpredigt* was to admonish the *Faust* (fist); by means of the Turks the devil seeks not only to rule the political world, but also to destroy Christ's kingdom and his saints.[11] Similar themes are found in a wide variety of early sixteenth-century publications from German-speaking lands.[12]

When the threat of the Turks was mentioned, it was often connected to the material and political danger they posed to Europe. The size of the Ottoman army was always of interest; the exaggerated numbers were intended to frighten and awe the reader.[13] Several writers mentioned fear of a 'domino effect': if the Ottomans capture Hungary, they will take Austria; Austria will be used as a base to ravage Germany, Germany as a base to ravage the Rhine, etc.[14] The Turks desire nothing less than world domination and will not stop until they have destroyed Christianity.[15] Large numbers of *Neue Zeitungen* on the Turks both reflected and fueled these fears.

The same theme was repeated over and over: the political and material threat is much more serious than Germans believe. There have been books which have warned and admonished us, Justus Jonas wrote, yet "with us it is vain security, as if a father sees with his own eyes his own house burning and hears inside his poor wife and children pitifully call and cry out, and then slowly sits at a table, glances at the fire and begins to play chess."[16] But the penalty of not discerning the urgency of the Turkish threat is clearly seen in "the laughing and dancing of Austria which turned to sadness and crying as they realized that they were not defending against 'Paper Turks' from a *Fastnacht* play, but rather the mighty army of Sulaiman."[17] Germans were instructed to learn from the tragic mistakes of the Greeks and not to underestimate the Turkish threat.[18]

It was not only the viciousness of the military attacks of the Turks, but also the spiritual danger they represented that made them an enemy in a class by themselves. When the spiritual aspect of the threat was taken away, the Turks became much less frightening.[19]

The spiritual danger was evident in three areas. The Turks were widely believed to be a tool of the devil designed to destroy the Church. Second, German preachers knew that the reputation of the Ottoman Empire caused some to admire or even desire Turkish rule. This Turkish 'evangelization' was dangerous; not only did it encourage people to leave Germany for Turkish-controlled lands, but it also raised the specter of fifth-column, pro-Turkish activity within German society. Finally, the Turks were a spiritual threat because they enticed their Christian captives to repudiate Christ and forfeit their salvation.

The danger to the Church was believed to be both real and serious. The Turks were characterized as the "enemy of the Christian name" and *Werkzeug* [tool] of the devil.[20] News that the Turks converted churches into mosques in Hungary brought fear of similar experiences in Germany. Several authors stated that the desire to destroy the Christian church was the primary reason for the Turkish advance. The Turks wanted to conquer the entire world and force all to accept their *Machmetische Glaube*.[21] They intended to silence Christian worship and replace Christ with the devilish Muhammad, as they had already done in the Eastern lands.[22]

Especially for persecuted Protestants and suffering peasants, however, a Turkish presence in Central Europe was something to be hoped for, not feared. Some even openly stated their desire for Turkish overlordship, believing it to be less harsh and more tolerant than that of their current Christian rulers. To the majority of the writers of the *Türkenbüchlein*, however, such comments seemed both treasonous and blasphemous. Several pamphlets loudly broadcast the eternal spiritual danger that such an overlordship would have. It was simply too easy to convert to Islam when under the political yoke of the Turks.[23]

A similar argument was made concerning the spiritual threat posed to Turkish captives. Freedom of the soul could not be separated from freedom of the body.[24] If the Turks captured an individual, he or she was in serious eternal danger.[25] This danger was not because the Turks forced them into hell, however, but because captives were likely to convert voluntarily to Islam. "There is a great danger that a person in Turkey will fall from the Christian faith to the Turkish faith, to the devil in hell."[26] *Türkenbüchlein* reported that such conversions were common.[27]

But why would someone forsake Christ for the devil and eternal punishment? It was known that the Turks made serious attempts to convert their captives and honored those who did. For sixteenth-century Germans, however, persuasive evangelization could not account for the conversions. Deception or force had to be involved. Some Christians were deceived by the 'glittering' external righteousness of the Turks, their ecstasies and false miracles; others were enticed by the Turkish military successes. Some simply converted in an attempt to escape their oppressed status. Children were especially at risk. They did not know how to spiritually defend themselves and were easy prey for the Turks.[28]

In an effort to save their souls, a considerable amount of spiritual counsel (most of it by Lutherans) was written to those who might be captured or otherwise fall into the hands of the Turks. Strategies for spiritual survival in Turkey were developed and stipulations were made concerning what one could and could not do and still retain their salvation. Luther recommended that soldiers prepare for the possibility of capture by memorizing the Catechism, especially the Ten Commandments, the Lord's prayer, and the Creed, especially the second article.[29]

The best strategy, however, was never to be captured. It would be better for both men and women to die defending their homes and go to heaven as saints than to allow themselves to be captured and risk eternal damnation. It was considered better by some to kill their own children (and presumably send them to heaven) than to allow them to fall to the Turks and thereby damn them to hell.[30]

Causes of Ottoman Success

If the Turks were in *Werkzeug* of the devil, and if they were threatening to destroy both the material and spiritual life in Christendom, why does God not stop them? It was clear to many authors in Reformation Germany that the seemingly unstoppable Ottoman advance was not due to innate Turkish advantages or even Satan's assistance. Rather, God was permitting the continued Ottoman victories because of the internal failings of Christendom.

Some Turkish advantages were recognized. Their military was disciplined, obedient, hardy, and bloodthirsty. In every battle they seemed to have superior numbers. Their lack of scruple permitted the use of all kinds of trickery and deception.[31] The devil himself was empowering the Turks, raging at Christians through them. Yet, in the minds of early sixteenth-century Germans, these factors could not account for the Ottoman success. After all, the Turks were Asiatics, effeminate (they wear long robes and silk turbans), uncivilized barbarians compared with Christians. "Twenty Christians should always defeat forty Turks."[32]

But there were very few Christian victories in the first half of the sixteenth century. Because it was psychologically impossible to hold that the enemy was simply superior, another interpretation for the Turkish advance had to be found. It was repeated again and again in the literature that the sins of Christians were the primary cause of Ottoman success. Some authors stated that sin had deprived Christendom of God's blessing and left it vulnerable to the devil. For most, the Turks were not just the devil's tool but also God's rod of punishment. They were a holy terror: "It is a dreadful thing to fall into the hands of the living God (Hebrews 10:31)."[33]

This cosmological interpretation of the Turks was reflected in the vocabulary of the *Türkenbüchlein*. They were called *Gottes Zorn* [wrath], *Toben* [rage], *Rute* [rod], *Strafe* [punishment], and *Geissel* [scourge].[34] Osiander's analysis and language from *Unterricht und vermahnung* is typical of much of the literature on the Turks written in the early sixteenth century:

> For a long time we [Christians] have attempted to check this raging tyrant by a variety of ways and means, by word, deed and force of arms. But unfortunately, to tell the truth, we have never yet succeeded in winning a decisive victory . . . it is the ardent wrath and fury of God,

provoked by our grievous, horrible, protracted sins and unrepentant lives, that now strikes us and oppresses us in these last, perilous times. In his divine majesty He is inflicting the power of the Turk upon us, giving him so much success and victory against us that neither our prayers in heaven nor armies on earth have been able to achieve anything considerable against him.[35]

The literary and theological influence of the Old Testament is clear. With analogies to Pharaoh and Egypt, the Turks were often an element in sixteenth-century lists of calamities, along with drought, plague, and pestilence.[36] Most often, however, the Germans identified themselves with Old Testament Israel and Judah. Old Testament prophets were frequently quoted in *Türkenbüchlein*, especially Jeremiah. When the ancient Hebrews failed God, He sent a foreign power to discipline them. Both Roman Catholics and Protestants understood their contemporary situation to be another example of this kind of divine chastisement. It was not unusual for God to use the wicked to punish the wicked; both Assyria and Babylon had performed this role. That God would use the Turks as His scourge was only an indication of the depth of German degradation.[37] Some Radical Reformers were even saying that only a 'Babylonian captivity,' a Turkish conquest of Germany, could purify the Church. It is too late to pray; like Jeremiah we must simply open the gates and let them in.[38]

The concept that a foreign threat, hardship, or military defeat was the result of God's punishment certainly was not new. The Turks were connected directly to God's punishment throughout the Late Middle Ages by church leaders and theologians.[39] However, the early sixteenth-century *Türkenbüchlein* broadcast this interpretation with an intensity and anxiety that far exceeded that of the Middle Ages.

A significant discontinuity with the late medieval period is also found in sixteenth-century discussions of the *nature* of the internal failings that we causing God's wrath. Not only were new emphases and understandings of the causes of Christendom's failure advanced, but this also became an issue in the confessional division. Roman Catholics and Protestants blamed different 'sins' (each other's) for the Turkish advance. In this respect the Ottoman threat also provides insight into the religious situation within Reformation Germany.

In the sixteenth century there were nearly universal demands for general moral improvement, both in and beyond the context of the Turkish threat. These demands were found frequently in the Catholic *Türkenbüchlein*. Gluttony, drunkenness, lust, pride, vanity, robbery, murder, hatred, and avarice were frequently mentioned. No class of society was fulfilling its responsibility: nobles will not fight, merchants are greedy, burghers dress like nobles in pride and vanity, even the *geistlichen* [spiritual estates] accumulate worldly possessions and offices.[40] At times considerable religious reform sentiment was displayed, particularly in the more popular pamphlets.

A strong critique of the Imperial military was also prevalent in many of the Catholic pamphlets, largely because of the close connection between the Hapsburgs and the most Catholic *Türkenbüchlein*. As in medieval criticisms of the Crusaders, the success of the Turks was due to the failings and the sins of the Christian soldiers. They have completely forgotten how to fight and are generally lazy. They are unreliable, disobedient to authority, and ask for too much money. How can God grant victory to armies composed of men who are among the worst sinners? They eat and drink too much, even on military expeditions. Drunkenness, use of prostitutes, looting, gambling, and blasphemous oaths rob them of God's blessing.[41]

Another Roman Catholic interpretation of the cause for the Turkish success was that God was punishing Christendom for tolerating the cancer of heresy and false teaching. In the Leipzig Disputation (1519), Johann Eck argued that the fall of Constantinople was God's punishment for the heresy of the Eastern Church. In his 1532 *Sperandam esse in brevi victoriam adversus Tucam*, he claimed that the Lutheran heresy had similarly provoked the wrath of God and was the reason for the recent Turkish advances.[42] Other Catholics echoed Eck's assessment. Just when it looked like a Crusade against the Turks was getting under way (referring to the 1517 agreement), the devil sent a messenger to ensure that it would not be accomplished. If Lutheranism and the other heresies were not destroyed, the divine judgment of God could allow the Turks to take all of Germany.[43]

Catholic authors also emphasized Christian disunity as a cause of Turkish success. Roman Catholic writers repeatedly stated that Christendom was filled with a divisive selfishness that leads to an abandonment of Christian responsibility for neighbors and brothers. Like the late medieval call for a general peace as a prerequisite to successful crusading, early sixteenth-century Catholic pamphleteers called for unity and Christian brotherly love as a prerequisite for military success.[44]

Christian disunity was evident in selfish betrayal. Hungarian treason was often blamed for Christian losses in the East. It is no surprise that in the context of the struggle for the Hungarian throne, German pamphleteers would call Zapolya a traitor to Christendom. Other Hapsburg foes, including gypsies, Hussites, and the Venetians, were castigated similarly.[45] Protestant hesitance to fight against the 'enemy of Christianity' also was portrayed as treasonous.

More examples of disunity were wasteful internal wars. Princes only think of themselves, their hearts have been turned away "from the honor of war and the common good.[46] Instead of helping Ferdinand, Christians squabble and fight among themselves.[47] The popular broadsheet *Ein newes Lied* (1529) almost pleaded with the German people: although Turkish pride is great, he has little power; if only you had unity and peace in your lands God would stand beside you and you would be victorious. Christian unity would provide incredible measures: an international armada from Spain, France, the Italian States, and England would drive the Turks out Mediterranean;

a land force would drive them out of Europe and provide a permanent 100,000-man defensive garrison in Hungary and Austria. On the other hand, Christian disunity would cause disastrous consequences: exploiting the divisions, the Turks would capture Hungary, Bohemia, Poland, then Germany, and finally Italy, France, and Spain. All of Europe would be lost to the infidel.[48]

There was some measure of Protestant agreement with these Catholic interpretations of Turkish success: from their own perspective Protestants also called for moral improvement and the end of selfishness, disunity, and neglect of Christian duty. In addition to these sins, Protestants blamed Catholic false teaching (idolatry) and the general German apathy toward the Gospel for the Ottoman advance. In contrast to the Catholics, however, Protestants much more strongly emphasized that the Turks were the scourge of God.[49] Christians did not simply need to regain His blessing; many Protestants declared that it was impossible to defeat the Turks by military force under *any* circumstances. This was a spiritual battle that would be won only with spiritual weapons.[50]

With significant influence from the Old Testament prophetic calls for justice and righteousness, Protestants (both Lutherans and Radical Reformers) considered the sins of Christendom to be a significant cause of the Turkish successes.[51] One of the best examples of early Protestant thought concerning this is found in the *Conterfaction Theseus der izt Turckischen Keyssers*:

> Truly the Turk is God's scourge by which He disciplines us because of our sins and misdeeds. . . . It is a wonder that God has endured us this long, since we have had his word, clear as day, in writing and preaching yet we continue in our sinful ways. . . . It is demonstrated that we do not have the true faith when there is no improvement.[52]

To the Protestants it is no wonder that God punished Christendom with a foreign power, it was more surprising that they were not completely destroyed.

Disunity was also a cause for the past and the present Turkish victories. For Luther and Melanchthon, the fall of Constantinople was caused by a combination of selfish preoccupation in the West and the conflict between the Greeks and Rome.[53] Due to this disunity, God had punished both of the quarreling parties: the Greeks through Muhammad and the Turks, Rome through the papacy and the Decretals.[54] Furthermore, Luther could not understand why cries of his ravaged and captive subjects did not move the Emperor to more rigorous action. It was the God-given responsibility of the secular government to protect their lands from such raving murderers.[55]

Even more strongly than the Catholics blamed them, Protestants blamed Catholic false teaching for God's punishment. In his 1526 *Vier tröstliche Psalmen,* Luther expressed sympathy with the sufferings of the widowed

Queen Mary of Hungary, but specifically blamed the collapse of the kingdom on divine punishment for the sins of the Roman Church. Similarly,
Melanchthon tied the rise of the Turks to the Catholic acceptance of the
doctrine of transubstantiation at the Fourth Lateran Council in 1215.[56]

According to Luther, the reason that all past military efforts against the
Turks have failed is because they were led by the church. This confusion
of spiritual and temporal authority is blasphemy and disobedience against
God. It angers Him, and as scripture says "There will be no success where
one is disobedient to God."[57]

Other Protestants reiterated these condemnations. Veit Dietrich in *Wie
man das volck* largely blamed Catholic 'idolatry' for the Turkish advance.
God is punishing us because of those who persecute the Gospel and yet
remain in their idolatrous ways.[58] At times the rhetoric could become very
strident. Osiander's *Unterricht wider den Türken* simply took advantage of
the Turkish theme to criticize Roman Catholics:

> The sins that have made God so angry with us are, in brief, the follow-
> ing: contempt for, falsification of, and persecution of his holy, divine
> word; abuse of his holy sacraments, false doctrines invented by human
> beings in divine matters of faith; enforcement of these doctrines at the
> point of the sword, shedding innocent blood, idolatry, heresy, simony,
> black magic, and the pagan Epicurean life of those who care not for
> God, do not go to hear sermons and cannot be persuaded to learn either
> the Our Father or the Creed or the Ten Commandments.[59]

As early as 1530, Protestants were also blaming apathy, unthankfulness, and
the rejection of the Gospel for the Turkish success. Radical Reformers such
as Hofmann claimed that the Turks were God's wrath for the insufficiency
of the Reformation.[60] Melanchthon wrote that is was certain that the
Turkish scourge was due to the despising of the Gospel.[61] Luther called it
a blasphemous "despising of the blood of Christ" and stubborn refusal to
submit to God that fully deserves the Turkish plague.[62] According to Jonas,
when a land is filled with wickedness (as is Germany), God has always sent
a messenger there to preach the gospel as a warning (like Jonah in Nineveh).
If the preaching was rejected, punishment followed. The Gospel has now
been preached in Germany, but largely ignored. "A divine punishment is
at hand but can still be turned from us through amendment of life."[63] Veit
Dietrich even alleged that God caused the Turk to conquer Hungary in order
to punish the Magyars for elevating the Virgin to the status of a goddess.
According to Dietrich, had Hungary reformed after the preaching of the
gospel, there would have been no Turkish visitation. However, "if we persist
in our sins and refuse to change, we and our children must surely expect
from God the same wrath and punishment [as Hungary]."[64] Without the
acceptance of the Gospel and improvement, Protestants believed that God
was more than justified to punish or even destroy Christendom.

Eschatological Limits of Turkish Power

Under such conditions it was natural to seek positive news, to establish some limit to God's punishment and to Turkish power. This hope for a better future was discovered in prophecy. Throughout the history of Christian-Islamic relations, as Richard Southern argued, whenever "the situation became really menacing, and particularly when the menace of complacency within was matched by the measure of danger without, the apocalyptic interpretation of Islam had a new lease on life."[65] This was particularly true in the early sixteenth century, especially due to the importance of prophecy and astrology in the period.[66]

Despite sharing common elements and sources, Catholic and Protestant interpretations and use of prophecy were fundamentally different. Roman Catholic prophecy was encouraging and optimistic. It predicted the rise of a mighty emperor who would definitively destroy Islam. Protestant hope, on the othe hand, was much more apocalyptic. Islam and the Turks were interpreted in eschatological terms. The devil-inspired Turks would not be defeated by mankind, but from outside the system, by God in a cosmological drama that would usher in the Last Judgment.

Sixteenth-century predictions of the destruction of the Turks were grounded in the fact that their rise had also been predicted. The medieval prophecies of Pseudo-Methodius, Merlin, and others were frequently quoted. According to these medieval predictions, Alexander had driven these "Red Jews"[67] into the Caspian Mountains, but a fox (a symbol of Muhammad) would show them a hole by which they might escape from this confinement. In their murdering they would spill much innocent blood, and ravage Christendom even as far as Cologne.[68] Through their celestial observations, early sixteenth-century astrologers Lichtenberger (in 1503) and Gruenpeck (in 1524) confirmed these predictions: The Turks would continue to be successful against the Christians until they had reached the Rhine.[69]

But according to Catholic authors there was a limit to Turkish power. All of the Ottoman gains were temporary. Both medieval prophets and contemporary miraculous signs in the heavens proved this. Since God only punishes to the third or fourth generation, after about eighty years of Turkish control Constantinople would be freed by a mighty emperor. Through God's help this mighty emperor will gather a huge army and destroy Turkish power forever.[70] "Thereafter the banner of our Lord Jesus Christ will be taken to the East with great honor. The *Machometicschen glaub* will cease and everywhere Muslims and Indians will run to Christian baptism.[71] The entire world will be conquered for Christianity, and "whoever will not adore the Holy Cross, he will kill."[72] Finally, the emperor will come to Jerusalem and in the thirtieth year of his reign die on the Mount of Olives.[73]

These eschatological predictions derive directly from late medieval prognostications regarding Islam. Joachim of Fiore and Spiritual Franciscans such as Peter John Olivi and John of Rupescissa all predicted a future conflict followed by the mass conversions of Muslims to Christianity.[74] Sixteenth-century Roman Catholic eschatology involving the Turks did not significantly alter this received tradition, but simply updated it in light of the contemporary Hapsburg-Ottoman conflict.

As might be expected, the Hapsburgs were not unaware of the value of these apocalyptic predictions as political propaganda.[75] As early as 1518 Maximillian's court poet, Jörg Dappach, wrote a *Lied* in which the Hapsburg emperor was the fulfillment of the Methodius prophecy.[76] After his accession, Charles V knew that many considered him to be the great emperor who would definitively defeat the Turks; he courted this interpretation and perhaps even believed it himself.[77] Whenever a rare victory was won against the Ottomans (as in 1535 at Tunis), a flurry of pamphlets were published that confirmed Charles's role.[78] The Hapsburgs used this to their advantage. It was no coincidence that the pamphlets that contain the 'mighty power' prophecy also include appeals to fight the Turks in obedience to Charles and/or Ferdinand.[79]

For Luther, in contrast, the Turkish problem would not be solved through a mighty emperor or any human power, but only through the direct apocalyptic intervention of God. The Turks were an important part of a 'last days' drama that ended only at the final judgment. This eschatological interpretation of Islam proved to be very influential in later Protestantism although it was not accepted by all.[80]

Like the Catholics, Luther's eschatology shared significant continuities with medieval positions and many of his eschatological themes were based on medieval ideas.[81] Luther was aware of and interested in the predictions and prophecies found in the writings of the Middle Ages. For example, he made a considerable effort to secure a fragment of the writings of the Franciscan monk Johann Hilton who supposedly had predicted both the Reformation and the Turkish advance.[82] Ultimately, however, Luther turned to the authority of scripture and offered his own explanations.

Comparing the contemporary condition of the world to scripture, it was clear to Luther that he was living in the last days. "For the scripture is completely fulfilled: so many signs have been seen and so great a light of the Gospel has shown forth, yet there is such great wickedness in the world as never before; things could never get any worse, the world must come to an end."[83] He likened contemporary Germany to the days before the flood when wickedness covered the earth. God will no longer bear it; the Last Judgment is at the door.[84] The Turks played an important role in this interpretation of the *eschaton*. Because the end of the world is near, the devil rages with his two weapons: the antichrist (the Pope), and the tribulation prophesied in Matt. 24:21 (the Turks). "The Turks are certainly the last and most furious raging of the devil against the Christ . . . after the Turk comes the judgment and hell."[85] When he heard rumors that the Turks and the Pope had entered an alliance, it confirmed his suspicions: "Now the world comes to its end."[86] Other theologians agreed; the Turkish *Reich* is indeed the biblical "final tribulation."[87]

In the eyes of these theologians, it was fortunate that scripture contained a wealth of information on the last days. One of the most important descriptions was found in the Book of Daniel. Luther, Melanchthon and Jonas all wrote interpretations of this book in relation to the Turks.[88] Since they were actually experiencing the events in Daniel, Lutheran theologians thought it was completely valid to mine the book for information on the contemporary situation concerning the Turks.

The four beasts of Chapter 7 were interpreted historically to represent the four kingdoms of Assyria-Babylon, Medo-Persia, the Greeks, and the Romans.[89] The ten horns represented the ten provinces of the Roman Empire: France, Italy (Welshland), Spain, Africa, Germany, England, Hungary, Greece, Asia, and Egypt. The Turks entered the interpretation in verse eight: Muhammad and his faith was the little horn that arose in the midst of the ten horns, the eyes of the horn are Muhammad's *Koran odder gestz* with which he rules. "In whose law there is no divine eye, but mere human reason without God's word and spirit." The mouth that speaks blasphemous things is Muhammad exalting himself over Christ. The statement that the little horn will oppress and rule over the saints was clearly true of the Turks. "For no people are more the enemies of the Turks than the Christians, the Turks fight against no one with such bloodthirstiness as against Christians." That Luther considered the majority of the people conquered by the Turks not to be 'real Christians' was no hindrance. Just a few true Christians in the military make the Turkish campaigns an oppression of the saints. Christian prisoners fulfilled the prophecy that the Turk will rule over the saints. In the end, the battle will culminate in the Last Judgment, and Luther provided a nasty eschatological picture of the sudden change in fortune for the Turks and their being thrust into an eternal punishment in hell.

Despite its appearance, this exegesis of Daniel gave Lutherans a great deal of confidence. Although Luther would not publically declare an *ad terminus* date for Turkish power, he predicted that the Last Judgment would happen in the very near future.[90] Privately he suggested c.1558 based upon his numerological interpretation of Daniel 7:25 (a time, two times, and half a time).[91] Not only were the Turks limited chronologically, they were also limited geographically. Daniel stated that the little horn uprooted only three of the ten horns. The Turks had already captured three 'provinces': Egypt, Africa, and Asia. According to scripture they would take no more territory; although they may be attacked, Hungary, Germany and the rest of Europe were safe![92]

The Book of Revelation also offered valuable insights on the contemporary situation.[93] In Lutheran analysis, Muhammad and the Turks appeared prominently in several portions of St. John's prophecy. Marginal comments of the *Deutshe Bibel* stated that Muhammad was the second woe (Chapter 9:13–21) between Arius and the Pope.[94] Although Luther finally reserved the designation 'Antichrist' for the Pope alone,[95] other theologians saw the Turks as participating in or part of the antichrist. Some declared the Turks

Figure 6.1 Turks Destroyed Before the Holy City, Matthias Gerung, 1530

Used by permission of the Universität- und Forschungsbibliothek Erfurt. UB Erfurt, Dep. Erf. 03-Na 4° 00287 (29)

to be one manifestation, the 'physical' or corporal, as the compliment to the 'spiritual' manifestation of the antichrist in the papacy.[96]

The most direct reference to the Turks in the Book of Revelation was in relation to Gog and Magog in Chapter 20. Lutheran theologians understood Gog/Magog to be the biblical designation for the Turks, as had been established by Luther's separately published translation of Ezekiel 38 and 39.[97]

Revelation 20 declared that after 1000 years the devil will be loosed to make war on the saints. He will gather Gog and Magog to besiege the city of God's people, but they will be destroyed with fire from heaven and cast into eternal damnation. (20:7–10). Luther interpreted the 1000 years of the binding of the devil to be a past event. This 1000 years was from the writing of the Book of Revelation until the founding of the Turkish kingdom c.1300 (he stated that the figures do not have to be exact.) Therefore, the devil's last time of raging is the period of the Ottoman Empire. Even though the Turks may attack the city of God (thought by some to be a reference to Vienna), they will not succeed. They will be destroyed not by military force, but by fire from heaven. (See Figure 6.1) As in the Book of Daniel, after the destruction of the Turks there is only one more event in human history: the Last Judgment.

Lutheran interpretations of the Turkish advance became increasingly pessimistic during the difficult years of the 1540s. If God did not intervene soon, they believed Europe might be destroyed by Islam. Melanchthon considered the situation so hopeless that he looked around for secure cities where at least a remnant of the Gospel could be preserved.[98] Luther wrote on the wall of his Wittenberg study that by 1600 the Turks would conquer all of Germany.[99] This extreme sense of despair represents a significant divergence from the medieval views of Islam and, in the end, one of the Reformation Era's primary contributions to the history of Christian-Islamic relations.[100]

Notes

1. Martin Luther, *Resolutiones disputationem de indulgentiarum virtute*, 535.
2. Some Radical Reformers, including Hofmann, Hut, Ziegler, Servetus, and Müntzer, minimized the territorial aspects of the Muslim challenge and emphasized a common interior spirituality. Williams, 1266–67.
3. Ebermann, 14.
4. Ulrich Hutten stated in *Ad Principes Germanos ut bellum in Turcas*, "You want to overthrow the Turk: I laud the ambition, but I fear you are going astray—seek [the enemy] in Italy, not in the East! Each of of our kings is strong enough to defend his own frontiers against the Turk. But all Christendom does not suffice to win out over that other [the pope]. Quoted in Setton, *Papacy*, 189. See also Carl Göllner, "Der Türke in der dramatischen literatur des 16. Jahrhunderts," 136.
5. Luther, *Resolutiones disputationem*, 535. The entire statement read, "Die meisten Grossen in der Kirche träumten von nichts anderem als von kriegen gegen die Türken, das bedeute aber, vom Kampf nicht gegen die (eigenen) Sünden, sondern gegen, Gottes Rute wider die Sünde und damit gegen Gott selbst, der durch diese Rute unsere Sünden straft, weil wir das nicht selber tun." See also Bobzin, 267.

6. This argument of Stephen Fischer-Galati. It was Fischer-Galati's often repeated thesis that German Protestants were largely unconcerned with the Turkish threat and took advantage of the Ottoman distraction to wrest religious liberties from the Hapsburgs. Fischer-Galati, "Peace of Augsburg", 49–50; Fischer-Galati, *Ottoman Imperialism*, 17–18.

7. Westermann, 16, Ebermann, 19.

8. Luther, *WA Br 5*, 163 (#1481). See also Mau, 653.

9. Luther, *Vom Kriege*, 146.

10. Luther, *Vom Kriege*, 145.

11. Luther, *Heerpredigt*, 160–161. See also Göllner, *Turcica*, vol. 3, 190.

12. For example, in the introduction to *Turcken puechlein*: "Warlich allein das gedicht ist gemacht Das man den vient nit zulang veracht." Kuripecic, *Itinerarum*, a1b-a2a: the wrath of God is not sincerely enough appreciated, "die Straf uns vor der thürs steet." *Ein kleglich ansuch*, a2a: "the threat is far greater than is thought."

13. Fear-driven exaggeration of the Turkish military was very common. In reality the Turkish army was never larger than 250,000 men, but, for example, *Copey und Lautter Abschrifft* claimed that 330,000 had participated in the 1532 campaign; *Ein Summarie der Türckischen Bottschafft* counted over 600,000 (not counting irregulars!) in 1537.

14. This was a very common argument, especially in the *Lieder*. Among others it is found in *Auszug eines Brieffs*, Sachs, *Ein klag zu got, Ein vermanung kaiserliche majestat, Ain ermanung wider die Türken*, Kuripecic, *Itinerarium, Die Abschrift ausz dem Orginial*.

15. For example, *Ein kleglich ansuch*, c3b (particular desire mentioned to possess Christian lands, d1a), *Bapstilicher heylikeit*, a2a (desires nothing less than world domination and the destruction of Christians), *New zeytung Die schlact des Türckischen Keysers*, a4a (The goal of the Turks is world domination. They want the borders of their domain to extend 'to the end of the world'). In a letter of Jonas printed in Giovo, y1b, their desire is to destroy Christendom.

16. Jonas letter in Giovo, y1b-y2b. Jonas was particularly critical of the papacy who has taken much gold out of Germany under the pretext of fighting the Turk and has only used it to increase its own wealth.

17. Giovo, y2a.

18. According to an interviewed Greek, it was their own fault that they are under the "wütenden und tyrannischen hund," because they did not seriously enough consider the threat. Kuripecic, *Itinerarium*, g1b.

19. "It was religious beliefs and practices of the Ottomans, more than any other factor, which gave the confrontation its truly threatening aspect." Biechler, 2–3. Cf. Rodinson, 33, 37–38; Joseph Schacht and C. E. Bosworth, eds., *The Legacy of Islam*, 29.

20. Jonas, *Das siebend Capitel*, a4b.

21. *Babstlicher heiligkeit*, a2a.

22. For example, *New zeytung die schlact des Türckischen*, a4b-b3a, Dietrich, a2v, Giovo, b1b.

23. For example, Georgijevic reported that Christians willingly "ergibe sich in die Religion Mehemmets." Georgijevic, *Von der Türcken gebreuchen*, b4b. This concern was a primary stated motivation behind the writing of Luther's *Vom Kriege*.

24. See Stefan Basignat, *Oratio de Anime inmortalti cum exhortatio*.

25. The Turks not only put men under their heavy service and tyranny, but worst of all, from Christianity "zu seiner verdamlichen sect gefurt un bract hat." *Verzeichnusz ausz was ursachen*), a2a.

26. "Und ist grosse gefahr, das wir ynn der Tu(e)rckey vom Christlichen glauben zum Tu(e)rckischen glauben fallen wu(e)rden, zum teuffel ynn die helle hinein." Luther, *Heerpredigt*, 184.

27. Actually, Muslim missionary success was highly overrated. The travel writings of the fifteenth and sixteenth centuries leave no doubt that throughout the Balkans the Muslims were a minority. There was no great success in missionary efforts among the Christian population, and as can be seen from the construction of mosques, schools, etc., no widespread spreading of Islam outside of administrative centers. Babinger, 204.

28. Concerning 'glittering' works, see Jonas, *Das siebend Capitel*, concerning hardship, see Georgijevic, *Von der Türcken gebreuchen*, b4b, concerning children, see for example, *Volgend zway lieder der armen gefangen Christen*.

29. Luther, *Heerpredigt*, 186.

30. In Giovo, q1b-q2a, a story is told approvingly of a widow of Rhodes who had two small children. When it seemed certain that the island was lost, she killed the children herself "den Tu(e)rcken nicht wollen jnn die hende komen lassen, das sie von Christlicher Religion keme" and then fought on the front lines until she died.

31. "The Turks defeat us much more with their advantage of numbers and trickery than with strength or might." Giovo, g4a.

32. Kuripecic, *Ein Disputation*, c3b-4a. See also, Osiander, a3a-a3b, b4b, Ebermann, 11.

33. Jonas, *Das siebend Capitel*, b2a: "so viel stedte dorffen pfarren kirchen christliche gemein zerreist verstöret und zu bode vertilget die prediger erwürget . . . ein hoher schrecklicher zorn Gottes." Among many others, see for example: Spangenberg, *Der LXXIX Psalm*, Sachs, *Ein new lied vom Türcken*, *Ausz Rathschlage Erasmi*, 2a, 7b, Kuripecic, *Ein Disputation*, d3b.

34. Jonas, *Das siebend Capitel*, b2a: "ein hoher schrecklichen zorn Gottes." *Ein neues Lied*, a4a: "die rütten seiner staff Damit er schlahen thüt die schaff." Kuripecic, *Ein Disputation*, a2b. God "strafft sy [all christen] von jrer sünd wegen."

35. Osiander, b1b. Translation by Bohnstedt, 25.

36. For example, Piscatorus, a2b. See also *Erinnerung der verschulten plagen*.

37. Bohnstedt, 26, Setton, "Lutheranism", 157, Herrmann, 49.

38. Williams specifically mentions Hut's view that the Turks were God's rod of anger with which he would crush a morally and theologically derelict Christendom. Williams, *Radical Reformation*, 267–268, 298. Luther wrote *Vom Kriege* in direct response to this argument.

39. For late medieval interpretations of the Turks as God's punishment, see Pfeffermann, 162 and Kissling, 11.

40. Some of the harshest critiques come from the popular pamphlets *Turcken peuchlein* (especially e2b-g1b) and Kuipecic, *Ein Disputation* (d1b-b).

41. See *Turcken peuchlein* and Kuripecic, *Ein Disputation,* c1a, d3b. See also Herrmann, 70ff and Bohnstedt, 26–28.

42. Döpmann, 324; Setton, "Lutheranism", 157; Göllner, *Turcica*, vol. 3, 196.

43. See especially *Eyn sendbrief der Ungern* and Barlezio, a2b.

44. Sadoleto, b2b.

45. See especially *Ein neues Lied*, a1b-a2a. Also Zell and *Ein newer bergreie*, Ebermann, 38.

46. *Ein Oration des hochwyrdigsten Herrn Franciscen Graffen*, a2b.

47. Kurpecic, *Ein Disputation*, c1b; *Des türkische kaysers heerzug*, a3b. See also Herrmann, 79–80.

48. Quoted in Bohnstedt, 39.

49. According to Bobzin, 267, Luther was not the first Christian to place the growth of Islam in the context of the inner failures of Christianity, but added sharpness by his characterization of it as *Gottesstrafe*. "It is also decisive for Luther that the struggle against the Turks stood as a sign of sensational unrepentance, and again, therefore a revolt against an angry God." Mau, 648.

50. "Ist das darfur die beste waffen
Dar wir alleyn auff Gott thu(e)n hoffen
Darneben in seyn wort vertrawen
Unt gentzlich vns auff Christum bawen
Der die welt vberwunden hat
Durch jhn wir auch obsygen drat
Vnd endtlich kumen in der zeyt zu der ewigen seligkeyt."
Ein spruch wie man dem Thürcken macht widerstehen auch wie sich die Christen solcher nott sollen halten.

51. For example, Luther's marginal comment to Ezekiel 39:23, "Gog umb unser sunde willen mechtig sey und so viel glücke und sieg habe." Luther, *Das XXXVIII und XXXIX Capitel Hesechiel*, 235, *Ein schön geystlich lied*, Sachs, *Ein klag zu got uber die grausam wüterei*.

52. *Conterfaction* continued, "Auch ist der merste teyl noch feindt Dem waren claren gottes wort." This was followed by a long series of biblical examples from the Old Testament, including Rehaboam, Mannasah, Josias, Joiachim, etc.

53. Luther, *Vom Kriege*, 144; Melanchthon's introduction to Giovo, b4a-4b, cla-b.

54. Quoted in Döpmann, 325.

55. Luther, *Vom Kriege*, 129ff.

56. Melanchthon, *Danielem Prophetam Commentarius*, CR 13, 823–1003. See also Köhler, 79–82.

57. Luther, *Vom Kriege*, 114.

58. Dietrich, b1a. See also *Ein new Lied, von der Schlacht inn Ungern*: "lass uns . . . all abgötterei vertreiben, und bessern uns fürbas!"

59. Osiander, b1b.

60. Williams, *Radical Reformation*, 1266–1267. Also, the 'Zwichau Prophets' saw the Turks as "das göttliche Strafgericht an allen Gottlosen, besonders an der verdorbenen Obrigkeit." Other Anabaptists saw in the Turks "die Zetrümmerung des Römischen Reiches deutscher Nation und die Vorbereitung eines neuen apostolischen Reiches." Pfister, "Antistes," 72.

61. "[A]lso ist die welt die zeit gestrafft umb verachtung willen des Evangelij." Giovo, b3b.

62. From Luther's introduction to his translation of Ricoldo de Monte Croce, 274. Also Luther, *Heerpredigt*, 162; Richard Lind, *Luthers Stellung zu Kreuz- und Türkenkrieg*, 34–35.

63. Jonas, *Das siebend Capitel*, b1a.

64. Quoted in Bohnstedt, 51, See also, *Ein kleglich ansuch*, a2a.

65. Southern, 27.

66. These predictions were the "most characteristic element of popular belief during the age of Reformation." Scribner, 117. The most important overall study of early modern eschatology is Robin Barnes, *Prophecy and Gnosis: Apocalypticism in the Wake of the Lutheran Reformation.*

67. This was a common designation for the Turks in the prophetic literature of the early sixteenth century. Methodius called the Turks "Red Jews," Jonas explained, because they keep outward forms like Jews but are a "kriegen, morden eitel bluthund." Jonas, *Das siebend Capitel*, d3b-4b. On the designation "Red Jews" including but beyond the Turks, see Andrew Gow, *The Red Jews: Antisemitism in an Apocalyptic Age, 1200–1600.*

68. For example, *Die Abschrift*, a2b-a3a; *Eyn auszug ettlicher Practica unt Prophecceyn*, Ebermann, 57–58.
69. See Grünpeck. Concerning Lichtenberger, see Barnes, 27–28.
70. See *Zerstörung des Türckishcen Kayserthumbs* and Eberman, 60, 62–63.
71. *Weyssagung des hochberumbten Astrologi*, d2a.
72. Dappach, *Ain schön lied New gemacht* and *Weyssagung dis hochberumnten Astrologi*, d1a-b.
73. *Ain anschlag wie man dem Türke widerstand thun*, b4a, ends with a prophecy (in Latin and German) supposedly written by the monk Cobole in Bononie (Sant Salvators) in 1440 (d.1488) that this emperor shall conquer Palestine and order all to adore the Holy Cross or be killed.
74. Brett Whalen, *Dominion of God: Christendom and Apocalypse in the Middle Ages*, 223–226.
75. "Les prophetics furent comme une nouvelle branche de cette activite propagandiste." Jean Deny, "Les Pseudo-propheties concernant les Turcs au XVIe siècle," 205. Deny argued that these prophesies were not legitimate or even believed, but were inspired by Charles V and served as a branch of his propaganda campaign. Although I see no evidence that these prophecies did not reflect genuine popular belief, both their propaganda value and their use seems clear.
76. "Ain newer christen künig würt (sein nam Maximilian si redten) der hailig land esetten und füllen mit christen glauben." Liliencron, 212–215.
77. Eberman, 57–58.
78. As in *Weyssagung dis hochberumbten Astrologi,* a2b. See also Deny, 210–212.
79. For example, Dappach, *Ain schön lied.*
80. Zwingli's and Calvin's interpretations of the Turks were intentionally non-eschatological. See Barnes, 277 and Pannier, 283ff.
81. Barnes defends the originality of Luther's eschatology without denying the influences and continuities with the medieval period, Barnes, 36ff. For the influence of general medieval eschatological themes on Luther, see Preuss. Concerning the importance of Nicholas of Lyra's world-historical interpretation of the Book of Revelation, see Bousset.
82. Volz, "Beiträge zu Melanchthons und Calvins Auslegungen des Propheten Daniel," 111–112.
83. Luther, *Heerpredigt, 172.*
84. Luther, *Vermahnung, 592.* Luther also likened it to the last days of the Jews before the incarnation. Luther, *Vom Kriege*, 143–144.
85. Luther *Heerpredigt*, 162. See also Bobzin, 285 and Mau, 654.
86. Concerning the eschatological ramifications of a Papal-Turkish alliance: "Ibi sedet papa in tempolo Dei. Quodsi Turca eo venit, zo ists als schlecht, zo ist nichts mer dahinden den dies iudicii. Luther, *WA TR 1*, 135 (#332).
87. Melanchthon's introduction to Giovo, c2a; Jonas, *Das siebend Capitel*, g1a, Osiander.
88. Luther's interpretation is found primarily in *Heerpredigt*. Jonas and Melanchthon worked together to write *Das siebend Capitel*. Jonas, *Das siebend Capitel*, a2a and Volz, 96–109.
89. The following discussion is taken from *Heerpredigt*, 165–171. All Lutheran explanations of Daniel 7 basically concur.
90. "Ko(e)nnen wir sicherlich weissagen, das der iu(e)ngst tag mu(e)sse fue(e)r der thu(e)r sein."
91. This was calculated from 1453 using "time=30 years" (Christ's age), therefore 105 years. This would leave twenty years to go, but Luther emphasized that this was only a possible explanation. Luther, *WA TR 1, 453* (#904).

92. Luther *Heerpredigt*, 171. Also, Jonas, *Das siebend Capitel*, c4a.
93. According to Barnes, 41, the Turkish siege of Vienna was a primary motivation for Luther's formulation of his interpretation of the Book of Revelation.
94. Luther, *Vorrede auff die Offenbarung S. Johannis*, WA DB 7, 409.
95. "Aber wie der Endechrist so ist der Tu(e)rck leibhaffige Teuffel," Luther, *Vom Kriege*, 126.
96. For example, *Ein kleglich ansuch*, a2b. Evidently this was originally an articulation of Luther "papa est spiritus Antichristi et Turca est caro Antichristi. Sie helffen beyde einander wurgen, hic corpore et gladio, ille doctrina et spiritu." Luther, *WA TR 1*, 135 (#330). In general, see Preuss, 171–175. This characterization would become more widespread in the seventeenth century.
97. This special printing was perhaps the first work he did at Coburg. See Miller, "Preface," Ebermann, 9–10, and Köhler, 73–75. The equation of the Turks with Gog/Magog was not universal. For example, Biblander did not find the connection to be either historical or biblical. Pfister, "Bibliander," 445–449.
98. Benz, 27.
99. 'Millesimo Sexcentessimo veniet Turcus totam Germaniam devastaturus." Vogler, 119–120. See also Mau, 661.
100. J. Paul Rajashekar, "Luther and Islam: An Asian Perspective," 174–191 and Göllner, *Turcica*, vol. 3, 194–195.

References

Ain anschlag wie man dem Türke widerstand thun. n.p., 1522.
Ain ermanung wider die Türken und wie si die Christen durchechtent im land Ungern. n.p., 1522.
Ausz Ratschlage Herren Erasmi von Roterdam die Türcken zubekriegen Der ursprung unnd alle geschichten der selbigen gegen Römische Keyser unnd gemeyne Christenheit vo anbegin des türckischen namenn nach der kürtze new verteutscht. n.p., 1530.
Auszug eines Briefes wie einer so in der türkey wonhafft seinem freünd in dise landt geschriben un wessen sey und wie Türcken Regiment un wessen sey und wie er es mit den landen so er erobert zu halten pflegt kürtzlich in Teütsche sprach gebracht nützlich diser zeyt zu wissen. Wittenberg: Schirlentz, 1526.
Babinger, Franz. "Die Osman auf dem Balkan." In *Völker und Kulturen Südosteuropas: Kulturhistorische Beiträge.* Balwin Saria, ed. Munich: Südosteuropa Verlaggesellschaft, 1959, 211–217.
Bäbstlicher heilikeit sampt Römscher Keiserlicher Maiestat auch anderer kristlichen Künig un Fürste botschaffte anschlag wider die Türken. n.p., 1518.
Barlezio, Marino. *Des aller streytparsten un theüresten Fürsten und Herrn Georgen Casttioten genant Scanderberg.* Augsburg: Steiner, 1533.
Barnes, Robin. *Prophecy and Gnosis: Apocalypticism in the Wake of the Lutheran Reformation.* Stanford: Stanford University Press, 1988.
Basignat, Stefan. *Oratio de Anime inmortalti Cum exhortatio ad capessenda arma contra Infidele.* n.p., 1517.
Benz, Ernst. *Wittenberg und Byzanz: Zur Begegnung und Auseinandersetzung der Reformation und der östlich-orthodoxen Kirche.* Marburg: Elwert-Gröfe und Unzer Verlag, 1949.
Biechler, James E. "Christian Humanism Confronts Islam: Sifting the Qur'an with Nicholas of Cusa." *Journal of Ecumenical Studies* 13 (1976): 1–14.

Bobzin, Harmut. "Martin Luthers Beitrag zu Kenntnis und Kritik des Islam." *Neue Zeitschrift für Systematische Theologie* 27:3 (1985): 262–289.

Bohnstedt, John W. "The Infidel Scourge of God: The Turkish Menance as Seen by German Pamphleteers of the Reformation Era." *Transactions of the American Philosophical Society* NS 58:9 (1968).

Bousset, Wilhelm. *Die Offenbarung Johannis*. Göttingen: Vandenhoeck and Rupricht, 1896.

Copey und Lautter Abschrifft ains warhafftigen Sendbrieffs, wie der Constantinopel aussgezogen, unt gen Kriechischen Weyssenburg ankomen ist, wie volgt. Dresden: Stöckel, 1532.

Dappach, Jörg. *Ain schön lied New gemacht won den türkenn. Auss der prophecy daruon man lang gesagt hat*. n.p., 1522.

Deny, Jean. "Les Pseudo-propheties concernant les Turcs au XVIe siecle." *Revue des études islamiques* 10 (1936): 201–220.

Des Türckische Kaysers heerzug wie er von Constantinopel Mit aller rüstung zu Ross und Fuss zu wasser und land u gen kriechische Weyssenburg kummen und fürter für die königlichen stat Ofen yn Ungern unnd Wien yn Osterreich gezoge die belegert un gestürmt u mit angehenckter ermanung der grausamen tyranny des Türcken wyder christliche Nation. Nürnburg: Zell, 1530.

Die Abschrift ausz dem Orginial so der Turck sampt dem könig von Cathy vnd Persien allen stenden des Römischen Reychs geschryben haben. n.p., 1523.

Dietrich, Veit. *Wie man das Volck zur Busz und ernstlichem gebet wider den Türcken auff der Cantzel vermanen sol*. Nürnberg: Berg, 1542.

Döpmann, Hans-Dieter. "Das Verhältnis Luthers und der Lutheraner zu den orthodoxen Kirchen." *Theologische Literaturzeitung* 109:5 (May 1984): 321–334.

Ebermann, Richard. "Die Türkenfurcht: Ein Beitrag zur Geschichte der öffentlichen Meinung in Deutschland während der Reformationszeit." Ph.D. diss., Halle University, 1904.

Ein kleglich ansuchen des ausschus der V. nider osterreichischen lande belangend die grosse jtzige fahr des Türcken halben. Wittenberg: Klug, 1540.

Ein neues Lied, in welchem fürsten und herren und andere stend des reichs mit sampt allen frummen lanzknechten zu fryd ind einickeit, auch got, den allergrossmechtigsten Keiser und herren mit höchstem fleiss anzurufen und in seinem namen auch umb seiner eer willen ritterlichen zu straiten wyder den Türcken treulich vermant werden. Nürnberg: n.p., 1529.

Ein new Lied, von der Schlacht inn Ungern geschehen im 1537. n.p., 1537.

Ein newer bergreie von Künig Ludwig auss Ungern. Von dem Künig von Ungern, wie er umbkommen ist. n.p., 1526.

Ein Oration des hochwyrdigsten Herrn Franciscen Graffen von Frangenpaen Ertzbischoff zu Calitschon und Bischoff zu Agran Gehalten zu Regenspurg am 9. Junij anno 1541. Ingolstadt: Weissenhorn, 1541.

Ein schön geystlich lied, Zu Gott, in aller not, trübsal und verfolgung. Nürnberg: Linck, 1531.

Ein spruch wie man dem Thürcken macht widerstehen auch wie sich die Christen solcher nott sollen halten. n.p., 1531.

Ein Summarie der Türckischen Bottschafft werbung an die herrschafft zu Venedig in Welsch sprach beschehen sampt des venedischen Senats gegebene Antwort. Copia eins briefs dem Cardinal von Neapolis zugeschickt jnhaltend die anzal der Türckischen Armada und kriegszvolcks zu Rosz unf fus wider Italien. n.p., 1537.

Ein vermanung kaiserliche majestat sampt aller stend des römischen reichs eines hezugs wider die pluttürstigen türken. Regensburg; n.p., 1532.

Erinnerung der verschulten plagen, des Teutschlands, sampt ainer getrewen ermanung zu Christenlicher bekerung, unnd schuldiger hilff, wider des Türcken grausam fürnemen unnd erschrocklichen angriff, in dem Ertzhertzogtumb Osterreich gethun. n.p., 1529.

Eyn auszug ettlicher Practica unt Prophecceyn. Sibille, Brigitte, Arili, Joachim des Abts, Methodij, un bruder Reinhartz. n.p., 1518.

Eyn sendbrief der Ungern in welchem angetzegt wyrdt. n.p., 1526.

Fischer-Galati, Stephen A. *Ottoman Imperialism and German Protestantism, 1521–1555.* Cambridge, MA: Harvard University Press, 1972.

Fischer-Galati, Stephen A. "The Turkish Question and the Religious Peace of Augsburg." *Südostforschung* 15 (1956): 290–311.

Georgijevic, Bartholomew. *Von der Türken gebreuchen, gewonheyten und Ceremonien.* Nürnberg: Guldenmunde, 1544.

Giovo, Paolo. *Ursprung des Turkischen Reichs bis auff den itzigen Solyman druch D. Paulum Jouium Bischoff Nucerin an keiserliche Maiestate Carolum V. inn welcher sprach geschrieben er nach aus dem Latin F. Bassainatis verdeutschet durch Justum Jonan.* Augsburg: Steiner, 1538.

Göllner, Carl. "Der Türke in der dramatischen Literatur des 16. Jahrhunderts." *Revue des études sud-est européennes* 3:1–2 (1965): 131–153.

Göllner, Carl. *Turcica: Die europäischen Türkendrucke des XVI. Jahrhunderts. Vol. 3. Die Türkenfrage in der öffentlichen Meinung Europas im 16. Jahrhundert.* Bucharest: Editura Academiei, 1968.

Gow, Andrew. *The Red Jews: Antisemitism in an Apocalyptic Age, 1200–1600.* Leiden: Brill, 1995.

Grünpeck, Josef. *Ein Dyalogus Doctor Joseph Gruenpeck von Burckhausen: do des Türckischen Kayser Astronismus Disputiert mit des Egiptischen Soldans obristem radte, ainem verlaugnten Christen von dem glauben der Christen un von dem glauben des Machumeten.* Landshut: Weissenburger, 1522.

Herrmann, Ehrenfried. "Türke und Osmanreich in der Vorstellung der Zeitgenossen Luthers: Ein Beitrag zur Untersuchung des deutsche Türkenscriftens." Ph.D. diss., University of Freiburg, 1961.

Hutten, Ulrich. *Ad Principes Germanos ut bellum in Turcas concorditer suscipiant exhortatoria.* Augsburg: Wirsung, 1518.

Jonas, Justus. *Das siebend Capitel Danielis von des Türken Gottes lesterung und schrecklicher moderey mit unterrich.* Wittenberg: Lufft, 1529.

Kissling, Hans Joachim. "Türkenfurcht und Türkenhoffnung im 15/16. Jahrhundert: zur Geschichte eines 'Komplexes.'" *Südost-Forschungen* 23 (1964): 1–18.

Köhler, Manfred. *Melanchthon und der Islam: Ein Beitrag zur Klärung des Verhältnisses zwischen Christentum und Fremdreligionen in der Reformationszeit.* Leipzig: Klotz, 1938.

Kuripecic, Benedict. *Ein Disputation oder Gesprech zwayer Stalbuben So mit küniglicher Maye. Botschafft bey dem Türckischen Keyser zu Constantinopel gewesen Dieweil sy allda in jhrer beherbergung vo dem Türcken verspert beschehen.* Augsburg: Steiner, 1531.

Kuripecic, Benedict. *Itinerarium Wegrayss K. May. Potschafft gen Constantinopel zu dem Türckischen Kayser Soleyman Anno xxx.* n.p., 1531.

Liliencron, R. V. *Die historischen Volkslieder der Deutschen vom 13 bis 16. Jahrhundert.* Vols. 3 and 4. Leipzig: F. C. W. Vogel, 1867–69.

Lind, Richard. *Luthers Stellung zu Kreuz- und Türkenkrieg.* Giessen: Brühl, 1940.

Luther, Martin. *Das XXXVIII und XXXIX Capitel Hesechiel vom Gog. Verdeudscht durch Mart. Luther* (1530). *WA 30II,* 107–148.

Luther, Martin. *Heerpredigt wider den Türken* (1530). *WA 30II,* 160–197.

Luther, Martin. *Resolutiones disputationem de indulgentiarum virtute* (1518). *WA 1,* 522–628.

Luther, Martin. *Verlegung des Alcoran Bruder Richardi, Prediger Ordens. Verdeutscht und herausgegeben von Martin Luther* (1542). *WA 53,* 272–276.

Luther, Martin. *Vermahnung zum Gebet wider den Türken* (1541). *WA 51,* 585–625.

Luther, Martin. *Vom Kriege wider den Türcken* (1529). *WA 30II,* 107–148.

Luther, Martin. *Vorrede auff die Offenbarung S. Johannis. WA DB 7,* 404–421.

Luther, Martin. *WA Briefwechsel (Br) 5,* 163–164 (#1481).

Luther, Martin. *WA Tischrede (TR) 1,* 135 (#330).

Luther, Martin. *WA Tischrede (TR) 1,* 135 (#332).

Luther, Martin. *WA Tischrede (TR) 1,* 448–456 (#904)

Mau, Rudolf. "Luthers Stellung zu den Türken." In *Leben und Werk Martin Luthers von 1526 bis 1546.* Helmar Junghans, ed. Göttingen: Vandenhoeck and Ruprecht, 1983, 647–662.

Melanchthon, Philip. *Danielem Prophetam Commentarius. CR 13,* 823–1003.

Miller, Gregory J. "Preface to the Thirty-Eighth and Thirty-Ninth Chapters of Ezekiel on Gog." In *Luther's Works* (American Edition). Vol. 59, 277–286. St. Louis: Concordia Press, 2012.

New zeytung Die schlact des Türckischen Keysers mit Ludouico etwan König zu Ungern geschehen am tag Johannis enthaltung 1526. n.p., 1526.

Osiander, Andreas. *Unterricht und vermanung wie man wider den Türcken peten und streyten soll. Auff ansuchung etlicher gutter Herrn und Freunde. An die jhenigen gestalt bey denen der Türck schon angriffen und schaden gethon und sie desselben noch alle tag gewertig sein müssen.* n.p., 1542.

Pannier, J. "Calvin et les Turcs." *Revue Histoire* 62:3 (1937): 268–286.

Pfeffermann, Hans. *Die Zusammenarbeit der Renaissancepäpste mit den Türken.* Winterthur: Mondial Verlag, 1946.

Pfister, Rudolf. "Antistes Heinrich Bullinger über den Türgg." *Evangelisches Missions Magazine* 98 (May 1954), 69–78.

Pfister, Rudolf. "Das Türkenbüchlein Theodor Biblianders." *Theologische Zeitung* 9 (1953): 438–468.

Piscatorius, Johannes. *Herkommen Ursprung unnd Auffgang des Türckischen unnd Ottomannischen kayserthums unnd was die selben für künigreich Länder und Stett so in kurzen Jaren den Christen abgetrungen sollen haben.* Augsburg: Steiner, 1542.

Preuss, Hans. *Die Vorstellungen vom Antichrist im späteren Mittelalter bei Luther und der konfessionellen Polemik.* Leipzing: Hinrichs, 1906.

Rajashekar, J. Paul. "Luther and Islam: An Asian Perspective." *Luther Jahrbuch* (1990): 174–191.

Rodinson, Maxime. *Europe and the Mystique of Islam.* Roger Veinus, trans. Seattle: University of Washington Press, 1987.

Sachs, Hans. *Ein Klag zu got uber die grausam wüterei des grausamen Türken ob seinen viel kriegen und obsiegen.* n.p., 1532.

Sachs, Hans. *Ein new lied vom Türcken.* Nürnberg: Gutknecht, 1530.

Sadoleto, Jacob. *Eyn schone nutzliche und Christeniche rede nawlich geschehen ist.* Dresden: Stöckel, 1518.

Schacht, Joseph and C. E. Bosworth, eds. *The Legacy of Islam.* 2nd ed. Oxford: Clarendon Press, 1974.

Scribner, Robert W. *For the Sake of Simple Folk.* Cambridge: Cambridge University Press, 1981.

Setton, Kenneth M. "Lutheranism and the Turkish Peril." *Balkan Studies* 3 (1962): 133–168.

Setton, Kenneth. *The Papacy and the Levant.* Vol. 3. Philadelphia: American Philosophical Society, 1984.

Southern, R. W. *Western Views of Islam in the Middle Ages.* Cambridge: Harvard University Press, 1962.

Spangenberg, Johann. *Der LXXIX Psalm auff die weise, Aus tieffer not.* n.p., 1545.

Stocr, Niklas. *Conterfaction Theseus der izt Turckischen Keyssers.* n.p., 1526.

Turcken peuchlein. Ein Nutzlich Gesprech, oder underride etlicher personen, zu besserug christlicher ordnung un lebens. n.p., 1522.

Verzeichnusz ausz was ursachen der Künffig Reichsstag auff Egidij nechst fürnemlich aussgeschriben. Nürnberg: n.p., 1522.

Vogler, Günther. "Luthers Geschichtsauffassung im Spiegel seines Türkenbildes." In *450 Jahre Reformation*, Leo Stern and Max Steinmetz, eds. Berlin: VEB Deutscher Verlag der Wissenschaften, 1967, 118–127.

Volgend zway lieder der armen gefangen Christen zu Constantinopel, irer jämmerlichen Klag und ermanung an gemeine Christenheit. Nürnberg: Guldemunde, 1526.

Volz, Hans. "Beiträge zu Melanchthons und Calvins Auslegungen des Propheten Daniel." *Zeitschrift für Kirchengeschichte* 67 (1955–56): 93–118.

Westermann, Ascan. *Die Türkenhilfe und die politisch-kirchlichen Parteien auf dem Reichstag zu Regensburg 1532.* Heidelberg: Carl Winter Universitätsbuchhandlung, 1910.

Weyssagung des hochberumbten Astrologi und Artzen doctoris Antonij Torquanti von Ferrer. n.p., 1535.

Whalen, Brett. *Dominion of God: Christendom and Apocalypse in the Middle Ages.* Cambridge: Harvard University Press, 2009.

Williams, George. *The Radical Reformation.* 3rd ed. Kirksville, MO: 16th Century Journal, 1992.

Zell, Christoph. *Ein neues Lied in welchem aufz angebung deren so von anfang mit und darbey gewesen Die gantz handlung des Turcken in Ungern und Osterreych nemlich der belegerung der Stat Wien begryffen ist.* Nürnberg: Peypus, 1529.

Zerstörung des Türckishcen Kayserthumbs wie es Methodius lang zuvor durch den grossen roten Trachen mit sieben häuptern. n.p., 1524.

7 Holy War and Its Discontents
Responses to the Ottoman Advance

O Lord God in the highest throne
Look upon this great misery
That the Turkish raging tyrant
Has done in Vienna forest
Wretchedly murdering virgins and wives
Cutting children in half
Impaling them on posts
O our shepherd Jesus Christ
Turn your wrath away from the people
Save us out of the hand of the Turks.[1]
                                    Anonymous

Pamphlets, broadsheets, sermons, and ballads repeatedly broadcast a Turkish threat of supernatural proportions to the German people of the Reformation Era. These depictions were not simply descriptive but were intended to move people into action. Indeed, the severity of the threat demanded a serious response. But what was the appropriate response? In the Middle Ages, the obligation had been clear: it was the Christian's duty to fight against these heretics with force of arms. Due to the Reformation in early sixteenth century Germany, however, the traditional medieval response to Islam underwent devastating attacks. New ideas were articulated concerning the appropriate Christian response to the Turks. In the face of these criticisms, even traditional positions were modified. By 1545, the monolithic medieval view had broken apart along confessional lines and the earliest beginnings of modern approaches to Islam could be seen.[2]

Missions, Rapprochement, and *Türkenhoffnung*

As in the Middle Ages, some sixteenth-century writers, particularly those categorized as Christian humanists, hoped for the conversion of Turks through missions.[3] Erasmus is particularly important in this regard. His doctrinal simplification of Christianity had the consequence that the boundary between the *philosophia christi* and natural law morality was obscured, to the advantage of devout pagans.[4] For Erasmus, the noble pagan possessed a *religio naturalis*, and therefore it was possible that some moral and pious Turks were perhaps already part of the true Church and that others could be converted. However, as he wrote in the introduction to his 1518 edition of the *Enchiridion*, this evangelization should be by example, not conquest.[5]

On the question of possible salvation for Muslims, Bibliander in particular was significantly influenced by Erasmian Humanism.[6] In opposition to Zwingli,[7] Bibliander based salvation not on election, but rather in *"der universal Hilfswille Gottes."* Since God places the heart of man *semina religionis et sapientiae*, it is possible for some to become the 'friends of God' without carrying the name of Jesus. A partial revelation of God could come from a consideration of creation, the teaching of angels, by a special work of the Holy Spirit, or by being part of the *ecclesia primitivorum*. There were precious elements in all religions; Bibliander regarded these as gifts of a common heavenly father and not borrowings or thefts.

Yet, primitive religious impulses could only be fully satisfied through Christianity. Therefore missionary work was imperative. It appears that Bibliander intended to go to Egypt personally as a missionary, but was dissuaded with difficulty by his Zürich colleague Heinrich Bullinger. Since Bibliander considered Islamic missions to be primarily a problem of communication, language study was urged.[8] This was also the motivation behind his Latin edition of the Qur'an. Bibliander understood the Christian ingredients in the Qur'an to be a *preparatio evangelii*, and suggested that missionaries emphasize certain fundamental principles on which both religions could agree.[9] The Turks could become fully the sons of God simply if they cast off their beliefs in the false prophet. Bibliander was optimistic enough to believe that some were not so committed to Islam that this would be impossible.[10]

The sixteenth-century conflict with the Turks was also important for the development of Lutheran concepts of missionary work.[11] A chronological evolution in views of missions to the Muslims can be found in Lutheran Reformation Era writings. The 'early' position was developed primarily in relation to the conflict with the papacy. In the early 1520s Luther accused the Pope of always wanting to make war against the Turks but never sending them preachers of the Gospel.[12] Luther also expressed a desire that before the Last Judgment the gospel would be spread throughout the entire world, including Muslim lands. A similar argument was made by Hartmuth Cronberg. In *Ein Sendbrieff* he claimed that the conversion of the Turks to Christianity would be entirely within the grasp of reality, if they would be shown "that our faith stands on the foundation of Christ alone (as the entire Holy Scripture shows) and on brotherly love, not on Rome or the papacy or our own interests."[13] Under such conditions it was Cronberg's hope that "all the people of the world would be moved to the true faith."[14]

After 1526 Luther became directly concerned with the actual Turkish threat and its effect on Germans. With the growing eschatological identification of the Turk and the devil, it became impossible to conceive of wholesale conversions of Turks. However, it was still possible for a few individuals to be converted. Citing the biblical examples of Joseph and Daniel, Luther suggested that any Turkish conversions would not take place through professional missionaries, scripture, or preaching, however, but only through the example of Christian captives.[15]

In *Heerpredigt*, Luther offered counsel to those who might be captured: be patient in your imprisonment (this may be God's will), serve your master well, do not commit suicide, suffer your bondage as a cross. Luther concluded that since biblical evidence demands that slaves be obedient to their masters, if Christians disobeyed their Turkish lords, they shamed the name of Christ and only encouraged the Turks in their faith.[16] However, "if the [captive] Christians are a true, obedient, pious, humble, diligent people, this will shame the Turkish faith and perhaps convert many."[17] Even women could participate in this missionary work by submitting to their Turkish masters "at bed and table" for Christ's sake. They were not to think that they were damned for doing so: "the soul can do nothing about what the enemy does to the body".[18] There was only one qualification to this absolute obedience. Captives were to resist the command to fight against Christians, even resisting to the point of death. Cooperation with the Turkish army would put an individual on the wrong side of the eschatological battle (Daniel 7 again) and would damn them with the rest of the devil's minions.[19]

Late in life, Luther was much more pessimistic. In his translation of Ricoldo de Monte Croce, he changed his earlier opinion and stated that Turks and Saracens could not be converted because they were so hardened.[20] How can one be converted if they reject the entire scriptures, both Old Testament and New Testament and permit no argument from scripture?[21]

Pessimism was not universal among Lutherans, however. As Luther was declaring that the Last Judgment was at hand, Lutheran pastors in the Balkans were beginning to realize the advantages of Turkish rule and making confident predictions of large numbers of Turkish conversions. Reports were sent back to Germany that some Turks were coming to hear Protestant sermons and that the word of the Lord was spreading more quickly among the Turks than among the Catholics.[22]

In addition to missions, some Germans encouraged a rapprochement with the Turks. Humanists, including Erasmus and Vives, argued that military action may be necessary against the 'enemy of the faith,' but that non-violent solutions be attempted first: "the Turks are men like us."[23] In the wake of the Protestant Reformation, some Radical Reformers disavowed all violence. The pacifism of these Anabaptists was apparently also influential, despite the fact that pacifism toward the 'enemy of the faith' was considered a betrayal of Christianity itself.[24]

Radical Reformers were very much aware of the Turkish incursions into central Europe but in general maintained a strong non-violent stand. Radical Reformers minimized the territorial aspects of the Muslim challenge and emphasized religious similarities. This may have been slightly to their political advantage in negotiations with local Turkish lords,[25] but was primarily developed in response to theological positions, such as the *ecclesia spiritualis* and doctrine of love.[26] One must not fight against the Turks, Sebastian Franck wrote, "for whether outwardly they are called heathens, Jews, Turks, or Christians, whoever lives righteously, then let them be a true brother, flesh and blood in Jesus."[27]

It was widely believed that these Protestants, as well as many other peasants and commoners, actually desired the overlordship of the Turks (*Türkenhoffnung*). Some were willing to negotiate with the Turks on 'secular' terms, others to relocate to Turkish controlled territories, some perhaps even to support an Ottoman invasion of central Europe. In 1541 Joachim Greff reported that there were some who said "Ha—what do I care who conquers us—the devil, his mother, the Turk, or whoever! It's all the same to me who is my ruler . . . it's far better to live under the Turk than under some Papist tyrant."[28]

There is some evidence that these accusations were true, although the danger from a pro-Turkish 'fifth column' in Germany was greatly exaggerated. In *Neue Zeitung, Die Schlacht des Turckischen Keysers mit Ludovico* (1526), it was reported that "many of the peasants and knights have gone over to the Turks," and that even Italians and Germans were seeking protection in Turkish territories from "Christian tyranny."[29] It was widely known that Christian skilled laborers were well treated in the Ottoman Empire, and it appears that some specialists relocated to Constantinople.[30] Many pamphlets report similar defections.[31]

Pro-Turkish sentiment among the Radical Reformers and peasants certainly was not unjustified. The fortunes of the Anabaptists in Moravia, for example, rose or fell in direct proportion to the Turkish threat. The periods of greatest persecution (1527–29, 1535–37, and 1547–51) occurred when Ottoman attention was directed away from east-central Europe. Taxation for defense against the Turks in the Hapsburg crown lands and Hungary became so heavy that the peasants considered Turkish rule to be more secure and less oppressive.[32]

The majority of the writers in Reformation Germany were greatly alarmed by both pacifism and *Türkenhoffnung*, however. Catholics advised Germans not to be convinced by pacifist arguments. Resist the evil Turkish aggression vigorously, Bishop Nausea wrote, Christians were fighting for a just cause and could kill in good conscience.[33] Turkish treatment of the Hungarians was cited as evidence of "what kind of guests are invited home" when the Turks are supported by Christians. *Vier warhafftige missiue* asked the rhetorical question, "What true Christian would put body, goods, and everything in danger by making an alliance, peace, or other [rapprochement] with such an enemy of God?"[34]

Because Lutherans had been accused of supporting non-aggression against the Turks, they were particularly vociferous in their denunciations of pacifism. One of the primary reasons that Luther wrote *Vom Kriege* was to counter such criticism. Similar motivations prompted a strong statement in *Unterricht der Visitatoren*. Evangelical pastors were not to permit anyone to teach that the Turk is not to be resisted because revenge is prohibited for the Christian. Rather, people should be taught that the authorities have been given the sword and power to punish all murderers and robbers, including the Turks.[35] In *Türkenbüchlein* Luther an pamphleteers frequently repeated the argument that the secular government had a God-given right and responsibility to use violence against those who destroyed the public peace and order.[36] Only private revenge was prohibited by scripture.[37]

Protestants also made several arguments against those who would prefer Turkish rule. These people break God's law concerning obedience to authority; they are perjurers and traitors that deserve to be punished. The Turks are not a legitimate authority as other Christian princes:

> The scriptures instruct us here and make a distinction between the Turks and other authorities. All other authority is ordained by God to keep justice and peace on earth; this is the reason why government is praised in scripture and declared to be God's order. However, the Turk respects no justice, keeps no peace; therefore he is also no lord, rather a tool of the devil.[38]

People who go over to the Turks will not actually better themselves, but will instead become trapped in Turkey in a far worse state than they are now. Furthermore, anyone who willingly submits to the Turk and does not act in such a way as to show his heartfelt disapproval, participates in their evil and wickedness. Rather, it is a very good and Christian deed to resist any Turkish attempt to conquer Germany. For it is a Christian's duty to defend himself and obey his governmental authority, as commanded by God.[39]

Spiritual Warfare

Since the enemy had a fundamental demonic aspect, it is only natural that spiritual warfare was a recommended response against the Ottoman advance. Admonitions for prayer, repentance, and moral improvement were nearly universal in all genres and in all authors of the early sixteenth-century German literature on the Turks.[40]

The theme of the spiritual battle against the Turks was particularly prominent in ecclesiastical literature. Examples of sermons, hymns, and prayers that admonished spiritual exercises in the face of the Turkish threat are so numerous that they almost form a distinct category of Reformation Era religious publications. It is clear German preachers believed that threatening their congregations with Turkish capture was an excellent means of motivating them toward spiritual activity and improved moral behavior.

At times, the demand for participation in the spiritual war was extreme and used a great deal of fear. A set of Stoer broadsheets show women with ropes around their necks led by two Turkish horsemen. The accompanying text reiterates the worst of the anti-Turkish rhetoric, and then adds the warning:

Awake oh Christian,
if you don't turn from sin,
the same will happen to you.
Your unthankfulness will also be punished.
"The ax is laid at the tree."[41]

In his sermon on the Turkish campaign, Matthias Kretz issued a similar warning: "To lazy people who do not like to pray, one should preach a sermon concerning the terrible fury and cruelty of the Turks, explaining how inhumanely and lamentably they would treat us if we should fall into their hands."[42]

Although these appeals may not have been very effective, they were repeated through the entire period. In the wake of each Turkish campaign in Hungary/Austria, the number and urgency of this kind of published admonition increased significantly.

Although all confessional groups advocated spiritual activity in response to the Turkish threat, some differences in the treatment of spiritual warfare in Catholic and Lutheran publications should be noted. Catholics generally urged prayer and moral improvement as a preliminary step to regain God's protective and military blessing. Lutheran authors placed little emphasis on spiritual aspects of military campaigns and were more interested in spiritual activities as weapons in their own right.

The Pope, Charles V, and local princes frequently mandated traditional Catholic practices such as special masses, processions, and bell-ringing. The 1532 command of George of Saxony was typical: every day at noon, each church was to sound a special bell to admonish the people to pray the Lord's Prayer and the Ave Maria three times against the Turks.[43] At the very least, each person was admonished to pray daily to God: "Lord have mercy upon us; give us grace to amend our lives; preserve us from falling into the hands of that horrible fiend, the Turk."[44] It was particularly important to Catholic authors that the unity of the Church be restored if the Christians were to offer successful resistance to Turkish attacks. Pray that "God may give us grace, unity, and conversion." Similar exhortations were made frequently.[45]

The goal of all the prayers, repentance, and reform was victory over the Turk in the field of battle. To this end, continual prayers were urged because the battle was believed to be continuous. However, a definitive victory could be won. The Catholic pamphleteers taught that if Christians simply reformed their behavior, they would find it easy to defeat the Turk because his "scimitars would soon become dull." If the Turks ceased to be an agent of divine chastisement, they would become incapable of any further notable military success.[46]

Like the Roman Catholics, Lutherans strongly advocated prayer and hymns[47] of repentance, but this was generally not done as a prerequisite for successful military action. In response to governmental requests in 1532 and 1541, Lutheran pastors did admonish their congregations to prayer against the Turks during Imperial military campaigns.[48] But even in this context, their recommendations were not very martial: rely on God and not on the power of armies, do not be confident because the Turk is God's enemy, for we are also unjust, do not seek glory or fame but only the glory of God.[49]

Most Lutheran authors counseled absolute reliance upon God and placed no hope at all in military success.[50] The broadsheet *Ein spruch Wie man dem Thürcken macht widerstehen* (1531) was typical:

> It is therefore the best weapon
> That we hope in God alone
> Trust in his word
> And completely build upon Christ
> Who has overcome the world.
> Through him we will be victorious
> And in the end gain eternal salvation.

The proper response is repentance, a plea for grace, and complete reliance on Jesus's help. Military might was not even mentioned.

Military might was not the answer because the struggle was a spiritual one, a battle not between the Turks and the Empire, but between God and the devil.[51] The important participants in the actual fighting were real angels and the powers of darkness.[52] Knaust did not see enemy soldiers on the field of battle, but "a field full of devils that only God can fight against and overcome."[53] (See Figure 7.1) Jonas called the Turks a "Satan" that one cannot overcome with cannon, guns, or armament.[54]

How could such an enemy be defeated? Pastors and preachers were to call the people to earnest repentance and prayer as the Old Testament prophets had done, only by this can one take the scourge from God's hand.[55] Luther denounced processions, masses, and the long insincere prayers of the monks; these things were only "affen spiel" [monkey business]. The truly powerful prayers are frequent and short sighs with one or two words. "'Oh help us dear Father God, have mercy our dear Lord Jesus Christ' or something similar."[56] Psalms of lament were frequently adapted for private and public use against the Turks. "For Christ's sake save us, oh God, we are your baptized and your honor is at risk."[57]

In response to prayer and genuine conversion, Lutheran authors promised that God would end the threat. Like the Old Testament destruction of Assyria and Babylon, this victory would come not through force of arms,

Figure 7.1 Jesus Driving the Turks into Hell, Matthias Gerung, 1530

but by God's judgment of "thunder, lightning, and hellish fire."[58] The victory would be miraculous and definitive. The Last Judgment will follow immediately after the defeat of the Turks. Luther ended *Vom Kriege* with this eschatological hope:

> So help us, dear Lord Jesus Christ, and come down from heaven with the Last Judgment. Strike both the Turks and the Pope to the ground together with all tyrants and the godless. Deliver us from all sin and evil, Amen.[59]

Military Response to the Turks

Except for some Radical Reformers and humanists, all early sixteenth-century responses to Islam had a military aspect. A significant continuity with medieval ideas of the Crusade remained, especially in Catholic *Türkenbüchlein*.[60] The cross was a common symbol in early sixteenth-century art and literature on the Turks and was used frequently on military banners (as in the 1542 campaign of Joachim I).[61] Historical examples of past Crusades were also published to encourage support for the war and to model appropriate Christian behavior.[62] Eternal salvation was promised to anyone who died in battle against the Turks.[63] Further ties to crusade ideology are found in descriptions of the role of Christian leadership and in the discussion of justifications for the war. Although the term *Kreuzzug* [crusade] was generally only used in relation to papal pronouncements, the intention was clear: the sixteenth-century conflict with the Turks was another chapter in the holy war with the infidel.

In the Catholic *Türkenbüchlein*, both Pope and Emperor were expected to be the "defenders of the faith." *Eyn schone nutsliche und Christenliche rede* (1518) stressed that the fight against the infidel was to be led by the two heads of Christendom: the Pope and the Emperor. This was visually portrayed on the cover illustration where the Pope and Emperor are seated together above a group of secular and sacred princes. Other popular pamphlets pleaded with the Pope to use the weapons at his disposal (including the *cruciat*) to be the "defender of Christendom."[64]

However, over the period the appeals were increasingly directed toward the Emperor, even by Catholic churchmen.[65] After the 1520s many Catholic pamphlets did not even mention the Pope; the title "defender of Christendom" was left for Charles V alone.[66] Although Charles eagerly accepted the role, this was more than political propaganda. Many popular pamphlets pleaded with the Emperor to be more active in the fight.[67]

Continuities with traditional crusading are also found in the justifications used for this holy war. The conflict was often put in terms of the protection of the Christian faith in a contest for world domination. As in *Nottel oder Verzeychnuss* (1526), it was every Christian's duty to defend the faith and the common good.[68] Preachers were admonished to stir people's consciences:

"every Christian is responsible to contribute to the fight with everything they have available, either fighting ability or (especially) money."[69] In *Ein vermanung kaiserliche majestat* a separate stanza is dedicated to every possible social group in Germany to do their share.[70] One popular pamphlet, *Ain anschlag wie man dem Türcke widerstand thun mag*, confidently demonstrated that a Christian army of 250,000 could be put together simply through the payment of a weekly penny by every adult communicant in Christendom.[71] Even monks and clergy were admonished to take up weapons and fight the Turks.[72] Everyone was responsible, because if the followers of Muhammad were not destroyed, Christendom would be destroyed by them.[73]

One frequently mentioned justification for the war against the Turks was to rescue enslaved Christians and those in the occupied territories.[74] The fact that the majority of them were Greek Orthodox was brushed over; all Christians under Turkish control were called 'brothers in the Christian faith.'

According to these *Türkenbüchlein*, brotherly love required military action. Description of Turkish slavery and atrocities were almost always followed by appeals on their behalf. For example, after a particularly brutal description in *Volgen zway Lieder* (1529), the author appealed to Christian honor and conscience: "These poor people are our disgrace. All Christians on earth, all Germany and the Roman Church are slandered because of it."[75] Pamphleteers also argued that the love of neighbor was the best self-defense. Fight against the Turk in the occupied territories, or fight against them in your homes. "It is best to put out the fire while it's on your neighbor's wall."[76]

A similar motivation is found in calls to drive the Turks from territories which rightly belonged to Christians. In the Catholic *Türkenbüchlein*, the best defense was clearly a good offense.[77] Despite the impossibility of the task, Catholic plans for military action against the Turks almost always included the territorial expansion of Christianity (often involving forced conversions). Driving the Turks out of Europe was most frequently mentioned, but dreams of a Christian Holy Land (specifically Jerusalem and the Holy Sepulcher) still moved individuals in sixteenth-century Germany.[78]

Although the hope of Christian unity was fading fast in the early sixteenth century, pamphleteers continued to develop military and economic plans of international scope. Some writers were optimistic.[79] If Christians would just unite their resources and change their behavior, they could easily overcome the enemy of the faith.[80] According to the Roman Catholic tract *Des Türckische Kaysers heerzug*, after the reform and reunion of the Church, all religious and political strife would end, with the result that:

> All the treasure hoards of Christendom would be opened and willingly placed at the disposal of the Emperor. Many pious Christians would abandon all their possessions and go into battle under the knightly

banner of St. George, to avenge the atrocities perpetrated by the Turk upon so many hundreds of thousands of innocent Christians. . . . [T]he Jews and all other sects in Christendom would lend their support to the Christian campaign, to say nothing of the pious little old grandmother, who would unearth the treasures long buried beneath the soil, so as to take part in such a laudable enterprise.[81]

As a result of the Reformation, however, the hope of Christian unity under one Pope and one Emperor was dealt a serious blow. Other means of dealing with the Turks had to be developed.

The Lutheran military response to Islam differed significantly from sixteenth-century Roman Catholic crusading. This was primarily due to the ramifications of Luther's unequivocal denunciation of the traditional Crusade as an appropriate response to Islam.

Luther's criticism of the Crusade developed early in the Protestant Reformation. German response to the announcement of Papal-Imperial Crusade plans in 1517 was generally not favorable. Anti-clericalism was growing, and nationalists were concerned that the war would never become reality. Many considered the Turks to be simply a pretext for the Roman 'extortion' of money from Germans.[82] Luther shared these concerns,[83] and many lauded his 1518 statement that "to fight against the Turk is to fight against God who is punishing our sins through them."[84]

Luther's criticism went far beyond papal finances, however. Three issues were involved. First, although he did not frequently mention the Crusade in relation to his anti-indulgence argument, he did occasionally criticize Crusades and Crusade bulls along with other forms of 'works-righteousness.'[85]

When the Turkish threat was more remote (prior to 1526), Luther also dealt with the Turks in relation to the religious situation in Germany. His response to the papal demand for help against the Ottomans was typical. It is meaningless, he said, to fight an external war when one is overcome at home by a spiritual war.[86] Since the reason for the Turkish advance was the sinfulness of the Germans, without reform any military campaign could not be effective. The first action against the Turks must be for Christians to genuinely repent.[87]

Luther's most important criticism, however, was that the Crusade was a blasphemous confusion of the heavenly and earthly kingdoms.[88] Christians *qua* Christians were not to lead or even participate in battle. Scripture commanded believers not to resist evil; fighting against the Turks would be a protest against martyrdom.[89] Furthermore, ecclesiastical attempts at military leadership angered God and were a prime cause of defeat in battle (e.g., the loss at Mohács).[90] Clergy were to preach and pray, not to bear arms and fight. According to Luther, soldiers even had a right to protest this kind of a Church-led Crusade through disobedience. "If I were a soldier and saw in the battlefield a priest's banner or cross, even if it were the very crucifix, I would run away as though the devil were chasing me!"[91]

Related to this argument was the criticism that Christ, not the Emperor or secular rulers, was the defender of the Church.[92] The Emperor was neither "the head of Christianity" nor the "the defender of the Gospel or the faith." To rely on the *Kaiser* was looking to man for salvation, an abomination to God. In essence, there was no religious justification for any military action—be it against false Christians, heretics, or even Turks.

> There are Turks, Jews, heathens, and all too many non-Christians, both with public false teaching and with outrageously shameful life. Let the Turks believe and live as they will, just as one allows the papacy and other false Christians to live. The Emperor's sword has nothing to do with faith—it belongs to corporal earthly things.[93]

Spiritual enemies must be fought with spiritual weapons alone.[94] No Crusade or holy war was permissible.

Luther's argument was quickly criticized by Catholic theologians, but was highly influential.[95] Other justifications for military action and even arguments against violent responses came into being. Some understood Luther to be advocating pacifism and declared that lordship over the body was not intimately related to lordship over the soul. In addition, a nationalist-defensive attitude toward the Turks emerged that was quite secular. In this conception, long-term negotiations were legitimate, and the only justification for military action was the violation of established borders.

The roots of the national-defensive response to the Turks in Germany can also be found in the arguments of Hutten and others against papal Crusade taxation. According to Hutten in *Ad princeps*, Rome should pray and proclaim the Gospel, but not order a Crusade. The princes, however, and above all the *Kaiser*, should seize the initiative and so bring honor to the German name.[96]

Luther's denunciation of the Crusade accelerated this process among German patriots.[97] At first, Hapsburg calls to military action were highly critical of Luther and forcefully reiterated Medieval Crusade ideology. Over the period 1520–1545, however, the combination of German anti-clericalism and the need to involve Lutheran princes in the Ottoman campaigns caused a shift in rhetoric. In the face of the impossibility of the true unity that was necessary for a Crusade, temporary arrangements were made to provide for defense during times of crisis.[98] Beginning in 1526, whenever *Reichstäge* voted an aid against the Turks, they added the stipulation that the money and military were for defensive purposes only. Gradually, popular ballads appealed more to German honor and fighting ability than to God's power.[99] During the few military victories, such as 1535 at Tunis, God was praised, but not nearly as much as Charles V. Pamphlets, such as *Treffenlicher und hochnützlicher anschlag* (1541), even discussed the conflict with the Turks with a distinctly non-religious approach.[100] When long-term peace negotiations were begun between the Hapsburgs and Sulaiman, Crusade rhetoric was intentionally muffled. Although references to the Crusade are found throughout the period, by the end of the first generation of Reformers, the number and ardor of German Crusade supporters had faded significantly. As was the case with Venice and France, the Ottoman Empire was beginning to be considered a legitimate European political power in Germany as well.[101]

Luther had not intended his disavowal of the Crusade to go so far, however. He was no pacifist, but also he was not a proponent of a secular *Realpolitik*.[102] In place of the Crusade, Luther saw a spiritual eschatological battle. However, military action was still necessary because Christians were not only citizens of heaven, but also citizens of an earthly kingdom. War against the Turks was justified (a *jus bellum*) based on God's dual political commands: governments must preserve peace and order, Christian subjects must obey established authority.[103]

According to the Lutheran 'just war' (*Notkriege*) theory, it was the duty of legitimate rulers to defend society against the Turks, just as they would oppose all domestic criminals and disturbers of the peace.[104] In his introduction to *Ursprung des Turckischen Reichs*, Melanchthon emphasized that "Christian potentates and princes are responsible with all their ability to do their best to drive out all poison and wickedness [like the Turks]."[105] Moreover, in fulfilling this commandment, princes were doing a godly, righteous work.[106] However, Lutheran *Türkenbüchlein* were particularly critical of the lack of rigorous military action by the Hapsburgs. It leads the Christian to think, Luther wrote, that the emperor is the enemy of his own people or perhaps has a secret alliance with the Turks.[107]

Christian subjects also had responsibilities in the conflict with the Turks. Citing Romans Chapter 13, Lutheran theologians stated that it was the duty of all groups and classes to obey divinely appointed civil authorities and assist them in any way, whether it be special war taxes or military service.[108] In *Heerpredigt*, Luther warned

> If you hold back and refuse to pay to ride [in battle], look out—the Turk will teach you when he comes in your land and does to you like what was done at Vienna [1529]. Namely, he won't demand taxes or military service from you, but instead attack your house and home, take your livestock and provisions, money and goods, stab you to death (if you are so lucky), shame or strangle your wife and daughter before your eyes, hack your children to death and impale them on the fence-posts. And, what is worst of all, you must suffer all this with a wicked, troubled conscience as a damned unchristian who has been disobedient to God and his government.[109]

If you do not pay now, you certainly will pay later. If commanded to, men and even women should fight to the death, sacrificing their own homes if necessary. They can fight in good conscience, certain that they are killing God's enemy and someone condemned to hell.[110]

Because Christians who died in the conflict with the Turks did so in humble obedience to their rulers, they were assured of their eternal salvation (provided all other evangelical criteria were met). "If a person dies in obedience, they die well. If they otherwise have repented and believe in Christ, they will be saved."[111] These faithful persons could even be called martyrs and saints, since Daniel 7:25 had declared that the "little horn will oppress God's saints." Many martyrs will be made in this conflict, Luther asserted, but this is God's plan.[112] In essence, there is no better way to die than in fighting the Turks, against God's enemies, in temporal obedience, with righteous companions on your way to heaven. "Oh, how precious to the Lord is the death of his saints."[113]

For many in the sixteenth century, this sounded very similar to what the Roman Catholics were teaching. Pacifists accused Luther of abandoning his early position against war; Catholic theologians accused him of contradicting himself.[114] Some modern historians have come to similar conclusions.[115] In fact, this subtle application of the Two Kingdoms doctrine was difficult for even some of Luther's colleagues to maintain consistently. The more popularly oriented the pamphlet and the more martial the context of the writing, the more likely that the distinction between the Crusade and the just war was obscured. Especially in 1542, some Lutheran *Türkenbüchlein* sounded like traditional Crusade pamphlets.[116]

Some Lutherans also drifted toward the national-defensive war in response to the Ottoman advance. After the Turks failed at Vienna in 1529, those Protestants who did not share Luther's intense eschatological urgency became more inclined to use the Turks as a bargaining tool to force an internal settlement of the German religious situation. It was no coincidence that most Imperial acts from 1532–1545, which reconfirmed the Religious Peace of Nürnberg, were influenced by Turkish pressure in the Balkans.[117]

It is clear that Ottoman Imperialism did play a role in the development of legal guarantees for Protestants, but not nearly to the extent that some historians claim. Ferdinand was not above granting temporary privileges of many kinds in return for immediate military assistance for his Imperial ambitions in the East. However, the opinions that "Protestantism might conceivably have gone the way of Albigensianism" without the Turks, and that the "consolidation, expansion and legitimizing of Lutheranism in Germany by 1555 should be attributed to Ottoman Imperial power more than to any other single factor" are clearly overstated.[118]

These conclusions reflect contemporary Catholic (Hapsburg) anti-Protestant rhetoric that Luther was a hindrance to the war effort.[119] Luther and many other Protestants, however, intensely supported the war, though later in life Luther became increasingly pessimistic about its success. Lutherans were caught in a dilemma: they knew that they were being blamed for the lack of response to the Turkish threat; at the same time, they realized the danger of contributing to an Imperial military force without first gaining promises that they would not be attacked. *Ein kleglich ansuchen* clearly reflects this frustration:

> It is laid on our side as if we have hindered the help against the Turks—this is a blatant lie. For the princes and people of this side have always requested such help . . . [this is despite the fact that] a great lord has suggested that forces should be gathered as if they were to campaign against the Turk, but then first conquer those that are opposed to papal doctrine.[120]

Despite the risk, Lutheran theological position required obedience.

For the most part, the evangelical princes and cities decided questions of *Reichstürkenhilfe* according to the good of the empire and not their particular interests.[121] Lutherans did not desire Turkish rule, as some modern historians have argued.[122] "I will always struggle to the death against the Turks and the god of the Turks."[123] Clearly, Protestant leaders did not "relentlessly exploit the opportunities arising from the secular conflict between Hapsburg and Ottoman"[124] for religious privileges. In fact, when asked to give his definitive expert advice for Johann Friedrich in 1538 as to how much should be demanded by Protestants in return for military assistance against the Turks, Luther made his position very clear:

> The Turks are a punishment from God on Germany against which there is no defense. King Ferdinand will most likely not have much luck in the war against the Turks. However, whatever is not merely in the interest of Ferdinand but also concerns the Fatherland: you are responsible for this help against the Turks, even if it is to be feared that after a victory over the Turks the Protestants would be attacked.[125]

Despite their pessimism about the outcome of military action against the Ottoman Empire, Lutherans remained convinced that it was their duty to battle the Ottoman enemy to the bitter end.

Notes

1. Ach Herre Gott in dem ho(e)chsten thron
    Schaw disen grossen jammer an
    So der Thürckisch wu(e)tend Thyran
    In Wiener walde hat gethan
    Ellendt ermort junckfraw vnd frawen
    Die kindt mitten entzwey gehawn
    Zertretten vnd entzwey gerissen
    An spitzig pha(e)l thet er sie spissen
    O vnser hyrte Jhesu Christ
    Der du gnedig barmhertzig bist
    Deyn zoern von dem volck ab wendt
    Errett er auss des Thürcken hendt.
    Der arme Leut Klag

2. Cf. Herrmann, especially 103, 11, 26. Herrmann claimed that there was no confessional distinction in sixteenth-century *Türkenbüchlein*.
3. Radical Reformers also were concerned about missions, but this tended to be a continuation of the medieval hope in the apocalyptic conversion of Turks and Jews. Williams, *Radical Reformation*, 1266–1267.
4. Williams, "Non-Christians," 336–367; Pfister, "Reformation."
5. "Es gehe nicht darum, viele Türken zu töten, sondern viele zu retten." *Enchiridion militia christiani*, quoted in Mau, 647. See also Williams, "Non-Christian", 328, Göllner, *Turcica*, vol. 3, 218. Cf. Herrmann, 38–41.
6. Williams, "Non-Christian," 360–361, Pfister, "Bibliander," 451–452; Clark, 6.
7. Zwingli had broad views of pagan salvation based on primordial election. He saw virtue as *signa elections*, even in pagans. Williams, "Non-Christian," 357–359.
8. Vives shared this desire. "Oh that God would have given the Agarenen, Turks and us a common language! Then I would hope that in a short time many would give themselves to our faith." Juan Luis Vives, *Wie der Türck die Christen haltet so under jm leben Sampt der Türcken ursprung fürgang und erweiterung biss auff den heutigen tag*, e3b.
9. See Miller, "Bibliander." Bibliander's list of shared beliefs included: 1) humans possess both body and soul, with the latter more important, 2) there is life after death, 3) the afterlife is preferred, 4) God is creator and sustainer of heaven and earth, 5) God is judge, and 6) God's will is to be followed. See also, Brenner, 231–234.
10. Similar positions were adopted by other thinkers influenced by humanism, including Vives, Bucer, and Bullinger. See Warneck, *Abriss einer Geschichte der protestantischen Missionen von der Reformation bis auf die Gegenwart*, 18–19; on Bullinger, Pfister, "Bullinger," 73; on Bucer, Williams, "Non-Christian," 356.
11. In general, missiologists, including Gustav Warneck, Julius Richter, Wilhelm Oehler, K.S. Latourette, Walther Köhler) have argued that the Reformation had no concept of missions in the modern sense. Luther and Melanchthon considered the Great Commission to have been already fulfilled, and the presence of Christian survivors and captives in Ottoman lands reinforced this view. (Cf. Benz, 192, note.) However, a significant minority of scholars led by Karl Holl have argued that the structure of Reformation theology was missionary—but the 'heathens' it sought to convert included all non-Christians, even those in the visible Church. See, for example, Warneck, 9–19; Pfister, "Reformation," 365; Holsten, *Christentum*, 10–14.
12. Erasmus made similar suggestions. Bobzin, 268; Heutger, 498.
13. Hartmuth von Cronberg, a3b-a4a.
14. Cronberg suggested that after vanquishing the Turks, the Christians should preach to them. Cronberg, a3b-a4a.
15. Luther, *Heerpredigt*, 192–95. See also, Holsten, *Christentum*, 144, Göllner, *Turcica*, 217, Osiander also made the same argument, Bohnstedt, 31.
16. Luther, *Heerpredigt*, 194.
17. Luther, *Heerpredigt*, 195.
18. "[N]icht verzweifeln, als weren sie verdampt. Die Seele kan dazu nichts, was der Feind an dem Leibe thut." Luther, *Vermanung*, 621.
19. Luther, *Heerpredigt*, 196–197.
20. Luther's introduction to Ricoldo de Monte Croce, *WA 53*, 276. For an exceptional discussion of this, see Francisco, 175–210.
21. Luther's introduction to Ricoldo, 274. See also Bobzin, 283.
22. This was after the 1545 peace negotiations. For example, the reports of Johannes Keyerthory (1551) and Gallus Huszor (1555), Pfister, "Reformation," 375. Some Lutherans equated the Turks with Jehu in Ottoman lands for

driving out the 'priests of Baal' (the Catholics). Leslie C. Tihany, "Islam and the Eastern Frontiers of Reformed Protestantism," 57. See also, Sturmberger, 143–144; Ebermann, 34.

23. "[D]ie Türcken auch menschen als wir." Vives, *Wie der Türck*, a4a. See also, Bainton, 133.

24. Bainton, 122–151.

25. Williams emphasizes the importance of inter-religious tolerance for those Radical Reformers who lived on the religious frontier of Eastern Europe. Williams, *Radical Reformation*, 1150–1153.

26. Williams, *Radical Reformation*, 1266–1267, 1270–1271.

27. Quoted in Capesius, "Francks," 121. See also, Herrmann, 20ff.; Göllner, *Turcica*, vol 3, 191.

28. Quoted in Bohnstedt, 20.

29. See also, Göllner, "Mohács," 72.

30. Kissling, 16.

31. Luther, *Vom Kriege*, 137. Also, *Auszug eines Brieffs*, a4a, *Ernstliche werbung*, a3b-a4a, *New zeytung Die Schlacht des Türckischen*, a2b, b3b, and Setton, "Lutheranism," 161.

32. Cyril Horacek, "Die wirtschaftlichen und sozialen Aspekte der Türkenkriege im 16. Jahrhundert," 105 and Vocelka, 16–17.

33. Bohnstedt, 16. The *Turcken peuchlein* was also strongly opposed to voluntary submission and advised readers to vigorously resist the Turkish aggression.

34. "[W]as für eyn gast am Türcken sie zuhause geladen." *Vier warhafftige missiue*, a2a, a2b.

35. Luther and Melanchthon, *Unterricht der Visitatoren*, WA 26, 236–240. See also, Mau, 649. In *Unterricht der Visitatoren* a separate section was dedicated to the Turks. The Turks were used as a chief distinction between evangelicals and Anabaptists.

36. Brenz, *Türcken Büchlein*, b2a–3a.

37. Brenz, *Türcken Büchlein*, b3a.

38. Jonas, *Das siebend Capitel*, b3b.

39. Luther, *Vom Kriege*, 138–140. Similar arguments were presented by Jonas, *Das siebend Capitel*, g1b; Brenz, *Wie Prediger*, a4a-b. See also, Bernhardt, 265 and Holsten, *Christentum*, 141.

40. Among many others, for example, *Ausz Ratschlag Herrn Erasmi*, 3b, 8a, *Hernach volgt des Bluthundts*, a3b, *Turken peuchlin*, c3b, g2b, *Des Turkisch Kaysers heerzug*, b2b. See also, Bohnstedt, 17, Pfister, "Bibliander," 350.

41. "O Christen mensch sey auffgeweckt Wirstu von sunden nit absteen So wirdt es dier gleich also gen Gestrafft wirdt dein undanckparkeit Die Axt ist an den Baum geleith."

42. Quoted in Bohnstedt, 43.

43. Alfred Moschkau, ed., "Das Türkenglocken," 32 and Ebermann, 19.

44. Quoted in Bohnstedt, 42.

45. For example, *Des Turckisch kaysers heerzug*, a3b, b1a, Kuripecic, *Ein Disputation*, c4b and *Hernach volgt des Bluthundts*.

46. To win a victorious campaign one must repent, pray, and fight. Sin is the reason for the Turkish success, and sin "would be cancelled through repentance and reform; and with the reason removed, God would cease to be angry and would drop the scourge from his hands. Then the Turk would stand alone and would become powerless and incapable of further victories." Kretz, *A Sermon*, translated in Bohnstedt, 41. See also, Stern, *Warhafftige handlung*, d3a; *Ein Lied wider den Türgken*.

47. Luther recommends in *Vermanung*, 607 to sing Psalm 79 or 20 against the Turk. Psalms and hymns against the Turks were particularly important for

Lutherans. For example, Spangenberg, *Der LXXIX Psalm; Zwey Schöne Lieder* and Luther, *Ein Kinderlied.*

48. Jonas, *Das siebend Capitel*, g3a-b. In 1541 both Elector John Frederick of Saxony and the city fathers of Nürnberg gave directives that clergy were to exhort their congregations to prayer against the Turks. These directives were the motivation behind Luther's *Vermahnung*, Dietrich's *Wie man das volck*, and Osiander's *Unterricht und vermanung.*

49. Luther, *Zwen torstbrieve*, a2a-3a.

50. Osiander, *Unterricht wider den Türken*, c2a. In *Vom geringem*, a2a-b, Knaust emphasized the need for a spiritual response and criticizes those who mock the severity of the threat or the ability to defeat it by prayer. Cf. Göllner, *Turcica*, vol. 1, 344.

51. Luther, *Vom Kriege*, 121. Cf. Köhler, *Melanchthon*, 8ff.

52. Osiander, *Unterricht wider den Türken*, c2b; "Wir mussen gegen die Teuffel Engel bey uns haben, Welchs gschehen wird, so wir uns demu(e)tigen, Beten und Gotte vertrawen in seinem wort." Luther, *Vermanung*, 618. See also, Lamparter, 64.

53. Knaust, a3b.

54. Jonas, *Das siebend Capitel*, b2b.

55. Luther, *Vom Kriege*, 117. See also, Mau, 651.

56. Luther, *Vom Kriege*, 118–120.

57. For example, Sachs, *Ein klag zu got uber die grausam wüterei.*

58. Hans Sachs attributed text accompanying *Ein ware Contrafactur oder verzeychnus der königlichen stat Ofen.* Also, *Luther, Das XXXVIIIund XXXIX Captiel Hesechiel*, 235, Luther, *Heerpredigt*, 171, and Knaust, c1a.

59. Luther, *Vom Kriege*, 148.

60. There has been some debate on this point. Herrmann, 16–19, 53 and Bohnstedt, 32 argued that Catholic writers were strongly under the influence of traditional crusading ideology. In contrast, Göllner, "Zur Problematik," 98–109 and Pfeffermann, 172 argued that crusade ideology played only a propagandistic role in the sixteenth century. According to Göllner, "Zur Problematik," 108–109, there was no mention of the crusade in Germany and the "Eroberung des Heiligen Landes spielte somit nur noch als propagandistiche Phrase eine Rolle."

61. Schreiber, 25–33.

62. Türck, *Das der Turck ein Erbfeind*, Barlezio, *Scanderberg*, a2b, and Kretz, *A Sermon*, 44.

63. Kretz, *A Sermon*, 44.

64. *Bapstlicher heyligkeit*, b1b, d2b; *Turcken peuchlin*, g2a; "[D]er Bapst thet als ein vatter des vatterlandts die macht seiner heiligkeit zu erlosung seiner kinder prauchte." Georgijevic, *Türckey*, h2b.

65. This was often due to the financial difficulty of the papacy. For example, Francesco Chieregato, *Francisci Chaeregati electi Episcopi Aprutini Oro habita Nuribergae in senatu Principum Germaniae.*

66. *Die Abschrift*, b1b-b2a. In an open letter to Pope Adrian VI, Hartmuth von Cronberg made a similar argument. He called upon the Pope to abolish the papacy and secularize the wealth of the Church making funds available for a grand military and naval offensive against the Turks. Cronberg, *Eyn Sendbrieff*, a3a-b. After 1529 Charles increasingly came to believe that the *imperator Romanorum* was *princeps paci* and *advocatus ecclesiae*, with the tasks of assembling the Christian power of the West to destroy the "Erzfeind der christlichen Religion." Hantsch, 62–63.

67. In *New zeytung Die schlacht des Türckischen*, b2a-b2b, Christian leaders are responsible "Erstlich kegen Got unserem herren Zum anderen kegen gemeynem Christlichen nutz." They are to follow the example of Ludwig who "seyn

blut umb Christliches glaubens willen vergossen." Also, Dappach, *Ein lied, gemacht; Ein kleglich ansuchen*, a2b.

68. Conscience was used to admonish people to contribute, see *Nottel oder Verzeychnüss*, c3a. Also, *Des heylige Römischen Reichs beharrliche hilff,* a3b; *Warhafftige*, b4a, a3a-a3b.
69. The *Türkenbüchlein* were often very detailed about this participation. In *Welcher gestalt des Churfürsten*, the orders of society that were to participate in the 1542 tax included: prelates, spirituals, lords, knights, widows from knights, city councils, citizens, farmers, merchants, day workers, craftsmen, miners; in short, everyone with the exception of poor people and those who had suffered a fire in the last two years. Se also, *Nottel oder Verzeychnuss*, b3b; *Verzeichnusz ausz was ursachen*, a4b; Kuripecic, *Itinerarum*, a2a; *Des Turckisch kaysers Heerzug*, b1a-b1b.
70. See *Ein vermanung kaiserliche majestat.*
71. The *Anschlag* estimated that there were 40,000 (Franciscan) cloisters which can contribute 36,000 soldiers. The other orders can do the same, for a total of 144,000 men (it considers the number of cloisters in Christendom to be c. 160,000). In addition, each of the 288,000 churches could contribute one soldier. If every cloister (average 30 spiritual and 30 secular persons) gives one pfennig per week per individual this would equal 648,103 Hungarian gulden. Similarly, if each church (average 93 men) gives one penny per week per individual, this would total 19,468,092 gulden. At a cost of 2 gulden per horse, 1 per foot-soldier, 249,094 soldiers could be financed. *Ain anschlag*, a2a-a3a. To do this required an inter-European currency standardization, about which the author goes into great lengths to describe. This was a very popular pamphlet; it was reprinted in various guises in response to every Turkish advance: 1518, 1522, 1523, 1532, 1541, and 1542.
72. *Anzeigung ze erobern die Türckey* was a legend of the victorious campaign of the monks of Ebertin's well-known *Wolfaria* against the Turks.
73. *Warhafftige Copey*, a3a. *Ein kleglich ansuch*, d1b, put the situation in similar terms: either drive out the Turks, abandon the land, or put yourself under his authority. Also, *Verzeichnusz ausz was ursachen*, a3b; Georg Agricola, *Oration anred und vermanunge.*
74. This was perhaps the most frequent motivation. *Ein kleglich ansuch*, d1a. Also, Kretz, *A sermon*, 44; *Des Künigs von Hungern sendprieff*, a3a-b; *Beschreibung Aller Turckischen*, c2b-c4a.
75. Also, Kuripecic, *Itinerarum*, c4a and *Erinnerung der verschulten*, a4a.
76. "[N]ach dem gemeinen Sprichwort das fewr am Besten zu leschen dieweil es noch an des nachbarn wand ist." *Auffgebot unnd warnungss*, a3a; Giovo, *Ursprung*, v2a-b.
77. *Christliche bündnuss un kriegssrüstüng*, a2a; *Römishcen Keiserlicher Maiestat*, a4b, b2a. See also, Herrmann, 30-31.
78. *Ain anschlag*, b2a. Also, *Des Turckisch kaysers heerzug,* b1b-b2a; *Bäbstlicher heilikeit*, a2a.
79. For example, *Ein christenlicher zug wider den Türken* is a ballad in praise of Charles V that optimistically predicts world domination and victory against the Turks.
80. Agricola was one of the most exaggerated concerning the success of the Germans. In *Oration*, he claimed that Germans had better weapons, spears, and armor compared to the Turks. He predicted the freeing of those under the Turkish yoke, the conquering of Turkey, then even the holy grave, followed by the possible mass conversion of Turks. Only a serious will is needed. Also, Kretz, *A Sermon*, 44; Senol Özyurt, *Die Türkenlieder und das Türkenbild in der deutschen Versüberlieferung vom 16. bis zum 20. Jahrhundert*, 22.

81. *Des Türckische Kaysers heerzug*, b1b-b2a.
82. Hutten, *Ad princeps*.
83. In *Vom Kriege*, Luther claimed that the Roman curia never really wanted war against the Turk, but only to extort money from the German people.
84. Luther, *Grund und Ursach*, 140.
85. Luther, *Vom Kriege*, 131.
86. In a letter to Georg Spalatin 21 Dec 1518, *WA Br 1*, 282. In a letter to Linck 18 Dec 1518 he stated that the antichrist dominated the papacy and this was worse than the Turk, WA Br 1, 270.
87. See for example, *Grund und Ursach*, 443.
88. Luther had established his division between spiritual and secular regiments as early as the Roman lectures of 1515–16. Lamparter, 6. In the 1523 *Von Weltlicher Obrigkeit*, "Die geistliche und die weltliche Macht dürfen nicht willkürlich miteinander verflochten warden." See also, Göllner, *Turcica*, vol. 3, 188, Bohnstedt, 32, and Holsten, *Christentum*, 142.
89. Lamparter, 76–77.
90. The Hungarian troops at Mohács were lead by the Archbishop of Kolocsa, which is the reason that Luther characterized it as a 'Pfaffenherr.'
91. However, "Wenn Keyser Karolus panier odder eins Fu(e)rsen zu felde ist, da lauffe ein iglicher Frisch und fro(e)lich unter sein panier . . . ist aber ein Bisschoffs, Cardinals odder Bapsts panir da, so lauff davon und sprich: Ich kenne der mu(e)ntze nicht." Luther, *Vom Kriege*, 115.
92. "[D]er Kaiser ist nicht das heupt der Christenheit noch beschirmer des Evangelion odder des glaubens." Luther, *Vom Kriege*, 130.
93. Luther, *Vom Kriege*, 131. According to Jonas, *The Seventh Chapter*, 33, "Although the Turks are non-Christians, there would not be sufficient cause to make war on them if they kept the peace . . . [no ruler had a mandate from God to start a war against non-Christians on purely religious grounds. . . . We can kill non-Christians with our fists—but we cannot make Christians of them with our fists—we cannot, in this way, put faith and the Holy Spirit into their hearts." (Bohnstedt translation)
94. Lind, 44–45.
95. Cuspinianus, Eppendorf, Eck, Anderbach, and Cochlaeus wrote criticisms of Luther's response to the Turks. Mau, 649 and Göllner, *Turcica*, 195.
96. Mau, 647. *Nottel oder Verzeychnuss*, b2b made similar arguments. Cf. Fischer-Galati, *Ottoman Imperialism*, 10.
97. "Die Reformation hat zur Frage der Neugestaltung der Beziehungen eines Teils des Abendlandes zu den Türken vor allem einen ideologischen Beitrag geliefert. Dem Prozess der Metamorphose des Kreuzzugs in den Türkenkriege hat sie das ideologische Gewand gegeben." Pfefferman, 172.
98. "Religion" began to be used as a term in the confessional conflict. *Treffenlicher unnd Hochnützlicher anschlag*, a2b, stated that there was a need to come to some kind of "religious" understanding, or at least not to dispute, in order not to lose this opportunity to fight against the Turks (1542).
99. For example, *Ayn neües Lyed wie der Türgk Wien belegert hat* and *Wie der Türke vor Wien lag*. A very interesting 1566 re-make of *Ein schon geystlich lied*, edited out the central theme of the Turks as God's punishment and added a prayer for defensive military help in the last stanza. "O Heere Gott heiliger Gaist, Wir bitten dich allsamen. Das du elösest allermeist, Das Landt in deinem Namen. Das wir wider die Fainde sein, Gerüst vnd wol gewapnet sein, Durch dich das Feld behalten" as opposed to the original "die feinde dein, den thu, O Herr, behilfflich sein, in deinem wort erhalten!"
100. *Treffenlicher vnd hochnutz*, a4a, b4b, c1a.

101. Fischer-Galati, *Ottoman Imperialism*, 39–40.
102. In *Ob Kriegsleute*, 661–662, Luther ended with an attempt to demonstrate his willingness to fight against the Turks against those "who have twisted my words." In 1529 Luther wrote *Vom Kriege* to clarify his position on the Turks, especially against those that thought he was pacifist or ambivalent about the Turkish advance. He defended his 1518 statement by stating that it was written in a specific context when the world situation was different. Luther, *Vom Kriege*, 108–109.
103. Buchanan, 146–147 and Bohnstedt, 33.
104. "Dann wie wol die Türcken unchristen sein so were doch das selbig nicht ursach gnug sie zu bekriegen so sie frieden hielten und nicht offentlich gewalt und frevel ubeten . . . Das ist aber ein recht ursache den türcken mit heeres krafft anzugreiffen das er ynn frembde lender einfellet." Jonas, *Das siebend Capitel*, g4b. See also, Brenz, *Wie Prediger*, a3b-4a, Luther, *Vom Kriege*, 116, 129, and Lind, 52–53.
105. "Die christlichen Potentaten und Fürsten schuldig sind mit all jrs Vorzügen und macht, das bey ir bestes zutun, das solche gift und grewel werde ausgetrettet." Melanchthon's introduction to Giovo, b4a-b3b. See also, Göllner, *Turcica*, vol. 3, 188–189.
106. For example, in *Zwen Trostbrieve*, 4a-5a, Joachim should have no small comfort because: "das es nit allein recht ist wider solchen bosswichtische mörder Kriegen sonder es ist ein erstner unnd gewisser befehl gottes vom himel herunder. Den die Türcken sindt Gottes feindt und kriegen nit wider uns sonder wider Gott selb im himel." Also, Jonas, *Das siebend Capitel*, g3a-4a.
107. Luther, *Vom Kriege*, 133.
108. Göllner, *Turcica*, vol. 3, 189; Bohnstedt, 32–33.
109. Luther, *Heerpredigt*, 181.
110. Luther, *Heerpredigt*, 173.
111. Luther, *Vom Kriege*, 130–131. Also, Osiander, *Unterricht wider den Türken*, c3a: if you die in the "rechtmessigen notkriege . . . stu(e)rben doch dieselben ehrlich, lo(e)blich, christlich und seligklich, als die nit allein in einem guten christlichen werck des gehorsams und beschu(e)tzung des vatterlands erfunden würden, sonder auch ir blut fornemlich umb Christus namen willen vergossen hetten."
112. In his introduction to Ricoldo de Monte Croce Luther declared that the Turks will make "viel Marterer als nie gemacht sind, das er so viel unschuldiger kinder und sonst frome Christen grewlich erwürget." Luther, *Verlegung*, 274–276. In *Heerpredigt*, 178, Luther told people not to be anxious about wives or children being sawed in two or impaled; for the angels wait to bear them up to heaven in their arms—and this brings even more damnation to the Turks.
113. In *Heerpredigt*, 176–77, Luther quoted Psalms 116:15 to comfort the anxious.
114. The majority took this to mean that Luther was propounding a new teaching. Johannes Cochlaeus in *Dialogus de bello Contra Turcas in Antilogias Lutheri* judged the Reformer to have a "Zweispältige Haltung in der Türkenfrage." Luther was a "Janus-like menace to Christendom, a double-headed source of evil, terror and confusion." In the dialogue "Lutherus" represented the early position of Luther (1518) against the *Türkenkrieg*, und "Paidonus" represented Luther from *Vom Kriege* that supported the war. Cochlaeus claimed to have found some fifteen different contradictions in Luther's writing concerning the Turks. Göllner, *Turcica*, vol. 3, 196 and Mau, 653.
115. Holsten, *Christentum*, 137 and Wallmann, 54–55.
116. According to Brentz, *Wie Predigen*, b1a, German emperors of old waged "praiseworthy and Christian wars at Jerusalem to weaken the Saracens, and

succeeded in checking them, delaying the growth of their power in Asia. These Christians wars are highly praised by St. Bernard, who rightly calls them "sanctam et tutam militiam." Translated by Bohnstedt, 24. See also, *Vom geringem*, a4a and Dietrich, *Wie man das volck*, b4b.

117. Fischer-Galati, *Ottoman Imperialism*, 116–117.
118. Setton, "Lutheranism," 133 and Fischer-Galati, *Ottoman Imperialism*, 116–117.
119. Kuripecic, *Ein Disputation*, d1a. Also, *Copey unnd Lautter*, b1b-b2a and Göllner, "Mohács," 71.
120. *Ein kleglich ansuchen*, a4a.
121. Bobzin, 263 and Wohlwill, 11.
122. Despite the very strong understanding of the Turks as a demonic power in the Lutheran *Türkenbüchlein*, some historians continue to argue that Lutherans supported or were at least ambivalent to Turkish rule. According to Pfeffermann, 167, "man kann sich schwerlich dem Eindrucke entziehen, dass er sich mit der Türkenherrschaft nicht nur Abfand, sondern zufrieden gab, ja, sie herbeiwünschte." Similar arguments are found in Schwob, 243.
123. Luther, *Heerpredigt*, 150.
124. Fischer-Galati, *Ottoman Imperialism*, 116–117.
125. Quoted in Göllner, *Turcica*, vol. 3, 193.

References

Agricola, Georg. *Oration anred und vermanunge, zu denen Grossmechtigsten Durchleuchtigisten von Kriegsrüstung und Heerzuge wider den Türcken geschrieben.* Dresden: Stöckel, 1531.

Anzeigung ze erobern die Türckey, un erlösung der Christenheit. Auch wie die Insel Mahumeta durch die ordenslüt dess Künigreichs Wolfarie erobert ist. n.p., 1523.

Auffgebot unnd warnungss schrifft so die Chur und Fürsten zu Sachssen des grawsamen Erbfeynds der verschulten. n.p., 1541.

Ausz Ratschlage Herren Erasmi von Roterdam die Türcken zubekriegen Der ursprung unnd alle geschichten der selbigen gegen Römische Keyser unnd gemeyne Christenheit vo anbegin des türckischen namenn nach der kürtze new verteutscht. n.p., 1530.

Auszug eines Briefes wie einer so in der türkey wonhafft seinem freünd in dise landt geschriben un wessen sey und wie Türcken Regiment un wessen sey und wie er es mit den landen so er erobert zu halten pflegt kürtzlich in Teütsche sprach gebracht nützlich diser zeyt zu wissen. Wittenberg: Schirlentz, 1526.

Bäbstlicher heilikeit sampt Römscher Keiserlicher Maiestat auch anderer kristlichen Künig un Fürste botschaffte anschlag wider die Türken. n.p., 1518.

Bainton, Roland H. *Christian Attitudes Toward War and Peace: A Historical Survey and Cultural Re-evaluation.* New York: Abingdon, 1960.

Barlezio, Marino. *Des aller streytparsten un theüresten Fürsten und Herrn Georgen Castrioten genant Scanderberg Hertzogen zu Epiro und Albanien etc. Ritterliche thaten so er zu erhalten seiner Erbland mit den Türkische Kaysern in seinem leben glücklich begangen.* Augsburg: Steiner, 1533.

Benz, Ernst. *Wittenberg und Byzanz: Zur Begegnung und Auseinandersetzung der Reformation und der östlich-orthodoxen Kirche.* Marburg: Elwert-Gröfe und Unzer Verlag, 1949.

Bernhardt, Karl-Heinz. "Luther und der Islam." *Standpunkt* 11 (1983): 263–265, 328–330; 12 (1984): 87–91.

Beschreibung aller Türckischen Khayser. Von jrem ursprung un anfang her weevil derselben biss auff dise unser zeit und jar geregiert was auch derselben jeder von Landt und Leüt Bestritten uberkhomen und in seinen gwalt unnd herschug gebracht. n.p., 1531.

Bobzin, Harmut. "Martin Luthers Beitrag zu Kenntnis und Kritik des Islam." *Neue Zeitschrift für Systematische Theologie* 27:3 (1985): 262–289.

Bohnstedt, John W. "The Infidel Scourge of God: The Turkish Menace as Seen by German Pamphleteers of the Reformation Era." *Transactions of the American Philosophical Society* NS 58:9 (1968).

Brenner, Hartmut. "Protestantische Orthodoxie und Islam. Die Herausforderung der türkischen Religion im Spiegel evangelischer Theologen des ausgehendes 16. und des 17. Jahrhunderts." Ph.D. diss., University of Heidelberg, 1968.

Brenz, Johann. *Türcken Büchlein. Wie sich Prediger und Leien halten sollen, so der Türck das Deudsche Land uberfallen würde. Christliche und nottürfftige unterrichtung durch Johann Brentz*. Wittenberg: Rhaw, 1537.

Buchanan, Harvey. "Luther and the Turk, 1519–1529." *Archiv für Reformationsgeschichte* 48:1 (1956): 145–160.

Capesius, Bernhard. "Sebastian Francks Verdeutschung des *Tratatus de ritu et moribus Turcorum*." *Deutsche Forschung in Südosten* 3:1 (March 1944): 103–128.

Chieregato, Francesco. *Francisci Chaeregati electi Episcopi Aprutini Oro habita Nuribergae in senatu Principum Germaniae*. Vienna: Singriener, 1522.

Christliche bündnuss un kriegssrüstüng Keyser Carls wider den Türcken zu Rom beschlossen den 8. Febraurii anno 1538. Dresden: n.p., 1538.

Clark, Henry. "The Publication of the Koran in Latin: A Reformation Dilemma." *Sixteenth Century Journal* 15:1 (Spring 1984): 3–12.

Cochlaeus, Johannes. *Dialogus de bello Contra Turcas in Antilogias Lutheri, per Ioannem Chochleum. XV. Contradictiones, ex duobus primis Quaternionibus Libri Lutherici de bello, contra Turcas*. Leipzig: Schumann, 1529.

Cronberg, Harmuth von. *Eyn sendbrieff an Bapst Adrianum: daryn mit christlichen warhafftige grund angetzeigt wurd eyn sicherer heylsamer weg zu ausreuttung aller kettzereyen: un zu heylsamer rettung gantzer christenheyt vo des Turken tyranny*. Wittenberg: n.p., 1523.

Dappach, Jörg. *Ein Lied gemacht wie es im Osterlandt ergangen ist, als man schreibt tausent fünfhundert im neun und zwainzigsten jar*. n.p., 1529.

Des heylige Römischen Reichs beharrliche hilff, und Christenliche Kriegrüstung wider den Türcken. n.p., 1542.

Des Künigs von Hungern sendprieff an Kayserlich Statthalter und Regiment zugesagter hilff gegen Türkischer Tyrannei merung betreffennde. Vienna: Singriener, 1523.

Des Türckische Kaysers heerzug wie er von Constantinopel Mit aller rüstung zu Ross und Fuss zu wasser und land u gen kriechische Weyssenburg kummen und fürter für die königlichen stat Ofen yn Ungern unnd Wien yn Osterreich gezoge die belegert un gestürmt u mit angehenckter ermanung der grausamen tyranny des Türcken wyder christliche Nation. Nürnburg: Zell, 1530.

Die abschrifft ausz dem Original so der Turck sampt dem könig von Cathey vnd Persien allen stenden des Römischen Reychs geschryben haben. n.p., 1523.

Ein christenlicher zug wider den Türken. n.p., 1530.

Ein kleglich ansuchen des ausschus der V. nider osterreichischen lande belangend die grosse jtzige fahr des Türcken halben. Wittenberg: Klug, 1540.

Ein Lied wider den Türgken, zur Besserung uns manend, Und in Gott unser vertrawen zusetzen. Augsburg: n.p., 1542.

Ein new Lied, wie der Türk; Ayn neües Lyed wie der Türgk Wien belegert hat. n.p., 1529.

Ein vermanung kaiserlicher Majestat sampt aller stend des römischen reichs eines herzugs wider ain pluttürstigen türken. Regensburg: n.p., 1532.

Ein ware Contrafactur oder verzeychnus der königlichen stat Ofen. Nürnberg: n.p., 1541.

Erinnerung der verschulten plagen, des Teutschlands, sampt ainer getrewen ermanung zu Christenlicher bekerung, unnd schuldiger hilff, wider des Türcken grausam fürnemen unnd erschrocklichen angriff, in dem Ertzhertzogtumb Osterreich gethun. n.p., 1529.

Ernstliche werbung bit un beger, der lobliche Legation oder bottschafft der bayden Königreiche Ungern unnd Sclauonien, An unnsern aller gnedicten groszmechtigsten Herren den Kayser Karolum. n.p., 1530.

Fischer-Galati, Stephen A. *Ottoman Imperialism and German Protestantism, 1521–1555.* Cambridge, MA: Harvard University Press, 1972.

Francisco, Adam. *Martin Luther and Islam: A Study in Sixteenth-Century Polemics and Apologetics.* London: Brill, 2007.

Georgijevic, Bartholomew. *Türckey oder von yetziger Türcken kirchen gepräng, Sytem unnd leben, auch was grausamen jochs, was unsäglichen jamers die gefangnen Christen under den selben geduldten müssen, sampt Namenbüchlein Persischer in der Türckey gängen sprachen.* Basel: Cratander, 1545.

Göllner, Carl. "Betrachtungen zur öffentlichen Meinung über die Schlacht von Mohács (1526)." *Revue roumaine d'histoire* 6:1 (1967): 67–76.

Göllner, Carl. *Turcica: Die europäischen Türkendrucke des XVI. Jahrhunderts. Vol. 3. Die Türkenfrage in der öffentlichen Meinung Europas im 16. Jahrhundert.* Bucharest: Editura Academiei, 1968.

Göllner, Carl. "Zur Problematik der Kreuzzüge und der Türkenkriege im 16. Jahrhundert." *Revue des études sud-est européennes* 13:1 (1975): 97–115.

Hantsch, Hugo. "Zum ungarisch-türkischen Problem in der allgemeinen Politik Karls V." In *Festschrift Karl Eder zum Siebzigsten Geburtstag.* Helmut J. Mezler-Andelberg, ed. Innsbruck: Universitätsverlag Wagner, 1959, 57–69.

Hernach volgt dess Bluthundts der sych nennedt ein Türckischen Keiser gethaten so er und die seinen nach eroberug der Schlacht auff den xxviij. tag Augusti nech stuer gange geschehe an unsern mitbrüdern der Ungrische lant schaffen gatz unmeschlich tribe hat un noch teglichs tut. n.p., 1526.

Herrmann, Ehrenfried. "Türke und Osmanreich in der Vorstellung der Zeitgenossen Luthers: Ein Beitrag zur Untersuchung des deutsche Türkenscriftens." Ph.D. diss., University of Freiburg, 1961.

Heutger, Nicolaus. "Luther und der Islam: Scharfe Äusserungen blieben glücklicherweise ohne Nachwirkung." *Luther Monatsblatt* 22 (1983): 397–498.

Holsten, Walter. *Christentum und nichtchristliche Religion nach der Auffassung Luthers.* Gütersloh: C. Bertelsmann, 1932.

Horacek, Cyril. "Die wirtschaftlichen und sozialen Aspekte der Türkenkriege im 16. Jahrhundert." In *Charisteria Orientalia Praecipue ad Persiam Pertinentia,* Felix Tauer, et al., eds. Prag: Nakladatelstvi Ceskoslovenske Akademie VED, 1956, 103–112.

Hutten, Ulrich von. *Ad princepes Germanos ut bellum in Turcas concorditer suscipiant exhortatoria.* Augsburg: Wirsung, 1518.

Kissling, Hans Joachim. "Türkenfurcht und Türkenhoffnung im 15/16. Jahrhundert: zur Geschichte eines 'Komplexes.'" *Südost-Forschungen* 23 (1964): 1–18.

Knaust, Heinrich. *Von geringem herkommen schentlichern leben schmehlichem ende des Türckischen abgots Machomets und seiner verdamlichen und Gotteslesterischen Ler.* Berlin: Weisen, 1542.

Köhler, Manfred. *Melanchthon und der Islam: Ein Beitrag zur Klärung des Verhältnisses zwischen Christentum und Fremdreligionen in der Reformationszeit.* Leipzig, 1938.

Kretz, Mathias. *Ein sermon von dem Turckenzug durch Doctor Mathiam Krecz zu Mosspurg in sant Castelsstifft gepredigt.* n.p., 1532. Translated in John Bohnstedt "The Infidel Scourge of God: The Turkish Menace as Seen by German Pamphleteers of the Reformation Era." *Transactions of the American Philosophical Society* NS 58:9 (1968): 41–46.

Kuripecic, Benedict. *Itinerarium Wegrayss K. May. Potschafft gen Constantinopel zu dem Türckischen Kayser Soleyman Anno xxx.* n.p., 1531.

Lamparter, Helmut. *Luthers Stellung zum Türkenkrieg.* Munich: Lempp, 1940.

Lind, Richard. *Luthers Stellung zu Kreuz- und Türkenkrieg.* Giessen: Brühl, 1940.

Luther, Martin. *Assertio omnium articulorum M. Lutheri per bullam Leonis X. novissimum damnatorum* (1520). WA 7, 91–151.

Luther, Martin. *Das XXXVIII und XXXIX Capitel Hesechiel vom Gog. Verdeudscht durch Mart. Luther* (1530). WA 30II, 107–148.

Luther, Martin. *Ein Kinderlied, zu singen, wider die zween Ertzfeinde Christi und seiner heiligen Kirchen, den Bapst un Türcke, etc.* Wittenberg: Klug, 1543.

Luther, Martin. *Grund und Ursach aller Artikel D.M. Luthers* (1521). WA 7, 299–457.

Luther, Martin. *Heerpredigt wider den Türken* (1530). WA 30II, 149–197.

Luther, Martin. *Ob Kriegsleute auch in seligem Stande sein können* (1526). WA 19, 616–662.

Luther, Martin. *Resolutiones disputationem de indulgentiarum virtute* (1518). WA 1, 522–628.

Luther, Martin. *Verlegung des Alcoran Bruder Richardi, Prediger Ordens. Verdeutscht und herausgegeben von Martin Luther* (1542). WA 53, 272–276.

Luther, Martin. *Vermahnung zum Gebet wider den Türken* (1541). WA 51, 585–625.

Luther, Martin. *Vom Kriege wider den Türcken* (1529). WA 30II, 107–148.

Luther, Martin. *WA Briefwechsel (Br)* 1, 270–272 (#121).

Luther, Martin. *WA Briefwechsel (Br)* 1, 282–283 (#125).

Luther, Martin and Philip Melanchthon, *Unterricht der Visitatoren*, WA 26, 175–240.

Luther, Martin and Philip Melanchthon. *Zwen trostbriefe geschriben an der Durchleuchtigen und hochgebornen Fürsten und Herrn Herrn Joachim Churfürste und Marckgraven zu Brandenburger vom Türcken zuge.* Nürnberg: Berg, 1532.

Mau, Rudolf. "Luthers Stellung zu den Türken." In *Leben und Werk Martin Luthers von 1526 bis 1546.* Helmar Junghans, ed. Göttingen: Vandenhoeck and Ruprecht, 1983, 647–662.

Miller, Gregory J. "Theodor Bibliander's *Machumetis saracenorum principis eiusque successorum vitae, doctrina ac ipse alcoran* (1543) as the Sixteenth Century 'Encyclopedia' of Islam." *Islam and Christian-Islamic Relations* 24:2 (April 2013), 241–254.

Moschkau, Alfred, ed. "Das Türkenglocken." In *Saxonia: Zeitschrift für Geschichts—Altertums—und Landeskunde des Königreichs Sachsen.* Leipzig: Louis Senf, 1877.

New Zeytung. Die Schacht des Türckischen Keysers mit Ludouico etwan König zu Ungern geschehen am tag Johannis enthaltung. 1526. Item des Türken feyndtsbrieff König Ludouico zugesandt vor der schlacht. n.p., 1526.

Nottel oder Verzeychnüss eyner beharlichen hilff wider den Türcke biss auff künfftige versamlung aller Stende des heylige Reichs. n.p., 1526.

Osiander, Andreas. *Unterricht und vermanung wie man wider den Türcken peten und streyten soll. Auff ansuchung etlicher gutter Herrn und Freunde. An die jhenigen gestalt bey denen der Türck schon angriffen und schaden gethon und sie desselben noch alle tag gewertig sein müssen.* n.p., 1542.

Özyurt, Senol. *Die Türkenlieder und das Türkenbild in der deutschen Versüberlieferung vom 16. bis zum 20. Jahrhundert.* Munich: Wilhelm Fink Verlag, 1972.

Pfeffermann, Hans. *Die Zusammenarbeit der Renaissancepäpste mit den Türken.* Winterthur: Mondial Verlag, 1946.

Pfister, Rudolf. "Antistes Heinrich Bullinger über den Türgg." *Evangelisches Missions Magazine* 98 (May 1954): 69–78.

Pfister, Rudolf. "Das Türkenbüchlein Theodor Biblianders." *Theologische Zeitung* 9 (1953): 438–468.

Pfister, Rudolf. "Reformation, Türken und Islam." *Zwingliana* 10:6 (1956): 345–375.

Römischer Keiserlicher Maiestat Christenliche Kriegsrüg wider die Unglaubigen, Auszug inn Hispanien und Sardinien. Ankunfft in Africa, und eroberung des Ports zu Tunisi. n.p., 1535.

Sachs, Hans. *Ein Klag zu got uber die grausam wüterei des grausamen Türken ob seinen viel kriegen und obsiegen.* n.p., 1532.

Schoen, Erhard. *Der armen Leut Klag.* (broadsheet) Nürnberg: Guldemunde, 1530.

Schreiber, Georg. "Das Türkenmotiv und das deutsche Volkstum." *Volk und Volkstum* 3 (1938): 9–54.

Schwob, Ute Monika. "Vom Kriege wider die Türken." *Südostdeutsche Vierteljahresblätter* 23 (1974): 240–244.

Setton, Kenneth M. "Lutheranism and the Turkish Peril." *Balkan Studies* 3 (1962): 133–168.

Spangenberg, Johann. *Der LXXIX Psalm auff die weise, Aus tieffer not.* n.p., 1545.

Stern, Peter. *Warhafftige handlung Wie und welcher massen der Türck die stat Ofen und Wien belegert.* n.p., 1530.

Sturmberger, Hans. "Türkengefähr und österreichische Staatlichkeit." *Südostdeutsche Archiv* 10 (1967): 132–145.

Tihany, Leslie C. "Islam and the Eastern Frontiers of Reformed Protestantism." *Reformed Review* 29 (Fall 1975): 52–71.

Treffenlicher unnd Hochnützlicher anschlag, Bündtnusz und verainigung. Augsburg: Ulhart, 1541.

Türck, Bernhardin. *Das der Türck ein Erbfeind aller Christen, weder traw noch glauben halte, klare beweysung aus den geschichten bisher in kurtzen jaren von jme begangen.* n.p., 1542.

Turcken peuchlein. Ein Nutzlich Gesprech, oder underride etlicher personen, zu besserug christlicher ordnung un lebens. n.p., 1522.

Verzeichnus aus was ursachen der Künfftig Reichsstag auff Egidij nechst fürnemlich ausgeschriben. Darauff dan die Stende des heylige Reichs, sonderlich wie den grawsament ernstliche fürneme des Turcken zubegenen. Nürnberg: n.p., 1522.

Vier warhafftige Missiue, eyne der Frawen Isabella, Künigin un nachgelassne Wittib in Ungern, wie untreulich der Türck und die jhren mit jhr umbgangen. n.p., 1542.

Vives, Juan Luis. *Wie der Türck die Christen haltet so under jm leben Sampt der Türcken ursprung fürgang und erweiterung biss auff den heutigen tag.* Strassburg: Beck, 1532.

Vocelka, Karl. "Die inneren Auswirkungen des Auseinandersetzung Österreiches mit den Osmanen." *Südostforschung* 36 (1977), 13–34.

Wallmann, Johannes. "Luthers Stellung zu Judentum und Islam." *Luther* 57:2 (1986): 49–60.

Warhafftige Copey so zu Speyr auff jüngst gehaltnem Reychstage der bewilligten Türcken hilff. n.p., 1542.

Warneck, Gustav. *Abriss einer Geschichte der protestantischen Missionen von der Reformation bis auf die Gegenwart,* 7th ed. Berlin: Verlag Martin Warneck, 1901.

Welcher gestalt des Churfürsten zu Sachsen die Anlage dem Türcken zu widderstandt gewilliget haben. n.p., 1542.

Wie der Türke vor Wien lag. n.p., 1529.

Williams, George H. "Erasmus and the Reformers on Non-Christian Religions and Salus Extra Ecclesiam." In *Action and Conviction in Early Modern Europe.* Theodore K. Robb and Jerrold E. Seigel, eds. Princeton: Princeton University Press, 1969, 319–370.

Williams, George H. *The Radical Reformation.* 3rd ed. Kirksville, MO: 16th Century Journal, 1992.

Wohlwill, Adolph. "Deutschland, der Islam, und die Türkei." *Euphorion* 22 (1915): 1–22.

8 Escaped Slaves of the Turks

George of Hungary and Bartholomew Georgijevic

At the same time that Martin Luther was preparing for an apocalyptic confrontation with the Turks, others in Europe seem to have been more interested in the developing commercial possibilities of the Ottoman Empire. There was no sudden shift from 'medieval' to 'early modern' understandings of the Turks during the Reformation, but there were clear signs of development and of a growing ambiguity that called into question received understandings and created space for new information to be accepted. A confluence of growing commercial, diplomatic, and military contact with the Islamic world combined with Protestant suspicion of the received tradition and the explosion of print created an important transitional time in the history of Christian-Islamic relations. Nowhere is this clearer than in a comparison of the two most important captivity narratives published in this period. The remarkable parallels between the two authors despite their seventy-year interval make them an almost ideal basis for marking developments in the depictions of Islam and the Turks in Reformation Germany. Appendices two and three contain the only modern English translations of these authors.

It is important to note that these accounts are significantly different from standard medieval travel writing, although they are sometimes lumped together in scholarly analysis. Medieval travel writing is characterized by what has been termed a 'temporal geography,' that is, the present read through the past.[1] The current ('surface') culture was either opaque or even entirely invisible. Instead of seeing and describing the Turks, medieval travelers tended to see instead only ancient Greece and biblical Israel. Firsthand accounts were not considered a necessary source of information and the cultures through which medieval travelers passed in the present were less evident (or important) than what their sources had told them about the ancient past.[2] In addition, in much of medieval travel literature, fantastic elements are emphasized, as, for example, in the case of the travel narrative of Ludolf von Sudheim.[3] None of this characterizes the writings of these two escaped slaves of the Turks.

George of Hungary

George of Hungary's work[4] was recognized in the sixteenth century to be of singular importance in helping to make sense of the Turks and Islam. However, his name was not known (he was often referred to as Septemcastrensis Captivus, after his place of capture).[5] Based on internal documentary evidence it is presumed that he was captured by the Turks in 1438 and remained a Turkish slave until 1458. The book evidently was written late in the life of the author, most likely in 1480 or 1481. Through reading the preface one can easily picture an old monk painstakingly writing this manuscript in Rome, recalling the troubles of his younger days. His wide-ranging survey of Turkish culture (including everything from toilet practices to religious beliefs) was extraordinarily popular and a prime source in subsequent publications on the Turks. At least twenty editions were published in German-speaking lands, including a translation by Sebastian Franck (with an introduction written by Martin Luther).[6] It was also included in the sixteenth-century equivalent of an encyclopedia of Islam, Theodor Bibliander's massive 1543 (and 1550) compilation *Machvmetis Saracenorvm Principis, eivsqve svccessorvm vitae, ac doctrina, ipseqve Alcoran.* As a part of composite works concerning the Turks, it remained in print until 1600.

The author presents the following biographical information: He was a student about fifteen years old in Mühlbach when the Turks besieged the city. The author claims that he attached himself to a small group of resisters including some of the local aristocracy. George states that he was prepared to die for Christ rather than to surrender to the Turks. In the end, this particular group was shut up in a tower as their last place of refuge. However, the Turks set fire to the tower and he was among the dazed survivors who ended up being sold to slave handlers. In Adrianople he was first sold in the slave market to merchants from Asia Minor who took him there and sold him to a farmer in Pergamum who lived up to his worst expectations in terms of cruelty. He undertook two attempts to escape even though he knew what kind of a horrible punishment he would face.

The second phase of his life occurred after he made arrangements with a slave trader to whom he escaped and who resold him three times before granting his freedom. After a few years wandering around Asia Minor, he was caught as a fugitive and served fifteen years imprisonment with his last master. At this point, he seems to have had a deep crisis of faith. He states that he felt all hope of liberation was lost and that he been abandoned by God. He was exhausted and broken and wondered whether he had in fact been following the false faith. Then follows a period in which he intensively studied Islam, conversed with Mevlevi dervishes, and participated in Muslim prayers and ceremonies.[7]

George's last owner was the complete opposite of his first. He made a pact with George to release him after serving his term. George calls him wise and good, and says that he treated him more like a family member than a slave, allowing him to participate in common mealtimes and giving him the time to dedicate to his religious interests. Much of what George later reports came from this owner whom he described as an eloquent man and a good storyteller. After his release, George traveled for a time, perhaps returning to Transylvania, and finally ended up most likely as a Dominican in Rome. The immediate context for the writing of the *Tractatus* appears to be the successful landing of Turks at Otranto (across the Italian Peninsula from Rome) in 1480. George's stated purpose for the composition is that he wrote to steel his determination to remain committed to Christianity as well as to give important information to those who may be captured by the Turks so that they will not abandon their Christian faith.

Although there has been no English version of this work beyond my translation excerpts in Appendix 2, our understanding of this author and his book has been enormously enhanced through the work of Reinhard Klockow's 1993 German scholarly edition of the *Tractatus*. Other than Klockow, only a handful of scholars have published specifically on this pamphlet, primarily as a part of much larger projects on late medieval and early modern *Türkenschriften*. Consensus appears to be universal lauding its originality, accuracy, and value.[8] It is recognized most for the important information it gives concerning the devshirme, various types of Ottoman troops, and perhaps the first extant record in the West of the dance of the Mevlevi dervishes.

Bartholomew Georgijevic

In 1544 another escaped slave, Bartholomew Georgijevic, published in Antwerp two short Latin pamphlets on the Turks which were also to become international bestsellers among *Turcica*.[9] Within a year these pamphlets were translated into French and German in two places separately (Nürnberg and Basel) something that was unique in the history of translation in that era.[10] Both *De Turcarum ritu et caeremoniis* [On the Rituals and Ceremonies of the Turks] and *De afflictione tam captivorum quam etiam sub Turcae tributo viventium Christianorum* [On the Afflictions of the Captive Christians Living under the Tribute of the Turks] were frequently republished and widely distributed. These publications are only a portion of a much larger collection of writings attributed to him. No fewer than eighty-two different editions of his works were printed from 1544 to 1686, including translations into seven European vernaculars.[11] In even as far removed (temporally and geographically) a publication as the British scholar Alexander Ross' 1655 *Pansebeia: Or a View of all Religions in the World*, Georgijevic is the most mentioned source in his section on Islam.

There are remarkable biographical parallels between George of Hungary and the sixteenth-century escaped slave, Bartholomew Georgijevic, which sometimes has led to confusion between the two. What we know of

Georgijevic comes almost entirely from his own writings. Georgijevic presents himself as a fascinating figure. A Croatian from the minor nobility, he claims (like George) to be captured by the Turks in Hungary (Georgijevic at the Battle of Mohács in 1526). According to a separately published autobiographical comment, he was sold seven times and lived as a slave both in European and in Asian Turkey. After several unsuccessful attempts, he finally escaped, traveling through Armenia, Damascus, and ending up in Jerusalem in 1537. After touring the traditional pilgrimage sites, and evidently becoming a Dominican, he then traveled to Santiago de Compostela in Spain, to continue his tour of major pilgrimage sites. Rather than going directly to Rome from Spain, however, he went instead to the Netherlands, where in Antwerp in 1544 he published *De Turcarum ritu et caeremoniis*.

He seems to be a professional seeker of preferment, dedicating his writings to a series of nobles, including Charles V and Maximilian Archduke of Austria. Georgijevic even traveled to Wittenberg expressly for the purpose of obtaining letters of reference from Luther and Melanchthon, a curious move for a Dominican monk. His knowledge of Luther's edition of George of Hungary's booklet on the Turks must have given him hope that Luther would be a patron of his own work. He left with a recommendation letter (Appendix 1), although it was not as ringing of an endorsement as one might have expected.[12]

From this point on in his life, we can make some conjectures concerning his peregrinations through the printing locations of his series of pamphlets. It seems that he made his living writing and talking about his captivity, going on the sixteenth-century equivalent of the talk-show circuit as an expert on Islam and the Turks and as an agitator for Christian military action in the East. He likely traveled to Louvain, Cologne, Mainz, Worms, Vienna, and Grosswardein in Hungary where he claims to have held a public disputation with a Turkish Dervish, Krakow (where he published his account of the disputation), perhaps Uppsala even, then back to Vienna, and finally to Naples and Rome in 1566 where he evidently died (or at least stopped publishing). We can follow the course of his travels so closely because everywhere he went he utilized local printers to put out editions of his works. He seems to have had no problem finding an audience. Europe was hungry for information about the Turks, and Georgijevic it seems was more than happy to satisfy it.

Georgijevic has been less intensively studied than George of Hungary, although *De Turcarum* has been published in a modern German edition with commentary by the Turkish scholar Melek Aksulu. The only other important publication on Georgijevic remains a brief Austrian National Library booklet. It contains a valuable chronological listing of Georgijevic's publications and their various translations and a short biographical sketch based on internal evidence.

I have reservations about the veracity of Georgijevic's story. Despite his stature among sixteenth-century European writers on the Ottoman Empire, there are elements of his narrative that raise questions both due to erroneous material in his writings as well as suspicious similarities with some specific items found in George of Hungary. However, in historical terms Georgijevic' writings are important for many reasons. He was important in the development of the use of the term Muslim, one of the first to use that term rather than Mohammedan (or the equivalent).[13] His writings contain the oldest transcriptions of Turkish words in Western literature.[14]

Theodor Bibliander's Qur'an

By their very nature, pamphlets are ephemeral, no matter how many copies or editions are produced. However, both George of Hungary's and Georgijevic's writings had an influence of Western views of Islam for more than two centuries because of their inclusion in the *Machumetis saracenorum principis eiusque successorum vitae, doctrina ac ipse alcoran* (1543, second edition 1550), compiled by the Zürich theologian Theodor Bibliander. This publication has long been recognized as one of the most significant texts on Islam published in the Latin West in the Early Modern era. The Qur'an translation it contained (the first ever to be printed), was not superseded for over one hundred years.[15] Bibliander's compendium was widely used as a scholarly resource, even for example, by Jesuit missionaries at the court of the Mogul Emperor Akbar, despite having been placed on the Index.[16]

Theodor Bibliander (1505?-1564) was Ulrich Zwingli's successor as teacher in the Zürich scriptural training institution known as the *Prophezei*. His lectures were greatly admired and were sometimes transcribed and circulated to pastors throughout the canton. He has been described as the father of exegetical theology in Switzerland.[17] Over the course of his career he published twenty-four books and left thirty volumes of unpublished materials (now located in the archives of the Zentralbibliothek Zürich). Bibliander's primary reputation, however, was as an expert on languages. No less a luminary than Guillaume Postel held him in the highest regard and even expressed the desire to relocate to Zürich so that the two could collaborate on research projects.

Islam particularly intrigued Bibliander, possibly as a result of his early experience in Silesia during a period of Turkish aggression. Beginning with the time of the Turkish offensive that culminated in the siege of Vienna in 1529, Bibliander seems to have sought sources on Islam and even had learned some Arabic. In addition to his compendium on Islam, he published one short work specifically on the war against the Turks (*Ad nominis christiani socios consultatio, quanam ratione Turcarum dira potentia repelli possit*, 1542).

Bibliander's interest in Islam was two-fold. He believed that the Turks were a real threat, both militarily and religiously. In this regard, he maintained that an accurate knowledge of Islam is the best weapon against it. But Bibliander also held a missionary motive in regard to Islam. In general, he maintained that there was hope for those outside of the visible Church, based on the expressed desire of God that all would be saved. Bibliander considered ignorance of the religion of the Turks to be the chief barrier both of defending Christendom against them as well as to proclaiming the Gospel to them.[18]

Although Bibliander was able to secure the services of the Basel printer Oporinus for his 1543 edition, a subsequent controversy concerning the danger that the publication of the Qur'an might cause the Christian community jeopardized the entire project.[19] All printed copies were seized and Oporinus was briefly jailed by the Basel magistrates during the fall of 1542. It took a concerted effort of support from several Protestant leaders including Bibliander, Bucer, Melanchthon, and Luther before the printing was allowed to continue.

The work is extraordinarily large. It was printed in three volumes bound together, each containing over 200 folio pages (2°), many filled with marginal comments or in double columns. The paper size and volume length is itself a sign of the perceived significance and importance of the text. Bibliander's third volume contains cultural and historical works, including George and Georgijevic. (See Figure 8.1) The inclusion of this kind of material is significant. The kind of engagement with Islam it represents goes beyond the theological. In several of the pamphlets in volume three, the Turks are not defined solely in terms of Christian theological categories (heresy, Antichrist) and *Heilsgeschichte*. Clothing, eating habits, and furniture are also examined alongside religious belief and practice. The very structure of the compendium is an expression of the ambiguous understanding of Islam in the early modern West, the very instability of the self-contradictory contents opening possibilities for new perspectives in the future. Translations of significant portions of George and Georgijevic from Bibliander's 1550 edition are found in Appendices 2 and 3.

Developments in Tone

While on the surface Georgijevic' and George of Hungary's publications appear similar, there are deep differences which may in part be attributed to individual personality but also reflect important historical developments in Christian-Islamic relations in the intervening seventy years, especially concerning perceptions of relative power. For George, the primary problem is conversion to Islam. One might think while reading this that Christendom was hemorrhaging renegades, especially priests and monks. George places much blame on Christians for this, but the central argument is that the Turks appear as an 'angel of light' through whose positive qualities Christians are led astray. As a result, George is compelled to show all of the 'good' aspects of the Turks and Islam to explain just how they could be so attractive. And then he demonstrates that the devil lurks under this appearance of probity and goodness. This means that George paints a remarkably positive picture of the Turks and Islam. Martin Luther, and presumably others in the sixteenth

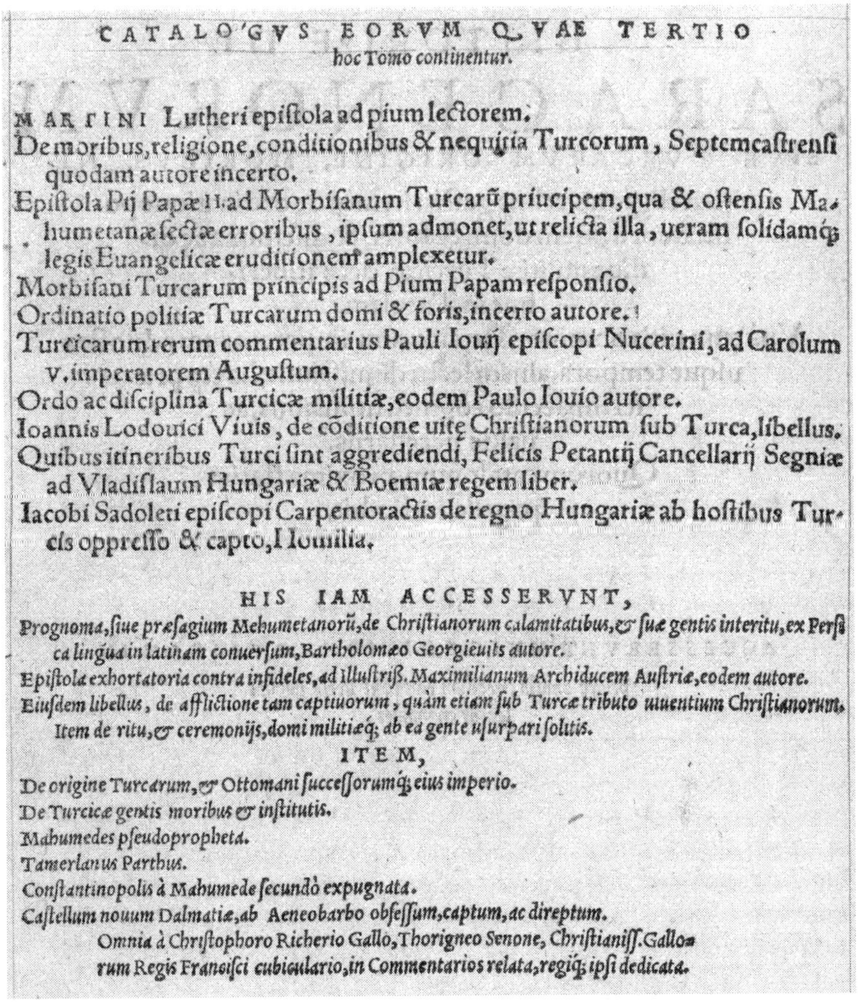

CATALO'GVS EORVM Q VAE TERTIO
hoc Tomo continentur.

M AR r I N I Lutheri epiftola ad pium lectorem.
De moribus, religione, conditionibus & nequitia Turcorum, Septemcaftrenfi
quodam autore incerto.
Epiftola Pij Papæ II. ad Morbifanum Turcarũ priucipem, qua & oftenfis Ma-
humetanæ fectæ erroribus, ipfum admonet, ut relicta illa, ueram folidamq;
legis Euangelicæ eruditionem amplexetur.
Morbifani Turcarum principis ad Pium Papam refponfio.
Ordinatio politiæ Turcarum domi & foris, incerto autore.
Turcicarum rerum commentarius Pauli Iouij epifcopi Nucerini, ad Carolum
v. imperatorem Auguftum.
Ordo ac difciplina Turcicæ militiæ, eodem Paulo Iouio autore.
Ioannis Lodouici Viuis, de coditione uitç Chriftianorum fub Turca, libellus.
Quibus itineribus Turci fint aggrediendi, Felicis Petantij Cancellarij Segniæ
ad Vladiflaum Hungariæ & Boemiæ regem liber.
Iacobi Sadoleti epifcopi Carpentoractis de regno Hungariæ ab hoftibus Tur-
cis oppreffo & capto, I lomilia.

HIS IAM ACCESSERVNT,

Prognoma, fiue præfagium Mehumetanorũ, de Chriftianorum calamitatibus, & fuæ gentis interitu, ex Perfi
ca lingua in latinam conuerfum, Bartholomæo Georgieuits autore.
Epiftola exhortatoria contra infideles, ad illuftriß. Maximilianum Archiducem Auftriæ, eodem autore.
Eiufdem libellus, de afflictione tam captiuorum, quàm etiam fub Turcæ tributo uiuentium Chriftianorum,
Item de ritu, & ceremonijs, domi militiæq; ab ea gente ufurpari folitis.

ITEM,

De origine Turcarum, & Ottomani fuccefforumq; eius imperio.
De Turcicæ gentis moribus & inftitutis.
Mahumedes pfeudopropheta.
Tamerlanus Parthus.
Conftantinopolis à Mahumede fecundò expugnata.
Caftellum nouum Dalmatiæ, ab Aeneobarbo obfeffum, captum, ac direptum.
Omnia à Chriftophoro Richerio Gallo, Thorigneo Senone, Chriftianiß. Gallo-
rum Regis Francifci cubiculario, in Commentarios relata, regiq; ipfi dedicata.

Figure 8.1 Contents page of Bibliander's Qur'an listing George of Hungary and Georgijevic, 1550

Courtesy of Houghton Library, Harvard University. GC5 B4716 543md, Houghton Library, Harvard University

century, understood this to be evidence of a praiseworthy lack of bias. Because George was unusual in his presentation of positive aspects of Islamic practice (piety, prayers, fastings, etc.), Luther considered him to be an essential, welcome addition to Christian understandings of Islam. Luther, of course, claimed to know all about the devil lurking under the appearance of piety and did not hesitate to connect his discovery about Islam to his claims about

Roman Catholic practice. By his interpretation (and subsequent framing publication) of George of Hungary, Luther praises the Turks as a way of damning the Papists. According to Luther, in this comparison the Turks easily come out on top. In this regard, Luther is much more medieval than early modern.

In addition, George of Hungary's work is rooted in the Apocalypse. In the first paragraph alone he cites both Old Testament and New Testament prophetic books. Dragons, beasts, pestilences, and Joachim of Fiore keep appearing throughout the text. The teachings of Islam are an infection, a poison which is both seductive and lethal. George's book is filled with anxiety over conversion. Islam is seductive, in large part because it is not forced and seems to be based upon freewill choices. On the surface it appears pious but in reality it is devilish. The tone is pessimistic and determined, as though George expected at any moment to see the Turks marching over the Apennines giving him the chance for martyrdom that was denied so long ago. His memoir is a work of self-justification, explaining his flirtation with Islam and exorcising his personal demons by demonstrating just how seductive Islam and the Turkish culture could be.

The contrast is striking with Georgijevic. Dedicated to the Holy Roman Emperor Charles V himself, Georgijevic's work reads more like valuable commercial and military intelligence than apocalyptic apologetics. This opening description is remarkable by its attempt to create an objective tone. Only the briefest biographical information precedes this description of the initial moments after capture (found in Georgijevic's dedicatory epistle), and there is no attempt to over-dramatize the situation of war captives. His rhetorical strategy is to begin with straightforward description although later sections utilize more derogatory language. *De afflictione*, complete with woodcuts emphasizing Turkish cruelties (one of them shows a captured fugitive being hamstrung), is explicitly intended to stir the princes of Europe to military action and *De Turcarum ritu* seems intended to be lessons on the enemy by a self-proclaimed humanist and demonstrates the growing commercial interest in Ottoman realms. It seems somewhat self-contradictory when Georgijevic rails against the cruelty of the Turks but then also teaches the reader how to count in Turkish and provides a practical phrasebook for various kinds of goods and services. Because it was published late in Luther's career (or perhaps because of the ambivalent personal response Luther had to Georgijevic himself), Luther did not edit and re-publish or even write an introduction to Georgijevic' pamphlets. Perhaps he felt like they did not significantly add to the knowledge base. Certainly George of Hungary's late-medieval work suited his rhetorical purposes much better.

Organization and Content

A comparison of the organization and contents of these two documents reveals significant parallels. George of Hungary in its original printing is the longer of the two documents, containing seventy full pages. It begins with a discussion of the origin of Turks and how they came to establish an Empire. He then warns the reader about the fearsome nature of these Turks and how they represent both a physical and spiritual threat to Christians that should not be taken lightly. To reinforce this point, George of Hungary goes on to describe the Turkish demand for slaves and uses his own experiences to paint a brutal picture of abuses by slave owners and the humiliations of the slave market. The difficulty and dangers of escape are described. At this point, however, the narrative shifts, as George details the rationales of those who freely convert to Islam, even when this brings them no great social advantage and is, of course, putting their eternal souls in danger. In the entire section that follows, encompassing about one-half of the total pamphlet, the Turks and their religion are described in a strikingly objective, even positive way. The Turks are described as just, proper, and avoiding vain display (in contrast to what the Turks perceive as frivolousness and crudeness in Christian dress and decorum). They are models of cleanliness and bathe frequently. In their churches there is a reverence that should shame Christians. In particular, Turkish women are modest and honorable in contrast to the loose women of Christendom. Even their horses are disciplined and don't prance about like Christian horses.

After discussing their external uprightness, George details the spiritual attractiveness of Islam. He describes their doctrines, prayers, ascetic practices, and miracles. It is no wonder that those Christians living among the Turks would be tempted by such outwardly pure, but deceivingly diabolical errors, to renounce their faith and convert to Islam. In fact, the author himself admits to doing so—but only for six or seven months. But in conclusion, the author examines the reasons why one can be saved from these errors by recognizing the falsehood of Islam as revealed through its many internal divisions in contrast to a unified Christianity (this is one argument that won't work a hundred years later), their lack of theological sophistication, and their near total ignorance of matters pertaining to salvation and the "cure of souls." The pamphlet concludes with a summary of the advantages of Christianity over Islam and a plea to believe his testimony because of his extensive personal experience, so great in fact that he completely forgot his mother tongue and became completely acculturated. In an appendix of sorts, some short selections were added by the author to the text. The author has been highly regarded by linguists for his inclusion of two short transliterated Turkish sermons with Latin translation. This is followed by a short selection from the Apocalypse commentary of Joachim of Fiore concerning the "sect of Muhammad."

Immediate parallels can be seen between the structure and contents of George of Hungary's and Georgijevic's works. Although there seems to be no overt copying, the similarities between these works point to Georgijevic's familiarity with the prior document, despite his specific denial. *De afflictione* begins with a description of how captives are treated and the various destinies to which they are assigned. This includes descriptions of sexual abuse and the humiliations of the slave market. The author then describes various ways that slaves attempt to flee (distinguishing between escape attempts launched from Turkish Europe and those from Asia Minor) and the severe penalties inflicted when caught. Georgijevic describes how the memory of Christ has little by little faded away in the one-time provinces of Christendom and concludes with a plea directly to Christian kings and princes to aid those suffering in Turkish slavery and the Christians under Turkish tribute.

Part II, *De turcarum ritu*, is divided into three sections. The first describes the origin of the Turks and of the Mohammedans and summarizes what Georgijevic evidently deemed the essentials of their religion, including sections on "temples" (which includes a transliteration of the Arabic confession of faith and a discussion of prayer), the Turkish "lent" and "Easter" (the Ramadan fast and Eid al-Fitr), circumcision, priests, schools, monks, marriage, pilgrimage, almsgiving, and burial. The second section deals exclusively with the Turkish military, giving information on leaders, foot soldiers, archers, cavalry, military discipline, and hunting. The third section describes domestic life, including towns, agriculture, clothing, and food. Like the *Tractatus, De ritu* also concludes with a linguistic appendix of which I will speak later.

Religious Themes

In combination, these two documents give us a well-rounded snapshot of the state of knowledge concerning Islam/the Turks during the fifteenth and sixteenth centuries, a critical period in Ottoman history and a time of significant development in European intellectual history. Perhaps even more importantly, when some specific themes found in these two documents are examined side by side, a number of interesting points emerge concerning important continuities and discontinuities in Western views of Islam.

Both authors display a mix of accuracy and error, the mundane and the bizarre in their treatment of religion, a theme of central importance in both documents. First, completely absent are the medieval notions of Muslims as worshipping idols or Muhammad. In fact, George sees the strength and durability of this 'sect' due to their doctrine of the unity of God and denigration of idols. Both authors consider Islam a kind of false belief; there is no use of the name "Islam" or an understanding of it as a self-contained body of belief and practice separate from Christianity. Many connections are made to Christianity, as though Islam were a dark shadow of the truth. However, there is a kernel of accuracy in George's description of Moses as the first major prophet of Islam, David as second major prophet, and then because of corruption, Jesus was sent as the third major prophet. According to George, for each of these at that time their law was the basis for salvation. Therefore, Islam is neither understood to be a Christian heresy nor paganism, but something in between these two options.

Aspects of all of the Five Pillars can be found mixed together with other material in various sections of these writings. In both authors, a rough approximation of the confession of faith (the *shahadah*) is included. Five times daily prayers are mentioned along with washings in preparation and George includes a somewhat accurate description of a raaka (the structure of prayer). Georgijevic's account is more confused and one might get the idea that only the *sacerdotes* [sic: priests] need to pray five times daily. Both authors emphasize prayer in mosques, with Georgijevic demonstrating accurate linguistic knowledge by correctly naming them *meschit* [*masjid*] in Arabic. The decorum and reverence during prayer in the mosques (especially in contrast to Christian churches) is emphasized. Sermons and the offices of muezzin and imam are known to both authors. Georgijevic includes accounts of two-hour long sermons, petitionary chanting of young boys, and late-night prayer services for women, all of which call into question the validity of his claims to firsthand experience. He also adds that Friday is the most sacred day because it was the day of the week on which Muhammad was born.[20] George also mentions a kind of "church police" to discipline those who do not participate.

Both authors mention a period of communal fasting, although neither identifies it with the month of Ramadan. They do know that this is a fast during daylight hours and that it travels through the year since it is based on a lunar calendar.[21] Both naturally compare the fast to Lent and comment about the 'Easterfeast' (Eid al-Fitr) that follows. Neither author places much emphasis on pilgrimage. Although the worst of the medieval misunderstandings are missing (particularly the myth of the iron coffin of Muhammad suspended in mid-air), both state that Mecca is the location of the tomb of Muhammad. George highlights the fact that those who have completed the pilgrimage are held in high esteem ("the testimony of a pilgrim is worth three others"). Georgijevic' treatment of the pilgrimage is almost entirely commercial; there is nothing that is particularly devotional or religious. The pillar of Islam least commented upon by these two authors is almsgiving. Both authors mention hospitality, alms, and the liberation of animals as good deed, but a fifteenth- or sixteenth-century reader of these writings would not learn much about religious aspects of Muslim economics or of the central place of *zakat*.

George's discussions of Islamic theology contain a similar mixture of truth and error. For example, he claims that Qur'anic law requires marriage, that Muslims don't believe in original sin, but that they believe in a kind of universalism through the power of Muhammad after the Last Judgment. George turns the tables on traditional Muslim apologetics. He states that Muslims avoid reason; they do not defend their beliefs with arguments but with the sword. Everything is treated as a law of God and cannot be questioned. Georgijevic is much more interested in what we refer to as life-cycle rituals than in traditional articles of belief or practice. His description of Islam spends much more time on circumcision, marriage, and funerary practices than theology. Both writers emphasize popular (certainly hetero-dox) religious practices. George mentions vows made at the tombs of saints, each with his own miraculous specialty. Georgijevic relates that when a Turk is sick or in danger, he takes a sheep or ox/cow to a certain place and sacri-fices it as an offering. He states that they are not held to their vows if they are not rescued from sickness or danger, for their vows are always "I will give as you give to me (*do ut dares*)." He adds, though, that this is common among the Greeks, Armenians, and other Christian peoples of Asia as well. Both authors mention the use of talismans, mystical practices (interestingly, both mention mystical pregnancies), curses, vows, and incantations. Georgi-jevic seems to think that the Turks commonly appeal to goddesses, and use votives, animal sacrifices, and offerings for the dead.

Georgijevic begins by making a comment about the origins of the Turks, and then immediately moves to Muhammad and Islam. He begins with a description of worship and emphasizes that Christians desecrate the temples of the Turks, at least in part because they do not complete the ritual wash-ings. He begins with a variation of the *shahadah* and then discusses prayer and fasting during Ramadan. He then discusses circumcision and distin-guishes it from Jewish circumcision. This crucial act marks conversion to Islam. He states that women are not made Muslims in this way, however, but by the confession of faith. Here he clearly links conversion to liberation, and even a financial reward. He emphasizes a different understanding of clergy, emphasizing that they are not as educated as Christian clergy, have little sacerdotal power, can be married, and often work at side occupations.

Washings, including the cleansing of the privates after urination or def-ecation, is emphasized. Georgijevic states that there were severe penalties for coming to the mosque with genital hair (for both men and women). For him these washings are of central importance and a key distinguishing factor, even though "the washings while making them clean on the outside do not clean the wicked filth which fills their souls."

Both authors consider Islam a kind of false belief rather than a false 'religion' in the modern sense. There is no use of the name 'Islam' or an understanding of it as a self-contained body of belief and practice separate from Christianity. Many connections are made to Christianity, however, as though Islam were a corruption of the truth. George uses the terms "law of Muhammad" and "sect of the Saracens" and "sect of the Turks."

In regard to this, each writer's treatment of circumcision is informative. George deals with circumcision in Chapter 21 in the context of reasons why one should turn away from the errors of the Turks. In an extended complaint he states that the Turks know nothing about original sin, the mysteries of faith, or forgiveness of sins. They have such a high regard for washing, bowings, and other religious activities that they think these gain salvation for them. They may punish sins like theft and murder, but they ignore others, both hidden and open sins and have no confession, absolu-tion, justification, or sacrament of purification. Even circumcision is not treated as a means of salvation, despite that the Turks consider the lack of circumcision to be a sure sign of heterodoxy and commonly demean people by calling them 'uncircumcised.' However, they take no great pains to circumcise a boy before he dies. George concludes by saying that it seems to him that the whole purpose of circumcision is to make the required whole-body washings easier.

For Georgijevic, circumcision plays a much more important role in Islam.[22] (See Figure 8.2) It is the third religious subject he describes after temples and fasts. He contrasts this with Jewish circumcision in that Muslim circumcision takes place in the boy's seventh or eighth year and is the pretext for a big family celebration that includes gift-giving and a naming ceremony. Georgijevic also highlights the role that circumcision plays in conversion to Islam. If a Christian converts of his own free will (as Georgijevic states that he has personally seen), then they demonstrate this through a circumcision ceremony that is followed by a procession, the receiving of gifts, and the official canceling of the 'unbeliever's tribute.' He also mentions forced conversions/circumcisions (specifically the case of an unnamed Greek bishop), which bring the same benefits except that there is no party or receiving of gifts. What is most important in this passage is the designation that Georgijevic gives these newly circumcised boys and converts: he states that they are called Muslumanlar. He mistakenly translates this as 'circumcised.' As I noted earlier, this is the first instance in Western European literature that I am aware of where Muslims are referred to as such, rather than as Mohammadans and its variations. Georgijevic is even closer to the truth when he states that since women cannot be circumcised, they are considered Musluman only after they have publicly sworn the Islamic confession of faith: "there is no God but God and Muhammad is his prophet." For Georgijevic, circumcision was the critical identifying marker, but he was not alone in recognizing the centrality of this as a cultural distinguisher. Islamic circumcision placed a mark on the body that seems to have limited some conversion.

Ascetic and Mystic Religious Practices

George of Hungary's firsthand experience with Muslim ascetics is demonstrated through his detailed, four-page description of their sects and practices. While he asserts that there is so much devilish power in them that they "almost appear to be living devils," still he credits them with miracles both during and after their deaths. One group reaches such a state of oblivion that they become inured to physical conditions, going about naked in heat and cold with only their private parts covered. To demonstrate their lack of concern for bodily sensation, they put fire on their bodies or cut their flesh with swords ("facit sibi apponere ignem vel incidere carnem cum gladio"). Some fast so that they practically go without food or drink. Others live in great poverty. A group called the "czamutlar" go entirely without speaking.

De Circuncifione.

VTuntur circuncifione eo-
rū lingua *Tfuneth* dicta, non
octaua die, more Iudæorum, fed
quamprimùm natus feptimū aut
octauum annū exegerit, fermo-
nis iam peritus : idq; ipfis myfte-
rium eft, propter verba côfefsio-
nis, quæ ante circuncifionem re-
quiruntur, erecto pollice manus
Parmach dicto, hæc videlicet, quæ
fuprà

Figure 8.2 Georgijevic, On Circumcision, 1558

Some receive revelations and others experience ecstasies (the Dervishes are here specifically mentioned and their dance is accurately and sympathetically described). In one description, while watching the Dervish dance his family was so awestruck that it was as if they were hit by lightning and there was not a dry eye in the house. In what seems to be a *non sequitur*, George hastily concludes that they are "angels of Satan" masquerading as "angels of light."[23]

Georgijevic's account, on the other hand, possesses no theological context or framing. He describes three orders of monks (all called Dervishes). The first possess nothing, go about naked except for a covering on their private parts, and beg alms. They ingest an herb called "matslah" which makes them oblivious to pain. They can hold a burning branch on their head, breast or hand until it turns to ash. The second order bores a hole through their penis and hangs a three-pound ring on it, in order to preserve their chastity.[24] The third order seldom comes out of their churches, but begs alms there and daily prays for a revelation from God, which the king of the Turks uses in times of war. Although similar to George's description, there is no sympathetic treatment here. No awe. No miracles. Although the two descriptions have much in common (and the latter may have drawn upon the former), Georgijevic's account is more straightforward, although exaggerated and quite reminiscent of typical later Orientalist accounts.

The Turkish Military

One of the key functions of these two publications is to attempt to make sense of the expansion of Turkish power from a Christian perspective. This includes, naturally, a discussion of Ottoman military training, political structure, martial values, etc., but also goes beyond temporal explanations to ask deeper questions about the role of the Turks in salvation history. It is simply a given that a phenomenon as significant as the rise of the Ottoman Empire is ordained by God for some discernable purpose. For George of Hungary, the primary framework is apocalyptic. He begins his treatise with a rhetorical flourish filled with dramatic imagery of beasts and dragons from the Book of Revelation. Joachim of Fiore is alluded to in his introduction and then quoted at length in his conclusion. As a whole, George's perspective is dark and foreboding. He is convinced that he is living in the last days, as evidenced not only by the power of the Turks, but also by Renaissance humanism which he sees as a grave evil. The Turks are fundamentally a God-permitted raging of the devil against the Church. There is some allusion to the Turks as punishment from God (certainly there is enough criticism of Christendom in this writing), but chastisement is not a central theme. This is not so much a call for repentance as it is a call to martyrdom in the face of overwhelming power. God is using the Turks not to purify Christendom, but to create opportunities for eternal rewards for those who remain faithful. It seems that for George, the Turks cannot be defeated. Their conquests will continue and be even greater than Alexander or the Romans.

This strongly apocalyptic framework of understanding does not exclude a discussion of more mundane reasons for Turkish military success, however. George does not go into detail about the Turkish military, but does extol their discipline and endurance. He seems particularly impressed with their skill in stealthy horsemanship. According to George, the Turks have an unlimited number of soldiers available, due in part to captured Christian slaves turned into the elite fighters called Janissaries. Further adding to their success is the fact that it doesn't take any effort to raise a large army because of the Turks' zeal for war.

The change in the writings of Georgijevic is astonishing. Apocalypticism does not provide an interpretive framework, is much reduced, and actually carries almost an opposite connotation of the potential of an ultimate Christian victory. In a dedicatory epistle to Holy Roman Emperor Charles V, Georgijevic claimed that even in Turkey a prophecy circulates that he is the one who will destroy Ottoman power. Georgijevic states explicitly that he published this material to move the emperor concerning the misery of captive Christians in Turkish lands and that he prays that the health and life of the emperor be preserved until the Christian flag flies over Asia and Africa, even throughout the world. The Ottoman military is described to be an awesome force. In fact, Georgijevic goes into great detail, using eight chapters to discuss the military and their campaigns in highly positive terms. However, in the end Georgijevic remains optimistic concerning Charles's success. Twice he states that if the Imperial army would simply attack and not turn back at the outset of the battle, the Turks would flee at once. For Georgijevic the hardest part is motivating the Christians to fight and getting them to the field of battle; and he offers a (highly unrealistic) strategic plan that he is certain would succeed.

Virtues and Vices

In George of Hungary, a significant part of the explanation of the power of the Turks vis-à-vis Christians can be found in a discussion of Turkish virtues in comparison with Christian vices. Some of his discussions of the virtues of the Turks does seem to be an attempt to critique his own society, with which he is clearly at odds.[25] However, it is not surprising that in what is basically a personal defense for his flirtation with Islam its attractiveness would be highlighted. According to George, the virtues of the Turks could fill volumes; but he hastens to add that they do this with the help of the devil. As with this example, he finds it necessary every so often to add pious boilerplate that this appearance of piety is really just a sham.[26] But one cannot but get the feeling that he does seem to be genuinely impressed with many aspects of piety found among the Turks. He is particularly taken with their cleanliness and lack of display—both of which are understood to be spiritual virtues. George relates that the Turks abhor the frivolity of Christian clothing, calling them goats or monkeys. Among the Turks there is nothing vain or superfluous. The sultan does not go about with a retinue and no one shouts 'long live the king' or so forth. Rather the sultan is benevolent, mild, and just. The Turks' buildings are simple even if they have a lot of money. It is almost, compliments George, as if they had taken vows of poverty. Except for the most important public buildings, they rarely use stone and ridicule the vanity of Christian architecture—"do they poor heathen think that they will live forever?" Their simplicity is seen also in the fact that they eat sitting on the ground, paying tribute to the fact that all are born equal. Their cleanliness is even more impressive. They allow no animals in houses or mosques and use the baths continually. They stay away from what they consider to be polluting (wine, swine) and will not pray until they are fully clean.

Georgijevic also mentions the Muslim lack of building adornment and the fact that they dress more modestly than Christians, in a manner that further supports a borrowing from George. And likewise he characterizes them as using frequent external washings in hopes of salvation, but that on the inside they are full of filthy sin. However, there is much more animosity and venom in Georgijevic and much less respect for Muslim piety. In a concluding statement to the reader he ends with a bitter rhetorical flourish: if someone praises the Turks, keep in mind that as much as light differs from darkness, so the Christian religion differs from the abominable barbarian superstition. He adds that he has not discussed everything so as not to dirty his paper with their filthy practices, which not only to write and read, but even to hear soils you.

There is also a salacious element in Georgijevic not found in George. Early in his description Georgijevic mentions various kinds of sexual violence inflicted upon captured slaves, this includes a variety of possibilities depending on age, gender, physical appearance, and skill-set, including the removal of male genitalia, concubinage, and child rape. Although Georgijevic seems to praise the discipline of the Turkish army on the march by noting the lack of camp followers, he does say that the Sultan and his nobles bring catamites along for their pleasure.

However, Georgijevic does seem to respect Turkish legal discipline, or perhaps he simply uses this as a further way of demonstrating the harshness of Turkish culture. It is interesting that this is one place where what appear to be personal anecdotes enter the text. Georgijevic claims that no soldier steals anything from another or takes as much as an apple from a tree while on campaign. He claims that he was once with the Turkish army marching against the Persians and saw a knight, his horse, and servant beheaded simply because the horse trampled on a field. As a further example of Turkish justice, he tells the story of a woman in the market who had some milk that was taken without compensation by a Janissary and drunk. When the woman accused the man before the judge, the Janissary was hung up by his feet, vomited the milk, and was strangled on the spot.[27]

Views of Turkish Women

It is not surprising that both George of Hungary and Georgijevic note differences in gender roles between Christendom and the Ottoman Empire. George has a particularly positive evaluation of the honorableness of Turkish women, although this is based fundamentally on a deep misogynism. He basically calls the women of Christian countries prostitutes, as with their "open necks, flirting eyes, flowing hair" they go about the city causing men to have adultery with them in their hearts. In contrast, the Turks are true men, according to George. They keep their women well. If they cannot watch over their wives continually, they have eunuchs to do this. George praises the veiling of women, their simple adornment without vanity. He applauds the fact that women would never dare to be seen in a gathering of men, do not buy or sell in the market, have separate places of prayer in the mosques, rarely talk together in public, and do not ride.

Georgijevic's descriptions of Turkish women do not go beyond what George had written, although he does add the accurate qualifier that only rich women are secluded and do not go to market. He adds an anecdote, however, concerning the double standard in judicial cases of adultery. If a man commits adultery he is imprisoned; after some months he pays money. However, if a woman is an adulteress she is taken street by street on a donkey, flogged naked, around her neck they hang cow's intestines and she is stoned to death. In both cases Muslim women are found to be much more upright than Christian women and neither author makes much of Islamic polygyny, although George does state (inaccurately) that Muslims can have up to twelve wives (though rarely do they have two under the same roof because it leads to disputes).

Conversion to Islam

According to George of Hungary, it was a combination of the outward attractiveness of Islam with the hopelessness of a slave's condition that induced him to (briefly) convert to Islam.[28] George's description of the slave market emphasized humiliation. With this kind of enormous hopelessness, is it any wonder that people fall from faith, he asks? In answer to the question, 'why did he doubt?' he tells of his sale to the other side of the sea (Pergamum) to a cruel farmer. After his first escape attempt he was beaten and threatened, after his second he was beaten almost to death and would have been left in chains had it not been for the intercession of the women of the household who pledged for him. After many failed attempts to escape he finally gave up hope and began to pray as a Muslim and study (secretly)

Muslim spirituality. The piety of the Sufis seemed more angelic than human and their practices and writings clearly intrigued him. He practiced Islam only for a brief time, he claims. After six or seven months he returned to Christianity more convinced than ever.

Even though the Turks do not force conversions, many Christians willingly become Muslim to avoid persecution or in an attempt to better their condition, according to George. In particular, monks and priests received more generous stipends from the royal chamber if they converted.[29] But George is skeptical about how much conversion helps slaves. A denial of Christ won't save you from being re-sold if you are a slave. Not every slave converts: some simply hold to the Christian faith—and either dies in it or escapes home. George admits the danger, but also the importance of deep inquiry: a little knowledge about Islam is the most spiritually dangerous. Much of the latter sections of George of Hungary's tract is an apologia for re-conversion to Christianity. However, in the end he holds little hope once an individual has converted to Islam. In a description of a conversation with a renegade, George asked him the question: why don't you re-convert? He received in response only a very quiet "It's not possible." He holds even less hope for the conversions of native Turks.

Georgijevic did not agonize over religious questions as did George. According to him, the first thing the Turks do is try to get slaves to convert by threats, flattery, and promises of an improved life. He states that whoever does not get circumcised is mocked and claims that he endured this mockery for fifteen years and never even pretended to convert. However, Georgijevic is quite concerned with the plight of other Christian slaves and the native Christian populations under Turkish rule. Much of his writing is dedicated to a description of their condition, often in the most emotive terms possible. This is also where Georgijevic can be the most salacious.[30] He describes how the memory of Christ, little by little was obliterated in lands that were formerly Christian. There are those who still remember the Turkish conquest and remain steadfastly Christian; however, the young people are forgetting Christ and in the future Christianity will be obliterated here. This is also cause for concern for the newly conquered lands of Croatia and Hungary, and is a prime motive force in his advocacy of Imperial military intervention.

Georgijevic includes a significant amount of information about what might be termed religious identity markers. Just because they are captives and have crossed into the geographical space of the Turks and are their possessions, does not mean they have become Muslims. He identifies three factors that make them Muslims. First, they must renounce Christian faith. Georgijevic emphasizes here the theoretical voluntary nature of conversion. Second, they are circumcised. For Georgijevic, this is the key. By whatever means if they can get the captive to allow himself to be circumcised, then he has permanently crossed a religious boundary. Both factors seem to be necessary. A renunciation without circumcision seems not to be able to make a Muslim. It does not seem that one can be a 'Muslim in the heart' without also the physical sign of circumcision. However, the conversion needs to be actualized by initiation into the ceremonies/rituals of the Turks through a confession of faith. Although he mentions that female captives 'always' convert, he does not detail a conversion process for them beyond the confession of faith.

Like George of Hungary, Georgijevic is keen to emphasize that converting to Islam does not better the status of a slave. He seems to grudgingly admit that allowing oneself to be circumcised might produce a little more humane treatment, but that it does not eliminate the status of slave immediately for the person or for his children. And he does state that becoming circumcised makes a return to Christian lands impossible, stating that the penalty for even attempting this is being burned to death. However, those who refuse to be circumcised are treated even worse.

For Georgijevic, conversion is not only personal, but also territorial. Wherever Turkish imperialism has come, Christians have been pushed to the margins and Christianity itself has been gradually effaced under Muslim rule because the youth grow up surrounded by a different culture. In addition, just like human bodies, territory is marked as a result of religious conversion. The transfer from Christian to Turkish control is marked by the removal of bells and organs from the churches, church desecration, and then the re-consecration of these buildings to Muhammad.

For Georgijevic, the term 'Christian' is broad enough to include Balkan Christians, Armenians, Greeks, and "other Asian nations of the Christian religion." His focus on Armenians is particularly interesting. Armenia is mentioned in several passages, including in the opening of the second book. The Greeks and Armenians come out as helpers of slave fugitives just because they have been treated well in Rome and Compostela(!). He includes a relatively sound summary of dhimmi status. Most important of all, he claims that if the West would only attack, the Eastern Christians under Turkish rule would rise up like a fifth column to help them destroy the Ottomans.

Framing Materials

The most important evidence of development in Western views of the Turks and Islam concerns the supplementary materials that were added as an appendix to Georgijevic's work. In the very first of Georgijevic's publications a kind of early Berlitz-type travel phrase book was included. Religious terms in Arabic and/or Turkish are given along with their Latin equivalent, for example, angel, prophet, saint, paradise, and God (which is given as Allah). But the vocabulary list goes far beyond theology to include words for times, seasons, natural objects, currency, relationships (mother, wife, etc.), body parts, colors, food and drink, clothing, eating utensils, numbers, and other common words. The word list is followed by a guide to simple conversations, including a greeting, a valediction and a thank-you. (See Figure 8.3) My favorite sample dialogue (in Latin and Turkish) is this: Turk: "Where are you going, O Christian?" Christian: "I'm going to Constantinople, sir." Turk: "What business have you there?" Christian: "I'm going to

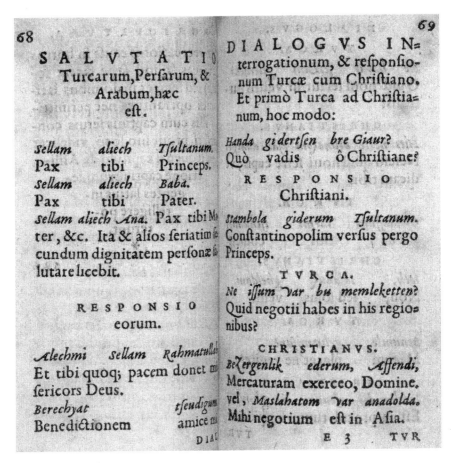

Figure 8.3 Georgijevic, Dialogue, 1558

conduct commerce, my lord." Etc. etc. The dialogue sounds like an exchange with a customs officer. It is no coincidence, I think, that Georgijevic's first publication was produced in Antwerp. The grammatical notes that follow are intended specifically for the purpose of trade with not only the Turks but also various Christians who live under their rule (Greeks, Armenians, etc.). The supplementary materials attached to George of Hungary's work are samples of Turkish sermons and an excerpt from Joachim of Fiore. The comparison between the two bestsellers of Turkish captivity narratives published in Germany during the Reformation reveals more than just a difference in focus. They represent evidence of a paradigm shift beginning to take place in the West's relationship to the Turks.

Continuity and Change

Despite the differences between these two documents, there remains a great deal of continuity. At the very least, Georgijevic was influenced greatly by George of Hungary, whom he may have read and whose work may have inspired him to write his own account. One telling example of this possible borrowing concerns both authors' descriptions of mystical pregnancies. While such tales did circulate in Ottoman lands, descriptions of it were relatively rare and it is suspicious that both of these writers would have heard such similar stories, despite Georgijevic's claim to have heard firsthand accounts. Other aspects of Georgijevic could even have been borrowed or learned after he returned to Christendom.

The continuity represented by these two authors goes far beyond the fifteenth and sixteenth centuries, however. As one example, a 1688 Magdeburg publication by one Wilhelm Burchard who, as an urgent reminder to his 'dear Germans' of Turkish gruesomeness, recounts the experiences of a 19-year-old Saxon who had been captured by the Ottomans:

> If among the captured males there are cute ones, the signs of their maleness are cut off so that not the slightest mark of their masculinity remains, and when they are healed, the arch-enemy uses these poor slaves for shameful and sodomitical fornication; once they have become plain, they are put in the women's chamber or made to do dirty work in the kitchen.

Compare this with Georgijevic's description of captives from *De afflictione*:

> If there are any cute ones, they are cut so that on their entire bodies nothing male appears, to the great peril of their lives. If they recover, they are kept for no other purpose than for gruesome, depraved fornication. When their beauty fades as they become too old, then they are put in the women's chamber to keep it, or they must groom the horses and mules, or do the dirty work in the kitchen.

Most of the Burchard book simply reorders and summarizes the (by then) century old Georgijevic work in a similar manner to this excerpt. But why create a false identity of a recently captured Saxon in order to communicate these ideas? An easy bestseller? A more compelling argument for military action against the Turks in the aftermath of the second siege of Vienna?

Scholars of Western-Islamic relations such as Norman Daniel and Edward Said both emphasize (for different reasons) a fundamental continuity in Western views of Islam from the Middle Ages to the beginnings of Western Imperialism. As Edward Said pointed out several times in *Orientalism*, even when European authors had considerable personal experience from which to draw for their descriptions of the Middle East, they instead repeatedly turned to stock images and stereotypes from their libraries rather than relate what their own eyes and ears had told them. Much continuity is indeed evident between George of Hungary and Georgijevic (not to mention Burchard). It seems clear, however, that essential transformations in European attitudes also took place during this period in Christian-Islamic relations, transformations that are highlighted by a comparison between these fascinating and in many ways parallel publications. However, the discovery of this textual and sub-textual development should be tempered with the knowledge that, as evidenced by Burchard, the broader structures of the depiction and understanding of the Muslim world long persisted, and in some measure persists still.

Notes

1. Rosamund Allen, ed., *Eastward Bound: Travel and Travelers, 1050–1550*, 204.
2. Allen, 214.
3. The earliest manuscript is 1380. Allen, 206.
4. The tract is itself anonymous. The authorial connection to the Roman Dominican monk George of Hungary seems first to have been intermittent until an article by Florio Banfi in the journal *Memorie Domenicane* in 1939. In the Bulletin of the John Rylands Library, J.A.B. Palmer supported this designation and added more evidence pointing toward George of Hungary O.P as the author. Klockow assumes that this is correct.
5. Evidently due to similarities in geographical origin and theme, I have found the works of George and Georgijevic sometimes to be confused or lumped together in archival catalogs.
6. Both Franck and Luther seem to have been interested both in the information on the Turks itself, as well as the rhetorical role which this information could play in confessional controversy. Franck molds George's account to argue the equal value of all religious institutions. Luther praises the Turks in order to draw unfavorable comparisons with Roman Catholics. See Palmer, 56.
7. In fact, much of this tract seems to have been written as an explanation why he would have momentarily converted to Islam. See Albrecht Classen, "The World of the Turks Described by an Eye-Witness: Georgius de Hungaria's Dialectical Discourse on the Foreign World of the Ottoman Empire," 257–279.
8. Palmer goes as far as to state that it is "the most valuable account of life and institutions among the Ottoman Turks in the fifteenth century which we possess." Palmer, 44.
9. Höfert, 213: "Georgejevic' Schriften wurden im 16. Jahrhundert zum unangefochtenen Bestseller unter den Turcica."
10. Melek Aksulu, *Bartholomäus Georgievics Türkenschrift "De Turcarum ritu et caeremomiis" (1544) und ihre beiden deutschen Übersetzungen von 1545: ein Beitrag zur Geschichte des Türkenbildes in Europa*, 19.
11. The number of editions is based on a composite of Göllner, *Turcica*, Kidric, *Gjorgjevic*, and my own archival research.
12. Luther, *WA Br 10*, 624–625, (#4019).
13. See also Höfert, 305.
14. See Foy and Heffening.
15. For example, until Du Ryer's 1647 French translation (re-translated into English in 1649), the 1698 Latin translation by Paduan Ludovico Marraccio, and George Sale's 1734 English edition.
16. Bobzin, 274.

17. This praise is from a founding father of Swiss Church history, Johann Heinrich Hottinger.
18. See Miller, "Bibliander."
19. The story of this controversy has been told several times. See Clark, 11–12 and Bobzin, 181–209.
20. This is certainly an advance from the understanding that Friday is the day of congregational prayer because it is the day of Venus (with all the additional connotations).
21. Although neither author quite gets all the facts correct, according to Georgijevic, they fast for a month and a week every year, this varies by one month every year and is done in place of the tenth as an offering to God.
22. Although perhaps expressed most frequently in popular pamphlets and in plays, across Europe circumcision seems to have served as a deterrent from a too-casual conversion to Islam. In Philip Massinger's *The Renegado* (1624) when a character is asked his religion he responds:

> "I would not be confined
> In my belief: when all your sects and secretaries
> Are grown of one opinion, if I like it
> I will profess myself—in the mean time,
> Live I in England, Spain, France, Rome, Geneva:
> I'm of that country's faith
> But what about in Tunis?
> No, so should I lose
> A collop of that part my Doll enjoined me
> To bring home as she left it: 'tis her venture,
> Nor dare I barter that commodity
> Without her special warrant." See Vitkus, 54–55.

23. See Appendix 2, "Concerning Supernatural and Religious Reasons."
24. Such practices of self-mutilation are not unknown, but are exceedingly rare and practiced by only a very limited number of Sufis. By emphasizing these practices, Georgijevic accentuates the exotic and lays the foundation for Orientalist approaches to Muslim practice. A modern Las Vegas act ("Zamora the Torture King") even claims to be following Sufi principles in his body piercings.
25. For example, corruption within the Church, especially simony, weakens Christendom. Christians themselves are responsible for the beginnings of the slave trade in which the Ottomans engage.
26. For example, the "exterior moral piety of the Turks is the whitewash that covers the stench of unbelief that infects the entire East."
27. He says he saw this in Damascus when he was leaving Armenia for Jerusalem.
28. The most important study of conversion to Islam in the Balkans in the early modern period is Tijana Krstic's *Contested Conversions to Islam*. Her study is particularly important because it emphasizes an Ottoman perspective and relies heavily on Ottoman sources. Although the focus of her study is different from mine, she is familiar with George of Hungary and mentions his narrative occasionally. Interestingly, she almost completely neglects the impact of conversion to Islam on male bodies through circumcision.
29. Tijana Krstic, *Contested Conversions to Islam: Narratives of Religious Change in the Early Modern Ottoman Empire*, 71.
30. However, in passages other than those concerning sexual abuse, the restrictions on these slaves does not seem to match his description of them willing to die "a thousand deaths" rather than being subjected to this slavery.

References

Aksulu, Melek. *Bartholomäus Georgievics Türkenschrift "De Turcarum ritu et caer-emomiis" (1544) und ihre beiden deutschen Übersetzungen von 1545: ein Beitrag zur Geschichte des Türkenbildes in Europa.* Stuttgart: Verlag Hans-Dieter Heinz, 2005.

Allen, Rosamund, ed. *Eastward Bound: Travel and Travelers, 1050–1550.* Manchester, UK: Manchester University Press, 2004.

Bobzin, Harmut. "Martin Luthers Beitrag zu Kenntnis und Kritik des Islam." *Neue Zeitschrift für Systematische Theologie* 27:3 (1985): 262–289.

Clark, Henry. "The Publication of the Koran in Latin: A Reformation Dilemma." *Sixteenth Century Journal* 15:1 (Spring 1984): 3–12.

Classen, Albrecht. "The World of the Turks Described by an Eye-Witness: Georgius de Hungaria's Dialectical Discourse on the Foreign World of the Ottoman Empire." *Journal of Early Modern History* 7:3/4 (August 2003): 257–279.

Foy, Karl. *Die ältesten osmanischen Transscriptionstexte in gotischen Lettern.* Berlin: Reichsdruckerei, 1902.

Heffening, Willi. *Die Türkischen Transkriptionstexte des B. Georgievics.* Nendeln, Liechtenstein: Kraus Reprint, 1966.

Höfert, Almut. *Den Feind beschreiben: "Turkengefahr" und europäisches Wissen über das Osmanische Reich 1450–1600.* Frankfurt: Campus Verlag, 2003.

Klockow, Richard, ed. *Georgius de Hungaria. Tractatus de moribus, condicionibus et nequicia Turcorum. Traktat über die Sitten, die Lebensverhältnisse und die Arglist der Türken. Nach der Erstausgabe von 1481 herausgegeben, übersetzt und eingeleitet von Reinhard Klockow.* Cologne: Böhlau, 1993.

Klockow, Richard, and Monika Ebertowski, eds. *De captivitate sua apud Turcas.* Berlin: Druckwerkstatt im Kreuzberg-Museum, 2000.

Krstic, Tijana. *Contested Conversions to Islam: Narratives of Religious Change in the Early Modern Ottoman Empire.* Stanford: Stanford University Press, 2011.

Luther, Martin. *Briefwechsel (BR)* 10, 624–625 (#4019).

Miller, Gregory J. "Theodor Bibliander's *Machumetis saracenorum principis eiusque successorum vitae, doctrina ac ipse alcoran* (1543) as the Sixteenth Century 'Encyclopedia' of Islam." *Islam and Christian-Islamic Relations* 24:2 (April 2013): 241–254.

Palmer, J. A. B. "Fr. Georgius de Hungaria, O.P. and the *Tractus de Moribus, Condicionibus et Nequicia Turcorum*." *Bulletin of the John Rylands Library* 34 (1951): 44–68.

Vitkus, Daniel. "Poisoned Figs, or 'The Traveler's Religion': Travel, Trade, and Conversion in Early Modern English Culture." In *Remapping the Mediterranean World in Early Modern English Writings.* Goran V. Stanivukovic, ed. New York: Palgrave, 2007.

9 Early Modern Transformations of the Image of Islam in the West

Although the period of intense contact was brief, the Ottoman advance into central Europe in the early sixteenth century formed an important chapter in the history of Christian-Islamic relations. While continuities with the medieval period remained, new images of Islam began to emerge in the early sixteenth century. The Turks also played a significant role in the internal struggle between Protestants and Catholics. In response to the Ottoman threat, both Catholic and Protestant scholars of this period formulated long-influential positions concerning religious identity and religious conflict in the West.

Several factors were involved in the development of these new views. Decades of intense contact due to the Ottoman push into Central Europe brought a degree of increased knowledge. *Türkenbüchlein* and broadsheets circulated eyewitness descriptions, captured Turks were interviewed, and Christians who had escaped from Turkish slavery reported their experiences. If this kind of contact had taken place in the Middle Ages, its overall effect would have been significantly less. However, with the rise of the mass print media Germans throughout the Empire rapidly could be made aware of the Turkish threat and exhorted to action. The short *Neue Zeitungen* circulated extensively and kept Germans abreast of the latest developments in the struggle against the Turks. In *The Book in the Renaissance*, Andrew Pettegree has described the impact of the Protestant Reformation on the development of the printing industry in Germany. The same *Flugschriften* printers who produced religious tracts also published writings on the Turks, and large numbers on both topics.

Neither intense contact nor the interest represented by coverage in the print media can alone account for the development of new images of the Turks in the early sixteenth century, however. Some pamphleteers simply repeated medieval depictions of Islam, and many echoed traditional responses to the Ottoman threat. However, the primary reasons for the development of new views of Islam were ideological changes within Christendom. One important factor was scholarship influenced by Renaissance humanism.[1] The influence of humanism was demonstrated, for example, in the frequent publication of histories of the Ottoman dynasty. The humanistic interest in the exploration of the unknown, the same interest that would later produce an abundance of literature on the New World, is also evident in the *Türkenbüchlein.*

The most important ideological change in early sixteenth-century Germany, however, was the Protestant Reformation. This may not have been the case if Luther himself had not have been so intentionally engaged with Islam, as Adam Francisco in *Martin Luther and Islam* has demonstrated. Luther's interest in the Turks and his wide-ranging publications caused understandings of Islam to become embroiled in the confessional conflict. The differences between Catholics and Protestants were particularly noticeable in their interpretations and reactions to the Ottoman threat. Protestants not only reworked and distrusted medieval (Catholic) sources on Islam, they also interpreted the Ottoman advance based on different theological presuppositions. In place of a dominant image, as was the case in the Middle Ages, the Reformation generated multiple interpretations of Islam.

As summarized in the classic work by Norman Daniel, the late medieval view of Islam which provided the background for sixteenth-century depictions was a relatively consistent 'canon' of beliefs that had developed since the twelfth and thirteenth centuries. Drawing on a wide variety of sources, medieval scholars collected a body of knowledge concerning Islam and detailed permissible responses to the Islamic threat. A few important beliefs composed this canon of the medieval view of Islam. Scholars knew Muhammad's claim to be the last and most important of God's messengers, and therefore focused their attack on the validity of his prophethood. Muhammad was shown to be grasping, lecherous, influenced by heretics and Jews, and a lover of violence. They also demonstrated that the Qur'an (although flawed) did confirm both scripture and Christianity and therefore disproved Islam. Not all of the teaching of Muhammad was evil, however; rather, the Qur'an must be 'sifted' to distinguish the true from the false. Points of agreement between Christian orthodoxy and Islam were to be the basis for the missionary conversion of the Muslims. Medieval Christians clearly did not understand Islam to be another 'religion' (in the modern sense), but rather some sort of treacherous Christian heresy. Although not the only response, in the late medieval period the Crusade was still the paradigmatic Christian reaction to Islam.

As in the Middle Ages, early sixteenth-century German writers continued to be interested in the religion of the Turks. The area in which the most dramatic development in Western knowledge concerning Islam took place was in new depictions of Islamic rituals and spirituality. Considerable attention was paid to the practices of the 'monks' of the Turks, as well as anything to do with sexuality. Other topics that received significant treatment include Muslim corporate prayer, almsgiving, and for the first time, extended discussions of Islamic mysticism and the divisions within Islam. From what is known of Muslim life in the sixteenth century, these descriptions of Islamic rituals and spirituality are often exaggerated and only partly accurate, but they do seem to reflect a Christian interpretation based on contact with genuine Islamic spirituality. Even though comparisons continue to be made with Christian practices, in contrast to medieval depictions the overall tone of these publications on the Turks is investigative.

However, highly derogatory comments came from the ecclesiastical literature of the Lutherans. Luther always used the same argument: no matter how spiritual it looks, without Christ they are damned. Miracles are no evidence of authenticity, for satanic power is great and can appear as an 'angel of light.' The Lutheran attack on the genuineness of Muslim spirituality was not only to protect people from converting to Islam (though this was believed to be a very real danger), but most importantly to prove the vanity of any works-righteousness, be it the rigorous discipline of the Turks or the comparatively shameful hypocrisy of the Papists.

German pamphleteers of the early sixteenth century knew the exclusiveness of the claims of Islam, but it is not clear if they understood the assertion that Islam was the successor to corrupted forms of religion found in Judaism and Christianity. Although the medieval idea that Islam was a type of Christian heresy remained influential, Islam was viewed by some as putting aspects of Judaism and Christianity together to create a new religion. Luther, for example, deliberately avoided designating the faith of the Turks as heresy. For him, it was worse; the Turks worshipped a different god, the devil himself. Although it shared some characteristics of the true faith, Islam was something essentially different from Christianity, a faith 'created' from 'Jewish, Christian, and Heathen faiths.' The Radical Reformer Sebastian Franck went even further toward a modem conception of religion. In his writings the beginning of an understanding that Islam was a separate religious system can be found.

Most of the time when pamphleteers related the *glaube* of the Turks to Christianity it was in the service of confessional polemic rather than as an investigation into the nature of Islam itself. Both Catholics and Lutherans used the image of the Turks as a weapon against their ecclesiastical opponents. There are numerous references in the Catholic literature to the equation of 'Turks and Lutherans.' The Catholic equation of Lutheran and Turk was not intended to describe Islam. Rather, whenever a Catholic representative wanted to malign an opponent no epitaph was more derogatory than calling them a 'Turk.'

Many Protestant writers also drew parallels between Catholic and Turkish doctrine and morality and used *Türkenbüchlein* to attack not only Turks but also their Catholic opponents (See Figure 9.1). In demonstrating the religious 'superiority' of the Turks over the Papists, Luther wanted to highlight not only the meaninglessness of works-righteousness, but also the fact that Roman Catholics did not do very well even at what they claimed to honor. The concept of the 'Turk' became a Lutheran metaphor for any 'anti-Christian' activity within the church. Not only Catholics, but also Anabaptists and stubborn, unbelieving Germans were called 'Christian Turks.'

Figure 9.1 Turks and Papists in Hell, Matthias Gerung, 1530

Used by permission of the Universität- und Forschungsbibliothek Erfurt. UB Erfurt, Dep. Erf. 03-Na 4° 00287 (08)

During the Reformation Era, the history, character, and culture of the Turks also received sustained attention in German publications. For sixteenth-century Germans, the confrontation between Islam and the West stood in a close connection with the question of the ancestry and history of the Turks. This is a continuation of the same focus that Margaret Meserve in *Empires of Islam in Renaissance Historical Thought* found among fifteenth-century humanists from across Europe. Reminders of the increasing power of the Turks, the past greatness of Christian kings and kingdoms, and the occasional vulnerability of the followers of Muhammad could serve as powerful encouragements for a war or crusade. The character of the Turks was also a common theme. In most of the literature of the early sixteenth century, the Turks were not simply considered evil, cruel, barbarous—but the very epitome of these characteristics. This was due in part to rhetoric in the service of the Hapsburg-Ottoman military conflict. Crusade propaganda alone does not fully explain the extreme nature of these judgments, however, especially since they are found in those who emphasized a spiritual rather than a military response. Rather, in the Ottoman advance Germans faced a cultural and religious 'other' that struck holy terror deep within the social consciousness of the people. In Luther's language, the Turks were the devil incarnate: inhumanly violent, treacherous, and demonically lascivious. They were an enemy of cosmic proportions.

Alongside these denunciations, pamphlets also reported positive aspects of Turkish society. According to these reports, the Turks did not drink wine, gorge themselves as the Germans, wear flashy clothes, build pretentious buildings, or swear very much. Rather, they were humble, disciplined, modest, unpretentious, hospitable, and obedient to authority—in short, everything that the German Christians should be, but were not. Much of this admiration must be seen in the context of Protestant attempts to reform Christian living or to discredit Roman Catholicism. However, the rigorous organization and disciplined life of the Ottoman Empire also held an attraction for many in Christendom. When German pamphleteers examined Turkish society and government, they examined it mirror in hand, and consciously related Christian weaknesses to supposed Turkish strengths. In the final verdict, however, the Turks were 'barbarians' compared with the Christians. This paradoxical combination of grudging admiration alongside sharp denunciation is found throughout the early sixteenth century writings on the Turks.

The ringing denunciations did not stop German pamphleteers from being interested in every conceivable aspect of Turkish society from personal toiletry to military organization. Most of this information was gained through contemporary reports from the Balkans or from escaped Turkish captives like George of Hungary and Bartholomew Georgijevic and then widely circulated. Both of these authors added to as well as corrupted European understandings of Islam. In combination, they demonstrate considerable advance in knowledge about Islam and the Muslim world from the worst inaccuracies and calumnies of the medieval period. It should be noted that in particular that in their writings salacious tales about Muhammad and/ or Muslim sexual deviance are missing. There is no mention of idol worship or of Islam as a kind of paganism. Although not entirely accurate, they contain some of the most accurate discussions, for example, of prayer, circumcision, and Turkish piety to that date in Western Europe. The accuracy of George of Hungary's description of dervish worship and Georgijevic's linguistic contributions would not be surpassed in Europe until the Enlightenment. However, even though some aspects of these author's descriptions were even laudatory, it should be emphasized that neither presentation is charitable. Greater knowledge about Islam did not automatically lead to a greater appreciation of Muslims or of Muslim belief and practice. Even the most favorable sections were ultimately interpreted as Satan masquerading as an 'angel of light.'

The real value of the George and Georgijevic documents however lies in a comparative analysis. In this perspective, the following points can be made. Although similar in their geographical location of origin and, to a degree, their experiences in the Ottoman Empire, the post-slavery lives of each author significantly shaped their presentation. George of Hungary writes as a combination of warning and confession. Georgijevic writes to encourage military action and very likely for preferment or remuneration. George explicitly rejects Renaissance humanism with its classicalizing and secular tendencies and lives in a world of mystery and the unknown. Even though George's first hand observations form the core of the work, he still uses the perspective of Joachim to frame the entire work. Georgijevic on the other hand repudiates all other sources and relies entirely on first-person observations.

It is important to note that both of these writings circulated in published editions (and translations) simultaneously in the middle and late sixteenth century. The knowledge of this should lead to caution when interpreting these sources as to their reflection of sweeping changes in European attitudes toward Islam and the Turks. In fact, Almut Höffert has argued that there was much more continuity with medieval understandings in Geogrgijevic and other similar writers than discontinuity. She is correct in the assertion that not much new information was presented, although the amount of the information was significantly greater.[2] Even taking this into consideration, however, the difference between these two writings demonstrates that certain developments were taking place, and important changes in the structure of the presentations is evidence for this. Particularly important is evidence that there was a change in perceived power relations between the Ottoman Empire and Christendom, along with the religious significance of this change. The Turks were still a power to be reckoned with in Georgijevic, but the temporal hopelessness and apocalyptic framework of George of Hungary is gone. In Georgijevic, the Turks are still cruel and fearsome, but the seduction of Islam is gone and military success against them is a real possibility. Through these two documents it is almost as though we can see analogically the rising and then passing of the high-water mark of the Turkish advance, as was indeed the case in reality between the Turkish attack at Otranto and their failure at Vienna. The world is a different place in 1544 than it was in 1480, as Daniel Goffman has argued, and the Protestant Reformation played a central role in these changes.[3]

Also significant are the framing materials appended to Georgijevic's writings. It is a strange thing to include a Turkish dictionary for greetings, numbers, and mercantile exchange in a document that calls for the destruction of the Ottoman Empire. This internal inconsistency in a sense subverts the explicit intention of the text itself. This lends a certain ambivalence to its interpretation that actually demonstrates the growing integration of the Ottoman Empire into the European economic and state system. The inconsistency and ambivalence about this part of the Muslim world demonstrated in Georgijevic, in my opinion, does an excellent job highlighting early modern European ambivalence as a whole to the Muslim world in this transitional period in the history of Christian-Islamic relations.

Of all the aspects of Turkish life and society discussed in the early sixteenth century, German publications, including George and Georgijevic were most concerned with the slavery of Christians. It is clear from the tone of the writings that the possibility of becoming a Turkish slave was believed to be very real. Entire pamphlets were written instructing people what to do if they should be captured. Why should Germans be concerned about the Ottoman Turks? The sixteenth-century Turkish military realistically could not have attacked beyond Vienna. Yet, Germans all over the Empire felt threatened by the Ottoman advance. This social fear transcended political propaganda. Even those who did not support Hapsburg Imperialism believed the danger to be real. As in all times of social stress, German writers sought a cause, a reason why Christendom was so severely threatened. Almost never did the Turks receive credit for their successes. Because it was seemingly psychologically impossible to hold that the enemy was simply militarily superior, another interpretation for the Turkish advance had to be found. Although different confessional groups offered different reasons for the Ottoman advance, the *Türkenbüchlein* universally cited internal causes. Catholics primarily blamed Christian disunity (especially the Lutheran rebellion) for the Turkish success; Protestants blamed Catholics for rejecting the Gospel. All pamphlets blamed the sins of Christians and admonished repentance. Catholic authors stated that sin had deprived Christendom of God's military blessing and left it vulnerable to the devil. For Lutherans, Old Testament analogies were appropriate: the Turks were not just the devil's tool but also God's rod of punishment.

Under such conditions it was natural to seek positive news, to establish some limit to God's punishment and to Turkish power. This hope for a better future often was discovered in prophecy. Despite sharing common elements and sources, Catholic and Protestant interpretations and use of prophecy were fundamentally different. Roman Catholic prophecy was encouraging and optimistic. It predicted the rise of a mighty emperor who would defini-tively destroy Islam. Georgijevic is part of this tradition and published a pamphlet translation of the Red Apple prophecy, a supposedly authentic Muslim prediction concerning a future Christian leader who would triumph over the Turks. Protestant hope, on the other hand, was much more other-worldly. Islam and the Turks were interpreted in eschatological terms. The devil-inspired Turks would not be defeated by mankind, but from outside the system, by God in a cosmological drama that would usher in the Last Judgment. A close identification of Christian-Islamic conflict with an escha-tological confrontation between God and the devil has remained very influ-ential among some Protestant groups. When they are threatened by Islam, some modem evangelicals still see their contemporary events forecast in the biblical prophecies of Daniel and Revelation. Coexistence is not possible with this kind of cosmological enemy. Rather, they see God as directing events toward the ultimate eschatological confrontation and the absolute and final destruction of Islam.

During the Reformation Era, pamphlets, broadsheets, sermons, and bal-lads repeatedly broadcast a Turkish threat of supernatural proportions to the German people. These depictions were not simply descriptive, but were intended to move people to action. Indeed, the severity of the threat demanded a serious response. But what was the appropriate response? In the Middle Ages, the obligation had been clear: it was the Christian's duty to fight against these heretics with force of arms. Due to the Reformation in sixteenth-century Germany, however, the traditional medieval response to Islam underwent devastating attacks. New ideas were articulated con-cerning the appropriate Christian responses to the Turks. Publications in German-speaking lands in the early sixteenth century emphasized three pos-sible responses to the Turkish threat: missions/rapprochement, spiritual war-fare, and military action. Pacifists and humanists were most concerned with peaceful solutions to the Turkish problem, although there is also evidence of some Germans who actually desired and/or advocated Turkish overlord-ship. The spiritual weapons of prayer, repentance, and moral improvement were a universal theme in the early sixteenth-century literature. Roman Catholics tended to view spiritual warfare as a means of regaining God's protection and military blessing. In contrast, Lutherans were much less con-fident in military solutions and advocated absolute dependence upon divine apocalyptic intervention.

Military responses to the Turks continued to be a dominant theme in these writings. Crusade ideology remained strong in Catholic literature well into the sixteenth century. Historical examples of past crusades were pub-lished to encourage support for the war and to model appropriate Chris-tian behavior. Eternal salvation was promised to anyone who died in battle against the Turks. Further ties to Crusade ideology are found in descriptions of the role of papal and Imperial Christian leadership and in the discussion of justifications for the war as the defense and/or extension of Christendom.

The Lutheran military response to Islam differed significantly from sixteenth-century Roman Catholic crusading. This was primarily due to the ramifications of Luther's unequivocal denunciation of the traditional Crusade as an appropriate response to Islam. Luther repudiated the Crusade not only because it represented works-righteousness but also because it was a blasphemous confusion of the heavenly and earthly kingdoms. Christians *qua* Christians were not to lead or even participate in battle. Scripture commanded believers not to resist evil with force; fighting against the Turks would be a protest against martyrdom. Furthermore, ecclesiastical attempts at military leadership angered God and were a prime cause of defeat in battle. Clergy were to preach and pray, not to bear arms and fight. According to Luther, soldiers even had a right to protest this kind of a Church-led Crusade through disobedience. Related to this argument was the criticism that Christ, not the emperor or secular rulers, was the defender of the Church. To rely on the *kaiser* was looking to man for salvation, an abomination to God. In essence, there was no religious justification for any military action- be it against false Christians, heretics, or even Turks.

With the advent of this first significant, sustained critique in the Western tradition of crusade theology (and not just crusade practice), the medieval response to Islam began to break down. Other justifications for military action and even arguments against violent responses came into being. Some understood Luther to be advocating pacifism and declared that lordship over the body was not intimately related to lordship over the soul. In addition, a nationalist-defensive attitude toward the Turks emerged that was quite secular. In this conception, long-term negotiations were legitimate, and the only justification for military action was the violation of established borders.

Luther had not intended his disavowal of the Crusade to go so far, however. In place of the Crusade Luther saw a spiritual eschatological battle. However, military action was still necessary because Christians were not only citizens of heaven, but also citizens of an earthly kingdom. War against the Turks was justified *(a jus bellum)* based on God's dual political commands: governments must preserve peace and order, Christian subjects must obey established authority. For many in the sixteenth century, this sounded similar to what the Roman Catholics were teaching. Pacifists accused Luther of abandoning his early position against war; Catholic theologians accused him of contradicting himself. In fact, this subtle application of the two kingdoms doctrine was difficult for even some of Luther's colleagues to consistently maintain. The more popularly oriented the pamphlet and the more martial the context of the writing, the more likely that the distinction between the Crusade and the just war was obscured.

Some Lutherans also drifted toward the national-defensive war in response to the Ottoman advance. After the Turks failed at Vienna in 1529, those Protestants who did not share Luther's intense eschatological urgency became more inclined to use the Turks as a bargaining tool to force an internal settlement of the German religious situation. It was no coincidence that most Imperial acts from 1532–1545 which reconfirmed the Religious Peace of Nurnberg were influenced by Turkish pressure in the Balkans.

After the Truce of Adrianople in 1547, the Ottoman-Hapsburg confrontation shifted its focus from the Balkans to naval encounters on the Mediterranean Sea. Intermittent attacks continued (both small-scale raids and two inconsequential campaigns, 1552 and 1566), but the danger from a massive invasion from the East declined. However, through their connection with Ferdinand and the Hapsburg claims on Hungary, in the early sixteenth century Germans throughout the Empire had been brought face to face with the Islamic Turks in a more significant way than ever before. Years of intense interest in Turkish themes produced new views of the nature of Islam and re-examined permissible responses to the Ottoman advance. With the decline of the threat in the mid-1540s, however, these views solidified into new, but standardized conceptions. Petitions continued to be made to the *Reichstag* for aid against the Turks, pamphlets on Islam continued to be published in Germany, but little that was original was added to the knowledge and ideas which had been put forward during the first generation of Protestant reformers. For example, among those German Christians who continued his legacy, Luther's understanding of the Turks and Islam became almost canonical. Not until the late 1600s with the re-acquisition of Hungary and the gradual retreat from the Balkans of the declining Ottomans did a changing political situation cause Germans to reevaluate and alter their view of Islam.

The early sixteenth-century German confrontation with Islam continued to have significant long-term consequences, however. Medieval Crusade ideology suffered a mortal blow due to the Protestant critique. The Christian unity that was seen as a necessary prerequisite for successful crusading was definitively destroyed. Papal military leadership was no longer possible for parts of Europe. Protestants denied that a war against the Muslims was in itself pleasing to God. Many followed Luther and denounced religious wars for any reason. Agreements were made for the defense of Europe, but not Christendom; the change in vocabulary is significant.

Perhaps one of the most important contributions of this literature to the history of Christian-Islamic relations was its role in the development of the concept of religion. In the Radical Reformers search for the 'essence' of religion, aspects of the beginning of the modern concept of world religions can be found. More generally, Almut Höfert has made a strong argument that because Georgijevic's and similar captivity narratives could not structure their writings in the traditional itinerary format, they had to create a different organizational structure and that this had an enormous impact of the conceptual categories of Europeans.[4] In particular, these writings contributed significantly to the development of the Western (neutral) concept of religion, as 'religion' began to be used as a non-evaluative descriptor which could be applied to Christians and Muslims alike.[5] This use of 'religion' as a *topos* was neither conscious nor modeled after prior texts, nor was it recognized at the time as new. There is an important paradox here: writings which were done in the context of conflict between Christendom and the Turks actually produced the religious concepts which permitted Christians and Muslims to be described in the same terms.[6]

An analysis of Reformation-era German publications on the Turks, then, can help us understand the ambiguous and transitional character of this period in Christian-Islamic relations. One of the most important results of recent scholarship has been to challenge the dominant metanarrative that early modern Europeans simply carried forward a 'medieval' binary under-standing of their relationship with the Islamic world. These new studies highlight the complexity of Western perceptions of Islam in the period.[7] They move beyond the central analytical focus being the posthumous awarding of merit for positive attitudes and accuracy about Islam or, more often, denigrating sources for distortions and mendacity. Instead, the ana-lytic focus has been on examining the ambiguity and ambivalence of many early modern Western European texts on Islam and the role of these sources in reflecting and shaping culture beyond understandings of Islam itself. The wide range of publications I have examined, and especially the pamphlets by George of Hungary and Georgijevic, support this perspective on early modern writings on the Turks. Sometimes even within themselves, publica-tions contained ambiguity and self-contradiction in their descriptions and understandings of Islam.[8] The contradictions are further compounded by the fact that although these writings on the Turks often disagree with one another, they were seen as part of a common project and often even pub-lished together.

In the history of Christian-Islamic relations, the early modern period can be seen therefore as a time of de-stabilization where multiple, competing perspectives lead to the breakdown of an earlier synthesis and make pos-sible a paradigm shift. This is parallel to what Edward Bruner has written concerning narrative shifts in ethnography:

> It takes time, however, for a new narrative to become dominant. For such a change to occur there must be a breakdown of previously accepted understandings, a perception that a once familiar event no longer makes sense, a penetration of the previously taken-for-granted. Stories oper-ate not simply in the realm of the mind, as ideas; to be convincing they also must have a base in experience or social practice. It is the perceived discrepancy between the previously accepted story and the new situa-tion that leads us to discard or question the old narrative; and it is the perceived relevance of the new story to our own life situation that leads to its acceptance.[9]

As we have seen, many factors were responsible for the breakdown of the West's medieval synthesis concerning Islam and the Turks, including the growing emphasis on an empiricism that privileged firsthand accounts, interest in the exotic, expanded mercantile and diplomatic contacts, and, of course, direct military engagement. Especially important was the explosion of print, especially early newspapers and pamphlets. However, in German-speaking lands the most significant factor was the Reformation. This was not simply due to the permanent fracturing of Christendom that resulted, although this, too, was significant. Rather, intellectual shifts like the Protestant suspicion of Roman Catholic sources, new theological ideas (for example, Luther's denunciation of the Crusade as a blasphemous confusion of the temporal and the spiritual), and the '*sola scriptura*' approach that encouraged Protestants to engage the Qur'an more directly—all these questioned prior narratives and created space for new ideas to emerge. This makes it particularly important to study this period in its own right, and not simply as an extension of medieval Christendom's views of Islam nor as an Orientalism waiting for Imperial opportunity.

Notes

1. Although the time period of her study precedes mine, in *Creating East and West* Nancy Bisaha does an excellent job demonstrating the complicated and multi-faceted legacy of Renaissance humanist interest in the Turks both on the early modern period and beyond. See especially, 174–187.
2. Höfert, 226.
3. According to Goffman, "changes in the balance of power in Europe also stimulated Ottoman integration. The fragmentation of first Italy and subsequently the rest of Europe destroyed even the semblance of a Christian cohesion and replaced it with princes and despots who paid little more than lip service to the idea of a religious ecumene. Fast on the heels of this emergence of secular politics was the development of principles to serve it in the form of Protestantism, which accomplished ideologically what the Renaissance had done politically." Daniel Goffman, *The Ottoman Empire and Early Modern Europe*, 232.
4. Höfert, 227.
5. Höfert, 303–309. "Die Weichen für diese Entwicklung wurden mit dem Entwurf des ethnographischen Ordnungsmusters im 15 und 16. Jahrhundert gestellt." Höfert, 308.
6. Höfert, 314–315: "Dieser wertungsfreie Raum eröffnete sich vielmehr unmerklich als eine nichtreflektierte Folge des ethnographischen Ordnungsmusters."
7. In terms of late medieval Western scholarship on the Qur'an, Thomas Burman in *Reading the Qur'an in Latin Christendom* has also demonstrated that scholars used a wide range of reading strategies and not simply hateful polemic.
8. This is also the conclusion of Charlotte Colding Smith in *Images of Islam*.
9. Edward M. Bruner, "Ethnography as Narrative," 276–277.

References

Bisaha, Nancy. *Creating East and West: Renaissance Humanists and the Ottoman Turks*. Philadelphia: University of Pennsylvania Press, 2004.
Bruner, Edward M. "Ethnography as Narrative." In *Memory, Identity, Community: The Idea of Narrative in the Human Sciences*. Lewis P. Hinchman and Sandra K. Hinchman, eds. New York: SUNY Press, 1997, 264–280.

Burman, Thomas. *Reading the Qur'an in Latin Christendom, 1140–1560*. Philadelphia: University of Pennsylvania Press, 2007.

Goffman, Daniel. *The Ottoman Empire and Early Modern Europe*. Cambridge: Cambridge University Press, 2002.

Höfert, Almut. *Den Feind beschreiben: "Türkengefahr" und europäisches Wissen über das Osmanische Reich 1450–1600*. Frankfurt: Campus Verlag, 2003.

Smith, Charlotte Colding. *Images of Islam, 1453–1600: Turks in Germany and Central Europe*. London: Pickering and Chatto, 2014.

Appendix 1

Martin Luther and Philip Melanchthon, Recommendation Letter for Bartholomew Georgijevic

Grace and Peace to the reader from Martin Luther and Philip Melanchthon!

This Hungarian guest, Bartholomew Georgijevic, a pilgrim to Jerusalem, came to our university. He told us that he had been captured by the Turks in the battle in which King Ludovico perished, was a slave in Constantinople for seven years and then six years in Asia. With skill, he described the names of the places and the character of the regions and inhabitants, along with the customs of the Turks, the Armenians, and the Greeks. And he told us with such agreeable trustworthiness and dignified accounts that we consider him to be genuine and the reasons for his journeys to be legitimate. We were most pleased to hear that in Armenia the Church of Christ and the study of Christian theology continues to flourish. Therefore, we would commend good men everywhere to take care of this guest, that is, those who understand duty toward strangers, the grace of God, human nature, and who are reminded of our own exile. For we came into this world as strangers and suffer various hardships. But we seek a fatherland and peaceful habitation governed by Christ. And God mercifully will ease our own exile if we would have mercy on these strangers. Dated Wittenberg, 11 August 1544.

Martin Luther Dr.
Philip Melanchthon
by their own hand
[WA BW 10:624–225]

Appendix 2

Selections from George of Hungary, *Tractatus de moribus Turcorum* [Booklet on the Customs of the Turks]

[Bibliander's Prefatory Summation:

Although the author of this book about the religion and manners of the Turks withholds his name out of modesty, he indicates his homeland and when and where he was abducted—which is the reason he was able to examine the things concerning the Turks. It would appear from all circumstances that he merits trust in this history. Indeed, it seems to me to be the benevolent plan of God that an adolescent equipped with these talents and spirit would be taken from the region of Septemcastrensis and preserved through twenty-two years in exile, just like Daniel. He was taken into their homes where he was able most accurately to learn all the Turkish institutions and communicate them to the churches of Christ, so that perceiving the condition of the Christians under Turkish bondage, people would be stimulated to build their lives to all godliness by the Word of God, so that they would never be handed over to these enemies. Neither should it offend pious readers that his speech is not in perfect, elegant Latin, since it can be clearly understood. For many writings in the most barbaric speech are read which nevertheless are not able to offer suitable fruit to readers.]

Preface to the Tractate on the Manners, Customs, and Wickedness of the Turks

Of the immense persecution, tribulation, fears, and terrors of most recent times, of a kind not so much human as satanic, which the prophets predicted and even today are proclaimed in the writings of the Old and New Testaments with their images of dragons and beasts, astounding shaking of the heavens and earth, unusual acts and deeds of the heavenly spirits—all this we have read about in books. But now there is no need of many books, as it is manifested before us clear as day. What was formerly taught is now upon us, incessantly and undoubtedly falling on our heads. Or perhaps we do not see the most bloodthirsty beast, the enemy of the cross of Christ, the most savage dragon—by this I mean the sect, the herd of the most infidel Turks who has destroyed all the lands of the East and through his breath has poisoned an infinite multitude of Christians and infected them with his unbelief. He is now approaching the boundaries of Italy with all the strength of his desire to bring about the collapse of the Roman church, which has alone escaped. O! Who does not grieve over the deaths of so many souls, whom daily he devours down his insatiable open throat and makes the heirs of his damnation? O pernicious and exceedingly savage persecution! O what wickedness, unheard of through the ages! For this is not a persecutor of the body as others but one of the soul, for this persecutor preserves the exterior body under the guise of piety and does not kill it, but stealing the faith within, strives to kill the soul through his diabolical cunning.

Of this an innumerable multitude of the faithful can attest, of whom many were most willing for faith in Christ and the salvation of their souls to die in the Christian faith but who, because their bodies were saved from death and they were led into captivity and over time were infected by its poison and shamefully renounced their faith in Christ.

I learned by my own experience that these things are true, for I anticipated undergoing death for my faith in Christ with great inner happiness. But nevertheless, as I will show in what follows, after being pulled out of the fire half-dead and brought back to life, over the course of time while I was held captive in their hands like an infection I was poisoned by their errors and I came to doubt the Christian faith no small amount. And except that the mercy of God was with me and kept me protected, I would have shamefully renounced my faith.

Therefore, my intention in this tractate is to relate the deeds, customs, manners, and wickedness of the Turks according to my experience, to remember them and to put them down in writing so that if a second time — may God prevent it, although I still fear it—even now in my old age that it happens that I fall into their hands, I might better prevail in keeping myself from their errors than I did when I was younger. And I believe that likewise this is able to be of great usefulness if every believer in our times endeavors to hear, study, and read these things. For it is clearly apparent that many, even innumerable Christians have renounced faith in Christ because they didn't understand or even didn't believe what they had been told of their craftiness, until they find out through their own experience what they earlier neglected to understand.

Introduction

First I would like to present my unfortunate story, that is how and when I was captured by the Turks and brought into their captivity so that each one can have a sure confidence that what I say is not a fable or fiction but the simple truth from my own experience. After the death of the Roman Emperor Sigismund in the year of our Lord 1436,[1] there arose a great dissention between the Hungarians and the Germans concerning who would be made king because the emperor had not left a legitimate successor. The Great Turk, who was called Moratbeg, the father of the one who is currently reigning, namely Mechemetbeg, invaded that land with a huge military force—it was said to have had 300,000 riders—with the intention of devastating all of Hungary. And it would have happened had not a certain river been flooded by God thus causing him to be stopped. Since that intention was frustrated, he directed his aim at the province on the other side of the mountain which is known as the Seven Fortresses[2] and savagely devastated and destroyed all which he encountered there. No one was able to withstand him.

At that time I was a youth of 15 or 16, born in that province. In the preceding year I had left the place of my birth and had come to the castle or town which is called Schebesch by the Hungarians and Muelenbag[3] as a student. At that time the town was somewhat well-populated but not well fortified. The Turk came, set up his camp and assaulted the town. The Duke of Walachia[4] who had come with him, because of an old friendship which had earlier been made with this town, came to the wall and silencing the weapons, called the citizens together in order to persuade them to follow his counsel and not to fight against the Turk because the town did not have sufficient defenses to resist him. This was his counsel: that they would hand over the town peacefully and that in return he would seek to obtain from the Turk an agreement that the leading citizens would be taken with him into his land and that later, they would be able to either stay or return, as they desired. The remaining common people, without any harm to their things or persons, the Turk would take to his land and would be given land to possess and then at an appropriate time they could return or continue to live there in peace as they wished. Everything that he promised, we saw fulfilled.

Along with this agreement, a cease-fire was established until the next day so that each one might be able to make arrangements to leave peacefully with his possessions and family. A certain nobleman, together with his equally brave brother who had been a castellan and had fought against the Turks numerous times, said that he would never agree to this kind of agreement and pact and that he would rather die a hundred times than to hand over his wife and son into the hands of the Turks. He convinced many others and having chosen one of the towers, he went in and all that night brought weapons and victuals inside and strengthened its fortifications. And I went into the tower with these, and awaited with great longing to die rather than to live. As it was now morning, the Great Turk came personally to the gate of the town and going out, each one with his family, he ordered that they be registered and led by an assigned guard into his land without any damage to his person or goods. He allowed the leading citizens to be taken in the same manner by the Duke of Wallachia into his land. But since his entire army was not permitted to have any part in these spoils, with great vigor and unbounded rage, together they ran to the tower in which we were, hoping for some gain. No tongue can express how great and powerful this storm was. So thick flew the arrows and stones that they appeared to be like rain and hail. So loud was the clamor of battle, the clash of weapons, the din of the attack, that it seemed at that moment like the heavens and the earth were crashing against one another. Because the tower was considerably sloped, the roof was soon destroyed by arrows and stones. But no one was able to penetrate its walls. As the hour was getting late and it was past noon and they had not been able to accomplish anything, they took counsel. While some fought, others gathered wood and piled the wood almost as high as the tower. And lighting it on fire, they baked us like bread in an oven. When they saw no more movement in the tower and presumed everyone was dead, they extinguished the fire and forced their way inside. If they found anyone half-alive, they dragged him out. By this means I was dragged to a merchant and handed over to be sold. He put me in chains with the other captives and brought me over the Danube to Adrianople, the residence of the Great Turk. From the year mentioned above until the year of our Lord 1458 I endured the harshest captivity, the heaviest burden and unbearable anxiety not only of the body but also to the peril of my soul. In the end, with God's help, as I shall describe below, I overcame and became free.

Chapter 1: How the Turks Came to Occupy and Settle the Lands of the East

According to all historians it is clearly agreed that the law of Muhammad and the sect of the Saracens began in the seventh century when Boniface V was pope[5] and Heraclius was emperor[6] and flourished in the ninth century when Leo IV was pope[7] and Louis II was emperor.[8] At that time the number of Saracens grew to such a magnitude and savagery against the church that coming to Rome they invested it and savagely burned everything which they found outside the city walls (they had already captured Jerusalem and ruled it). They turned St Peter's church into a stable for their horses and destroyed it to its foundations. On their return, they destroyed Italy and Sicily. Around the year 1280 they began to receive the fruit of all this malice and evil in lying signs and wonders which even now they have in abundance. At that time, the Great Sultan with God's permission went out from the South against the East and all the region and its fortifications to the Sea. When he saw that the land was spacious and suitable for many inhabitants, he divided it into seven parts and gave each part to one of his chiefs as a hereditary possession. The first one was named Othmanbeg, the second Ermenbeg, the third Germenbeg, the fourth Czarchanbeg, the fifth Andinbeg, the sixth Menthessebeg, and the seventh Karamanbeg. While each one in the time following lived, ruled, and held his land in peace, the one called Othmanbeg began to expand his land and borders by invading the lands of his neighbor to the east. As he was not able to resist him, he left his land and fled to the one called Karamanbeg who took him in. After he had obtained those lands, he turned to invade the lands on his other side and drove him out in the same way. He turned likewise against the third, fourth, fifth, and thus held all of the lands himself except those of the one called Karamanbeg alone. This was because all those who fled were allied with him and because his land was very difficult to conquer. Besides, and this is easier to believe, it pleased God that it would be so. For just as once in the desert God caused some peoples not to be conquered so that they might challenge Israel, so he wanted to do the same with him. For until the present day it has remained unconquered and has been the source of much treachery and problems for him.[9] For unless there is peace between them, the Ottomans don't dare to go to war against anybody else. Because if they do, immediately their lands are invaded. Three times while I lived there he came and invaded that land and devastated, burned, and plundered much. Many times the Ottomans went up against them but accomplished little. Once he went out against him full of rage and anger to destroy him with a vast army (it was said to contain 20,000 foot soldiers armed with axes and other weapons). His intention was to thoroughly destroy the land by cutting down the trees and vines and making it uninhabitable. Nevertheless he had to retreat, make peace, and leave everything intact. From this came a certain saying which became proverbial among them that Karmanbeg would stand forever. That Othmanbeg and his descendants (who took his name and are called Othmanogli, that is, sons of Othman) up to today are kings and lords of all of Turkey. And they made and continue daily to make such gains that they are feared not only in the East but also even in the West. Although once the Great Tartar[10] from the East did defeat him, as my master used to tell me, because at this time he had not conquered any lands on the other side of the sea[11] and therefore did not have the strength to withstand him. However today his power has become so great that no one could find or hear of any in the eastern regions more powerful. Moreover, the entire kingdom on the other side of the sea today is today divided into seven regions called by the names of its original inhabitants, namely Othmaneli, Ermeneli, Germeneli, Czarchaneli, Andingeli, Menthescheli, Karmaneli.

Chapter 2: How the Sect of the Turks Has Increased and How They Received the Name of 'Turk'

Concerning the sect of the Turks, as was mentioned in the previous chapter, the fruit of their evil could clearly only have been because of the guilt of Christians who denied their faith in Christ. This course of events is daily most clearly obvious and can be doubted by no one. From which, as has been said, when the Saracens or Mohammadans began to persecute the Christians and occupy their lands, many Christians in a desire to avoid persecution voluntarily handed themselves over. And this is evident in that today in Turkey there are many fortresses and towns which used to be Greek but gave themselves over to Turkish lordship in order to be preserved. As a result of which those Christians became allies to the persecution of other Christians. Their guilt began to grow because they did not heed ecclesiastical warnings. Because they themselves were Christians they began under the guise of piety to forbear from conquering Christians and to keep them as slaves and servants. From this began that impious lust to possess slaves and servants which remains up to today in that sect. Finally, by that fake piety their guilt grew so much that the evil of Christians persecuting other Christians exceeded the evil of the unbelievers: in this they were their teachers and leaders and in wrongdoing they had them as students who had earlier been their own teachers on the destruction of souls. From there entered that new, spiritual Muhammad, the herald of the Antichrist and they began then to be called not Saracens but 'Theorici,' that is 'spirituals' because they are seen to have an almost supernatural ability to draw Christians to their evil and turn them away from faith in Christ and the society of the church.

Because the ability of the church to correct them by means of public censure diminished, it began to excuse their guilt and to justify them, saying that the church performed a great service in this because they protected Christians from the attacks of the Saracens. Thus was added to them a second evil, that is, a false humility and rebellion against the church under the guise of humility. The reward is an exterior appearance of morality and the presentation of a false model and fictive piety. From this they are called hypocrites, and rightly so.

Chapter 3: How Frightening this Sect of the Turks Is and How Much They Are to Be Feared

Much, in fact almost everything which happens or comes to mind today, warns us to be careful and teaches us to fear the end of the world, especially since we are certain that we are living at the time when the end of time has arrived. Holy Scripture in both testaments, especially the Book of Revelation and the frightening and horrifying images of Daniel and Ezekiel, were given not just for us to learn and understand but also to fear the dangers of the end times. The images themselves are terrifying, but the reality is without doubt even more terrifying. Likewise, the disposition of this world teaches us this, whose old age and soon approaching end is clearly demonstrated in the propensity for evil among all orders, the lack of good, the greed of the leadership, the reluctance to obey, likewise inquisitiveness in the arts, many kinds of extravagance in buildings, the presumptive novelty in learning, and finally, added to this, in everything a new foolishness for antiquity. But among all these it is that savage beast, I mean the Turks, who ought to concern us the most. Their continual growth, constant war and persecution, and long duration warn us of nothing but great crisis, scandal, tribulation and extreme misery. Nevertheless, we are not concerned about all these things, because they are hid from our eyes, as Abbot Joachim states concerning Revelation 13 'Who is like the beast and who is able to fight the beast?' where he says: "Woe! Woe! How many children born in this world are there who will not escape this great calamity which is now hidden from their eyes? O, unfortunate mothers who bear these sons and the breasts which nurse them. Wretched are the parents who gather great riches but do not realize the evil which the Lord intends for the wealthy of this world. Listen, listen, I beseech you, all of you who love their children. Listen, all of you who nourish your little ones with dainties. Teach your sons to inhabit forests, to survive in the desert on the roots of herbs, to set aside abundant delicacies and to avoid dishes of meat, so that they may learn to live with the wild animals until the wrath has passed."

Thus, Abbot Joachim. For I certainly believe that just as in the time of Noah when the waters of the flood suddenly overtook the unbelievers, so in these times the great vengeance and universal, unavoidable, and eternal divine wrath will catch them unaware. Also, in the Gospel, the savior teaches us to avoid and flee this dire situation, saying, 'Don't fear those who kill the body" etc. And following, "Fear him who after death has the power to send you to Gehenna." Note that he says "after he is slain" without further delimitation. For that persecution kills not in a human, but in a devilish way. The usual way that one kills is to separate the soul from the body. The inhuman, that is devilish way is to kill the soul and let it decay like a putrid cadaver, buried in a living body. For just as in the elect the external exemplariness of virtue for the perfection of souls is the good odor of Christ for the holy soul who remains in the body, so without doubt the appearance of external virtue of the reprobate to deceive souls is the stench of the souls which remain in living bodies. These are the whitewashed tombs whose stink of infidelity infects the entire East, and now is beginning to be carried to the West.

Chapter 6: How They Maintain, Buy, and Sell Captives

In order to be able to handle captives easily and conveniently, they have special merchants in all cities for buying and selling humans. Just as other kinds of merchants have privileges from the king, they are able to buy, sell, bind, or loose any captive to or from anyone according to royal statute without any kind of hindrance. They do this not only in the cities, but they bring chains and go into camp with the army. They buy captives directly from the hands of those who captured them. For those who seize the captives are not able to hold on to them, so they sell them immediately for a higher or lower price according to the abundance or paucity of captives. I have heard that sometimes there are such a large number of captives that a man can be sold for the cost of a single cap. The merchants buy them and bind them, ten or twelve on a single chain. There isn't a doctor or physician who can compare to their ability to ascertain the physical attributes or the characteristics of people. As soon as they look into someone's face they know their value, vocation, and history.[12] They take not only the mature and elderly, but even the little ones and children, even suckling infants and those whom the plunderers usually threw aside. So that they would not be a burden, they carry them in sacks and care for them with great diligence and astounding effort.

In addition, just like for other types of merchandise, in all cities there is a specific market and official location for the buying and selling of humans. The poor captives are brought to this marketplace in chains and tied with rope just as sheep led to the slaughter. There they are examined and stripped naked. There these rational creatures made in the image of God are most vilely bought and sold for money just like animals.[13] There (it is shameful to say) the genitals both of men and women are fondled and openly displayed before everyone. They are forced to march, run, walk and jump naked in front of everyone in order to demonstrate whether they are infirm or healthy, male or female, old or young, virgin or not. If they are seen to blush, all the more they are compelled, beaten, struck with rods, and punched[14] until finally they are forced to do in front of everyone what they of their own free will were ashamed to do. This is not the worst of it.[15] There the son is sold in front of his suffering mother. There the mother is bought to the shame and humiliation of the son. There the blushing wife is taken from her husband and given to play the harlot with another man. There the baby is ripped from the bosom of its mother and taken away from her while she is shaken to her very core. There is no deference for rank or consideration of status. There clergy and commoners are valued with the same coin. There soldiers and peasants are weighed on the same scale. This is just the beginning of their misfortunes. See what follows: one is sold, lead away, and condemned to the most wretched perpetual slavery with a vile farmer, a disgusting villager. There is no more hope of freedom or rest, no solace or consolation. The desolation is increased by the disgrace of having the burden of the entire household, and all who are in it, placed on his shoulders. And if he falters, you will see him whipped like an ass and with this whipping they are mocked with the reproach of the cross and passion of Christ. I will be silent about the intolerable work and say nothing about the hunger, thirst, and shame of nakedness. I will add only this: the affliction of the soul and spirit caused by this servitude is so great that death itself cannot be compared with it. For what can the poor soul do when he realizes that he is cut off from all good and exposed to all evil? He sees himself subjugated by the enemy of the cross of Christ. He sees himself oppressed by so much work and all of the various tasks he has to do. He understands himself to be separated from the flock of Christ and handed over to the claws[16] and jaws of wolves. Finally, he sees himself shut up in a perpetual prison with all hope of freedom extinguished. In the end he sees himself as abandoned by God and handed over to the devil. Clearly, if given the choice he would choose to die rather than to live. O, how many are not able to bear the test of this calamity and fall instead into the hell of despair! O, how many try to escape, exposing themselves to various kinds of death on mountains or in forests dying of hunger or thirst, or what is worse, to strike themselves or to extinguish their lives with a noose or to throw themselves into a river, destroying both body and the soul at the same time.

Chapter 7: Concerning Their Greed for Possessing Male and Female Slaves and Concerning the Flight of Slaves and Their Liberation

So great is their greed for male and female slaves that in all Turkey everyone has the opinion that whoever has at least one slave will no longer be poor. And they are not wrong. For I am convinced that if the curse of God is upon one's house and he has no hope of eternal happiness, he celebrates temporal pleasures. For such a great insatiability seizes his heart that once he possesses one slave immediately his whole heart longs for a second, and when he has a second, a third, and when he has a third, a fourth. And so his guilt grows infinitely along with his greed. For that reason many villages can be found which are made up entirely of slaves. The slaves are permitted to establish households, and the sons and daughters which are produced as a result somewhat slakes their insatiable desire.[17] In all of Turkey one can hardly find a single household that does not have at least one male or female slave. Because of this, despite the increasing amount and number of slaves their price or value never decreases but rather increases. As a result, the skill of the plunderers and merchants is kept sharp because they realize that the price of their merchandise and value of their goods never decreases but only increases.

Just as the masters have a great desire to possess slaves, so the slaves have a great desire to escape from their hands. For nothing among them is discussed nor is anything thought about or talked about except how they might be able to flee and escape. But as soon as their masters become aware of this as a result of overhearing and understanding the slaves' constant conversation, they begin to reduce the amount they give them to eat so that they would not be able to set aside food for the escape.

There are many modes of escape, although nothing which works. For hardly anyone is able to escape, especially those who are taken to the other side of the sea.[18] The Turks have discovered many different ways to impede, seek out, and find them. When slaves are discovered after an escape attempt and brought back, their misery is doubled. If they flee a second time and are discovered, there is no longer any restraint[19] and they are mercilessly berated, tormented, and beaten. If they continue to try to escape, they are sold or the various things needed for escape are withheld from them. Some restrict food, drink, and clothing to such a degree that the slave dies; others fasten large irons on their feet. Some put chains around their necks; others burn through their tendons to cripple them. Some cut off their ears and noses making them deformed and worthless as well as recognizable; others brutally cut them down and kill them.

However in the face of these problems a solution has been found, although only the wiser and milder masters make use of it. In order to restrain the urge to escape and keep them in place, they compel them to agree to a pact for the granting of their freedom. If they agree, the master takes them before a local judge and the master and slave agree together to a certain length of time and amount of money. These are established before the judge and made official by oath and seal. The slaves come back having a guarantee for their liberation. When the agreement in the pact is completed, by imperial authority the judge grants the slave his or her freedom through this solemn instrument which no one may infringe upon in the least. I myself received freedom by this means. In past times this form of liberation was widespread and abundant, because it allowed them to either remain in Turkey or to return to their fatherland according to their desire. At this time is it restricted, because even when freed the slaves must remain in Turkey and are no longer permitted to return home. For this reason the freed slaves have enormous difficulty in leaving Turkey. Everywhere, whether in ports or in other places, the emperor has declared a prohibition that the freedmen are not permitted to return to their homelands.

There are some other ways to attempt escape, of which two are most often utilized. The first is when they are able to gather enough money to purchase from a pilgrim a letter giving them permission to travel and by this means secretly to return home. The second is through certain conmen who pretend to be the kind of slave traders who go from land to land selling men. When they find a slave who wants to escape, they take them secretly and sell them in a remote place. If they find the slave to be especially capable, they make a pact with them, and after three or four times selling him then in this way, they let them go free with a certificate. Of those who are freed, few return to their homeland because they have already established relationships or because of the difficulties associated with returning that we have described above.

Chapter 8: Concerning Those Who Not Against Their Will nor By Force, But of Their Own Accord Expose Themselves to This Danger

This sect is supported and grows as a result of those who daily are conquered and against their will led away. Nevertheless, immeasurably greater is the guilt of those who hand themselves over without resistance like dry wood on an insatiable fire. Concerning the large number of those who daily of their own free will deny their faith: they do not only destroy themselves, but also encourage the ruin of others. In the north there are four or five great kingdoms with people like this. These territories were captured and possessed long ago, but because of the extent and spaciousness of the land they have not yet been able to fill them with Turks. The names of these lands are: Bosnia, Arnaut,[20] Laz,[21] Slavonia,[22] and Albania. Up to the present time, the people of those lands live under the dominion of the Turks but because of the annual tribute, the heavy burden, and many inconveniences which they suffer, they are impoverished and hardly have enough food to stay alive. For this reason, compelled by their great poverty during the annual laboring season, they go to various cities of the Turks and try to ameliorate their poverty a little by the sweat of their brow as a day-laborer. And if bad weather is not a factor, they come in such numbers that they are content to work for nothing more than food to eat. It is easy for them to be persuaded not to go back, for the numbers of those who come from their stock and speak their language has grown so much, especially in Adrianople the imperial city, so that almost everyone, male and female, small and great, is able to speak this language. In the court of the king, the Turkish language is hardly ever heard, as the entire court and the greater part of the magnates are made up of renegades who speak their native language.

In addition, the Great Turk takes his tithe from the booty and plunder. When he learns of a good quantity of captives, he orders that all youths up to age twenty should be given to him in lieu of the tithe. In addition, throughout all the lands of his domain there are many of Greek and other ancestry who live in a large number of castles and towns. They are free and exempt from all statutes and burdens of the other lords, are directly subject to the emperor and are attached to his court. Every five years the emperor commands that they send their sons twenty years and younger to be divided among his magnates and educated and trained in manners, physical strength, and weaponry. When they reach the age of around twenty years or older, they are brought back to his court, given a stipend, and made his attendants. These are called "gingitscheri" and at times at court there are thirty or forty thousand of them. They have a certain insignia on their clothing and especially on their heads. They have white caps or mitres which no one is permitted to wear except those in the court of the emperor. From them five or six thousand are selected as archers who bear their bows in the left hand and are called "czolaclar", that is, left-handers. Their bows are so strong that the arrows can penetrate all shields and mail. They march immediately in front of the emperor and when he goes on campaign they serve as something like a shield wall for him. He doesn't engage in the fight, and even if his entire army happens to break apart, nevertheless because of his personal force he does not lose the victory. This is what happened as we heard in the great three day and night battle between him and the king of Poland. His general army was completely broken and defeated, but in the end with his personal force he gained the victory.

The above named servants who have proven their worth are promoted to royal benefices. As a result, all of the magnates and leaders in the entire realm are like officials and not lords or owner of their own fiefdoms. As a result, the emperor is sole lord and possessor and the legal dispenser, distributor, and ruler in the entire realm—all other executors, officials, and administrators serve at his will and under his imperial power. There are two great lords among them who have leadership over all the others, one on this side of the sea and one on the far side of the sea. They handle all business of the realm according to the emperor's will and under his imperial power. They are called "beglerbegi", something like "lords of lords." As a result, although there are innumerable people, there is neither argument nor resistance in the realm. Rather as one person everyone everywhere in unity respects, is subject to, and indefatigably serves his imperial power. Except by his authority, no one dares do anything. If someone tries, whether great or small, all of his benefices are taken away and are given back to the original recipient, that is, if they do not receive an even greater punishment. On the contrary, if the emperor wants, he can have them executed, put in prison, sold, or reduced to slavery without appeal or consideration of status.

Chapter 9: Of the Various Types of Reasons Why People Are Persuaded by This Sect and Prefer It to the Christian Faith

The reasons why people are persuaded to go over to this sect and its errors are twofold, namely natural and supernatural. The natural reasons are also twofold, namely the universal and the particular. The universal are of two kinds: conjecture and experience. By 'conjecture' is meant that which depends on information from afar and only through what is heard. By 'experience' is meant that which is seen and perceived by the senses. The Abbot Joachim speaks about conjectural reasons in his commentary on Apocalypse 13: "'And the entire earth wondered at the beast': In his day it must be fulfilled that there will be many who will wonder and begin to quake, saying, 'what is believed to be this evidence that such a great multitude opposes the faithful and is permitted to prevail against the people of Christ? Do you suppose that so many thousands of men are condemned as if they were one person? Do you think that God permits them to grow infinitely without cause? These wretched ones have fallen from the faith not knowing that it is written: 'How great are your works, Lord! No one can fathom the depths of your thoughts. The feeble minded do not know and the foolish do not understand that sinners spring up like the grass and all workers of iniquity thrive until they are destroyed forever. But you, oh Lord, are most high.' Truly, fools do not know this, those who are in awe of the beast and abandon faith in Christ. They bow before the power of the beast and partake of his uncleanness and make themselves heirs of his faithlessness." That is the quote. Abbot Joachim posits four conjectural reasons. Hearing of the power of the Turks and his victories over the Christians and the great evil which he does daily, they are in awe and say: 'how can such a great number oppose the faith? It is like they are saying, since truth always prevails against error, and is more greatly loved and desired by everyone, it is not possible that so many fight against it. Therefore, where the multitude is, there is truth.' The second is: 'how can truth be defeated when God is on its side and preserves it? Therefore, whoever is victorious, they have the truth.' The third is: 'How is it possible that they are able to multiply and grow when all error is groundless and thus unable to grow? Therefore, etc.' The fourth is: 'How could God allow such a great multitude to be damned when He wants all men to be saved? Therefore, etc.' To these reasons or ideas Abbot Joachim responds according to the Psalms where it says, 'How magnificent' etc., which is like saying: 'When nature in order to preserve and nourish a small seed allows the immeasurable increase of chaff and stubble and does not err in this, why do you wonder if God permits and supports many reprobates for the salvation of a few righteous? The foolish do not consider this, who want to judge incomprehensible divine operations by their own fantasies and thoughts.

The experiential reasons are twofold, namely universal and particular. Concerning the universal reasons it should be noted that temptations which are seen have a much more powerful effect than those which are heard or received by conjecture. Of these one can speak briefly. One must deal more diligently with those which come through sight and experience. As a foundational point, it should be noted that good and evil appear alike in external characteristics although they are different in terms of intention. For as every good thing works together for the good, so also all evil works together for evil. If good people demonstrate good morals, it is as an example of virtue. Bad examples preserve interior virtue and humility. But reprobates use good morals as a deception and bad morals to corrupt the souls of the faithful. Concerning the first is says 'Their words are soften than oil, but are darts.'[23] Concerning the second: 'Bad company corrupts good morals.'[24]

For who, and I am not speaking just of the simple but also of the wise, is not moved at the first glance by seeing such morality among the infidels? For all frivolity in every deed and action, in their clothing and equipment is detested like fire and despised like the plague. Seeing the frivolity of the Christians in clothing and riding gear and everything else, they mock them and call them goats and monkeys. They have the most honorable, even pious manner of clothing: men as well as women, great and small, members of the court as well as peasants and farmers. They have such a general simplicity that there is not a hint or note of anything indecent or dishonorable or superfluous or vain or frivolous. What shall I say concerning those things pertaining to piety and devotion? For they demonstrate such simplicity, unity, such remarkable appearance, such exemplarity in actions, deeds, demeanor, and clothing that one would believe that they had taken some sort of vows. In horsemanship and all riding apparel, not only the commoners but even the magnates avoid all shouting and commotion and ride only castrated horses. One does not hear even a single commotion or shout even in an army of one hundred thousand horses. In saddle and harness they have nothing at all extravagant, vain, or superfluous. They hold to the greatest simplicity in all their riding gear. No one goes out armed when they leave camp; all weapons are carried in packs on camels and mules. No one rides back and forth; no one dances about or jumps with his horse as is the custom of the Christians. The magnates and princes value simplicity so much that it is not possible to distinguish them from other classes. I saw the emperor going to church down the long way from his palace with two youths and I also saw him going to the baths. Neither on his return from the church to the palace did anyone dare to accompany him, nor did any one dare to run up to him or shout on the street like they are accustomed to do, saying "long live the king" and such things. I saw him praying in the church, not in a chair or on a royal throne, but on the ground on a spread out rug sitting like everyone else, with no ornamentation suspended, displayed, or extended around him. Nothing at all distinctive in his dress or with his horse that could distinguish him from others can be seen. I saw him at the funeral of his mother, and it would not have been possible for me to recognize him if someone had not pointed him out. He has most strictly forbidden anyone to accompany him or to run up to him on the street without his express permission. I will not mention much of what I heard concerning his affability in conversation, his maturity and kindness in judgment, largess in charity, and benevolence in other deeds. For example, the brothers in Pera said that he came into their church and sat in the choir in order to observe the ceremony and their means of officiating. As he desired, they celebrated a mass before him and demonstrated for him the elevation of a non-consecrated host. This was to satisfy his curiosity but at the same time not to throw pearls before swine. After he had had a discussion with them concerning the law and rituals of the Christians, and had heard that bishops lead the church, he wanted them to appoint some bishop for the consolation of the Christians. To this end, he promised them all the favor which he was able to give as emperor and his complete support. Who, hearing from afar of his victories, wars, his great army, his glory and his magnificence would suspect that there was such simplicity in him, or who, having heard, would not be in awe?

Chapter 10: Concerning Specific Experiential Reasons

The specific reasons are of two kinds, namely internal and external. The external ones are those which primarily pertain to cleanliness. For in all external matters they demonstrate such a love of cleanliness that it is almost as if they think everything they use makes them unclean. In the places where they eat in their houses no chickens or dogs are permitted and if by chance a dog or chicken touches a dish or jar, by no means will they ever eat from it again. When they want to eat a chicken, for six or seven days they tie it up and give it pure grain to eat. If any animal is killed and the neck is not cut with a sword or knife and the blood totally drained, they will absolutely not eat its flesh. So great is their concern for the cleanliness of their body, especially for those who pray frequently, that they will not tolerate the smallest spot on their clothing or their bodies. The washings which are required before prayer are discussed below in Chapter 13. For the same reason they drink no wine and eat no pork. They say that these make a person unclean. After any natural pollution[25] they are not permitted to speak with anyone or, as much as is possible, even be seen by anyone unless they first submerge or wash their entire body in water. As a result, the baths are always being used in the cities. Where there are no baths, they have a private place set aside in their houses for this purpose so that they may bathe as soon as possible before they leave the house. They call a polluted man a 'tschunzip,'[26] which means 'unclean.' They consider this to be most detestable.

The internal reasons are those which pertain to the appetites and desires. The first thing which strikes one is their great simplicity in architecture. They do not take any pleasure at all in buildings or constructing their houses, and regardless of whether they are rich in silver and gold or are poor, they nonetheless detest all superfluity and vanity to the degree that one would think they had taken a vow of poverty. In cities it is rare to find a building constructed of stone outside of those of the great lords, of the churches, and of the baths. Rather, houses are commonly constructed of wood and earth. Those who have seen the buildings of the Christians are extraordinarily scandalized by their superfluous luxury. When others are told of these buildings who have not seen them, in disgust they say. "[D]o those wicked pagans think they are able to live forever?" In fact, when there is no call to campaign even their great lords in the summer leave for pleasant areas. They don't care about houses but live in tents and dedicate themselves entirely to the hunt and leisure. In addition there is one type among them who dedicate themselves to nothing other than the feeding and care of their flocks just like the patriarchs. The number of these is so great, that even if they were dispersed through the whole of Turkey, the land could not contain the multitude of their flocks and herds. They take no concern for houses or buildings, but move around the land as needed for pasture and the other requirements of their flocks. In winter they descend to lower and warmer altitudes; in summer they ascend to higher altitudes. They are so rich and powerful that a single one of them with his family and wealth are able to arm and muster an army. Yet they live in worthless tents and yurts, demonstrating that they are not citizens of this world but pilgrims. They do out of natural instinct what Christians ought to do by commitment to Christ and faith.

The second reason is their simplicity. They abhor and detest pictures and sculptures of all kinds. They call Christians, who take so much delight in these, idolaters and worshippers of demons, and believe this to be true. When I was in Chios and the ambassadors of the Turks came to receive the tribute, going into our church I wanted to convince them about images. They acquiesced in nothing, but refuting all arguments and persevering in their stubbornness, they affirmed only: "you worship idols." They prohibit games of chance for money of any kind and those who are found participating in such are afflicted with many ignominies and punished. Concerning that great superstition of Christians, especially in Italian regions, of painting and engraving their equipment and writing on them their names and insignia—this is foreign to all Turks and not a trace of it is to be found among them. No seals or any other mark no matter how small are used in letters either from the emperor or anyone else. Trust is given immediately just by hearing the name of the sender of the letter or by inspecting the handwriting style.

They abhor all things of this kind which denote excessiveness or superstition and consider them to be vain, unhelpful, and unnecessary. This is also the reason why they do not allow the use of bells or permit the Christians among them to use them.

What can I say about the simple way in which they sit? Not only peasants or commoners, but all princes and magnates—no matter what their position might be, even the emperor himself—for eating or any other purpose, do not require a footstool, chair, or anything else for sitting, but rather in the manner of children yet with the most honorable and appropriate composure they sit on the ground, showing deference that nature has made all equal. For the most part their tables are made of common leather or deer pelt, preferably round, four or five palms wide, having metal rings around the circumference through which a tie is threaded so that it may be closed and opened and carried like a purse. No one enters a house or church or any other location in which they sit without first removing their shoes. They consider it to be dishonorable to sit with shoes on. In order to do this comfortably, especially women use a certain kind of sandal which in their language is called "baschmag" which are easy to take off and put back on. It is common in the places where they sit in houses or in churches to have laid out carpets of wool, thatch, or rushes, or even to use an elevated platform where it is necessary due to wetness or dirt. I will also not avoid describing how honorably they relieve themselves[27] outside of the house or in public view, as often happens in camp. They have really large and long outer garments and breeches which are open in the front. Thus, in the middle of the army they can squat and pull down their pants under the outer-garment and without anyone able to see their nakedness they can relieve themselves in such a way that it is hardly possible to know what they are doing. They also take great care when they are doing this not to turn their faces toward the south, the direction toward which they turn while praying. In addition, if anyone urinates or makes water while standing, it shows everyone that they are a heretic or an excommunicate.

Chapter 12: Of the Honorableness of Their Women

If anyone does not want to believe what I now desire to discuss, let him examine the precepts of right reason: these will be witnesses for me that the truth must not hide anything. For if according to right reason judgment proceeds from the head, how can it not be said that whatever is done in the body comes from the sexual impurity and lasciviousness of humankind, all of which is found in dishonorable and indecent women, as scripture attests that man is the head of the woman? Without doubt a great admiration was born in me when I saw how honorable the women were among the Turks, considering the shameful dress and accursed morals which are seen among Christian women. What I saw everywhere in Turkey I hold to be true because I never saw an exception wherever I went. Among Christians what

I see is not so common or universal so that all deserve reproach, but only among those who are not true men but effeminate men who have allowed their reason to be submerged in carnality so that they are not able to discern anything concerning what would aid the salvation of their neighbors but think only of themselves and their most lustful hearts and eyes take pleasure in the harlotry of their wives. Neither are the wives excused in that they are only pleasing their husbands, because they are not required to obey them in anything which is detrimental to their salvation. But because, as the proverb goes, all women are whores, the guilt of their husbands is doubtless greater than theirs, for their husbands did not direct their unrestrained shamelessness with the bridle of discretion. O what accursed, diabolical impurity that is not able to corrupt every male member so it tries to thrust its prostitution upon every eye and heart! Certainly a prostitute in secret in a brothel is much better than these most shameless women who go around destroying the souls of the entire city! O, you most wretched offspring of all women, do you believe that you keep the oath of marriage—you who commits adultery so often? You who so often cast before shameless eyes your naked throat and breast, your fluttering eyes, gentle face, erect neck, and flowing hair? But you, o man, whose most shameless wife is not yours alone but everyone's—o prostitute of Satan, you who greatly cherish and nourish the snare of the devil, do you think you will not have to give an account of such great evil? As it says in scripture: "Whoever looks upon a woman to lust after her, commits adultery with her in his heart."[28]

But now let us return to the intended theme of our message. Certainly the Turks deserve to be called 'men.' Although they say they are permitted to have twelve wives if they want, they do not display uncontrollable love toward any one of them. All of them equally serve him in bearing and nourishing his offspring. As they teach that one man is superior to twelve women, this proves the worthlessness of that most unfortunate sex and the statement by the creator concerning the woman: 'you shall be under the authority of the man.'[29] Those who allow themselves to be dominated by their women because of the ardor of their lust are rightly not called men but the worst kind of voluptuaries and the devil's helpers in the destruction of souls. Among the Turks it is considered to be greatly scandalous for a man if his wife is seen by other men with her face bared either in his own home or outside of it. The women dress with utmost simplicity without the hint of anything vain or superfluous. On their heads they wear hoods with a veil over them wrapped carefully and appropriately in such a way that the end of the veil hangs down the right side of their faces. This is so that if they leave their houses or if it happens that they are in the view of men inside their houses, they immediately are able to wrap it around and cover their entire face except for the eyes. This is true of everyone, even the peasants and the poorest of them. In the cities, indeed, it would be considered a great scandal if the wife of some noble was outside of her house without her entire face covered by fine silk in such a way that she could see others but no one else could see her face. A woman would never dare enter a gathering of men and it is considered to be illicit by everyone for a woman to go to market and buy or sell anything. In the larger churches they have an extensive place separate from the men and therefore private into which no one is allowed to look or by any means to enter. Only the wives of the great lords and no one else are allowed inside, and even they are only permitted on Friday during the noon prayer, which is considered among them to be sacred. A conversation between men and women together in public is so rare that even if you would spend a year among them, you would scarcely experience it. It is considered monstrous for a woman to ride a mule or a horse. Even in his own home with his wife there is not the slightest trace of lasciviousness or dishonorableness in action, behavior, or conversation. The men display such a great maturity in their own homes that fear and respect is always given to them, especially because they never relax their strictness with their wives. As it is not possible for the great lords to always be present with their wives, they have eunuchs as deputies who watch over them with such great diligence that they have no knowledge of any man except for their husband. I will cover the remaining reason briefly. It would take a long time to describe every single thing that I saw and experienced concerning women during the fifteen continuous years in which I was in the house of my last master. But nevertheless, I cannot be silent entirely about something so important. The wife of his son, who for twenty years had lived in the house, having sons and daughters, was never seen by the father of her husband, either eating or in conversation, with an uncovered mouth or unveiled face. And this strict reverence was from the first day that she entered the house and was never relaxed nor will ever be relaxed.

Chapter 13: Concerning Supernatural and Spiritual Reasons, and First of All Concerning the Profession of Faith and the Law of the Turks

The profession which is the foundation of the law of the Turks is the following: "layllaha hillallach mehemmet erczullach." According to the unanimous opinion of the commentators this means: "God is one and Muhammad is his greatest prophet." Everyone recognizes that there is a difficulty as a result of their manner of profession of faith. If by this one is able to be persuaded that they worship one god, the poison of their error can be spread more easily under the guise of piety. This is the stone of offense which is a stumbling block to many, casting them into a snare and causing the damnation of their souls. This is the millstone hung on the necks of many and plunging them in the hell of despair. For the simple have heard that they despise idols and all forms and images, rejecting them as if they were the fires of hell, that they always profess and preach the worship of one god.

This is the general opinion of almost all Turks concerning their law: they say that the first great prophet who received the first law from God was

'Missa,' that is Moses. He was given the book "tefrit" which we call the Pentateuch. All men of his day who observed that law are saved. Because over time this law was corrupted through human malice and negligence, a second great prophet was chosen to correct these errors. This is Daut, who we call David. He was given the book "czabur" which we call the Psalms. As this was preserved and then corrupted in the same way, a third great prophet followed, Yesse, whom we call Jesus. He was sent with a third law, the book "ingili" which we call the Gospel. It was the source of salvation for all people in his time. Finally, as this became no longer valid in the same way as its predecessors, a fourth was chosen, Muhammad.[30] He received from God the book called the "alcoranus." As all prior to it have been emptied of their authority, it alone is necessary for salvation until another comes after it. They preach and say that it is complete and indubitable.

The law of the alcoran has as its first precept that until old age everyone of both sexes should not live outside the bonds of matrimony. Furthermore, with equal strictness everyone is subject to prayer. The prayer is to be carried out five times a day at five specified times. The first prayer is at the rising of the sun. They do not compute the time exactly but approximate it. Because they have no means of calculating the time exactly, they simply go by natural instinct. In the first prayer they do four erkets and two czalamats. An "erket" is a double bowing with the same number of prostrations. A "czalamat" is the silent prayer done while seated after each "erket" by a greeting to the right and the left, and making the sign of peace which is done by putting both hands in front of the face. The time of the second prayer is around noon and is made up of ten erkets and five czalamats. The third prayer is done at the time of vespers as the sun is going down. It consists of eight erkets and four czakamats, etc. The fourth prayer consists of five erkets and three czalamats and must be done at the time when the sun sets. The fifth and last is longer than the others and consists of fifteen erkets and eight czalamats. It is celebrated after supper at a later hour. In their language, the first prayer is called "dangnamas," the second "oilenamas," the third "kyndinamas," the fourth "achsam namaz," the fifth "iaczinamas." Each one is supposed to pray these prayers with his pastor[31] and in his own church, unless a legitimate reason makes this not possible. In such cases it is permitted to do them anywhere. They have a dispensation concerning their observation of the times of prayer: they may add to one time of prayer what they missed at another. Friday is a feast day for them on which they pray most diligently without being absent from or failing to do whatever work they have. In the cities there is one main official church which is called "enemesgit." Everyone gathers there on Friday together with their king, if he is present, and other nobles. The noon prayer is carried out with great solemnity with a sermon and the distribution of royal alms. It would take too long to discuss all aspects of the proper order, uprightness, silence, and devotion which they display in church. Briefly I will say that when I compare the silence of the Turks in their churches with the tumult of Christians in their churches during the time of prayer, I am filled with great wonder at so great an inversion in the way things are supposed to be. The Turks have such great devotion and the Christians such a lack of devotion, although reason demands that it should be the opposite. They have inquisitors who punish through much public shame those who miss prayers. They lead them around with a sign decorated with fox tails hung around their neck. They don't release them until they pay a fine, especially if they missed prayers during their Lent.

They have a three-fold washing to prepare for prayer. The first is such a thorough washing of the whole body with water that not a single place the size of the head of a pin remains untouched by water. Otherwise, the washing is invalid. For this reason they frequently and diligently shave the hair of all parts of the body except the beards of men and the heads of women. These are washed very diligently and combed in such a way that the water is able to penetrate to the skin. They are very diligent about cutting their fingernails and toenails and I think that it is for this reason that they circumcise, as will be discussed below in Chapter 21. This washing, as was stated above in Chapter 10, is necessary after any blemish of pollution. It is called "czoagirmeg." The second washing is called "tachriat" and is necessary whenever one goes to the bathroom or passes gas. Then the genitalia and the rear are washed privately. The third washing is called "apatz" or "abdas" and requires a washing of the five sense organs, beginning with the hands. The arms are washed to the elbows as is the mouth and nose. Then the entire face is washed from the eyes to the ears. Water is poured over the head by hand. The feet and legs are washed to the shin. This washing may be done anywhere. It is not necessary that this be done before each prayer unless some uncleanness requires it. If after the first prayer one is able to remain free from any uncleanness, no other washings are required that day for all the other prayers. Some, however, for the sake of devotion or to be particularly careful are in the habit of frequently washing.

They have one month of the twelve regular months of the year in which they fast. Because the lunar year does not correspond to the solar year without adding additional days, and because they are ignorant of this computation, they reckon twelve months per year. Therefore the month of their fasting happens sometimes in winter and sometimes in summer. During the month of the fast they abstain by day from all food and drink. At night they can partake of all foods whenever they desire.

They have an Easter at the completion of the fast. At this time they visit the graves of their dead. They pray there and eat what they have brought with them. They exchange kisses and say "Baarom gutli oczong," which is: "May you have a good Easter." They do all of this also on a second Easter which is celebrated forty days after the first because on that same day their pilgrims celebrate it in Mecca as a conclusion to the ritual of their pilgrimage. For the grave monument and tomb of Muhammad is in the place which they call Mecca and annually it is visited by a great multitude of that sect, not just by Turks, but by all peoples which are obedient to that sect, namely Arabs, Saracens, Tartars. Mecca is forty days beyond Jerusalem and it is not possible to travel there except by camel because the way is sandy and very dry. For this reason the sultan has camels prepared for the pilgrimage. They hold these pilgrims who visit the tomb of Muhammad in great reverence and esteem and call them "hatschilar." They enjoy many privileges. That is the reason why in court one of their testimonies is worth the testimony of three others. Special prayer is offered on their behalf, just like that for military victors. Everywhere they have two kinds of inns for them, one on the roads and one in the cities. Those on the roads are called "kevvennc-zerey." They are the largest buildings in those areas where there are not large enough settlements to accommodate travelers and pilgrims. Those in the cities are called "ymart." They are large churches built by kings and princes. They are given so many possessions that every day they are able to provide two means to those who come: the first for the pilgrims and the second for the students who are registered there. If any food is left over, it is given indiscriminately to those present. This is done every day at lunch and supper times. The priests and the students who are registered there are obligated for their food to celebrate a special service on behalf of the souls of those who have built and instituted these places.

In addition, they have many large gymnasia[32] in which are taught the civil laws which were issued by the emperors concerning the government of the realm. The most proficient of these scholars are given offices in which they judge and rule the people. These are of two ranks. The lesser is called "minetschum"; the greater is called "muderis." The less experienced are called "tanisman." It is sufficient for them to know the Alcoran well and that which pertains to the prayers and the ritual law. They disperse benefits in the following way: Unless they are judges, registrars, or jurisconsults (who are called "calife") and who have no free time, they are not paid[33] except for being free and exempt from the service and burdens of the common people. Their priests are not responsible for the cure of souls, hearing confessions, administering the sacraments, visiting the sick or burying the dead. Nor do they have great responsibility for churches with relics, adornments, sacred vessels and altars—they do not have any of these. It is not possible to defile a church or destroy sanctity when there is no consecration. There is no difference between their priests and a common person or between their churches and ordinary buildings. The priests and everybody else can do the rhythm of prayer without leaving anything out from the completion of their work. Their free time is not spent in meditation or studies but in the comforts of their wives, sons and families, in their livestock and possessions, in their businesses and incomes, in their pleasures and their hunting with birds and dogs. None of this or other similar things are illicit for them or prohibited. As the law is, so are the priests; as the rituals are, so are the ministers.[34] Everything that should be said about these things exceeds the quantity of pen and paper that I have. I have covered it briefly so that I might give a reason for inquiring about the rest and diligently investigating it. For it shames and disgusts me to discuss the particulars of what I have seen and heard.

Chapter 14: Concerning Supernatural and Religious Reasons

In book twenty, chapter 19 of the *City of God*, speaking of deceiving signs and wonders, Saint Augustine says that they may be said to lie in two ways. One way is that human senses are deceived through the power and arts of the devil to believe that something is which in reality is not. These are fantasies. The second, because they lead believers into error, namely that they believe something to be done by the power of God which is actually done by the devil, or they believe something is beneficial for their salvation when it is actually for their damnation. As it was not a deception that fire came down from heaven and consumed the family and flocks of Job, even if it were the work of the devil permitted by God.

In the same way, each believer should consider the wondrous and innumerable signs done either done during their lives or even after their deaths by the monks of the perfidious Turks to be deceptions. For so great is the power of the devil in them that they would appear to be more devils incarnated than humans. Behind the distinction which they have in their external appearance lurks a diabolical power in them. Certain of them choose the harshest suffering. They do not wear clothes but go around naked, except for covering their genitals. Among that kind of religious are some who reach such a state of perfection that they are almost insensible and they are not able to sense any external stimuli at all. In the coldest winter weather they go about with their entire body naked and they do not feel anything. The same is true for the heat of summer. As proof of the truth of their sufferings they show on their bodies various burn marks and the scars of cuts. If anyone wants to test this, they will hold fire against themselves or cut their flesh with a sword. In all of this they show no more sign of sensation than if fire was held against a rock or a sword cut into wood. Others of them demonstrate great strength in abstinence. It is said of these that some reach such a level of perfection in this that they rarely eat or drink. Some reach such a state of perfection in this that their bodies are able to live without any food or water whatsoever. Others are greatly impoverished. They have no interest at all in worldly things and set nothing aside for tomorrow. Others keep perpetual silence. They are called "czamutlar," that is, the mute. They have no interaction with people so that they are not compelled to speak. I was able to see only one of them, but I was amazed. Some experience visions, others revelations of various kinds. Some have raptures, others have supernatural ecstasies. And so there are none among them who do not have some spiritual experience which can clearly distinguish them from the order of "dervishler"—the name for all who live in this state. They are distinguished in their dress and mode of life based on their type of spiritual or supernatural experience, for each one carries the sign of his profession. If you would see someone with feathers on their head, this denotes someone dedicated to meditations and revelations. If they wear clothing patched together with different colors, this denotes poverty. If they wear earrings, this designates spiritual obedience because of their frequent raptures. Having chains on their neck or arms denotes violent or powerful ecstasies. The insensate who go about naked were described above, as were many others.

They have various modes of life. Those who are less hindered by spiritual matters, namely raptures and so forth, live an ordinary life among the general population. Others live apart in communities like villages. Others live as solitaries in forests or the wilderness. Others dedicate themselves to hospitality in cities in houses which are called "tekye." They receive guests to sleep overnight, even if they have nothing to feed them. Others live entirely by begging. Others carry skins of the best water which can be found there around in the cities, offering drinks of fresh water and asking for no payment except freely given donations. Others, living around the tombs of well-known saints maintain them and live off of the donations of the devotees. I was not able to ascertain whether they all had wives, mainly because they don't follow the law of the Turks on this but have their own views, as will be discussed below in Chapter 20. Neither do they observe other rituals of the law such as prayers, washings, and the like. Since the appearance of other virtues in them is almost supernaturally pronounced, as had been said, one would think that a prodigious abstinence would not be missing. A great miracle which is widely rumored among them to happen to women who have not been corrupted by sexual contact, namely, that many are conceived and born without male seed. They are called "nefes ogli"—they will be mentioned in the following chapter. It may be that those mothers are the wives of religious who due to their amazing abstinence bear sons to them not by natural means but through a diabolical power hidden to humankind. For this reason, it does not seem unusual to the Turks when Christians say that Jesus was conceived and born of Mary without human seed. In fact, they say and confess the same thing. However this happens, even though it may sound unusual and miraculous, it is nevertheless not impossible to see this as done by satanic power, if their other works that they do are examined.

These religious also hold certain festivals, in response to the gifts of people or to honor the memory of their predecessors, or because of the needs of the general population such as pleading for rain or good weather or that kind of thing. When this happens they gather together all who are in the surrounding area and begin with a common meal for everyone. They butcher animals if they have them. If they don't have meat, they make as much food as they can as well as they can from beans or rice. After they have finished eating whoever is the leader takes a drum. When he has established a rhythm, the others rise and begin to dance[35] accordingly. This festival is called "machia" and the dance is called "czamach." In this the entire body moves in a rhythmic and well-measured motion, characterized by an appropriate, dignified, and immensely dignified movement of every part of the body. This is done according to the rhythm appropriately established by the musical instrument. Finally, this builds to a kind of a spinning, very fast circular movement by rotating or turning in which the entire power of the dance consists. They are turned by their fervency with such speed that it is not possible to discern by looking at them whether they are humans or statues. In this dance, they show themselves to have an almost supernatural bodily agility. Although others are able to imitate them in other movements of the dance, no one is able to imitate this kind of spinning motion, no matter how capable or agile he is. After each one has danced, they all rise at the same time and dance independently, making intercession with their voices for the salvation of those who gave them gifts or alms.

They have certain sayings handed down from their predecessors which they say under inspiration while they are enraptured or in a state of ecstasy. They are artfully composed in rhyme and easily remembered, longer or shorter depending upon the material which they treat. Some are six verses, some eight or ten, some more, some less. They treat all the ceremonies and rituals of the law of the Turks according to a spiritual understanding. I either copied or memorized a lot of them and enjoyed them because they better affirmed the Christian religion than the religion of the Turks. For this reason their priests do not accept them for the reason that those who said them did not know what they were saying because they were enraptured or in ecstasy and were out of their minds when they said them.

When these religious are among men, each one attempts to display his perfection or profession by means of a sign. Among the displays, nothing demonstrates their devotion or fervor like the dance mentioned above. There is also a spiritual meaning to it.[36] For even the holy prophets of antiquity used this kind of dance in their religious rituals, just as David did when he danced before the ark of the Lord as did many others in the Old Testament. When certain of them were guests in our house, after the meal they rose and girded themselves and began to dance. While they were spinning, such a sound from their voices was heard that everyone in the house was thunder-stuck in admiration and was hardly able to keep from crying. Another time while we were eating, one of them suddenly fell into a rapture and completely lost all his senses. He sat there like he was dead without moving or being aware of anything. Often when they were our guests they offered the sayings discussed above as encouragement for the listeners. They are so exemplary in everything they do and say and give such a display of religion in their morals and actions that they appear to be angels rather than men. Their faces have such a sign of spirituality, that even if you had never seen them before, you would immediately be able to recognize them.

But as we have said enough about their external appearance, now at last let us, in so far as we are able, examine the fruit by which we can know the inner person, as the savior says in Matthew 8.[37] For if one would investigate the details of their sayings and deeds, he will find in them so much ambition regarding their own reputation and so much venom of spiritual pride that one might think that the saying "an angel of Satan transforms into an angel of light" was about them. For they say of themselves that they are chosen by God before others and that they should be honored by everyone as friends of God. They say that they have special grace from God and that no one can be saved without the mediation of their grace.[38] Because of this they say that the gifts and alms of all people ought to be given to them. And if someone offends them in the least, they immediately call down the wrath of God upon them. When one of them once was staying at the house of a rich man in my region (the rich man's house was not far from our village), because he and his family were caring for his herd (as it was raining) and not giving him the hospitality he wanted, he immediately left the house yelling and calling the wrath of God down upon them. That same year the anger of God fell on them so hard that in that house neither person nor animal remained, but all died. I heard this kind of thing from many others. For this reason everyone tries hard not to offend them in anything. Considered from the standpoint of faith, those are not the characteristics of the friends of God who desires that all would be saved but rather of the friends of Satan who seeks to do nothing except to destroy. I will say more about this in the following chapters, here I want only to add that all evil and cunning of devilish deception, in fact all wickedness of his art in the destruction of souls is without doubt found in abundance in these reprobates.

Chapter 15: Likewise on Supernatural Reasons as Well as Deceptive Wonders and Signs

Among others of this sect who have displayed deceptive signs and wonders after death, and still display them daily, there is a main one who is greatly venerated and honored in all Turkey. His name is Sedichasi, which means "Holy Victor" or "Victor Among the Holy." His tomb and shrine is on the border between the Othmans and the Karmans. Although these two frequently quarrel and one invades the territory of the other, no one dares to approach his tomb or near the area with any evil intention. This is because they have often experienced that vengeance falls upon whoever dares do this. It is the general opinion among them that no one who pleads for his help in any crisis will be cheated of the fulfillment of the request, especially in war and in the midst of battle. This is demonstrated by the large number of offerings of all kinds of animals and other things and money which are annually given by the emperor, princes and the entire community of commoners, and flow to his tomb. For in fact, he has the greatest fame and esteem not only among the Turks but also among all peoples of this sect. I want to discuss his signs and wonders because he has a greater celebrity among all Muslims[39] than St. Anthony among the Christians.

There is another called "Hatschi Pettesch" which may roughly be translated as "helper of pilgrims." Many call upon and venerate him, especially pilgrims who it is said often receive help from him. Another is called "Ascik Passa." His name is derived from the word for love and he is said to be something of a patron of love. He is said to give aid concerning marital matters like childbirth or desiring offspring or marital discord with wives and many other similar needs. "Alivan Passa" helps those fighting to be reconciled. It is said of him that he appears to those who seek him sometimes as a young man and sometimes as an old man. "Scheych Passa" helps the distressed and troubled to be comforted.

In those areas in which I myself lived, there were once many who were considered to be saints but whose names were unknown. Nevertheless, their tombs were greatly venerated. If rain was needed or good weather desired or when there was any pressing need, they would gather at their tombs and make offerings and prayers and return in great hope of the fulfillment of their prayers. I often went with them in order to get something good from what they carried with them to eat there.

There are two among them whose names are known. One is "Goivelmirtschin," the other is called "Barthschun Passa." Miraculous works are told about them in that region, especially concerning the care and maintenance of herds and other animals, particularly the concerning the one called "Goivelmirtschin." My master's wife frequently told me about that saint's great help in the area of the care of their calves. For that reason annually a certain amount of butter was promised and taken to him. She also said, "If once I forget or neglect to fulfill my vow, immediately I would suffer some punishment." Even I was persuaded that I should call upon him when a wolf entered into the flock of sheep at pasture. Also, I do not think I should neglect to relate what my master frequently said. He said that one day one of his bulls was missing when the rest of the herd returned in the evening. As was the custom in the area, he immediately called together the neighbors, and just like a hunt, that same evening they went through the forest area nearby with quiver, bow, and dogs. They came back without finding any evidence at all of the bull. On the following day they went through the entire pasture in the same manner without any results. On the third day as evening was coming on they were returning tired and completely hopeless when suddenly and unexpectedly my master mentally made a vow. He vowed that for the love of Saint Goivelmirtschin, if his animal were returned to him he would eat with the pilgrims a hot bread known as a "paslama" with butter on top. As soon as he had this thought, there was a commotion, and behold, the bull was found. He had been caught by the horns in the fork of a tree. For him it was miraculous because for the last three days they had gone through that area while they were searching, neither was it possible that that the bull could have survived the wild animals. When my master told everyone about the vow which he had made, they were all amazed and returned in happiness and joy, giving glory to God and extolling the goodness and name of Goivelmirtshin, for they had not only found the bull but had also witnessed a miracle.

There is another whose name is "Chidirelles" who gives aid to travelers especially when they are in danger. So great is his reputation in all of Turkey, that there is hardly anyone who has not experienced his help in need, or who has not heard of someone receiving his help. He usually appears in the form of a traveler riding a grey horse and immediately helps travelers in need, either if they call upon him or even if they don't know his name but put themselves in the hand of God, as is known from the tales of many.

I need to also describe another evidently true miracle which was told to me by some people from their relations who were still alive at that time. At that time there were monks in the area around us who were maligned on account of suspicion that they were traitors to the emperor. In a fury, the emperor ordered that all of them be burned to death. When their leader could not appease the emperor, he swore his and their innocence before God and in front of the emperor was the first to enter the furnace to be consumed by the fire. He was there until the entire conflagration around him had cooled, but he remained completely uninjured. The anger of the emperor was assuaged. So he rescued himself and the others from the danger of death and left to his successors and to all people of that sect a solemn example. Until today in that remote region, they have the sandals which were with him in the furnace but remained undamaged from the fire as a testimony to the veracity of this story.

For sake of brevity, I will not say more about those who are called "neffes ogli" who I spoke of above (of which it is said that there were always two or three in the large city named Brusczia), and of whom it is said that someone receiving their hair or clothing is cured of disease. It is said that they are birthed in a miraculous manner, that is, without the man's seed, and as a result their entire life and actions must be believed to be supernatural and miraculous. A little is said about them in Chapter 14.

Chapter 20: How One Can Be Brought Back From the Errors of the Turks

Three kinds of Christians in Turkish captivity can be found. . . .

But if there are some of these renegades who have mental fortitude and are not quickly persuaded by the arguments of that sect but instead diligently investigate them, without doubt they would find much to bring them back from those errors and sufficient reason to demonstrate its infidelity. Of these reasons, three are primary:

The first is their spiritual discord. They may appear to have a great external concord and unity, and in fact they are unified in the persecution of Christian worship, the expansion of their religion, and the perpetuating of all evil. Nevertheless, in those things which pertain to salvation and to the understanding of truth there is so great diversity of opinions and spiritual divisions and ill will that no one can doubt that this religion has its origin not in God but in the devil. All things which pertain to their law are nothing other than inventions arbitrarily constructed and made standard through tradition and containing nothing of the mysteries or of truth. On the contrary, they abound in blasphemy, superstition, and the deceptive work of the devil. They use, or better misuse their Alcoran to justify all kinds of evil such as theft, murder, fornication, adultery, sexual sins, robbery, and similar things. If I chose to tell everything that I heard, saw, and experienced, it would become tedious and nauseating to the reader. They are so infected, disfigured, and corrupted by fortune-tellers, spell-makers, and diviners that there is hardly an elderly person who does not have some knowledge or skill in this area. There is so much disparity in what they say and diversity of opinion concerning their law, the Alcoran, and Muhammad that if you asked a hundred of them about these things not one would say the same thing as another. Their priests may make a great display of piety before men, but privately they are filled with so much evil that they enter into all kinds of wickedness. They make money by writing the certificates which are needed to do anything or transact business. They write many certificates of freedom for money so that slaves can flee and escape the hands of their lords, as said above in Chapter 5.[40] They also write certificates for those who go to war so that swords or arrows will not hurt them. They also write many talismans which are called in their language 'haymayly.'[41] All of them try to do this, but many are deceived especially by the wandering priests who flee from place to place after they have received money so that their evil is not discovered. In these and innumerable other ways they are filled with lies and deceptions so that as many different diabolical deceptions that they could think up, they are divided into so many types based on the errors which they have found.

Among other smaller divisions concerning ceremonies of the law, rituals, institutions, worship, and observations into which they are divided, there are four main opinions concerning salvation. Each group holds to these so strongly that not only are they not in agreement but one even attacks the other by force with weapons and with military fortifications. Often the entire realm is shaken and things do not settle down unless the king intervenes.

The first group is the priests. They enjoy a high reputation as leaders of the people and as the executors and dispensers of the law, as teachers, judges, and directors of spiritual, ecclesiastical, and educational benefices. They believe that one cannot be saved except through the law of Muhammad; they teach this and persuade everyone. And although this cannot be proven by reason or authority or example, nevertheless they try any possible method to oppose their opponents. They have much support among the people, especially among the princes and magnates.

The second group is those who are called 'dervishler.' They are monks who are held in high esteem by them as descendents and followers of the saints, as protectors of the entire realm, and as friends of God and Muhammad.

Much was said of them in Chapter 13.[42] Their opinion is that the law is not useful but that it is the grace of God that allows all men to be saved. This grace, which they call 'rachmatallach,' is sufficient for salvation without merit or law. Neither is their opinion based in reason or authority but they try to demonstrate it by signs and wonders, as was seen above in Chapter 20.[43] They, too, have many patrons and supporters, especially among those who live a more spiritual and devotional life.

The third group are those who are called 'czofilar.' They emphasize meditation and spiritual exercises and have a great reputation as the successors of the prophets and fathers who founded this sect. They are said to have a greater authority than the others. Neither do they have any basis for their opinions, except that they are said to have come from the ancient tradition. Their opinion is that everyone ought to be saved by merit and this is sufficient for salvation with grace or the law. This is called 'pereketetallach.'[44] They are greatly concerned with special prayers, spiritual exercises, vigils, and meditation. They never cease from doing continual prayer which they call 'czikir aitmach.'[45] At night they come together and sit in a circle saying 'Laylachillalach.'[46] They repeat this for some time, coordinating it with a movement of their heads. After this they say 'lahu' in the same manner. In the end they repeat 'hu, hu' until they collapse in exhaustion and fall asleep. Their opinion has many supporters, especially among those who pride themselves in their ancestry and nobility. These are called 'Eflieler embieler.'[47] These are considered to be genuine because they do not permit their kind to mix with any other nation and have not deviated from the founders of that sect.

These three groups with their opinions are known to all the people and they carry on their significant disputes both privately and publicly. Nevertheless, because each one is considered to be equal by all the people, one is not able to prevail over the others, but they are continuously forced to keep peace and concord.

A fourth kind is called 'horife'[48] in their language and are considered to be heretics. Their opinion is that everyone is saved according to his own law and that God has given to each people a law by which they must be saved. Each law is equally good for those who observe it; one is not to be preferred or is worse than the other. The Turks are suspicious of this group and consider them to be schismatics. If they are found, they are burned. As a result, they don't proclaim their opinions but keep them private. I met one of this kind when I was in Chios. He entered the church of the Christians, made the sign of the cross, sprinkled holy water on himself and openly said, 'Your law is better than ours.' No Turk who holds one of the other opinions would do this; it would cost him his life.

Having found, experienced, and truly proved such divisions in this sect, who in their right mind would not find it empty of all truth, or better who would not find it full of the devil and all superstition and would not consider it foundationless and condemn it as having no merit?

Chapter 21: Concerning the Second and Third Reasons for Bringing Someone Back From the Errors of the Turks, Namely Their Ignorance and Stubbornness

The second reason through which we clearly see the argument that the Turks are unbelievers is ignorance. Although they may be very astute in the carrying out of all evil and in natural things they have great, even supernatural skill and experience, nevertheless concerning those things which pertain to salvation and the knowledge of spiritual things, they are both ignorant and foolish. It seems as if they lack the use of reason like they were beasts and stubborn as stones. They are not capable of possessing spiritual intelligence. None of the liberal arts are taught in their schools. All of the other sciences are so foreign to them that neither the names of them nor their understanding can be found among them. For how could they understand the acts of God, the mysteries and the sacraments, the nobility of the soul and its salvation, when they do not know how to give a reason for the ceremonies of their law and institutions? For if it is said to them, 'Why don't you drink wine?' or 'Why don't you eat pork?' they are completely silent or they respond with some fiction or lie or, as was stated above in Chapter 9,[49] that is makes them unclean. They have such a high regard for the washings that they do, which were discussed above in Chapter 13,[50] the prostrations and all their other ceremonies, that they think they are a means of grace and the remission of sin, and that they earn eternal life by them. Concerning sins and violations of conscience and how the soul is polluted through sin and how it is cleansed again through penance, finally, how God is offended and how He is pleased, most of all about vices and virtues, none of them show the least sign of understanding or knowledge. They praise humility and other virtues and they condemn pride and other vices but they consider these only according to natural affections and not with regard to guilt or merit. They condemn and punish by law only crimes which disturb the concord of the community or the interest of private exchange, such as robbery, murder, and such others. Other offenses, either open or hidden, great or small are neither mentioned nor confessed. For them there is neither penance nor absolution, neither correction nor final purification. They do not utilize circumcision as a means of dealing with any guilt or sin because they are completely ignorant of original sin. They circumcise only due to their superstition. They consider it to be a great insult to be called "czunetsz,"[51] that is, uncircumcised. This is why they often insult another by saying "you uncircumcised." However, it appears to me that it is more likely that they use circumcision so that the washings with water which they are required to do would not be invalidated due to some dry spot which would remain under their foreskin, as was discussed above in Chapters 10 and 13. For this reason they also carefully cut their nails and shave their hair. However, it is certain that whatever is done, is done only out of superstition. For their sons frequently die uncircumcised, and neither are they concerned that they be circumcised. This certainly would not happen if they believed it were either harmful or helpful for salvation. When you ask them about this or anything else, in order for their ignorance not to be recognized, they conceal their opinions, and speaking in obscure ways, pull a veil of excuses over themselves. The priests do this when they are asked about spiritual things or about eternal life. But when this subject comes up among the laity, it causes various frivolous or insolent remarks. With derision and mockery they say to each other: 'maybe we will have beautiful wives' and 'maybe we will have lots of sweet things to eat and drink' and so forth. If someone wanted to say something serious, he would not be able to say anything appropriate on the subject because he would not be able to find anything rational on this topic or any other in their books. As a result each of them, whether priest or unlearned, speaks out blasphemously on this according to their own ideas. They make up lots of frivolous and absurd tales and prattle on about the antichrist (who they call "tethschel"[52]), the resurrection of the dead, the last judgment, hell and purgatory, all invented according to whatever they want. Among others they say: "After the judgment Muhammad will free all persons from hell of all sects and religions, leaving no one behind, because of the great power and authority which he has from God." For the sake of brevity, I do not wish to say anything else about the other innumerable fables and lies which circulate among them concerning spiritual things. Nevertheless, I do want to add this: just like in all other things, they conceal and hide their wickedness behind a veil of hypocrisy. And thus the ignorance of their priests is hidden, just like a gilded copper cup is named and thought to be gold because it is covered. For whatever they say and whatever they teach they want everyone to observe as if it were a command of God so that no one would dare in the least to contradict or resist them.

The third evidence of the unbelief of this sect is their stubbornness. For who would doubt that true faith increases the freedom of the will rather than limits it? For this reason in the Gospel the faithful are called "teachable" because they do not reject reason but use it. They reject evil after examining it by reason, and through examining the good they do not reject it. They bring forth good out of evil and turn adversity to their advantage. And all these things are done in the freedom of faith through which all things work together for good for those who are called according to his purpose to be saints. The faithless Turks do not do this but like beasts they strive to defend their sect not through rationality and argument but by means of swords and weapons because they say that this is commanded in their law. This sect has so much inherent pertinacity and stubbornness that they appear to have lost any use of reason and there does not seem to be anything which necessarily could move or bend them. For whenever something is seen, heard, or experienced which this sect does not command, they immediately condemn as insane and crazy, rejecting it and running away as if it were lethal poison. They are also incapable of any spiritual impressions, nor are any other kinds of truth able to move them. While this holds true for all, nevertheless it is especially the case for the hopeless renegade Christians whose consciences have been so blinded that it is like they have been bound with chains of iron by the devil which nothing can break. I asked one of them in private conversation "why in the name of God have you done this? What compelled you?" He was not able to respond other than to say "It was an evil day when I did this." I responded, "Why don't you return to Christian faith?" Shaking his head, he answered "It's not possible, not possible," and would say no more.

There are other things not less indicative of their stubbornness which should be noted. To be sure, there are no other nations among which are found no converts to Christian faith. But concerning this perverse people, it is held to be impossible for an adult to be converted to Christianity. As was said above in Chapter 16,[53] it would be considered to be greater than a miracle for this to happen. In the first year of Pope Sixtus IV when a naval expedition was launched against the Turks, many of them were brought to Rome. The better ones were presented to the Pope and the rest of them designated for the prelates of the curia. All were baptized. I came to know some of them. They demonstrated great devotion for the Christian faith, and as an interpreter asked me for confession and communion. I heard confession from one of them but I asked his priest to withhold communion from him because I was not convinced of the veracity of his conversion. Events proved me correct. For after some years they all found means and occasion to flee despite the fact that those in the papal court were well taken care of. By this it was made manifest that they had agreed to baptism falsely. From whence the opinion which I already had was now established beyond doubt: that it is impossible for a Turk to become a Christian.

Chapter 23: Concerning the Advantages of the Christian Religion

In the preceding the very briefest summary of the sect of the Turks has been given, namely how it is lacking all basis of truth, the evil and malice by which they persecute Christians, the reasons why they are persuaded that it is true, and how one can be brought back from them—and the description and interpretation of all these things with examples. Now in this last chapter I think I should describe the most holy religion of the Christians most briefly, so that any believer can compare its truth with the errors of that sect and can recognize clearly which one to choose and which one to detest. No tongue can sufficiently praise and glorify the most holy and worthy Christian law as it ought to be, nevertheless as much as the present material requires, I intend to commend it most briefly in seven main points. . . .

Notes

1. HRE Sigismund died Dec 9, 1437.
2. Septem Castra or Siebenbürgen.

3. Today Sebes in Romania.
4. This is Vlad II Dracul.
5. 619–625.
6. 610–641.
7. 847–855.
8. The Frankish emperor, 850–875.
9. In reality, the lands of Karaman had been subjected to the Ottoman Empire beginning in 1466.
10. Timur the Lame at the Battle of Ankara, 1402.
11. In reality, the Ottomans held territory in Europe as early as 1353.
12. Lat: Fortuna (fate).
13. Lat: animal irrationale.
14. Gr. collaphisando.
15. Lat: sed de hoc modicum dixi.
16. Lat: traditam in manus et in fauces luporum.
17. Lat: suo insaciabili desiderio aliqualiter satisfiat.
18. That is, Asiatic Turkey.
19. Lat: iam non est locus venie.
20. This refers to the first section of Albania captured by the Turks.
21. Serbia, from the name of the Serbian King Lazar Grebjanovic and his successors.
22. Between the Drav and Save Rivers in Croatia.
23. Ps 54:22.
24. 1 Cor 15:33.
25. That is, ejaculation.
26. Turk: cünüp, that is, ritually unclean (after intercourse).
27. Lat: ad secreta nature perficienda.
28. Matthew 5:28.
29. Genesis 3:16.
30. Lat: Mechometus.
31. Lat: parrochiano.
32. Gignasia; that is, high schools.
33. Lat: non habetur alie provisiones.
34. Lat: qualis enim lex tales et sacerdotes, et quails cultus, tales ministri.
35. Lat: ludere.
36. Lat: Nec caret misterio.
37. Correct: 7:20.
38. Lat: ita ut nemo posit saluvari nisi mediante gratia eorum.
39. Lat: Mechometistas.
40. Correct: 7.
41. Turk: hamayli for talisman.
42. Correct 14.
43. Correct 21.
44. Turkish-arabic: Bereketullah, the blessing of God.
45. Turk: zikir ayitmak, to recite the religious formulas.
46. That is, the first line of the *shahadah*.
47. Turk: eviya, saint; embiya, prophet.
48. Turk: hurufi, the name of a sect, from huruf, 'letter.'
49. Correct 10.
50. Correct 10.
51. Turk: sünnetsiz, uncircumcised.
52. Turk: Deccal, the antichrist.
53. Correct 17.

Appendix 3

Selections from Bartholomew Georgijevic, *De afflictione tam captivorum quam etiam sub Turcae tributo viventium Christianorum* [On the Afflictions of the Captive Christians Living Under the Tribute of the Turks] and *De Turcarum ritu et caeremoniis* [On the Rituals and Ceremonies of the Turks]

How Christians Captured in War Against the Turks Are Handled

When the Emperor of the Turks goes on campaign against Christians, among other merchants there is always a large group of slave traders riding camels. In hope of captives they carry long chains in which easily 50 or 60 in a row can be fettered together. Those not slain by the sword of the enemy are sold to these pillagers;[1] this is permitted by their law. If they give a tenth to the Emperor, they can either keep the remaining captives for their own use or sell them. There are no richer or more common merchants than these slave traders. This is just as in the time of the Romans, who bought this kind of merchandise openly and honestly, without having to fear a loss of legal title (this was called the "res mancipi"[2]).

For What Things the Captives Sent to the Turkish Emperor Are Intended

Old and young of both sexes which are due to him as a tenth are divided. The older ones are sold for agricultural use, although these are seldom among the captives as they rarely spare them, as they consider older people to be hardly marketable. Girls, however, and young men are sent to a certain place which is called Sarai in their language in order that they be taught certain skills which will be used later.[3] First of all they urge them to repudiate the Christian faith [*Christiana fide*] and be circumcised. After they are initiated into the Turkish ceremonies, through a careful study of the slaves' physiognomy and bodily features to discern their innate qualities, they are sent either to learn law or to the military if bodily strength appears to be their best quality. They are given a stipend of two or three Ahtse per day.[4] This is enough to buy food and clothing until a campaign begins. Their basic training consists of the following: to build the strength of the youths they are given first a light bow then heavier and heavier ones as their strength and skill grows until they are fit for battle. An incredibly strict trainer requires daily exercises, and they are whipped once for each miss of the target. These are enrolled under the order called SOLACLAR or archers.[5] Others are trained to be IENIZARI.[6] These have their own instructor who daily makes them spar in pairs with staves. The remainder are used for evil. The better looking ones have all traces of manliness removed from their entire bodies, at grave peril to their lives. If they survive, they are not otherwise harmed and are made to serve the most wicked lusts. As soon as they lose their beauty through aging, they are made eunuchs. These either serve the women, or are assigned to take care of the horses and mules or serve in the kitchens.

What Is Done With the Girls and the Rest of the Women

The spectacularly beautiful women are chosen to be concubines. The middling sort are given to serve as attendants of the wives. There they must do filthy services of which it is not proper to speak.[7] For they must follow the wives when they go to evacuate their bowels with a pitcher of water and clean them afterward. Others are given various tasks, some spin and weave, some work at milling. None of them are freed. None remain Christians, or have any hope of liberation as long as they live.

What the Rest of the Turks Do With Their Captives

So far, I have stated what the Turkish Emperor does with his slaves, now on to the common Turks. As soon as they get them they use all kinds of threats, promises, and flattery on these recent captives so that they will allow themselves to be circumcised. Those that are circumcised are treated somewhat more humanely, but all hope of a return home is destroyed—the penalty for attempting to do so is to be burned. Because these are believed to be more loyal and less likely to attempt escape, they are used by their owners on campaign. Eventually they get their freedom, either in old age[8] when they are dismissed (or rather thrown aside) by their owners, or during war if their owners grant it to them in the heat of battle. They are permitted to marry, but their children can be sold according to the will of their masters. Knowing this, they avoid marriage. Those that refuse to be circumcised are considered savages. I can vouch for this due to thirteen years of misery—words cannot express how horrible this kind of life is.

What Is Done With Christians Who Know No Craft or Trade

Those who learned no trade or craft have the hardest lot, for there craftsmen alone are held in honor. For this reason, it is most wretched for scholars, priests, and the idle rich—if they fall into the hands of the Turks. The slave traders consider them to be almost un-sellable and spend no money on their maintenance. Neither their heads nor their feet are covered and frequently they go about almost entirely naked. When their fancy clothes are stripped from them nothing is given to replace them. They are dragged through snow and hail, summer and winter, and this doesn't end until either they die or find a foolish master who buys what they consider to be bad goods. In addition, no one is so lucky, no matter if married, old, knowledgeable, or good looking, that if he or she gets sick during a journey that they are put in a hostel. First, they are forced by whip to go on, if that isn't possible, they are put on a mule. If they can't sit, they are tied on, like any other sack or piece of baggage. If they die, they are dragged off by their clothes and thrown into a near-by pit or hollow for the dogs and vultures.

How the New Captives Are Transported

The captives are not only tied together on long chains, but during transport their hands are bound by manacles. There is a gap between each one so that they don't trample each other. They do this so that they are not stoned by the captives. Since each slave trader can lead a large number of slaves this way, ten traders often have 500 slaves chained together. They fear the power of such a multitude, if they would have their hands free to throw something. In addition, when night falls, their feet are also bound, and they must lie down exposed to all the hazards of the open air. The condition of women is more humane. The stronger are marched on foot. The more tender are carried by mule. Those who are so sick that they cannot ride are carried like geese in baskets. Night is more wretched for them, for either they are imprisoned in the camp, or they suffer the impure lusts of the slave traders. A great wailing is heard through the darkness from the young of both sexes as they endure this violence. Even six and seven year olds cannot escape the misery of this great wickedness. This is the kind of violence that these vile people do by lusts against nature.

How the Slaves Who Are to Be Sold Are Handled

At dawn the slaves are led to the market like a flock of sheep or goats. The merchants gather and determine the price. If a slave interests a buyer, they are stripped and inspected by the future owner. Every limb is examined, poked and prodded; no defect of joint or limb is left unexposed. If the slave is not acceptable, they are sent back to the trader. They must endure this many times, over and over until someone buys them. If the slave is acceptable, they are taken away to hard labor as a plowman or shepherd, not to mention even harder labors. There are many examples of unspeakable misery. On the other hand, I never saw men bound to a yoke and dragging a plow. The slave girls are strictly cloistered and put to perpetual labor; they are cut off from their husbands and not even permitted conversation with fellow slaves. If a mother and children are captured, the nobles like to buy them. They put them in charge of their country estates where they care for the fields, vineyards or flocks. Anyone born of a slave becomes a slave. If a slave remains Christian, after a certain period of service they are freed. However, unless ransomed, their sons remain slaves subject to the will of the master, either remaining where they were or sent to another place. For the slaves do not have a specific place to which they are assigned for the term of their service. If they want to return to their fatherland after they have gained their freedom, they are given a certificate. But those who renounce our religion are not given a specific term of servitude nor any right to return to their homeland. Their hope of liberation is solely dependant upon the will of their lord. When they do obtain their freedom, they must pay the tenth[9] like other Turks, but they are free from the rest of the burdens which oppress the Christians.

Concerning Those Captives Who Are Made Shepherds

The life of the farmworker is hard, but the life of those bought to be shepherds is harder still. They must live in solitude, the entire day and night under the open sky. The lord and his wife alone stay in tents. In addition to their duties of watching the flocks, in their spare time they must weave carpets and gather supplies. Every month they change pastures, going from mountain to mountain. Those masters who are more humane give some pay to the slaves, termed "*dimensum*" by the Romans.[10] This is granted to them as their own property, and is either kept for traveling money if they want to return home after they have been granted their freedom, or used for the necessities of life. This is not done everywhere, but is the kind of enticement which keeps the wretched slaves from thinking about escape. They are not so indulgent to those who deny Christ and are circumcised, because they are sure that they will not flee.

The Flight of Captives Out of European Turkey

It is easier to escape for those who go to European Turkey than for those who are sold to the regions across the sea. This is because there are only rivers which are nothing to be crossed and can easily be swum, but it is very difficult to cross the Hellespont. Whoever tries to escape usually does it at harvest time, for it is both easy to hide in the grain field and nourishment is at hand. They flee at night; during the day they hide either in forest, swamp, or field. And they prefer to be eaten by wolves or other beasts than to be returned to their old masters.

The Flight Out of Asia Minor

Those who undertake escape from Asia head for the Hellespont, between Gallipoli and the fortresses formerly known as Seston and Abidon,[11] now called Bogazassar,[12] meaning fortresses at the neck of the sea, for this is where the sea is most narrow. These carry with them an axe and rope in order to cut down and bind together trees from which they make a raft to cross the sea. Taking salt with them, they board the raft by night. If they are favored by the winds and fortune of the sea, they cross in three or four hours. But if not, either they perish in the waters or are driven back to the Asian shore. Having passed through the sea, they head for the mountains. Looking toward the North Star and the constellation Boötes, they head north. When they get hungry, they use herbs seasoned with their salt to sustain themselves. If they are escaping as a group, at night they attack shepherds, whom they kill. They find supplies there and take them with them. Often they are killed by the shepherds, or captured by them and handed back to their original owners to be returned to their former servitude. The majority are consumed from the many perils suffered over a long time. Few survive shipwreck, or the teeth of beasts, or the swords of enemies, or they perish from extreme hunger because of the long wanderings of their flight.

Concerning the Punishment of Fugitives

There are many different penalties for fugitives. Some are hung by their feet and whipped so severely that it brings about their death. Others have multiple furrows cut into the souls of their feet and salt put into the wounds. Others have an iron collar put around their necks to which is attached a huge iron bar which they have to drag about day and night for a long time.

On the Kindness of the Greeks and Armenians Toward the Captives

The death penalty and the confiscation of all possessions is inflicted on those who help the captives escape. Nevertheless this does not stop the Armenians and Greeks from hiding captives, and in disguise, leading them to the ships of the Venetians or other Christians. And they give them nourishment and every necessity, not omitting any sort of kindness. For they say that they experience our kindness if ever they come to Rome or Compostella.

Concerning Turkish Incantations Against Fugitives

They have a kind of incantation which draws fugitives back against their will. They write the name of the slave on a piece of paper and hang it in the tent or house of the slave. Then they speak fearful words and cast spells against the slave that through demonic power the fugitive would think that he was encountering lions or dragons in the way, or that the sea or rivers rise up against him, or that darkness would overwhelm him so that in terror he would be driven back and return to his master.

How the Memory of Christ Is Being Effaced Little by Little in Formerly Christian Provinces

There are still some alive who remember the capture of Constantinople and the kingdoms of the Greeks, Albania, Walachia, Serbia (which the Turks call Bosnia). They have been driven into the provinces but they hold tenaciously to Christ. However, the young people are forgetting the faith and in a short time Christianity will be completely obliterated. Likewise the same will happen in Croatia, Hungary, and Slavonia which have been recently been put under the authority of Turkish imperialism.

The Situation of Those Attacked

When a province is captured, all goods of the inhabitants, both fixed and movable, become booty. Noble lineages are destroyed, especially royal branches. And now they control the son of the Viovode, for no other reason than if Hungary is taken from them, they will send him in to initiate some new uprising. When they have Hungary as a secure possession there is no doubt that they will kill him, for in Turkey in this kind of thing neither birth, nor relations, not even brotherhood is respected. If the clergy are not killed outright, all wealth and dignity are stripped from them, leaving them laughingstocks and beggars. All bells and organs, and other church musical instruments are seized; indeed they desecrate those churches and consecrate them to their Muhammad.[13] They leave poor, little shrines to the Christians, where the sacred rites may be done, although not publicly, but secretly and quietly. If they are toppled by earthquake, or burned in a fire, or decay through time, it is not lawful to rebuild them unless a great amount of money is given out. Preaching and proclaiming the Gospel is completely prohibited. Neither is any Christian[14] permitted to handle or bear arms, or adopt the same dress as Turks, or be festive, eat or dance publicly. If either they or Christ is abused by the most insulting words, they have to remain silent and endure it. But in contrast, if you speak slanderously against their religion, you are circumcised by force. Moreover if you speak against Muhammad,[15] fire and flames are prepared for you.

Concerning the Respect That Christians Show Toward the Turks

If a Christian rides up to a *Musulmannum*, that is, one initiated into the religion of the Turks, it is necessary that he gets off his horse, and with his face to the ground pay his respects to the seated Turk. If he does not, he is knocked from his horse by a blow from a staff. In addition, by law the messengers and emissaries of the Turks can seize a Christian's horse and use it to the point of exhaustion while the Christian follows on foot.

Concerning the Tribute of the Christians

Christians must give a fourth of all they produce. And this fourth is collected not only from the produce of the fields and flocks, but also craftsmen must pay a fourth of their profits. Then there is the other burden of a head tax of a single ducat per member of the family. If the parents cannot pay, their children are forced to be sold into slavery. Others are bound in chains and go from door to door begging for money, because if they cannot be freed by this, they are sold into perpetual slavery. In addition to all the other obligations which they must pay, the Turks always have the right to select the best children, whom they circumcise. And they take them away from their parents and raise them in the army, nor do they ever return to their parents. And right away, because this happens easily to a child, he forgets Christ. Soon he even forgets his parents and blood relations, and this to such a degree that even if he lives among them, he does not recognize any of them. Words cannot describe the tears, groans, and sobbing caused by this separation. A child is dragged away to live ever more among foreigners. Whatever love is caused by blood, dearness by association, friendship by familiarity, all this is left behind and they are counted among those who are called "the fatherless" and "the motherless" by the Greeks.[16] The father who trained his child in Christian ritual sees him seized to become a soldier of Satan fighting against Christ.

How Priests and Monks Live Under the Turks

The situation for priests and monks is the worst, as they are considered to be a sacrilege and a scandal to God and man. They get nothing from the church. On Fridays a little bit of bread is given them by some women; they are given nothing on the other days. They live by collecting firewood, for it is their custom to put deadwood from the forest on the backs of donkeys and to take this as merchandise through the streets calling out "wood for sale." If these people would have known in advance what kind of calamity awaited them, they would have preferred a thousand deaths than to suffer this way. If anywhere death is mixed with life, indeed, if anywhere life goes on for a long time so that one may die for a long time, it is in Turkey. No Egyptian bondage, Babylonian exile, African captivity, or Roman devastation can be compared with this misery where daily is heard the lamentations of Jeremiah, not just in words, but in reality.

Proclamation of the Captives and Tributaries to the Kings and Princes of the Christians

The wretched who are living like those in that fiery furnace of Ur of the Chaldeans entreat heaven with prayers and groans: How long will you sleep,

O God? Rise up and reject us not forever. Turn your eyes from heaven to our fatherland, bound in slavery. Although banished from their fatherland, they desire to serve their fatherland. Their prayer is not for liberation, but just to serve in a different place. Next they turn their eyes to the Christian kings and princes. They desire the Pope as the father of the fatherland to turn the power of his holiness to the liberation of his children. They desire the invincible fist of the Emperor to move his conquering forces against the Turk. They know that in war the Spanish are most keen, the Belgians most ferocious, the Germans most strong, and the Italians surpass all physically and mentally. They know that his brother Ferdinand King of the Romans is devoted to war against the Turks and, supported by Illyrian and Subalpine peoples, is very familiar with fighting them. They know that all Germany, so many imperial electors, equipped as powerfully as kings, willingly follow the leadership of the Emperor. Therefore they consider their prayers not to be in vain. Invincible Emperor, they consider that you will be as their Ezra and as their Joshua. For so many prophecies about you are circulating, not only among Christians, but also among the pagans. If only you would allow them to enter your army, you would see everyone springing to arms with you. No age, gender, or rank would be absent from your forces. In the house of each and every Turk would be assassins among his slaves. The Turk would have traitors in the fortresses and deserters in battle. For all Christians who are there hold the forces of the Turks in highest contempt, as they recognize that the Turks are fit only for irregular combat. They attack their enemies like one shoots a bird from a distance with missiles. If their enemies do not flee in terror, the Turks themselves flee. Except for shield and helmet they are mostly unarmored. They do not dare to come to hand to hand combat. They cannot wound anyone except at a distance. But if now the Venetians and the Portuguese would gather their naval forces, the princes of the English, Poles, et cetera, especially those who govern under the authority of the emperor, not for long would Suleiman be able to resist Charles, as Darius could not Alexander, as Xerxes could not Themistocles, and as Antiochus could not resist Judas Maccabaeus. This is what all the Christian captives think. Likewise, I learned in thirteen years of experience that the Turks are certainly most courageous in fleeing and are quick to run away from invaders. The Turks are therefore naturally prone to flee when they should fight. For the ungodly flee when no one is pursuing them. May God arise and cause his enemies to scatter, and may those that hate him flee from his face. Just as smoke vanishes, may they fade away; just as wax melts before the fire, so are sinners destroyed before the face of God. If only the great and mighty God would allow that monster the Turk, a mockery of human nature, to be suppressed and worn down by your power, invincible emperor, so that you might release to freedom the Christians oppressed by this heavy tyranny. For after God, in you alone all hope of liberty is bound together. The End. Praise be to God.

ON THE RITUALS AND CEREMONIES OF THE TURKS

Their Origin

The historians of the Armenians say that the Turks are a Scythian people, the Zmaildan, a kind of Ishmaelite. They were led through the Caspian Mountains and the Caucasus Pass up to Constantinople by a leader of a certain King of Armenia [in order to betray and injure him by carrying off these soldiers.][17] But I will not spin out the tale of their origin at length but I will only put down that which I experienced with my own eyes concerning the ceremonies, household structure and military, using nothing borrowed from other authors. Rather I have written down with the greatest care, according to my extremely limited and modest talent, only that which I saw before me and learned by long association.

Concerning the Origins of Muhammad

There is a great amount of uncertainty concerning the origin of Mehemmet (whom we call Mahomet).[18] Nor can it be known for sure whether he was a Persian or an Arab.[19] Nevertheless, they are correct who hold that he was an Ishmaelite from royal stock, whom they call OTHMANNI SAI and SVLTANLAR. At his birth they say that five thousand idol temples toppled. This omen predicted our decline, or rather pretended to predict our decline.

Of Their Temples

They have many large and sumptuous temples which are called MESCHIT in their language. In these temples there are no images at all except these words inscribed in the Arab language: LA ILLAH ILELLAH MEHEMMET IRESVL ALLAH TANRE BIR PEGAMBER HACH, that is, "there is no God except the One and Mehemmet is his prophet, one creator and equal prophets." Or this: FILA GALIB ILELLAH, which is, "nothing is as strong as God." After that one notices a great abundance of lamps burning with oil, the entire temple whitewashed, the pavement covered by a matting of rushes and ornate carpets. Around the temple are amazingly high towers which the priests ascend at the time of prayer. In a loud voice with their fingers in their ears, they repeat these words three times: ALLAH HECHBER, which is, there is one true God. Hearing this call, both noble and commoners gather in the temple for their required devotions. Then the aforementioned priest descends and prays with them for they are required by office to do this five times through the day and night. Whoever comes to prayer is required to wash their hands, feet, and privates, and finally to sprinkle water on their head, reciting these words: ELHEMDV LILLAHI, that is, glory to my God. Then, taking off their shoes (called PATSMAGH) and leaving them in front of the temple door, they go in, some with bare feet and others having clean shoes called MESTH which don't ever touch the earth. The women never gather with the men, but rather separately in a certain place where they are completely secluded from the sight and hearing of the men. And they rarely frequent the temple, except during Easter time and sometimes on Fridays which are called GSVMAAGVN in their language. They pray from the ninth hour of the night to the twelfth, or midnight. And during their prayers to an amazing degree they torment their bodies by continuous agitation and exclamations until often they lose their strength and consciousness and fall prone on the ground. If any from that moment perceive themselves to be pregnant, they claim that they have been impregnated by the grace of the Holy Spirit. And when they give birth these children are called NEFCS OGLV, that is, spirits, or sons of the Holy Spirit. This was told to me by one of their maids, for I myself did not see this, neither is it permitted that any man be present at this spectacle. But I was often at the men's prayers with my master, as was his custom. During prayer they do not remove their hats (which are called TSALMA in their language), but hold them with the tips of their fingers, as if they were going to raise them, and falling on their knees frequently kiss the ground. They consider it an abomination if a Christian is present during their prayers, for they believe (as they themselves say) that their temples are contaminated by filthy men, and certainly Christians according to their custom do not do frequent washings. Then their priest goes up into the pulpit and preaches for about two hours. After the sermon is finished two boys ascend and sing their prayers. After their song, the priest with all the people begins to sing in a low voice, turning their bodies from side to side, these words alone: LA ILLAH ILELLAH, that is, there is only one God and for almost half an hour he chants and moves. But this kind of prayers and ceremonies, as singing and preaching, is not used every day, except in the time of Lent and festivals, for example Thursday from the ninth to the twelfth hour at night. And likewise on Friday (on which Muhammad was said to have been born) which by some is most religiously observed.

Of Their Lent

Likewise, they have a Lent which is called ORVTZ in their language,[20] they fast a month and a week every year, but not always at the same time. But if (as for example this year) they fast in January, the following year they fast in February, so that in the course of twelve years one year and twelve weeks are offered to God in place of the tenth.[21] When they fast, they ingest nothing at all the entire day, neither bread nor water. When they can see the stars, it is permitted for them to eat everything, except if the animal had been strangled, or the flesh of swine. Strangled animals are called MVRDAR, that is, a dead body or unclean. Pork is called DVMVZ. When the Lent is complete they celebrate Easter, which is called BAIRAM in their language,[22] with great solemnity for three days. They anoint the nails of their hands and feet with a certain ointment called CHNA[23] which turns the nails red. Likewise they dip their horses' tails and hooves in the same stain. This pigment binds extremely well and can neither be washed nor wiped off. Otherwise, unless new nails grow from the roots, they always look red. But frequent washings will remove it from the hands. Women not only stain their nails, but also their hands and feet with this ointment.

Of Their Circumcision

They circumcise (which is called TSVNETH in their language) not on the eighth day as is the custom of the Jews, but seven or eight years after birth when he is able to speak well. This is because their rite requires a verbal confession before the circumcision while raising the thumb of his hand (called PARMACH[24]), namely that described above as displayed in the temples. But the boy is not brought to the temple, but is circumcised in his parent's home. I have often been to these celebrations which they do in this manner. First they gather friends and neighbors for whom plenty of fine dishes are prepared from all the different kinds of meats that are permissible for them, and everywhere (if they are rich enough) they slaughter an ox. After skinning and cleaning it, they put a sheep in it which has a chicken in it which has an egg in it. These are roasted together in honor of that day. Then, during the serving of the courses of the banquet, the boy who is to be circumcised is led in. A physician of this specialty uncovers the head of his penis and securing the skin with pincers, folds it back. Then to allay the fears of the boy, says that the circumcision will take place the following day and leaves. He quickly returns, though, pretending that he has forgotten something that must be done in preparation, and suddenly cuts off the foreskin. He puts a little salt in the wound and applies some quince fruit.[25] Henceforth he is called MVTSLVMAN—that is, circumcised. Their names are not given at circumcision, but on the day of their birth when they are brought into the light.[26] The names are such as these: first the king, TSVLEIMAN, meaning Solomon. TSVLTAN, TSCELIM which is prince of peace.[27] MVRATH BEGH, that is, a desired ruler.[28] MVTSTAFA and similar. Leaders, PIRIN, HAIRADVN, HADER, EBRAIM. Lesser lords are like these: TSPAHA-LAR, TSAVSLAR, EMINLER, BEHRAM, MEMMI, MEHEMMET, ALLI, AHMAT, TCIELEBI, PAIAZITH, CHATSVN, HVTSCREF. And for all the others: MVTSA, IONVZ, TSCHENDER, PERHAT, FERRO. The majority of captives and servants are called SEREMETH, which signifies bold and quick. After feasting for three continuous days, the circumcised boy is led to the baths with the greatest pomp. When he returns home, he is led by the guests who give him presents they have prepared. Some give silk garments, others give silver cups, others money or even a horse. The women also give him tunics, handkerchiefs and other things like this. Each guest gives according to his desire and ability. Women are not circumcised, but only confessing the previously mentioned words, are made MVSLVMAN. But if any Christian willingly confesses Muhammad, he is circumcised, which often happens because of the heavy yoke and onerous tribute. These are led through the streets and boulevards of the city with the greatest honor and to the joy of the people accompanied by the sound of drums. And a small gift is given to them, and afterward are freed from paying tribute, which is called HARACS in their language. And greedy for this lucre, many Greeks, called VRVMLAR[29] and Albanians, who are called ARNAVTLAR[30] are circumcised. If he is compelled to be circumcised by force, as for example because he struck a Muslumanum, or afflicted one with reproach, or blasphemed Mehemmetum (as I saw happen to a bishop of the Greek sect), none of this is given to him, but he is nevertheless released from the tribute and is free, just as the other MVSLVMANLAR, that is circumcised.

Of Their Priests

Truly the priests, called TALISMANLAR in their language, are distinguished from the laity by little or nothing, for neither are ceremonies by their leaders (like by bishops for us) required nor is great knowledge of their doctrine. It will be enough if they are able to read the Elcoranum and Mussaphum. But those who are able to interpret according to the text are held to be highly skilled, because it is not the common language of the Turks, but Arabic from Mehemmeto in which these are handed down. It is considered to be blasphemy if interpretations are transcribed in the common language. These ecclesiastical leaders are chosen by the people, but they receive a stipend for their work from the king. They have wives and are dressed as the laity. If their stipend is not enough because of the number of their children, they work a trade befitting the dignity of a free man like becoming a schoolmaster or transcribing books. Among them I saw no printing press, but they make the best paper. Others earn profit as a tailor, shoemaker, or similar.

Of Their Schools

And they have places for instruction called OCHVMACHGIRLERI[31] in their language. Their teachers, called HOGSIALAR, instruct both males and females, although separately: men teach the males and women teach the females. They teach astronomy, philosophy, and the art of poetry. During their lessons they call out in loud voice, turning their bodies from side to side. They don't know artificial music, but produce verse according to prescribed rules, which are: no matter the verse, each line must contain eleven syllables. And so it pleased me to include these small examples:

Verses Which They Call BETHLER
Birichen bes on eiledum derdumi
Iaradandan istemiscem iardumi

Terch eiledum zahmanumi gurdumi
Ne ilem ieniemezum gunglumi

These are love verses of their goddess called ASSICH,[32] that is goddess of love, of which the following is a word for word interpretation:

> Birechen is: out of one. Bes is: five. On is: ten. Eiledum is: made. Derdumi is: in my troubles.
>
> Iaradandan is: from the creator. Istemiscem is: I asked. Iardumi is: help.
>
> Terch eiledum is: I neglected. Zahmanumi is: of my country. Gurdumi is: a visit.
>
> Ne is: what. Ileim is: could I do. Ieniemezum is: I was not able to conquer. Gunglumi is: my mind.

Of Their Monks

Also, they don't lack monks. These are called DERVISLAR, in three different orders. The first order possesses no property and goes about almost naked, excepting their pudenda which they cover with a sheepskin hide (in cold weather they cover their backsides with a similar hide). Their sides, hands, feet, and head are never covered at all. They beg alms from Christians as well as Turks, saying ALLAHITSI,[33] that is, for the sake of God. They consume an herb called MATSLACH[34] that makes them so insensible that they can cut themselves across [or through] their entire breast or arm as if they felt no pain. From a tree they take a fungus, and lighting it on fire, they hold it against their head, breast, or hands, until it is turned to ash. The second order I saw[35] bores a hole through the penis and inserts a three-pound[36] copper ring to prevent coitus in order to preserve their chastity. The third order rarely goes out, but remains night and day in their temples. They have little shelters in the nooks and corners and have no shoes, clothing, or head coverings, except for a long shirt. They pray and fast for days on end that God would give them a revelation of the future, for the Turkish Emperor consults them when he goes on campaign.

Of Marriage Contracts

Marriage, called EVLENMECH in their language, is like this. They unite in marriage without an oath. They receive them entirely without a dowry and are pretty much forced to buy them, contrary to custom (which was formerly done among the Romans) where the son-in-law alone is bought, not the daughter-in-law. The bride has nothing in bodily adornment or ornament which he is not forced to purchase from the father-in-law. Divorce among them is because of moral impropriety or infertility. Their judges[37] are knowledgeable in these things. Also, marriage is permitted among servants, but the offspring of these unions become slaves.

Of Their Pilgrims

Pilgrims, called HAGSILAR[38] in their language, visit places where their saints have lived, namely MECHAM (like our Jerusalem) where Mehemmetum is said to have died. They do this, though, not less out of a desire for gain as for religion or devotional sake. Having seen a gilded shoe called TSAROCH[39] hanging from the vault of the temple, they buy the most intricate weavings, called CHVMAS, and return home with great gain. And when they are going back, some for devotion sake carry water skins in the streets, freely offering it to the thirsty that they meet along the way, while others go about their business.

Of Their Almsgiving

They have hostels called IMARET, founded by the legacy of the king, where food is given to the poor and to pilgrims. Elsewhere other things are given: places called PIRINCTS TSORBA[40] give rice with meat, elsewhere BOGH-DAIAS[41] which is made of wheat. For provisions they include plenty of bread. The drink which is supplied is water. Let me add, it is not permitted for them to spend the night there or sleep, but they have other places open to the public to spend the night called CHARVATSANRIE where they can receive free hospitality. These do not have beds, but they can sleep on hay or straw under a roof.

Of Their Sacrifices

They also offer sacrifices, but more often as votives, called CHORBAN in both Turkish and Arabic. In times of disease or danger, each according to his means, promises to sacrifice a sheep or ox in a particular place. The promised offering is not burned whole as was the custom of the Jews, but the hide, head, feet and a fourth part of the flesh of the slaughtered animal is given to the priest. Then the other parts are given to the poor, a third to neighbors.[42] Anything remaining is prepared by the ones who do the sacrifice for themselves and their companions to eat. They are not held to their vow if they are not saved from the disease or danger. For all of their sacrifices are conditional: I give if you will give. And similar rituals are observed by Greeks and Armenians and other Asian nations of the Christian religion.

Of Legacies and Testaments

If any dying Muslim[43] intends to set up a will, friends and neighbors are called in. Almost always the legacy is either to bring water from a distant place to some hospital or temple or an arid place frequented by men. These are called HAIRITSI—that is pious goodwill, or GSIANITSI, that is for the soul. Others as a legacy liberate slaves and the servants they have purchased.

Foolish women (as this kind is more superstitious than others) bequeath money to soldiers to kill a certain number of Christians. They consider this to be greatly advantageous for the salvation of their souls. Kings order temples and hospitals to be built, as do the other powerful men.

Of Funeral Rites

When one of the Muslims[44] dies, if a male, then men are responsible for the funeral rites, if a female, then women are responsible. They wash the body and clothe it in the brightest linen. Afterwards they carry it outside the city to a separate place, for it is impious to bury in the temples. Taper-bearers and monks with candles go in front, priests follow, singing softly, until they arrive at the place of burial. If the deceased was poor, they are accustomed to collect money and give it to the religious for their work.

Of Tombs Called TVLBE

Temples are built (for example by kings) over tombs, for the kings are buried in cities. The tombs of rich and poor are the height of an altar so that animals cannot jump on them or defile the place. Often they return there in lament, and put on them offerings of food to the dead: bread, meat, cheese, eggs, milk. This feast lasts nine days, according to the custom of the pagans. This food is eaten by the poor, or birds of the sky, or ants, for the soul of the deceased. For they say that it is equally pleasing to God to offer alms to the brute animals as to humans when it is given out of love of God. I saw many release small birds, giving an amount of money equivalent to the value of the bird and having them fly off, others throw bread into the river for the fish out of love of God. They say that they will receive a great reward for such pious activity on behalf of the needy.

Of the [Rituals] of the Turks, Part II Of the Military

All of them have one king, who in their language HVNCHER OTHMAN-LARDAN SAHI TSVLTAN TSVLEIMAN, as called by them today, which means: Emperor of the Ottomans Prince Solomon. His first born son is now around twenty-three years old called MVTSTAFA. He excels his forebears in tyranny and cruelty, often waiting in ambush for his father in order to kill him if possible out of a lust to rule. The king has under him two dukes or satraps called TSAMGIACH BEGLER, one for Europe and one for Asia, which have under them lesser leaders called TIMARGILAR to whom the ordinary soldiers are subject. If these are slow to come when they are called to campaign, they suffer the penalty of hanging. There are many BASSA-LAR, which interpreted means "head." Because they provide counsel to the king they always accompany him. And there are SVLIHTARLAR, his bodyguard who always follow behind him, together with CAPVGTSIBEGLER, that is, chamberlains, IAZIGTSIBEGLER, that is, chancellors, EMINLER, that is, tribute exactors, namely of boys and money, TSPAHALAR, that is, lightly armed cavalry, many VLACHLARIS, that is, messengers, and others of this kind who continually follow the court.

Of the Estate of the Nobility

None of the satraps possess provinces or cities as a result of the right of inheritance which after his death he may leave without consent of the king to his children or successors. But if any leader or prince desires a certain possession, it is given to him with this condition: he undertakes a reckoning of the value and it is given to him to possess. For the Turks know how many soldiers may be maintained a year by that assessment. Then that TSATRAPA has to gather that number of soldiers, having them always ready for all orders. Otherwise he loses his head. And nothing may excuse him from being present in war, except ill health. And if at any time it pleases the Turk to take away such benefices, it is within his liberty to do so. If, however, it is not taken, it is his until death. After his death, if his successors wish to observe the agreement previously made with the deceased, they are permitted. But if not, the benefice is given to others. If at some time one of these nobles wants to speak with the king, in humility they must lower their eyes, daring not to look in his face.

On the Estate of the Chazilars

The soldiers called CHAZILAR are strong and amazing in combat. At first contact they break their spears upon their enemy. They have absolutely no equipment except for a shield, spear, a sword,[45] and using them as we do, a coat of mail and helmet. When their spear breaks, they unsheathe their sword and defend themselves with their shield. They fight manfully, always striking at the head and hands of their enemies, endeavoring to destroy their enemies with all their might. It is regarded as ignominious, not praiseworthy, to strike their opponent or his horse with the point of their sword. They put their lives and safety into the care of the goddess of fortune, called NASSVP[46] in their language or CTSVTARA. This proverb is the best known among them: IAZILAN GELVR BASSINA. Translated into Latin this means: IASILAN,[47] that is, scripture; GELVR, that is, will come; BASSINA,[48] that is, on the head. As they would say, whatever the goddess of fortune inscribes on each individual's head on the day of birth is impossible to escape, even if one hides in an impregnable fortress.[49] Their deeds are written in verse in histories and recited by all in order to strengthen boldness (aroused by zeal for honor and praise) and so that they might attack their enemies fearlessly. And for all such victories, their stipend is doubled. Thus, the aforementioned cavalry are required to follow the king, equipped with their weapons: spears, swords, arrows, iron clubs. Some have shields, some not, and always receive a wage in times of peace as in war.

On Infantry

The first order of infantry is SOLACHLARVM,[50] that is archers. They use a bow, arrows, and sword, and wear a different headgear from the IANIT-SERIS. The second order is the IENITSERORUM. They have weapons similar to TSOLACHLARVM, but instead of bow and arrows the use arquebuses and an axe. They are collected from Christians who live under tribute. They are taken by force, circumcised, and educated in a place called a TSARAI. They fight against Christians most strenuously. They receive hardly enough of a wage to feed themselves, that is, some receive four, some five or six coins called AHTSE, sixty of which make a crown.[51] These are not permitted to ride horses unless sick, under pain of death. Also, there are found of the sons of the Turks many who are made IENITSERI. The third order of infantry is AZAPLARVM. Their stipends end at the end of the war and they are always sons of Turks. They use a long spear and sword, and wear a cloth cap of red or another color called TACHIA which has four crescent-shaped corners. Their uniforms and armament are different from the IEN-ICERIS and SOLACHLARIS. They strike enemy horses during battle. There are other types of infantry from Walachia of the sect of the Greeks called VOINICHLAR. These receive no stipend from the Turks, but are free from the payment of tribute or tithe. These have the responsibility to feed and care for the idle horses of the king of the Turks at their own expense and to bring them forth in times of war.

Of the Tents of the Turkish King

When the Turkish king leaves Constantinople in order to wage war, two tents, named SATORLAR, are used. When one is used, the other is set up at the next stop in order for him to be received there the following day. The magnitude of the tent is such that at a distance it seems to be a city. The princes camp next to the king's tent, surrounding it. The cavalry have their tents next, either singly or in threes. Likewise the infantry have their own tents, for they have the rule that no one sleeps under the stars. As the army is moving laborers prepare the way. These set up piles of stones or heaps of wood to show the way so that not even in the dark is it easy for them to lose their way. They move out in the middle of the night and march until noon the following day. The king marches among the cavalry between two BASSALARVM which whom he converses. They are preceded by some soldiers of the IENITSERORVM order on horses carrying burning candles. And this is done at the dark time of the night. Then TSAVSLAR, that is, captains, who have iron clubs covered with sharpened points to drive people out of the sight of the king to the distance of a throw or the flight of an arrow. There the SVLIHTARLARVM, that is, force of body-guards, among whom are wagons full of catamites for the use of the Turk and the nobles. Following and preceding the aforementioned leaders are an immense number of soldiers: cavalry, infantry, and various other orders. Some receive wages, others seek advantage and money. All are men, for no women march with them.

How Their Animals Are Cared for

Thereupon follow a multitude of camels, mules, and horses (here and there they lead elephants, called PHIL[52] in their language). These carry provisions, tents, and similar military necessities. And where the tent of the Turk is set up, everything is there ordered and set up just like a city. There are places for tailors, millers, and butchers. Some prepare dishes of all kinds of meat. If they do not have fresh meat then they use that which has been trans-ported by their animals, namely, twice-cooked bread, dried meat (called PASTARMA), cheese, and coagulated milk. They have the most incredible endurance of hunger, thirst, and cold. Rarely do they lodge in cities, but rather in tents in the field near hay and water. They are more concerned about their animals than they are about themselves. And they are content enough with a little common food, namely the aforementioned coagulated milk mixed with water and with some bread included, either fresh or twice baked. This is for the lords as well as the servants. They maintain a great silence at night; they even disregard escaping captives, not raising a clamor, so as not to incur punishment. But when they go to bed and when they arise and go out, they all cry out in a loud voice these words repeated three times: ALLAH ALLAHV, that is, O God.

Of the Exercise of Justice in War

There is such severe discipline in war, that no soldier dare seize anything unjustly, otherwise he is punished without mercy. For among them they have established custodians or defenders of things such as bread, eggs, fruit, and grain, which are carried by boys eight or ten years' old to sell along the route of the soldiers. The aforementioned officials preserve and defend the orchards situated along the way, so that no one dares to take a single apple or anything of this sort without permission of the owner. Otherwise they would pay the penalty even with their heads. When I was in the army of the Turks in campaign against the Persians, I saw a TSPAHIAM beheaded, together with his horse and servant, just because his horse had entered someone's field.

On the Celebrations When the Turks Are Victorious

When a report of victory is announced, cities break forth in all kinds of joyfulness. In the night, about the time of the first torch, they begin the triumphant festivities. Tapers, torches and candles are set up everywhere and carpets, tapestries, and silken garments cover the houses and the streets along the route of the emperor of the Turks. A proper triumph is celebrated in Constantinople, where he normally resides, as long as he is not currently waging war in other regions. Nevertheless, he is required by law at least every three years to personally undertake an expedition into Christian lands, either to enlarge the kingdom or to defend it.

Of Their Hunts

No nation under the sun enjoys the hunt as much as do the Turks. For they chase wild animals on horseback into rugged and mountainous terrain, taking various beasts. If the animal had been killed by having been suffocated by the dogs, it is not eaten, either by them or by the Christians who live in those regions. And if they kill a wild boar, they give it to the Christians of that place because Muslims[53] are prohibited to eat swine flesh.

Of Craftsmen and Agriculturalists

Provincials tend their fields by means of slaves, paying a tenth to their emperor.[54] Workmen, however, sustain themselves by means of crafts. Whoever is lazy wastes away with hunger. Trade is also vigorously practiced. They travel throughout Asia Minor, now called Natolia, Arabia, and Egypt conveying merchandise to Venice itself. There are baths in every city where according to their usual custom they wash themselves two or three times. If they urinate, they wash their penis. If they evacuate their bowels, they wash their anus. Likewise this is done by the women. The servants follow them carrying a vessel full of water: male servants for men, females for the women. And when they go to bathe, the women anoint themselves with a kind of ointment which after half an hour causes the hair to fall out. The men themselves shave their genitals, by no means allowing that hair to grow. They do this every month two or three times, both men and women, especially when they go to the temple. Otherwise they would be punished by fire as violators of a sacred place. Also, they have different craftsmen, such as tailors, shoemakers, gold and silversmiths and all kinds of metalworkers, likewise carpenters, painters, and masons, but neither as skilled or as outstandingly talented as those in our regions.

Of Their Justice Among Citizens

They all have the same judge, whether Christian or Turk. However, this one is chosen from the MVSLVMANIS, and is bound to minister justice equally to all. If someone commits murder, they are put to death. If he steals or takes anything by force, he is hanged. It so happened that a certain IENITZERO drank milk that a woman was carrying to the market to sell without paying for it. When he denied it before the judge, he was suspended by his feet and bound around the middle by a cord. He immediately vomited milk and was at once condemned to be hanged. This happened right before my eyes in Damascus when I was going from Armenia to Jerusalem. If anyone commits adultery, the men are thrown into prison (after a few months they can be released through a financial payment), but the woman adulteress in led on an ass through the streets and highways. She is scourged with whips naked and then stoned to death with the entrails of an ox hung around her neck.

Of Their Agriculture

Both Christians and MVSLVMANI tend fields, vineyards, and pastures. They have crops similar to our regions, such as wheat, millet, barley, oats, spelt, beans and all kinds of legumes. More than in these parts, in addition they have rice in abundance, flax, and quince. Also, both peoples have vineyards, the fruit being put to different uses. Christians make wine and the Turks make a honey-like drink called in their language PECHMEZ. Dried grapes are prepared in such a way that they always look and taste like they are fresh. These are called VZVM TVRSSI. They have fruit in great abundance. In season the gardens and fields are full of watermelon, melon, and cucumber. There one can find inexpensive nuts, apples, pears, pomegranates, chestnuts, figs, cherries, bitter orange,[55] and others of this sort, but not in every region. For there are places, as here and there in Cappadocia and Lesser Armenia where it is not possible to grow any of these, because of the extreme cold.

Of Different Animals

They have shepherds called TSOBANLAR[56] who always live in the wilds. For fodder they move almost every month and have no house at all or possessions except for tents and their herds of camels, mules, horses, cattle, sheep, and goats. They eat cheese and butter. They shear sheep and make little garments called CHEPENECH and carpets. They sell these and then buy grain and provisions for their families. All of the aforementioned pay a tenth to the king of the Turks of all the animals born each year. In addition to this, the Christians who live under Turkish tribute are forced to pay tax, namely one crown for each male. And what is the cruelest, every five years they search their homes, and seize by force all the sons who don't have wives.

Of the Building of Their Houses

There is no great magnificence in their construction. For the most part they are made of brickwork. The bricks are of two kinds: some are cured in a kiln, others dried by the sun. The roofs are built wedge-shaped, just as they are throughout Europe. But in Natolio the roofs are flat in the manner of a floor, without any ridge. Siphons and gutters distribute the rainwater which drains into them through pipes.

Of Their Clothing

Their clothing is made from wool, flax and silk and can be magnificent. Their garments, called CHAUTAN,[57] are close-fitting with fringes[58] and hang down to the ankles. They detest our trousers, because they display the privates too much. Their tunics, called GHVMLECH,[59] and handkerchiefs are dyed with a violet color. Their heads are covered with cloth built up as a tower and wound into a cone shape. This headdress is called a TVLBENT or CSALMA[60] in their language. Wealthy women wear veils, never allowing men outside their family to see their faces nor do they frequent the market. Their shoes are called BABVCS[61] or CSISME, the same for men and women, fastened underneath to the sole so that they may be used longer.

Of Their Meals

They have a good quality bread, called ECHMECH, both dark and white, just like we do, but they sprinkle on it a certain kind of seed called SVSSAM just after it is baked when it is fresh, which gives it a great taste of sweetness. This is not used by us, except some places in Spain, especially in the kingdom of Granada and around Seville. They have many different kinds of skills in their cooking and various ways of seasoning foods. It is most common for rice to be added to their food to such a degree that they are able to draw out portions with their hands. Remarkably, fish is absent. They eat all kinds of meat, except pork. They do not have designated taverns or inns as we do. Nevertheless, in the streets there are various vendors of food as well as all other necessities of life.

Of Their Beverages

They have three kinds of beverages. The first is made from sugar, called SECHER[62] by them, or honey diluted in water, this drink is called TSERBTH.[63] A second is made from raisins (with the seeds removed) put in boiling water and then rosewater added and a little bit of honey. This drink is called HOS-SAPH and it is sold in all places in Turkey. It is sweet and causes the belly to swell. The third is a type of syrup called PECHMEZ which is made from grape juice. In taste and appearance it is like honey. It is diluted with water and given to the servants to drink.

On Their Way of Sitting and Eating

When they eat, they put down a rush mat called HACTSER which is then covered with carpets or pillows. Others sit on the bare ground. Their table is called TSOPHRA and is made of leather. It is extended and drawn in like a pouch. They don't sit down like we do or recline like the ancients, resting on their elbows. Rather they sit cross-legged like tailors. Before they begin to eat, a prayer is given. They eat quickly in great silence. Meanwhile the women are kept separate. Menservants older than twelve years, however, are not permitted to go into the house where the women are, but boys less than twelve years old are permitted to go in and out. They bring the majority of necessities to the women who live separated in those other houses. Female captives do not have freedom to go out of the house except when they go with Turkish women when they go to the baths to wash or when they go outside the city for recreation to gardens or vineyards (which they are in the habit of doing often). Rather they are kept secluded in the houses nor are they permitted to speak with menservants. Good God! Who is able to explain or describe the afflictions and calamities of the captives and those Christians who live under the tribute of the Turks? Or who is able to tell of the cruel and most wicked abuse both in secular things as well as in the ceremonies of the Turkish faith? For you understand as you have read already about their washings and cleanliness in which they consider that in these alone are their only hope for the salvation of their souls, while inside they are filled with all kinds of wicked filth. Muhammad is a blind leader and they provoke God eternally. Much else instituted by Muhammad they are required to strictly observe, which I have studiously omitted so as not to make the readers sick by my loquaciousness.

On the Vocabulary of Greetings and Responses and Numbers

First, Names of the Heavenlies

Allah, God
Feriste, Angel
Pegamber, Saint
Irretsul, Prophet
Gugh, Heaven
Vtsmach, Paradise
Gunes, Sun
Ay, Luna
Iulduz, Star

Name of Times

Gil, Year
Ay, Month
Hauta, Week
Gun, Day
Kes, Winter
Tsoch, Cold
Kar, Snow
Buz, Ice
Iagmur, Rain
Dolu, Hail

Yaz, Summer
Itsigsiak, Hot
Tsabah, Morning
Dil, Noon
Aksom, Evening
Gegse, Night
Karanlich, Darkness
Aidanlik, Moonlight
Oth, Fire
Mum, Candle

[The vocabulary list extends several pages.]

Greetings of the Turks, Persians, and Arabs

Sellam	aliech	Tsultanum
Peace	to you	Prince
Sellam	aliech	Baba
Peace	to you	Father
Sellam	aliech	Ana
Peace	to you	Mother

Others may be greeted likewise according to their rank.
    Their response:

Alechmi	Sellam	Rahmatuallah
And to you likewise	peace	may be given by the merciful God
Berechyat,	tseudigum	
And blessing	to my friend	

A Dialogue of a Question and Response by a Turk With a Christian

Turk

Handa,	gidertsen	bre, Giatur?
Where	are you going	O Christian?

The Christian's Response

Stambola	giderum	Tsultanum.
Constantinople	toward I am going	Prince.

Turk

Ne issum   var   bu memleketten?
What—business do you have here?

Christian

Bezergenlik   ederum,   Affcndi
Trade—I am carrying on,   Lord.

Or

Maslahaton   var   Anadolda.
I have business   in   in Asia.

Turk

Ne . . . habar   tsizum   girlerden?
What—news   do you bring   from your lands?

Christian

Hits   neste   bilmezom   tsaa   dimege.
I don't know   any   news you want   that I could say to you.

Turk

Gioldassum   varmi   tsem ile?
Is there   with you   anyone?

Christian

Ioch—Ialanuz   gheldum.
No,   alone   I came.

Turk

Benumle   gelurmitsun?
With me   would you like to come?

Christian

Irachmider   tsenum iataghom?
Is it far   to your inn?

Turk

Iachender   bundan   gustereim   tsaa.
It is near   this   I will show   to you.

Christian

Gel ghusteriuere   Allaha tseuertson.
Come—show me   if God   you love.

Turk

Kalch—iochari tur   bonda.
Get   up,   stand   here.

Christian

Hanghi   daraftan   der   bilmezum
In which direction   is it   I don't know.

Turk

Tsagh   eline bacha ghun   doghutsine
Toward   the right   look   to   the east.

Christian

Bir . . . buch   ew   atsarghibi   gurunur omider
A tall—house   which looks like a fortress, isn't that it?

Turk

Gercsekson   oder, iaken   deghilmi?
That is correct, that is it,   close by isn't it?
Valediction

Christian

Allaha—tsmarlahadoch tseni, ben   oraa   gitmezom
To God   I commend you,   I   that way   will not go.

Turk

Bre neden korkartson   nitcie   gelmetson
What?—Of what   are you afraid that you are not coming?

Christian

Benum   iolum oraa   deghelder.
My way   that direction   is not.

Turk

Wargeth   staglogla   eier   ghelmetson.
Go with good portents, if   you don't want to come.

Christian

Gegsien   hair   oltson.
(May) night   be favorable   to you.

Turk

Aghbate   hair oltson.
And—to you   blessed.

Christian

Ben kurtuldom stoch   succor   Allaha.
I am free,   highest praise to God.

The Same Pilgrim to the Good Reader, Many Greetings

Kind reader, you have learned more than enough of the rituals and customs of the Ishmaelites, and in addition much vocabulary, salutations, responses, thanks, valedictions, together with numbers in the Persian language (which we call Turkish). The Persian language used by the Turks will not be hidden to you, which they corrupt, because those with complete understanding are able to benefit from all discussions. I certainly have not considered it to be valuable to describe at length the customs of the lay commoners or their filthy religious practices, which pollute our paper. But primarily for this reason we saw fit to explain a little of this omitted wickedness (which is shameful not only to write and to read, but even to hear) so that having read they may know (especially if someone stands up to commend their foul works) to what degree light is different from darkness, how different is the true Christian religion from that most nefarious superstition of the barbarians. Therefore, kind reader, I pray you might consider my attempt worthwhile (it is truthful, although clumsy), if you might be able to draw forth something pleasing or agreeable from my offspring. For I am able to swear that I have pursued the bare truth; I have not examined any writings about the Turks. I commit the judgment of its veracity to experts in the language and nation, and then to those who may have diligently examined those things about the rituals and customs of this people which have been brought to light.

Notes

1. Lat: praedatoribus.
2. *Res mancipi* was a designation of Roman property law concerning the requirements for legal transfer of ownership.
3. This is a reference to the Turkish seraglio.
4. Correct: Akche. This was a small silver coin and was the primary portable currency of the Ottoman Empire. The size was around 12–15 mm and a little over 1 gram.
5. Georgijevic is here confusing all Ottoman archers with the elite force of guards of the Sultan known as Solaklar (left-handeds).
6. Turk: Yeniçeriler.
7. This may also be a reference to female homosexuality.
8. Lat: annis inutilis.

9. This is a reference to the zakat. Georgijevic frequently utilizes Christian terminology in an effort to translate Islamic concepts.
10. This was the monthly (or daily) allowance of food given to slaves. It included grain (primarily), with some wine, fruit, but rarely vegetables.
11. Seston on the European side and Abydos on the Asian side are located at the Nagara Point on the Hellespont, the shortest distance across the entire Dardanelles (about 1 mile across).
12. The Turkish word for the Dardanelles is Bogazi.
13. Lat: suo Mehemmeto.
14. Lat: Christianum Rep[ublicam].
15. Lat: Mehemmetum.
16. Although misspelled, the Greek given in the text is close, apateras, amateras.
17. Lat: ob proditionem, atque iniuriam eius militibus illatam.
18. Lat: Mehemmeti, Mahometum, respectively.
19. At times he seems to confuse Persians and Arabs.
20. "Oruç" is the Turkish word for "fast."
21. This is not accurate, the lunar calendar is shorter than the solar calendar, not longer.
22. This is more commonly known by its Arabic name, Eid al-fitr, although it is called the Lesser Bairam in Turkish.
23. Kina in Turkish, or henna.
24. In Turkish, parmak can refer to any digit, not necessarily the thumb.
25. This appears to have been a common ancient anti-inflammatory and burn treatment.
26. Lat: quo in lucem eduntur.
27. Selim actually means "sound, honest, free from defect."
28. Amurath is Turkish for Murad.
29. This is probably related to rum(lara) which is a reference to Greeks.
30. Arnavutlar is "Albanian" in Turkish.
31. Okumak means to read or study; girleri has to do with funding.
32. Turk: Aşk.
33. That is, Allahiçin.
34. Correct: maslach. This is an opiate which was used by the Turks.
35. This is one of the few places in the text where Georgijevic writes in the first person. It seems that he believed that the incredible nature of his description needed firsthand verification for credibility.
36. That is, three Roman pounds (36 oz. total).
37. Lat: iudex ipsorum.
38. Turk: haci.
39. Çarik is Turkish for shoe.
40. This could mean "rice soup" in Turkish.
41. Buğday is Turkish for wheat.
42. Perhaps the intention of the author was to divide this into thirds, which would have been closer to the Hajj sacrifice.
43. Musluman.
44. Muslumanlaris.
45. Lat: framea. Most likely in this context a sword.
46. In Turkish nasip means "lot", "destiny", "foreordination."
47. Yazili in Turkish means both "written" and decreed by fate."
48. Baş in Turkish means "head."
49. This is an Islamic tradition which is credited to a pagan goddess.
50. Solak, meaning left-handed.
51. That is, a ducat.

52. Fil in Turkish.
53. Lat: muslumanis.
54. Generic for tithe; perhaps referring to a tax?
55. Lat: poma narranca. Naranca is Croatian not Latin. The Turkish word for this fruit is turunc.
56. Turkish: çoban.
57. This is probably "caftan."
58. Lat: laciniosa, perhaps pleats.
59. Turkish: gömlek, shirt or tunic.
60. This is Serbian, Croatian, and Hungarian for turban.
61. Pabuç is Turkish for shoe.
62. Şeker in Turkish.
63. This is evidently a reference to Şerbet, which was originally a Turkish drink made with sugar and spices or sugar and fruit juices.

Index